MESOPOTAMIA

MESOPOTAMIA

Writing, Reasoning, and the Gods

JEAN BOTTÉRO

Translated by Zainab Bahrani and Marc Van De Mieroop

THE UNIVERSITY OF CHICAGO PRESS
Chicago & London

The University of Chicago Press, Chicago 60637
The University of Chicago Press, Ltd., London

Paperback edition 1995
Printed in the United States of America
00 99 98 5 4
ISBN (cloth): 0-226-06726-2
ISBN (paper): 0-226-06727-0

First Published as *Mésopotamie. L'écriture, la raison et les dieux.*

Library of Congress Cataloging-in-Publication Data

Bottéro, Jean.
[Mésopotamie. English]
Mesopotamia : writing, reasoning, and the Gods / Jean Bottéro ; translated by Zainab Bahrani and Marc Van De Mieroop.
p. cm.
Translation of: Mésopotamie.
Includes bibliographical references (p.) and index.
1. Babylonia—Civilization. I. Title.
DS69.5.B6813 1992
935—dc20 91-25917

♾ The paper used in this publication meets the minimum requirements of the American National Standard for Information Sciences—Permanence of Paper for Printed Library Materials, ANSI Z39.48-1984.

CONTENTS

IV. "THE GODS": RELIGION

CHRONOLOGY

Note: all dates presented in this book are of course to be taken as "negative" and refer to the period before the Christian era. Before the fifteenth century these dates are subject to a degree of error that becomes larger the earlier the dates are.

Starting from the sixth millennium the region emerges little by little from north to south and takes on its shape of a great lowland between the Tigris and the Euphrates. It was populated by unknown ethnic groups who had descended from the piedmonts of the north and the east. There is no doubt that those groups also included Semites who had come from the northern edges of the great Syro-Arabian desert.

In the fourth millennium at the latest, after the arrival of the Sumerians (most probably from the southeast), a process of interaction and exchange started to form *the* local civilization. It soon developed into an urban society through the unification of more or less autonomous primitive villages.

Around 3000: first "invention" of writing.

Until around 2350: independent city-states. The *First Dynasty of Ur* (*Ur I*), the *Dynasty of Lagaš.*

Last third of the third millennium: the first Semitic empire founded by Sargon the Great (*Akkadian Dynasty*); then, after a century of "anarchy," the kingdom of Ur (*Third Dynasty of Ur—Ur III*) in the south. *Old Akkadian period.*

First third of the second millennium: a return to a system of city-states that fought for hegemony. Arrival of new Semitic tribes: the Amorites.

Starting from 1750: Ḫammurabi reunites the country in a kingdom centered around Babylon: *First Dynasty of Babylon. Old Babylonian Period* (in the north of the country: *Old Assyrian Period*).

Around 1600: invasion by the Kassites (and *Kassite Dynasty*) who pull the country into a political torpor, which favors a vigorous cultural development. *Middle Babylonian Period.*

Around 1300: the northern part of the country, Assyria (around Assur, later around Kalḫu and then around Nineveh) gains its independence. *Middle Assyrian Period.*

Starting from 1100: Babylonian revival. The battle for hegemony between Assyria and Babylonia. Even when the latter was politically dominated, it kept its cultural supremacy. Arrival of new Semitic tribes: the Arameans.

First third of the first millennium: Assyrian dominance. The Sargonids (Esarhaddon, Assurbanipal). *Neo-Assyrian Period.*

609: Nineveh is defeated by Babylon, which takes control over the entire country. *Neo-Babylonian Period.* The Aramaic language, written in an alphabetic script, starts to relegate Akkadian, which was still written in cuneiform, to the state of a literary and scholarly language.

539: Babylon in its turn falls to Cyrus, who incorporates Mesopotamia into his empire. *Persian Period.*

330: Alexander conquers Babylon and Persia. With the Seleucid rulers Mesopotamia becomes part of the Hellenistic world. *Seleucid Period.*

Starting with the middle of the second century the country is invaded and conquered by the Parthians and for a long time loses all political and cultural importance. Mesopotamia is dead and a new era begins.

RULES OF TRANSCRIPTION AND TRANSLATION

TRANSCRIPTION

Names of people and of places are usually rendered in their usual transcription (Ḫammurabi, Assurbanipal, Nineveh), except where it seemed better to show their component parts, for one reason or another (Âṣu-šu-namir; Atra-ḫasîs).

The same applies to divine names, which are usually written in italics (*Marduk; Utu; Nin.ḫursag*).

Sumerian nouns are transcribed into Roman characters and their elements are always separated by points, the way they are spelled in cuneiform (dam.kar). Akkadian nouns are in italics and their syllabic division in the writing is expressed by hyphens (*tam-ka-ru*).

For both languages most of the consonants and the vowels used in the transcriptions maintain their common values. But:

u is always pronounced *ou* (Uruk = Ourouk);

all the consonants are articulated (*Ningirsu* = *Ninn-girsou*);

all the consonants are voiced: (*Nin-girsu* = *Ninn-ghirsou*);

ḫ corresponds to a sound close to the Spanish *jota;*

š indicates our *sh;*

ṣ, ṭ, and q indicate so-called "emphatic" values that are unknown in our phonetic system.

The circumflex on a vowel in transcriptions of Akkadian indicates that the vowel in question is long: Atra-ḫasîs.

Diacritical signs, i.e. accents and numerical indicators that are found with certain syllables (šá, šà, u_4, unu_x), have no phonetic value whatsoever and only refer to cuneiform signs that correspond to different Sumerian words (see p. 95 n. 4).

A Roman lowercase letter, appearing as a superscript before a word, reflects the use in the cuneiform writing system of a "determinative" or a "classifier" (see pp. 59 and 89) that indicates the category to which the word belongs. Thus ^{d} in ^{d}*Šamaš* is used to indicate that Šamaš is the name of a god (^{d} is the abbreviation of the Sumerian word dingir: "god").

TRANSLATION

The numbers in the left margin beside a translated passage refer to the number of the line or the verse in the entire work.

The large Roman numerals refer to the *tablet* of a work that consists of more than one tablet in the original cuneiform version. The lowercase Roman numerals refer to the *column* if there is more than one on the tablet. Thus *Gilgameš* I/iv: 8–15 is to be understood as verses 8 to 15 of the fourth column of the first tablet of the *Epic of Gilgameš*.

Square brackets [. . .] enclose passages that are lost in the original, and that are reconstructed; if the reconstruction is almost certain, the passages are in italics like the rest of the citation. Otherwise the passages are in Roman letters, if we are only certain of the general sense. I have added in parentheses (. . .) some words that do not appear in the original language but that I have considered to be useful for our understanding of the text.

When the copyist was sometimes distracted and forgot a word or a passage, it appears in pointed brackets ⟨ . . . ⟩. If on the other hand he has written something that is superfluous, I have enclosed it with curved brackets { . . . }.

BLACK SEA
Caucasu
ARMENI
Urartu
Ankara
Boghazköy
Hatti
Hittites
KURDISTAN
Hurrians
LEBANON
Shanidar
Tell Billa
Arpachiya
Khorsabad
Karkemish
Şulṭan-tepe
Tepe Gawra
Assur/Assyria
Aleppo
Mosul
Kuyundik
Nineveh
Amurru/Martu
Mesopotamia
Ebla
Nimrud/Kalhu
Jarmo
Lattakia
Sagaratum?
Ḫariḫumba?
Ras-Shamra/
Ugarit
Jebel Hamrin
Aššur
SYRIA
Tigris
Nuzi
CYPRUS
Terqa
Ishchali
Tell Asmar/
Ešnunna
Diyala
Euphrates
Mari
Beirut
Behistu
Damascus
Khafadjeh
Tell Ag
Aqarquf
Tell Harmal
Baghdad
Sippar
Uqair
Djemdet-
PALESTINE
Kutha
Babylon
Kiš
Abu Salabik
Babylonia
Canaan
Fara
Akk
Canaanites
Jeruzalem
Nippur
Isiñ
Umma
Uruk
Sum
Sumer
Ur
Lars
al-Ubaid
Eridu
Ku'ar?
Ch
Syro-Arabian desert
Sinai
ARABIA
T
RED SEA
0 100 200 300 400 500 km
Medina

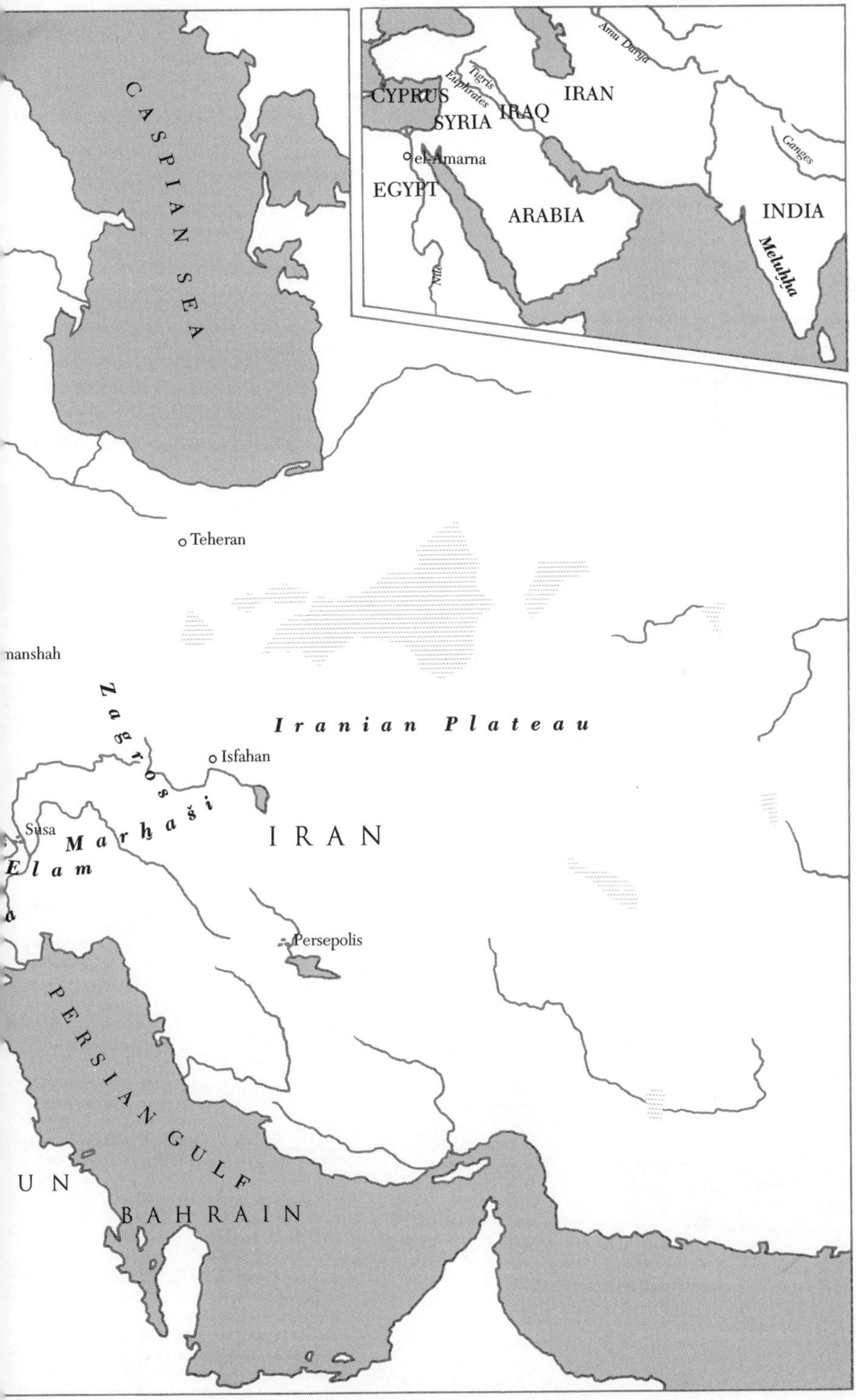
CYPRUS
SYRIA
IRAQ
IRAN
Tigris
Euphrates
Amu Darya
el-Amarna
EGYPT
Nile
ARABIA
INDIA
Ganges
Meluhha
CASPIAN SEA
Teheran
Iranian Plateau
Zagros
Isfahan
Susa
Marhaši
Elam
IRAN
Persepolis
PERSIAN GULF
BAHRAIN

THE BIRTH OF THE WEST

Beyond the recognized sources of our civilization, and the most easily explored sources of our thinking and our consciousness, i.e. Israel of the Bible and Ancient Greece, there is a much more distant source at the extreme horizon of history that influenced both the other ones. In my book *Naissance de Dieu* (since, at the moment, I seem to be devoted to origins), I tried to show the influence of this source here and there. But familiarity with this source, even the pure and simple knowledge of its existence, seems up till now to have been reserved for a handful of professionals who are not very eloquent and remain in obscurity. The source is ancient Mesopotamia, the land of Sumer* and Akkad,* of Babylon* and of Nineveh.*

The best term to indicate the area whose history I will consider here (the ancient inhabitants usually said "the land"—kalam in Sumerian and *mâtu* in Akkadian) is *Mesopotamia.* Literally it means "Between-Rivers" and, although in the past it had a more restrictive sense, it applies more or less to the territory of modern-day Iraq. We will find the term too often repeated in this book, by necessity, as I do not know a term that is equally appropriate. Sometimes I have replaced it by *Babylon,* because starting around the year 1750 that city became first the political capital, then the cultural metropolis of the country. But we could not extend the use of the term to the long period before 1750, as it would be anachronistic. *Babylonia* customarily indicates only the southern half of the Mesopotamian territory from the middle of the second millennium on. *Assyria,* with its successive capitals: Assur,* Kalḫu,* and *Nineveh,** was the northern half. Whatever may have been its later political destiny it was always culturally dependent on Babylonia, even starting in the mid-second millennium. For that reason the coupling of the two names in the term Assyro-Babylonia, as has sometimes been done, is more misleading than useful. I have avoided as much as possible the name *Sumer:* It referred in antiquity

*For the benefit of the uninitiated reader it has seemed useful to establish at the end of this volume a type of glossary for some technical and commonly used terms in Assyriology. I have usually tried to explain each of them when they appear in the text, but it seemed better to repeat their meaning when they appear several times. These words are indicated with an asterisk almost everywhere in my text: e.g. *Enlil,** etc.

only to the southernmost part of Lower Mesopotamia (the other part, in the north, had the name *Akkad*). It did not refer, as a naïve and simplistic fad has made us believe for too long, and still makes us believe, to an independent Sumerian culture that can be isolated as such. The existence of that culture cannot be doubted—the use of the Sumerian language vouches for it—but it existed *before* History—and in any case it falls outside our documentation. Our sources, from the earliest moment that we have them, reveal nothing but *one* coherent civilization, even if it had been formed by two influences that originally did not have the slightest element in common: the Sumerians* on the one hand and the Semites,* "Akkadians," on the other. And this does not take into account third cultures and ethnic groups that are also prehistoric and about whom we know almost nothing. Thus I refrain deliberately from talking as a historian about the Sumerians, about Sumerian culture, thought, and religion, and even about Sumerian literature. In ancient Mesopotamia only one composite culture existed that can be truly recognized. And thus one thought, one religion existed, where it is possible to reveal the features that were of probable Sumerian origin, and others probably of Semitic origin, by analysis, by comparison, and by conjecture. And also there was but one literature, written partly in the Sumerian language and partly in the Akkadian language, their proportional shares varying over time. One could, then, talk about a *Sumero-Akkadian* world, but I for my part have little affection for such a heavy dual noun.

It is also to the credit of Mr. P. Nora and Mr. M. Gauchet that they have encouraged me with kindness and intelligence to devote this volume to that culture. It gives me true pleasure to show them my warmest gratitude.

I have not wanted to devote to my subject matter a real synthesis, one that would flatter itself that it reproduces, or even attempts to reproduce, all the aspects of the subject. Precisely because I have haunted and surveyed the subject matter in every way for half a century, I have not felt like drawing up the Baedeker of this old continent. Ancient Mesopotamia is lost in the faraway past, immense and rough, badly explored, and difficult to explore, and large areas of it remain submerged in the mists of prehistory, while the part of it that emerges still remains, in places, imprecise and indiscernible to us, at such a distance. How can we pretend to draw the portrait of a civilization, attested by half a million intelligible documents at a low estimate, and often by many cultural vestiges that are so rich, so dense, so complex, so original, that their enormous vitality has kept them alive for at least three millennia, but from which we are separated by two thousand years of total oblivion?

It has seemed to me better to be less reckless and perhaps more certain, and suggest only a discrete silhouette of this civilization. By using somewhat better established features, I can indicate at least some contours that are at the same time more distinct and more unexpected, while some are also more important to us because we can recognize in them quite clearly, from far away and despite the differences, the most ancient state of our culture: the distant birth of the Western world.

For that purpose I have chosen a certain number of articles that I have devoted to Mesopotamia, especially in the last twenty years. I have reworked them here and there to various degrees in order to extract from them all bothersome erudition,[1] and to adapt them to my particular plan as well as to the actual state of our knowledge. As I will indicate for each of them, all these articles have appeared in specialized periodicals or collective works. I would like to take the time to thank the publishers of these periodicals and the editors of these works, who have allowed me with great generosity to take back my texts.

Two articles were unpublished, however; the first in its entirety ("The Religious System," chap. 12), the other ("Writing and Dialectics, or the Progress of Knowledge," chap. 6) I have entirely reworked on the basis of a very long and detailed study that, I fear, was almost entirely inaccessible to non-Assyriologists in its original form. During the preparation of this book I was thinking more about non-Assyriologists than about my accomplices in the field.

The plan that I have adopted reflects that.

First of all, it did not seem opportune to me to involve myself with the "material" conditions: geography, climate, economy, ethnology, sociology, and so on, and even less with what is called the "factual history" of the country, because all these elements are well described in a small number of books that are accessible to everyone and that I have listed in my bibliography. However, in order not to complicate everything, it was indispensable to have at least a preliminary and basic chronology before the eyes—which one will find here on pp. viif. But a time chart does not give the entire story; in the end it is nothing but a frame, a structure within which takes place the only history that is of real value with regard to the plan that I am pursuing here: to discover step by step the ways of seeing, of sensing, and of living, and the unpredictable thoughts and hearts, of our oldest recognizable ancestors. These changing conditions are more difficult to penetrate, more fascinating, and more evasive than the ephemeral avatars of dynasties and battles, *faits divers* that were unimportant in later days.

I have decided to draw attention first to Assyriology, the "scientific" discipline devoted to this very old country, in order to prudently introduce the proper subject matter of my book: the civilization of ancient Meso-

1. At the mercy of my subject matters and of my approach to them, I have ended up leaving in some places technical references and Akkadian and Sumerian terms, although as few as possible. The serious reader should not be scared off by them: they are there to remain credible, perhaps even useful, to my professional colleagues who might be interested in reading my work.

potamia. I have pointed out some rough indications of similarity—and sometimes of contrast—between Mesopotamian civilization and our own, in order that the oldest discernible state of a glorious cultural patrimony, which was digested, reworked, enriched, and transmitted to us through the long line of our ancestors will become recognizable. First, I will deal with Assyriology in itself, with its subject matter, its methods, and the value of its knowledge ("In Defense of a Useless Science," chap. 1). Then, I will stress the place it should occupy in a truthful and full knowledge of our past, a place that is still badly known ("Assyriology and Our History," chap. 2). Then I will establish a balance-sheet of the upsets caused by Assyriology during the century that the discipline has existed ("A Century of Assyriology," chap. 3).

The countless discoveries in this regard, most of them quite revolutionary, would not have been possible without the surprising decipherment of the cuneiform writing system, used in ancient Mesopotamia, the secrets of which had been lost for two millennia. I was eager to recall this exceptional adventure ("The 'Avalanche' of Decipherments in the Ancient Near East between 1800 and 1930," chap. 4), because perhaps the most often and most eagerly asked question put to Assyriologists is: "How were you able to break the impenetrable code of the cuneiform signs, without the help of any Rosetta stone?"

The writing system is impressive in itself. It is also the earliest one attested in world history, and was perhaps the most shining and generous contribution of the ancient Mesopotamians to the development and the progress of our understanding, when we consider, right now,[2] to what degree the transition into the written tradition has profoundly transformed our intelligence, by reinforcing and multiplying its capacities. Contrary to what one still seems to think, those who "invented" writing at the end of the fourth millennium, did not develop it all at once, and the history of the stages of the evolution ("From Mnemonic Device to Script," chap. 5) illustrates its strange and frightening complications very well, as well as its original down-to-earth character which was particularly "realistic."

It was precisely this "realism" of their writing system that so strongly marked, even modeled, the minds of its inventors and users. Being in the habit of taking their written signs as an immediate reflection, as a real substitute for what they represented, it was much easier for them to pass from the written sign to reality, and from the name to the object. They developed an entire system of dialectics and of hermeneutics, which allowed

2. Especially after the fundamental works of J. Goody. See especially *The Domestication of the Savage Mind* (Cambridge and New York: Cambridge University Press, 1977), and *The Logic of Writing and the Organization of Society* (Cambridge and New York: Cambridge University Press, 1986).

them, they thought, to go forward in the knowledge of things by scrutinizing and analyzing their written indications ("Writing and Dialectics, or the Progress of Knowledge," chap. 6).

Whatever we think of such outmoded and imaginary postulates, it remains a fact that they invited the ancient Mesopotamians to a rational examination and a profound study of things from various angles. The most surprising in our eyes, but also the best known because of an abundant documentation, is what I have called "deductive divination.*" In order to illustrate its mechanism better, avoiding the risk of excessive dilution of my explanations, I have devoted myself to one of the numerous divinatory areas explored in the country; an area which is especially captivating and well attested: the taking of omens from dreams ("Oneiromancy" chap. 7).

The innumerable documents related to deductive divination strike us first of all by the frivolity of their object and by the discouraging monotony of their presentation. If, however, we turn our attention away from the "superstitions" at work, and if we take our courage in both hands to confront a sleep-inducing list of words, we can strive at evaluating and analyzing with care the underlying mental operations. There we discover a strange wish to analyze the elements of the universe systematically and rationally, by obstinately searching in them what they hide that is permanent, necessary, and universal beyond their casual and fleeing materiality. And, all things considered, the first features appear to be at least the result of an awareness and an application, if not a theory, of causality and proof; in other words, the first serious rough outline of what was later taken over, expanded, deepened, and organized by the Greek thinkers, and developed into the "scientific mind." It is the oldest rough draft of this science and this type of reasoning that we still highly esteem ("Divination and the Scientific Spirit," chap. 8).

The authenticated custom of sometimes replacing the ruler of the country by a simple subject when the king's life was threatened by supernatural forces, and of killing the substitute in question without any form of process in order to ward off this danger entirely, had some type of divinatory origin, because the fatal destiny promised to the king was only recognizable through omens. But the recourse made to substitution obtained its validity from an entirely different institution, which was more immediately religious and which, if we judge by the enormous dossier in our hands, seems to have played a considerable role in the life of the ancient Mesopotamians. It is often called "magic," but it would be better to speak of "exorcism." By using different manual and oral procedures, its users sought to ward off from their person Evil: i.e. bad luck, suffering. The particular application of exorcism that I have chosen to highlight here ("The Substitute King and His Fate," chap. 9) has the advantage, in my opinion, of turning our attention to another essential parameter of the local civilization: the monarchical conception of power.

This concept bursts out from a famous monument, one of the few works of the literature of ancient Mesopotamia that is vaguely known outside the small circle of professionals ("The 'Code' of Ḫammurabi," chap. 10). However, this exceptional document, which is almost entirely preserved with its three thousand five hundred lines of text, has been taken since its discovery in the beginning of the century as something it is not, by relating its point of view and the thoughts of its authors and intended readers through a naïve anachronism to our own model. Thus it was worth the trouble to attempt to examine it once through the eyes of its authors and readers, not only to understand it better in itself, but also to find in it cultural elements, important in their own right, which are useful for helping us understand our ties to, as well as our differences from, these ancient people. It shows how they understood the knowledge, the "science," and the teaching of law, the exercise of justice and of equity, and the importance and the meaning of royal power.

We find also other notions and practices that are familiar to us as well as to them, but upon which they looked in a way different from our own. For example, all that involves love, carnal love, was understood in its free expression not to be "subjugated" to family life or to the propagation of the species. This love, homosexual as well as heterosexual, was practiced not only in a greater spiritual freedom than our own, which is still burdened by the heavy Christian curses that we have attempted to shake off with such an uproar, but it was also held in the highest esteem and devotion. Nonetheless, still without the least moral or religious connotation, they despised and kept at a distance its representatives: the prostitutes of both sexes that seem to have officially prospered in their society. In order to resolve such a contradiction ("'Free Love' and Its Disadvantages," chap. 11), we have to make reference to a primary notion in their system of thought: that of Destiny—or as we would say, of Nature. Because these professionals of free love were considered by the Mesopotamians to have strayed from the straight path of their "destiny," an attitude was taken towards them that was certainly not hostile or condemning, but ontologically pejorative, if we can use these words. It was an original view, and especially so because it reveals to us one of the major expressions of the "theology" of the believers.

Such a conception of nature and destiny, as well as the royal ideology, the beliefs and manipulations of exorcism, and even to a degree those of divination, all converge towards the same central point which is considerably particularized and reduced in our "disenchanted" world,[3] but which in ancient Mesopotamia still ruled as sovereign over the entire existence both

3. M. Gauchet, *Le désenchantement du monde* (Paris: Gallimard, 1985).

of individuals and of the state: religion. Their religion was boldly polytheistic and anthropomorphic. A multitude of testimonies about it, extraordinarily varied and difficult to penetrate, are preserved for us. They are from all periods of a long history but separated by large lacunae. Before such a mass of documentation we feel at first as if we are losing hold, as if we are being submerged by such a multiplicity of varied phenomena that most often seem to have no connections. I have preferred to avoid organizing them in a perspective that would be sufficiently objective and illuminating at the same time. As I am convinced that we can, and must, adopt a different attitude from that type of nonchalant phenomenology, I have tried to go further, on two levels.

First of all, I tried to see if, behind this apparent jumble of individual elements, there does not exist a central axis that ordered all of them and conferred on all of them their sense and their value. I think I have found this backbone in the principle of royal power, simply transposed from earth to the supernatural universe by mythological reflection. Around it, religion was organized in a real system that was coherent and, in its own way, rational and logical ("The Religious System," chap. 12).

The problem of arranging such a staggering mob of gods and goddesses, that at first view seems to be chaotic, is possibly more acute. Hence, it has seemed to me useful to show to what degree this pantheon itself has been systematized in a balanced hierarchy that was usually stable and in which each deity played an irreplaceable role in his position and with his prerogatives. Thus they contributed, each in their part, to making the gigantic, perfectly oiled machine of the universe function, like wheels in a mechanism. Also in that chapter the close study of one example has more value than a panoramic view, which would be much less clear and telling even though, numerically, more complete. Thus I have stressed one of the gods whose personality and actions are the best characterized, a god who by himself and by his own office reflects excellently the recognized priority given, in such a society of production and consumption, to technique and to practical intelligence ("Intelligence and the Technical Function of Power: Enki/Ea*," chap. 13).

A notion that is of concern to me, because I consider it to be essential to the religious feelings of the ancient Semites (in spite of its ancient Sumerian components, Mesopotamian religion was partly created and especially developed during at least two millennia by Semites!) is the propensity to vigorously reveal the distance between gods and men: the divine superiority in existence, in action, in duration, and in intelligence over mankind. To say it in one word: the *transcendence,* which truly culminated in the absolute monotheism of the ancient Israelites.[4] In order to better establish the pres-

4. *Naissance de Dieu,* passim.

ence in Mesopotamia of such an apprehension of the supernatural world, I have concentrated on a short literary piece that has an unusual presentation and a bearing which remains quite enigmatic among experts ("The 'Dialogue of Pessimism' and Transcendence," chap. 14).

And finally, as death terminates everything here on earth, I was inclined to finish with it. Not a single religion or philosophy in this world has escaped answering the anxious questions about death and what follows it that have been tormenting mankind, even if none of them has been able to answer these questions with anything by "calculated guesses." Hence, I have collected in rough outline in the last chapter what our texts show us about "The Mythology of Death" (chap. 15). In that chapter the oldest foundations of our own traditional imagination about the "final end" can be found easily.

I am not sorry that I have kept the texts of these studies as they were, even when one overlapped more or less with another, or repeated some aspects of it. In fact, when I repeated myself two or three times in order to discuss an issue of importance, my point of view was never entirely the same, to such an extent that these repetitions were more complementary than overlapping, encouraging us as a result to survey the subject in its entirety. I can say this without repeating the golden rule that repetition is the best guarantee of efficiency, in the communication of knowledge as well as in magic or exorcism.

Even if my subject is seemingly far removed, and much earlier than the one that I addressed in *Naissance de Dieu*, my methods of approach, of examination, and of reflection, as well as the balanced combination of stubbornness and of reservation in the methods, have remained the same, since they are imposed upon me by my professional duties as a historian. Historians and actors have this in common that they have to be able to step into the skin of their characters, not in order to play them better, but to understand them better. Thus it is not surprising that I show as much "sympathy" for the ancient Mesopotamians as I showed for the ancient Israelites.

But not for the same reasons, however.

In my earlier work I have so sufficiently praised the authors of the Bible that one cannot doubt either my inveterate admiration or the good reasons for it. In general I did not have the same motives for associating myself with the oldest inhabitants of the Land-between-Two-Rivers. It took me time to free myself from the deception that had taken me during my first contacts with original cuneiform inscriptions. Not to mention the difference in languages: biblical Hebrew, by far closer to the beautiful Arabic language, is phonetically richer, more vigorous, more sonorous, and more fascinating than is Akkadian. And with regard to Sumerian, it is so remote from us and so strange that one has to be a person with a very low melting point to be excited when listening to it. I came to this field from the warmth, the naturalness, and the color of the "Life of Elijah from Tishbi" in the Book of Kings;[5] from the powerful and commanding opening of Genesis;[6] from the impetuous and cursing convictions of Amos, Hosea, and Isaiah;[7] from the tenderness of Jeremiah;[8] from the prodigious outbursts of Second Isaiah[9] and of Job;[10] from the emotions contained in between the "philosophical" and the gloomy lines of Ecclesiastes.[11] I came upon an infinite formal and cold prosaicness; upon a formalist and conventional court poetry that is without real lyricism and where deep feelings themselves are often fabricated, if not stilted, the few times they are visible. Even the "scientific" works presented themselves to me as unending and gloomy lists of words or of propositions, juxtaposed with no clear connections between them, without the least apparent attempt to subsume this infinite number of pieces into larger units or synthetic concepts, into abstractions that are more familiar and more useful for our way of thinking. And then, I have to admit, although this polytheistic stirring was systematized, coherent, and "logical," it seemed to me to be earthbound, singularly lacking in absolute value. Was there not enough to discourage even the best will in the world, and to send me very soon back to the Bible, or to Greece, and their universe which was accessible to me?

By good fortune, I was soon able to overcome that original feeling of dejection. First of all, when I started to explore the literature of Sumer and Akkad, of Babylon and Nineveh, I was able to uncover more easily here and there parts that somewhat warmed my heart. But I soon became especially convinced that where warmth, glitter, and the power of *words* were absent, there ruled secretly the intelligence of *thought*, a strident need for uncovering, a thirst to understand, and an extraordinary creativity. In such a harsh country, deprived of almost everything except clay, bitumen, and reeds, with a muddy and fertile soil, and two rivers to irrigate it serving as the only earthly resource, these people, just emerged from the uncertainties, the poverty, and the primitiveness of prehistory, conceived and created everything. In a few centuries they developed for themselves an existence that was economically opulent, they constructed a political and military power that was for a long time unique, and almost always un-

5. *Naissance de Dieu*, pp. 68ff.
6. Ibid., pp. 160ff.
7. Ibid., pp. 75ff.
8. Ibid., pp. 94ff.
9. Ibid., pp. 102ff.
10. Ibid., pp. 126ff., 131ff., 167ff.
11. Ibid., pp. 229ff.

equalled, in the entire Near East. They were the very first to expend a considerable amount of energy not only for making use of the world by the ingenuity of their rapid technological progress but also for attempting to understand it by their observations, their comparisons, their thinking, and their interpretations. In a sense they made up a particular system of thought, unprecedented in those distant times, but also admirable in itself even if it is so remote from our own. And the system was especially fruitful if we judge it by the elements that have been retained from it until today.

I am not forgetting, nor do I want to belittle, the venerable and sumptuous Egypt which was as old, as magnificent, and undoubtedly much more fascinating with its numerous incomparable monuments. But we must recognize that in the Near East, where the cultured and exciting world was located at that time, in the opinion of historians, the kingdom of the Pharaohs, the window of Africa on the Mediterranean, was at first an edifice almost entirely closed off in our direction. Mesopotamia, in contrast, first of all by its geographical situation and by its people, seems to us from very early on entirely open to its environment which businessmen and warriors surveyed and explored in all directions. At the latest, since the middle of the third millennium, the Elamites* of southeastern Iran, and the Semites of Ebla* in Syria borrowed their script and, in part, their languages from Mesopotamia—a sign of a strong cultural dependency. In the second millennium the same situation appears among the Semites and the Hurrians* of Syria-Palestine and among the powerful Indo-Europeans of Anatolia, the Hittites.* We find almost everywhere, either in the original language or in translation into the local language, fragments of mythological, epic, poetic, literary, and scientific works (even plagiarisms) that had been produced with great effort in Babylonia. The extensive international diplomatic correspondence of the pharaohs themselves with all the courts of the Near East in the fifteenth century was found in Egypt, at el-Amarna, but written in the Akkadian language and noted down in cuneiform. In the first millennium the same Egypt borrowed its astrology from Babylonia, which had also spread out its age-old practice of extispicy (divination by the examination of entrails) to Asia Minor, and even to the Etruscans. All things considered, Egypt does not really seem to have transmitted very much that is substantial to the various authors of the biblical books, where on the other hand themes and structures developed in Mesopotamia are still recognizable despite the transformations that the convinced monotheists of Israel imposed upon them. Even ancient Greece did not escape the far-reaching but intense radiance of Babylonia. Its reflections appear more clearly in the period of the formation of Greek thought. The *Theogony* of Hesiod shows more than one element of the *Poem of Creation*,* and even Thales of Miletus, the ancient Ionian thinker, kept water as the primary matter of the world. But a sign of a more widespread and more radical dependence, even if we find the effects more and more rethought and reinterpreted over time, is the fact that all ancient Greek philosophers worked exactly within the path outlined by the earlier mythographers of Mesopotamia, for instance in the subject of cosmogony. They all postulated a unique primary matter for the universe, and by concentrating only on the problems of evolution and transformation, none of them even asked the question of the absolute origin of everything. For anyone familiar with Mesopotamia and its thought and literature, and who carefully considers those of Greece, there is no doubt that such connections will appear to be all the more numerous and strong. They will be understood better once the historians who direct their attentions to that faraway source will agree to expand their horizons far beyond the necessary philological quibbles and the supercilious study of the infinite number of contracts and administrative documents.

Those are the things that have kept me "by the rivers of Babylon," without romanticism, without parochial spirit, but with only my historical witnesses, in order to recognize there the homeland of the first discernible fathers of our Western world.

A last word: it is not because of a lack of interest, but because of a lack of space and opportunity that I have failed to present here a larger number of pieces or fragments of the enormous dossier of Mesopotamian writings. Let me say this so that one does not think that I am so much discouraged by the (real!) difficulties of translation. I hope as soon as possible to start working on a thick volume prepared in collaboration with the great Sumerologist S. N. Kramer, in which we plan to publish, in a succinct, annotated translation, all the remains—a few thousand lines and "verses"—of the fifty or so surviving myths in the Sumerian and the Akkadian languages, in order to give an idea both of the corpus and of the specific ways of mythological thinking of those forgotten and badly known ancestors of our own theologians and philosophers.

I

ASSYRIOLOGY

1

In Defense of a Useless Science

IT IS INEVITABLE THAT, WHEN ONE REACHES A CERTAIN POINT IN LIFE, one is tempted to look backwards in order to evaluate, and as a result justify, a road that is already long. I would like to confide in you, by fits and starts, a certain number of things that have been on my mind and that involve what I call my "profession": Orientalism. I am not unaware of the fact that this term covers an area much broader than the one with which I have been involved, i.e. ancient Mesopotamia; but I am convinced that even if I were not an Assyriologist, but an Egyptologist, or an Iranist, a Semitist, a Hebraist, an Arabist, an Ethiopianist, etc., I would base myself, certainly, upon different elements, but I would not say anything else. Hence, it will be easy for you to listen to all such scholars through my mouth.

When I entered the field of Assyriology—I am talking of a long time ago, as Rabelais said—I had just completed seven or eight years of study of the philosophies of Plato, Aristotle, and Saint Thomas Aquinas. I had learned there a number of lessons that since then have been very useful to me. Here are two or three of them, that can be used as a starting point.

The first lesson was that the highest nobility of mankind lies in knowledge, in knowing, and that man has it in his nature to want to know *everything:* everything about the order and the evolution of the universe. This pursuit is, at least, presented to us as an exalting and shining ideal, even if

A lecture given in Brussels (March 1982) on the occasion of the fiftieth anniversary of the foundation at the Free University of that city of the Institut de Philologie et d'Histoire orientales, and published in *Akkadica* 30 (November–December 1982): 12–26.

we can never attain its completion because of the vastness and the infinite character of its object. Secondly, on all levels including that of knowledge, all that is useful is servile and in itself inferior to what it serves. There was one consolation when I engaged myself in the unending, arduous, and fatiguing study of that frightening cuneiform writing system; of those languages extinct for millennia, so far removed from us, so loaded with pitfalls; of these endless texts, too often gloomy and deprived of any spark, and that at best excite us very little; of the strange outmoded mentality, which is often inaccessible to our present-day minds. My consolation during all this was the conviction that I was never going to learn anything that would be useful or usable for anything else than the enrichment of my mind. And this knowledge precisely gained its value from this awareness. At least such a point of view encouraged me to set off on this unending journey.

Afterwards I have never regretted this motivation nor the path it has led me to take. But I have reflected upon it—one tends to reflect more the older one gets—and I have slightly modified it, or, if you wish, I have specified my first opinions. I am still convinced that the chief greatness of mankind is to know, to store knowledge, and as it were to decant in one's mind if not the entire universe—that is the purpose of philosophy—at least the greatest possible part of this cosmos. Insofar as our actions are necessarily inspired by our knowledge, the higher, the larger, the more loyal and unselfish knowledge becomes in each of us, the more righteous and irreproachable our behavior could be. But, without trying to take away anything from the nobility and the detachment that I have assigned to Assyriology, I am not as convinced as I was before that it can be really useless and unusable, and as a consequence I am not so convinced of its independent and autonomous nature.

Let us quickly pass over a first use, or a practical use, that I have discovered. Assyriology made me neutral. Not only because when I was involved in it, lost in my illegible scrawls, surrounded by heavy books, by voluminous file cabinets and dusty tablets, I could not have a prejudice against anyone. In this day and age, when so many people spend their lives by getting involved with other people's affairs, by sticking their noses and their hands into their lives, by pestering them, by persecuting them or even worse, this is a great advantage—at least for other people. The discipline to which I have devoted myself has made me especially incapable of intervening in the lives of my contemporaries, as I have turned all my attention to the past. I do not know what wise man once said that there are two large categories of scholars, one that speeds up the world and brings its end nearer by its discussions, its inventions, its experiments, and its teachings; the other that goes back in its curiosity to the origins of the world and as a result leaves the universe and its inhabitants in peace. Without doubt,

Orientalists and Assyriologists fall into the second group. Their discipline acquires by that fact a negative usefulness, and how precious that is, especially in the present time! Perhaps you could even agree with me that it would be best for the proper development of the world if a number of our contemporaries would be converted and assigned to that discipline. Those people would then be able to spend their time without getting involved in that bickering, in that havoc, even in those massacres with which they are now so merrily involved—with the best intentions in the world, I am willing to believe if they say so, but to the greatest discomfort of all of us. I will not insist upon this generous, but unfortunately utopian, view on a possible use of Assyriology. I have to talk about a more realistic point of view which is clearly positive: the usefulness of Assyriology on the level of knowledge itself.

In order to explain to you what I mean by that, and what will be the essential part of the rest I have to tell you, I must recall the evolution of my own thoughts, with your permission. I have to admit first of all that I have always detested writing prose without knowing it, because that is a behavior, so to speak, for animals. Thus I have visited many archeologists, even a certain number of philologists, and in the beginning I was amazed (later I became used to it) to see to what degree even the smartest among them could undertake their activities with some kind of psychological automatism that was extremely surprising to notice. They worked with some kind of burrowing instinct that could be compared to that of moles, by all appearances without ever in their lives having had the slightest conscious idea of the real and the final purpose of their work, of the deep sense of their research, of the place and the value of their discoveries for knowledge in general. In order to guard myself from such a mistake—such a mess—I have asked questions only about Assyriology, and about what that science could teach me, in the very restricted area to which I was forced to limit myself, after my original, somewhat foolish, philosophical ambitions. I told myself: it is a *historical* science; thus it will give me access to a historical vision of the world. It involves the history of *ancient Mesopotamia:* thus my knowledge will be limited strictly to the borders of that country and its influence in the ancient Near East, from the "beginning of time" to around the beginning of the Christian era. But, still concentrating only on the subject of enrichment of the mind, what would be the advantages of compensating for these restrictions?

History (let us start there) grows out of human curiosity, as does all human knowledge. "By nature men want to know" Aristotle said, and men ask questions when confronted with things. They ask themselves "What is this?

How is it made? What is at the bottom of this?" They try to answer these questions by mentally isolating the simplest and most universal elements of what interests them, and when they try to draw from these elements the laws and the principles that govern their origin and functioning, they construct what we call "sciences" in the pure sense of the word. These sciences start out from concrete objects and end up with abstractions that are more and more removed from the obvious reality. I had just completed eight years of dealing with quintessential truths, and such an ascent did not tempt me. As a reaction I was more drawn towards recovering a contact that was as close as possible to living and individual material realities. Before them I was inclined to ask myself a string of questions: "Where does that come from? How did it become this way right in front of my eyes? What was there before it, in its place?" This inquiry did not involve "science" as described above, but it involved *criticism*, at least if we understand the resourceful control of answers to one's questions as such. The way of progressing in knowledge here is not by analysis. Analysis tends towards the general and the abstract, but it is *observation* which remains face to face with the tangible and moving objects, as they revolve around us, here on earth. It is involved with individuals, and especially with humans. Because in the end, and I do not want to displease the misanthropes and the most zealous members of the society of the protection of animals, the most interesting individuals on earth are still humans.

All of this pleased me immensely. After years of remaining in the thin air of the higher metaphysical altitudes, I felt like I lacked the full-bodied, odorous, warm, and moving air from the earth. After all, I told myself, still thinking if not of my philosophies, at least of my philosophers, once Aristotle had achieved his "metaphysics" he came back down to earth to keep himself busy with men and animals. If the entire universe is really the potential object of our inquiries, why should we limit our curiosity to abstractions? Why should we give a place of honor to the so-called "pure" sciences, when there are so many captivating and capital questions about living and moving human beings; when one of our most natural and most praiseworthy instincts guides our attention to those who surround us, and to those who preceded us and have left us such a rich heritage? Besides an explanation by laws and by principles, is there not a place for explanations by individual causes and by precedents? Do we have to understand a river only in terms of chemistry, hydrology, and the mechanics of fluids? Could we not also walk upstream to find its source? Genetics and psychology are all very well, but are there not among the children of mankind characteristics and resources that can be understood only by reference to their fathers? Do we not have to look in the past for vivid, concrete, and pertinent reasons for what is at issue in the present? This is why history at once became my business, without giving me the least impression—to the contrary!—that I had abandoned my first ideal of understanding things after having stored in my mind the largest possible wealth of information about those things.

Certainly, the fact that we deal with the "past" poses great difficulties. Our existence is short, and what we can understand of the past by having been there personally does not encompass more than a few decades. But there are witnesses older than us, and we can still question them. Also there are especially the remains, or even better the works, of our ancestors that have outlived them, often for a long time, and in which they have left behind much of themselves, even without wanting to do so. They are available to us if we make them speak to us. These remains include not only what our ancestors have built and what constitutes the enormous field of archeology: their residences, their dwellings, their defensive walls, their palaces, and their temples; the endless bric-a-brac of their tools, of their furniture, and their utensils; the remains of their labor and the debris of their undertakings; their works of art, monumental or miniature, dazzling or touching, this entire treasure that has been taken out of the earth and that gives us contact with its creators, definitively remote, but tridimensional and based on solid grounds. The remains also, perhaps especially, include written works when we deal with a civilization that knew and made use of a script and a language that are decipherable to us because they were based on elements that were solid enough to have survived. Those remains are only two-dimensional and are less imposing than the purely archeological remains, as if more ethereal and less real. But they *talk* of themselves, they reveal and they explain to us much more deeply, not only material life, but also the thoughts and the feelings of their vanished authors. Philologists who have learned how to read them, to understand them and to question them, are able to extract from them an enormous accumulation of precise elements. Because of those elements we can actualize the faded past, even the farthest away, as an immediate observation, thanks to which historians succeed in re-presenting the past, in more or less extensive sections. With luck they are able to do so with sufficient precision to allow us to recognize and evaluate in it what we received from our ancestors when we arrived in this world. Thus these elements give us an answer to the fundamental questions that haunt us always, to some extent, insofar as we are able to lift ourselves above the daily routine: "Whence do we come? How have we become what we are? What was there before us?" With such perspectives in mind I could remain faithful to my original intent after having associated it with more modest ambitions, and consequently I did not make a mistake by betting on history.

I also was not wrong in having chosen the ancient history of the Near East, more specifically of ancient Mesopotamia. True, it was not an easy field. Before I could enter it and could move freely around in it, I had to confront endless and often overwhelming initiation rites. I had to assimilate a chronological framework that was notoriously complicated, with a progression of elusive ethnic groups, a succession of cultures, of political vicissitudes, of dynasties with more or less strict hierarchies, and of countless rulers with complicated names that sound alien. I had to master a writing system with a discouraging complexity. It had between four and five hundred characters that changed in outlines from one century to another, and even became unrecognizable. Each of these characters usually can be read in more than one way, both on the level of ideography* and of phonetism,* and the choice of value can be determined only in function of the context, to such an extent that there is never a question of just reading, but only of deciphering. I had to be introduced to the mysteries not only of one language but of at least two, both dead and forgotten for millennia: Sumerian* and Akkadian.* These languages are as different from each other as French is from Chinese, and their usages became dissipated in an abundance of dialects over a dozen centuries. Finally, I had to familiarize myself with a monumental vocabulary that was partly twofold. At a low count it includes some twenty thousand words, a large number of which relate to concrete realities that we can pinpoint only with difficulty, as we have never *seen* them—not to mention those words that are even more difficult for us to understand.

But once I had overcome this thorny hurdle, once I was in possession of the keys, once I gained admission to the house and was allowed to move around freely in it, I discovered in it, day after day, an incomparable pile of riches. Without considering the immense archeological furniture, the booty of a century and a half of excavations in an inexhaustible soil, there is a gigantic library of at least half a million works. I have to outline a short catalogue of this library in order to give you some idea about it.

Four-fifths of it are occasional documents drawn up from day to day for a particular and ephemeral purpose, linked to the affairs of individual, collective, or political life, on which they throw a surprising light: lists and inventories of possessions; accounts of receipts and issues; of objects in storage or on hand; records of the regulations of communal life; price indices; international treaties and private agreements involving all imaginable types of transactions; sales and acquisitions, loans and deposits, marriages and "divorces," dowry agreements, wills and inheritance divisions, adoptions and contracts for nursing or for apprenticeship; official or private letters; commemorative and dedicatory inscriptions; property marks, etc.

The subject of the remaining part is more detached from immediate interests, and is more devoted to a certain duration in space and in time. It translates the thoughts and the feelings of its authors more than their material existence. We could call that part "literature," and it is also varied in form and sumptuous. The lion's share of it deals with religious preoccupations which are omnipresent at that time: myths, "theology," and catalogues of the supernatural hierarchy; hymns and personal prayers; rituals of the official liturgy and of "exorcistic" ceremonies for private use, etc. The person of the king and his exercise of power characterize a large part of the other literary works: celebrations in honor of the ruler; royal annals and historiographic documents, in their basic form or reworked in compilations or in chronicles; epical and heroic legends, whose protagonists were most likely ancient monarchs; and even political pamphlets. What remains is an entire "academic" literature, i.e. inspired mostly by the profession, the duties, the prerogatives, and the tastes of the association of scribes, who were the only ones with the ability to read and to write: portraits, satires, fables, character sketches, and various essays; literary disputes and proverbs, or advice on how to live well; an enormous mass of lists and classifications of words and ideas; bilingual dictionaries (Sumerian-Akkadian), even trilingual dictionaries; encyclopedias; catalogues; "treatises" on mathematics, on grammar, on law, on medicine, on divination; notes and calculations on astronomy; and finally technical formulas for the production of colored glass, of perfumes, of dyes, of beverages, and even—I hope you will allow me to crown such a glorious list with this—recipes of culinary preparations!

The oldest pieces of this amazing documentation were not that far removed in time from the moment when man had established, around 3000, in Mesopotamia the oldest known script. The documentation spreads out over three millennia. Inevitably, what we know of it was restricted by three processes: the recording of it in writing, the preservation of the works, and the rediscovery of the works. This is why large areas remain in the shadow or in the dark even if certain places and time periods are better known to us. We cannot compensate for such deficiencies; but philologists and historians have learned how to reduce the inconveniences by ingenuity and acuity in analysis of the remaining parts, by comparisons, analogies, and hypotheses, which they handle with precaution or skepticism, in short by the systematic use of this maxim of popular wisdom that has perhaps most inspired mankind towards progress: We have to make do with what we have!

This is how I, once I had entered the field of Assyriology, and thanks to the efforts of Assyriologists, discovered little by little a sufficiently deep and lively picture of ancient Mesopotamia. It was an original civilization, rich and complex, that survived for three millennia through innumerable vicissitudes, across generations of people, of whom I personally know a few thousand: by their names, their comings and goings, their businesses, sometimes by their loves and their hates, the luck and the mishaps in their lives. For someone whose original candid ambition was to collect in his mind as much information as possible on our world, and even with these much more moderate goals on which I had finally concentrated, I was not at all badly served.

But, and here I return to my original purpose, I soon discovered that, contrary to my first expectations, and by the proper logic of the history to which I had devoted myself, the accumulation of knowledge provided to me by Assyriology could not be treated as an isolated whole, closed in on itself from all sides, autarchical and consequently dressed up with the eminent dignity of a complete uselessness. We can isolate ideas, we can bridge unsurpassable gaps between abstractions, but we cannot so easily dissociate realities, and even less men.

In the evolution of the reconstructed history of ancient Mesopotamia itself, even if the reconstruction is imperfect, I did not only find before me, from the end of the fourth millennium on, between the simple, uniform cultures that were more or less rudimentary and surrounding it, a high civilization which was doubtless the first on earth—at least as known to us—that gave access to this density, this complexity, and this plentitude; I also encountered ubiquitous signs that this culture at a very early stage started to radiate, like a light, over its entire geographic and political horizon: from the Persian Gulf to the Mediterranean, from Iran to Syria, Palestine, and Asia Minor. From around the year 2500 on, the oldest documents found in the east at Elam* as well as in the west at Ebla,* show that the culture had spread out, together with its script and its languages, disseminating its inventions and its cultural values. Excavators have uncovered almost everywhere in this large area of the Middle East bits and pieces of cuneiform literature from the second millennium on: of its myths, its epics, and its scientific "treatises." And is it not highly significant that the two large collections of international correspondence in the second millennium, those from Mari* in the eighteenth century and from el-Amarna (in Egypt!) in the fourteenth century were drawn up in cuneiform script and in the Babylonian language? If the Bible, which for a long time was considered to have been more or less a product of the supernatural and to have preserved the oldest records of humanity, has lost this naïve privilege, it is because on December 3, 1872, the Assyriologist G. Smith announced in London that he had discovered on a cuneiform tablet an account of the Flood that was too similar to that of the biblical book of Genesis for us to deny the latter's dependence, both thematical and literary, upon the cuneiform account. All that we know of the impressive Hittite* empire, from the second millennium, shows us that this culture is also indebted to its Mesopotamian older brother: it received from Mesopotamia its script, a part of its vocabulary—and together with the words, the things to which they referred!—and a number of literary, juridical, and scientific models.

Moreover, the Hittites lived in Asia Minor, and Asia Minor borders on the Aegean and on Greece. Even if they do not think about it with pleasure, the most stubborn "patriots" among the Hellenistic scholars today cannot deny any longer to what extent Archaic Greece was influenced by the East on the cultural level—and in all other areas. And in the East they borrowed first of all from the honorable and grandiose culture of Mesopotamia.

For us, our "Western civilization" was inaugurated and launched by Christianity, whether we believe in it or not. Christianity itself finds itself notoriously in agreement with the biblical ideology on the one hand, and with the Greco-Hellenistic one on the other. Thus we too are remote dependents of the Sumerians* and the Babylonians* through this double relationship. Therefore the Sumerians and the Babylonians are our oldest recognizable ancestors in a direct line of descent. From afar, very far, they belong to our family, they are part of our past. The past has to be as indivisible in our knowledge as it was in its actual development. If we want to understand it on the genetic level, if we want to rediscover our ancestors, if we want to take account of the oldest and most fundamental part of our heritage, and if we want to find the irreplaceable and enlightening explanation of what we have become, the explanation that only history can provide us, i.e. "by individual causes and precedents," we have to go back as far as these ancient Mesopotamians, at the extreme limit of our horizon.

For a long time a double "miracle" (in any case, miracles are always suspicious) has prevented historians from going on this road of return to our origins: the image of the Bible, "the oldest book on earth," written by God and bestowed upon men in order to give a definitive answer to all their questions; and the famous "Greek miracle" which implicitly presupposes before the Greeks a universe of primates that had barely come down from their trees or nervously left their caves. No historian worthy of that title in its real sense, should see absolute beginnings either in the Bible or with the Greeks—only two great steps on a road that goes much farther, much earlier, and ends only between the Tigris and the Euphrates, right before the uncertainties, the twilight, and then the increasing darkness of prehistory.

This is why I have renounced assigning to Assyriology a total uselessness, which would in my opinion have amounted to recognizing in it an indisputable independence and preeminence. Since I have practiced the discipline and I have obtained an idea of all that it can bring to us, I have learned to consider it to be not only useful, but (objectively!) as indispensable for a correct and global understanding of our own history. Assyriology is not simply an enrichment of the mind. It should not have as its final goal our own pleasure and grandeur in discovery and learning. It is at our disposal to provide us with our oldest family documents, if we want to consult them. It is there to crown our past, to inaugurate our origins, and to lead us to the primal source of that enormous stream which still carries us.

In this regard, Assyriology takes its own irreplaceable position in the center of knowledge and learning that make up this *university of sciences*, a university which was the greatest and most noble ideal of the Middle Ages. As in Plato, Aristotle, and Thomas Aquinas, the medieval ideal also placed the dignity and the greatness of mankind before all else in the pursuit and the satisfaction of its hunger for knowing and understanding. And it thought that, just as we all have a brain in order to see, to perceive, to think, to prepare, and to direct properly the activity of our mouth, our arms, and our legs, all truly human society worthy of that name must have the capability of knowledge, of perception, of understanding, and of information that does not leave anything outside its field of vision, of research, and of study. As this cannot be done by a single man, it must be undertaken by a group: by scholars gathered to secure and to promote the university, i.e. the *totality* of sciences that form a system where nothing can be left out without compromising the whole. We have inherited this magnanimous and magnificent belief. The existence and the fame of your own university, and the efforts you are making to preserve and to develop this ideal, show to what degree you still believe in it.

And this is apparently not without merit. Because in our countries for some time now a great hurricane of subversion has arisen, pushed forward by I do not know what vicious demons—and doubtless in accord with the life-style that we have made our own, unfortunately. This hurricane tries to reverse our traditional order of values, to throw out all that we put forward as being unselfish, gracious and open to the world, open to things and to others, all that is active in dilating our minds and our hearts. It wants to replace it by the single, brutal, arithmetic, and inhuman motivation of profit. Henceforth, all that counts, all that is to be considered and preserved, is what brings profit. The truly ideal aspects of knowledge will not be more valuable than those of interest rates and of financial laws. The only sciences that are to be encouraged are those that teach us how to exploit the earth and the people. Besides that, *everything* is useless.

That is an entirely different notion of useful and useless, entirely in opposition to the one I took as a starting point. Taken literally, it reduces mankind in the end to the depressing state of the dismal mechanics of classifying and calculating. But even if it contradicts all that I have just explained to you, it leaves intact the fundamental and explicit principle: all that is useful is subservient.

We will say only that in this new perspective all that is useful for profit is thus subservient to profit. And that brings us back very deviously to my first naïve version of things which I have slightly adjusted, as I have told you, but which I have never decided to abandon. Thus I accept the verdict of these new standard-bearers and I urge you to accept it with me. Yes, the university of sciences is useless; for profit, yes, philosophy is useless, anthropology is useless, archeology, philology, and history are useless, oriental studies and Assyriology are useless, entirely useless. That is why we hold them in such high esteem!

2

Assyriology and Our History

FOR SOME TIME NOW WE HAVE BEEN EXPERIENCING A RENEWED INterest in history, especially in France. History is the controlled and "scientific" rediscovery of our own past, the ground where we meet our forefathers and whatever we owe to them, in order to measure our dependence on them at the same time as our own progress—or our own decline. This interest is witnessed by the noise made about certain historical works, even though they are thick and difficult, and by the success of some serious periodicals of high-level vulgarization.

But I would say that this interest remains selective. For example, Assyriology, which has existed for more than a century and whose innumerable discoveries are almost all surprising and very important, is still regarded, with a degree of reverence or reservation that is almost ironic, more or less as a pastime for pure scholars. And as a scholar is, by definition, a gentleman "who knows everything about nothing," the subject of the Assyriological discipline, i.e. the history of Mesopotamia, is as a result thought to be negligible. That was understood some years ago when the powers that be, always so well informed and so clairvoyant, excluded the field entirely from the program of secondary schools. At most, this outdated adventure deserved to be glanced at in passing, in the same way that one decides on a rainy Sunday afternoon to go through the Ancient Near East section of the Louvre Museum, in order to kill time.

To the extent that this attitude is not irrational, as are all fashions both positive and negative, the principal reason for this lack of interest, not so

This chapter first appeared in *Dialogues d'Histoire ancienne de l'Université de Besançon*, 7 (1981): 93–106.

much among the educated public, which is an obedient flock of Panurges, but among professional historians, cannot be the vague apprehension that the citadel of cuneiform script is guarded on all sides by an imposing wall of ultraspecialized competence. All sectors of serious history are more or less like that, each in its own way. This has never prevented the uninitiated from being involved with them, if they really want to do so, by falling into step with the specialists, the only certified guides in the labyrinths of this type. It seems to me that the real reason for this indifference is that the Assyriologists themselves have not been able (I think they have never seriously tried), to integrate the subject of their research into what concerns all of us: the history of our own past, what has made us the way we are. Assyriologists are too few in number and preoccupied with deciphering difficult documents that have been taken out of the earth by the hundreds of thousands for over a century, and that are inscribed on fragile clay tablets in a language and a script that were both dead and forgotten for two millennia. They give the impression of being astronomers who are fascinated only by an enormous globe that is wandering through the universe and is separated from us by thousands of light years. Such stubbornness can well be admired, but does not prevent us from leaving such touching eccentrics to their dusty unintelligible scribbles.

It may be useful to explain that the unintelligible scribbles in question, methodically nibbled on by these discreet rodents, really form the oldest documents of our family history, if we look at them closely.

We may want to trace our genealogy backwards in order to return to the origins of our own heritage, of our own ways of living and of thinking, to the origins of the Western civilization in which we still live, whatever some people may think. An age-old tradition that is difficult to uproot stops us on our way by confronting us with two "miracles" that are different from each other but that have at least this in common: they appeal enough to something supernatural and irrational to stop us on our way.

Whether we like it or not, Western civilization derives directly from Christianity. And Christianity is at the confluence of a double cultural stream: the Bible on the one hand, and Hellenism on the other. Let us start with the Bible. For too long it has been regarded as the "oldest book on earth" and, even better, as written down "under the inspiration of God" or "revealed" by him. Hence, it is considered to contain such an absolute and total truth that until recently few have thought, and many of our contemporaries undoubtedly still do not think, to search beyond what it tells us about our oldest ancestors of the Israelite branch—not to mention what it says about the very beginning of all things. With regard to the other branch, no Greek scholar would still refer in explicit terms to this "miracle" as the sudden appearance of the Greeks in a world of humanoids. No one would still claim that the Greeks invented almost everything, created everything in the real sense of the word, i.e. starting from nothing. But judging by what they write, many scholars are still more or less consciously indoctrinated by this amazing idea and do not feel any urge to investigate beyond the superhuman Greeks in the direction of the "Barbarians" to whom the author of the *Epinomis* (987–88a) already referred with a certain respect.

The Assyriologists have the material in hand to defuse this imaginary double postulate, that grants the status of absolute beginnings to what is nothing but a stage in an evolution.

The oldest documents, both biblical and Greek, do not date further back than the second half of the second millennium before Christ. The oldest "cuneiform*" documents that can be understood and used on a historical level are close to the year 3000. Even better, it is these texts that contain something of an unsurpassable limit in them: the oldest among them are very close in space and in time to the invention of cuneiform writing in Mesopotamia, probably even to the invention of writing itself. Besides, only *written* documents can give us an assured knowledge of our past that is precise, detailed, and analytical. Prehistorians and archeologists as such can only see a hazy and uncertain outline of the past. This is why *history begins at Sumer,* as is emphasized by the title of a popular book. In other words, history begins in Lower Mesopotamia in the first part of the third millennium.

And this history is our history! It is not divorced from us, as are the remains excavated in the depths of Australia or of Tierra del Fuego. It extends in time precisely the history of our ancestors, both Hebrews and Greeks. This is not only because the cuneiform documents present us with a historical framework that is earlier than both of them, and because the documents of a later stage redefine and complement what these people tell us about themselves; but also, and more importantly, because we are largely formed in all aspects of our culture by the Mesopotamian civilization which was born in the fourth millennium and was already well-developed in the third. This civilization is perhaps the oldest in the world that deserves this noble title. It radiated to its surroundings during its entire existence and generously inspired and enriched its neighbors: Israel directly, after and together with its Semitic congeners; the Greeks indirectly through the Hittites and the pre-Greeks of Asia Minor.

This is why Mesopotamia has its *organic* place in the lineage of our own past. This is why, on the historical and the genetic level, which explains children by their parents and rivers by their sources, we cannot understand anything of the past without going back to Mesopotamia, and without refusing to stop in Greece or in Israel on this road. This is why Assyriology should not be considered in itself as the pastime of a few obsessed scholars—whatever one's opinion on the hermits who make it their profession—but as great history, at the same level as "classical" history on the one hand, and as biblical history on the other. Both of these are crowned, completed, and seemingly "explained" by Mesopotamian history. Because in the end, if the ancient Mesopotamians are really recognized as our oldest discernible ancestors in a direct line of descent, why do we stop with their children, our older siblings, when we draw up our genealogical tree? Why do we consider futile and unworthy of attention and of study what the Mesopotamians have left us, and what was transmitted to us in a more or less altered fashion, enriched or improved?

As it is not very serious to keep on talking in the air, it will not be useless now to abandon the area of principles and return to the more mundane level of facts. Thus, I would like to bring in an example of how Assyriology can enlighten our own history, at least from a cavalier and elevated point of view. This example lies in an area that is really characteristic of us and that still is very valuable in our "Western" eyes, as things stand: the scientific spirit and the practice and organization of science.

Nothing would make it doubtful that the search in all possible areas of knowledge that surpasses material and actual objects in order to record whatever the objects conceal that is universal, permanent, necessary, and foreseeable, is one of the characteristics of our culture. No one will dispute that this search has been bequeathed to us by the Greeks, even if we have, especially in the last century or two, particularly deepened, expanded, and enriched the notion that they had extracted from scientific knowledge, especially on the experimental level. Thus, the creation of science has been credited to the Greeks, as so many other things. And the few historians who have been so rash as to ask openly "What existed beforehand?" and turned their attention to the pre-Hellenic east, have even increased the merits of the Greeks, so to say, by finding among these ancient peoples nothing but real *technical* progress, and no trace whatsoever of some sort of *theoretical* development. For instance, the Babylonians would have developed utilitarian calculations and surveying, but only the Greeks would have extracted mathematics and geometry from them.

This is not entirely how things present themselves to the eyes of someone who has firsthand acquaintance with cuneiform documents and has tried to follow step-by-step the long intellectual trajectory that they reveal.

Among the oldest cuneiform tablets, ones that are still almost undecipherable as they are so close to the mnemonic device that the script originally was, we can already find some Lists* amid hundreds of accounts. These lists are groups of words, classified in different ways. They may very well have served first as catalogues of characters, of mementos that are indispensable for learning and mastering the elements of the script. The continuing use of these lists, which were greatly expanded during the later history of the country, shows us that they had the ultimate purpose of arranging objects, of drawing up inventories of the numerous sectors of the actual world that were not only as complete as possible but that were, especially, methodical lists.

One of the most spectacular results of this ancient enterprise was a famous "encyclopedia," seemingly compiled in its essential parts in the first half of the second millennium, but based on older material. In nearly ten thousand entries this encyclopedia organized almost the entirety of the material and nonhuman universe, in its original form as well as in its form altered by human intervention, following a logic that naturally does not always correspond to ours but that by all indications had its own rules. We can find the following things in it in this order: all known trees and objects usually made of wood; the reeds and reed implements; clay containers; skins and articles in leather; various metals and what is made of them; animals, both domesticated and wild; parts of the body; stones and objects in stone; plants other than trees; fish and birds; fibers, fabrics, and clothes; all that can be found on the face of the earth—cities and dwelling places, mountains and waterways, in Mesopotamia itself and in the surrounding areas; and finally all things, natural or prepared, that were used as foodstuffs.[1] A similar list was made for all purely human things ("classes," occupations, professions, trades, etc.).[2] The considerable documentation that has come down to us from this "literature of classification," does not allow the least doubt about its fundamental character, however little one thinks about it. We have here the testimony and the results of an enormous and constant intellectual effort, typical for the state of mind of the ancient Mesopotamians, as an attempt to *understand* the universe by classifying and organizing its contents, itemized by common traits and by specific differences.

Other literary works testify as strongly in favor of this extraordinary determination to penetrate beyond the appearances of things. For example, starting from the turn of the third to the second millennium we have at our disposal some fifteen Disputations,* sometimes in several "editions." This was a popular genre of literature in Mesopotamia, and it consisted of confronting in a literary tournament two objects that were clearly taken as the prototypes and the representatives of their species and that were of a similar sort and were given a human personality. By turns each of them presented its own qualities, advantages, and prerogatives until one of them

1. The text is published in the lengthy and learned work by B. Landsberger, *Materialien zum sumerischen Lexikon* (vols. 5–11).

2. Ibid., vol. 12.

was declared the winner: Summer and Winter, Bird and Fish, Tree and Reed, Silver and Copper, Ox and Horse, Pickaxe and Plow, Millstone and Mortar, etc.[3] When we consider these short works carefully, we see that behind the mental games and the endemic passion of the "duel of prestige" there lies a real analysis of the objects presented, always with the same care to dissect, to compare, to classify, to understand things.

Of course these things appear only in their concrete and existential form both in the Disputations and in the Lists. They appear as they are visible and perceptible. Their generic or specific characteristics are never expressed in abstract terms, nor are their constant connections expressed in the form of laws. By all indications the ancient Mesopotamians balked at such formulations, which their language in any case hardly permitted them to develop. Their language is not rich in words that are purely abstract, and there is no term for a notion such as that of "law." But that is of little importance, as everyone knew, and we still know, that with "ox" in the Disputation or in the Lists one had to understand clearly what *we* would call the *idea* itself of an ox: what is common and characteristic of all bovines, in opposition to the *idea* of the horse, which represents all equids. Certainly, these people's mode of expression differed from ours, but it reproduced in effect the same mental processes that distinguish behind the physical appearance of things what separates and what unites them. Underneath the obvious, the ephemeral, and the unpredictable, these processes can recognize universal, constant, and permanent elements—what we would call concepts.

This desire to know and to understand is best expressed in a type of work called a Treatise* or a Manual which, by chance, represents the largest proportion of what remains to us from the literature of believers: several dozens of thousands of tablets at a cursory view. This type of work involves writings that are sometimes rather short—between fifty and one hundred lines on a single tablet, or even less; but usually they are much longer—we know of some that are spread over a hundred tablets or more, which would result in more than 10,000 lines at a low estimate. Each of these is devoted to one of the "intellectual" disciplines that the ancient Babylonians have explored: in addition to lexicography, grammar, and philology which were presented in Lists, there were also theology—we would almost say "philosophy" or "metaphysics"—partially also presented in Lists and in Catalogues, but more commonly explained in the form of mythological accounts, and astronomy (which probably developed rather late), also in part put down in Lists and spread out in a great number of observations, of

3. The texts of the Sumerian pieces are not yet accessible to the non-Assyriologist. One can find fragments of similar works in the Akkadian language in W. G. Lambert, *Babylonian Wisdom Literature*, pp. 150–212.

reports, and of accurate calculations. We also have to cite jurisprudence, whose manuals take the form of what we mistakenly call "law codes"; mathematics (arithmetic, geometry, and algebra), which was very well developed from the first half of the second millennium on, and for which, from that time on, there are amazing testimonies; diagnostic medicine, specially compiled in a great work of forty tablets (therapeutics was a technique treated separately); and especially "deductive divination." All of these were disciplines well suited for presentation in Treatises.

Deductive divination is one of the oldest known and, especially, the best attested of these sciences. Without any doubt, it presented in the people's minds a discipline of great importance during the entire history of the country, and its study is revealing to us in the highest degree. In any case, it has to be explained to readers of our time who may see it as nothing but a superstition, even though they take the puerilities of psychoanalysis seriously; therefore, I will concentrate my comments on it.

The ancient Mesopotamians were convinced that the world could not be explained by itself, and to give meaning to the world they were forced to set up superhuman personages who had to have created the world and who governed it. In order to represent these superhuman beings they did not find a better model than their own political powers, with the monarch at the top of a pyramid of subordinate authorities, whose power emanated from his. They transposed this system to the supernatural level in order to organize their pantheon and to represent the way the pantheon functioned. Just as their king governed the country, directly or through "vicars," by expressing his wishes, by making decisions, and by communicating them, the gods also made the world function according to their designs, by *deciding the destinies* of all beings, as individuals or collectively. And in this country with an ancient written tradition, where the decisions of the king were regularly promulgated in writing, the gods had to fix and memorialize their will in some way. How?

We cannot forget that the fundamental principle of the cuneiform writing system, invented in Mesopotamia and whose discovery and functioning profoundly marked the mind, was pictography, both originally and later always maintaining its power—in other words the possibility of representing objects by other objects. The drawing of a foot also evokes walking, standing up, and transport. The drawing of a stem with an ear of cereal also represents the products of agriculture. From that principle the conviction was born that the "script of the gods" consisted of the things themselves that they produced when making the world function. When things conformed to routine, as happened most frequently and most regularly, their message was also "normal" and undetermined, i.e. the signs announced a decision conforming to the routine. In other words, they represented a special non-decision, a purpose deprived of interest, as things did not do anything but follow their known and expected course. But when the gods produced either a creation that did not conform to its model, or a singular event that was unexpected and eccentric, they expressed with it their will to announce an equally unusual *destiny.* One could know the destiny if one knew how to decipher it through the presentation of the abnormal phenomenon in question—just as one deciphered pictograms and ideograms of the script.

That was the foundation of deductive divination. It involved reading *in* events or objects that were unusual and irregular, in order to draw and deduce from them divine decisions that touched upon the future of the interested party: either the king or the country, or any individual who was put in touch with the object of the divinatory action. It should be said that this future was not a "real" future, an absolute future which would take place inevitably. It was a future that the gods had decreed *hic et nunc,* and, just as the ruler was free to revoke his decisions, to give in to requests, and, for example, to put off the punishment of someone he had originally condemned, the gods also remained merciful. The people had invented and developed numerous recipes to urge the gods to alter the more or less cruel "destiny" that they could have originally fixed, and that had been read in the omens in a more positive sense.

Thus the essential act of this procedure was a "deduction," a judgment that started from one given fact and led to another fact that was considered to be contained in the first. From the aspect of a phenomenon that differed from the ordinary and as such played the role of an *omen,* the definition of a part of the future, a *prediction* was drawn by a way of discourse. One example can suffice here, but several more can be found in the book "Divination et rationalité" (pp. 70–193). This example is taken from an enormous "Treatise on divination through the accidents of daily life (in "Divination," p. 106): *If a horse attempts to mount a cow* (this is the event, one that is quite rare and that by its very abnormality would draw the attention and indicate that a message could be found in it: it is the communication of a divine decision): *there will be a decline of the land* (this constitutes the decision, the prediction, what one should expect as a result of the will of the gods. It was communicated in this fashion, and would take place unless precautions were taken in order to make the gods change it).

A certain number of considerations present themselves at this point. First, as the "medium of the script of the gods" is the entire world in its outlook and its development, so to speak, all areas of nature required close attention and observation in the divinatory perspective. We also find Treatises on mantic techniques* which have as object the stars and meteorites (astrology* and meteoromancy) in their presentation and their movements;

the days of the calendar (hemerologies and menologies, to the extent that the coincidental or accidental nature of a specific event on a specific moment of the calendar could be ominous, as it would be a singular occurrence in itself); the birth of creatures and their form when leaving the womb (tocomancy* and teratomancy*), both of animals and of humans, and for births on time as well as for premature births or for abortions; the configuration of the land, of rivers, of cities etc.; the appearance and the behavior of plants and of animals (divination through the accidents of daily life*); the disposition of the human body and the behavior of men, by themselves or in their interactions with others or with the rest of the world (physiognomy* in the narrow and in the broad sense; accidents of daily life); the contents of dreams (oneiromancy*), sometimes dreams that are induced or provoked (incubation*); accidents and their occurrences and especially unexpected noises that strike the ear (cledonomancy); not to mention other examinations after human intervention, such as the examination of the reaction of animals at the moment of their sacrificial slaughter, and the appearance of their entrails afterwards (extispicy* and especially hepatoscopy,* as the liver was considered to be a choice recipient of supernatural messages, perhaps because of the large variety of its possible appearances); or the examination of the configurations presented by drops of oil (lecanomancy) or of pinches of flour (aleuromancy), etc. In conclusion, during their investigations the authors of the Treatises could use the entire infinite object of the musings of the authors of the Lists: the entire earthly universe.

The universe thus explored was detailed and classified in its component parts, just as in the Lists, but more punctiliously and more deeply. Not only did one have to separate and to serialize the different formal objects: the Treatises on astrology dealt with the examination of stars; those on physiognomy dealt with the reading of the appearance of the human body; those on oneiromancy with the canvas of dreams, and so on; but each of these categories also had to be scrutinized and inventoried *in all its eccentric forms,* which presupposed a complete and exact notion of their normal appearances. When the *Lists* of the parts of the human body were satisfied with a few terms for the various parts of the face, the Treatise on physiognomy took into account all the individual aspects of the same face: was it abnormally long, or short; square or rounded; deformed, and if so, in what way; red or pale, or another unusual coloring; spotted, and if so, with what type of markings, etc. The first tablet of the Treatise (which comprised at least twelve tablets) devoted in that way more than one hundred and sixty observations to the head alone, most of them to the hair. In each Treatise a very well-developed operational diagram was systematically used, and it was adapted to the subject matter in question. It was a type of grid that was laid over the object or over elements of it that could be isolated. As a framework of inquiry, it permitted recalling anything of its abnormal appearance:

size, number or volume; absolute or relative position; shape; coloration; presence of adventitious elements, etc. And the various conjectures about these elements were methodically classified in a constant order with a painstaking rigor. Each eventuality was the object of a separate rubric, and all were exhibited in the same grammatical form, repeated ad nauseam, as so many hypotheses, or "protases,*" each followed by their results, or "apodoses.*" For instance, on a physiognomic tablet (translated and explained on pp. 174ff. of *Divination et rationalité*) there is question of the presence on the human body of a birthmark called *umṣatu*. It is catalogued from head to toe in more than seventy imaginable positions (and the tablet is even partly damaged) on an entirely uniform pattern: "If the *umṣatu* is located on that organ . . . "; "If it is located in the center . . . "; "If it is located on the right . . . "; "If it is located on the left. . . . "

Even if one needs a lot of patience to read these Treatises carefully and to think about them, and despite their sleep-inducing presentation which would easily put off even the most persistent of readers, they provide us in this way with analyses of an extraordinary minuteness. They involve numerous observations that are sharp and penetrating, and an eagerness to know that is even more impressive than the one that must have inspired the composition of the Lists.

In the same way that the Lists constitute simple inventories of objects that are present and that exist before the eyes of the observer, the Treatises also envision hypotheses about the future. They are based on observations of past events, but they project them into the future. *If a horse attempts to mount a cow* does not mean that *once when a horse wanted to mount a cow this was followed by a decline of the land*, but *each time that a horse attempts to mount a cow, one has to expect a decline of the land.* Just like the words in the Lists, the situations in the Treatises represent universal things; prototypes that are everywhere and always valid. Hence, they obtain their character of profound knowledge and of importance to objects in general, surpassing individuality, time, and space. In other words, these Treatises have a scientific character that is even more obvious than it is in the Lists.

This becomes much clearer when we see that the Treatises frequently surpass the field of observation to tread on that of conjecture. Take, for example, a short manual on hepatoscopy that takes into consideration the strange presence of *two* gallbladders in the liver of a sacrificed lamb, an unusual but certainly an observable occurrence and definitively observed once. The manual does not stop there, however, but goes on to foresee *three* and so on up to *seven*, a number not chosen because it is an unsurpassable limit but because one has to stop somewhere, and one has to allow the prospect of even more extraordinary quantities. Similarly, the Treatise on tocomancy does not stop with twins (it involves human births!), but also envisions triplets, quadruplets, quintuplets, and up to *nine* children together during one and the same delivery, a number that is to be regarded like the seven above. Such anomalies apparently had never been observed, but it is of the highest interest that they have been inserted into the Treatises. Precisely because the latter were not works of the simple recording of history, but of science, a discipline which bears not only on the past but also on all times, they had to note down both what had happened, in fact, and what could happen, by right. In our predictions on these matters, we have enclosed ourselves within our biological laws, which exclude such eventualities. But the Mesopotamian scholars, in whose opinion the universe was ruled not by laws of which they were aware (at least not aware of them as laws) but only by the wish and, in the end, by the free will of the authors of everything, did not see any possibility of imposing limits on those authors. If on a rare occasion the high beings decided that quintuplets or septuplets would be born, why not? This is a new characteristic that places next to the simple passive and detached knowledge of pure observation the desire to know *everything:* not only the observed reality but the possible; in other words the universal. This is a new characteristic that forces us to put forward the term Science.

Another important remark will take us one step further on this road. It involves the understanding of why the authors of the Treatises considered themselves to be authorized to go from the omen to the oracle, and with such a certainty that their propositions were always applicable, or, in other words, normative forever.

It seems to be beyond doubt that divination in Mesopotamia was based and created at first on some type of empiricism. The truth of the judgment by which one identified protasis and apodosis, by which one derived the oracle from the omen, was based upon the observation made at least once of the de facto consequence of two events. Traces of that survive in our Treatises when the deduction bases itself, for instance, upon a real experience. Thus we find in the Treatise on physiognomy in the broad sense (the behavior of individuals): *If a man has the habit of betraying secrets: he will never get access to an important office.*[4] Or, and this time it is with a certain irony or with a certain humor: *if there are many wise men in a city: that city will be ruined;* with the expected counterpart: *if there are many fools in a city: that city will be happy.*[5] Moreover, a certain number of oracles presupposes a "living being" by their precision and by the detail of their formulation. One of them is very intriguing, even moving, and appears in a Treatise on hepatoscopy: *If* . . . (it involves the appearance of a part of the liver): *the*

4. *Zeitschrift für Assyriology,* 43 (1936): 96f.; 2: 3.
5. F. Nötscher: *Haus- und Stadtomina:* 48ff.: 70 and 67.

wife of that man, pregnant by another man, will constantly pray to the goddess Ištar and say to her while thinking of her husband: "May my child resemble my husband!."*[6]

On the other hand, certain oracles recall events that are seemingly historical—and that almost all belong to one period (particularly the period of the dynasty of Akkad,* between the years 2350 and 2150) during which we can assume for certain reasons that the divinatory discipline was developed. For example, in a Treatise on extispicy put down in writing in the Old Babylonian period (first half of the second millennium) we find: *If the heart of the sacrificial animal resembles the testicle of a sheep: this is the omen of king Maništušu* (the third ruler of the Akkad dynasty, around 2250) *who was assassinated by his courtiers.*[7] It is possible that the murder of the king had really been associated with the somewhat earlier discovery of an abnormally shaped heart in a slaughtered animal. This is all the more likely as the Mesopotamians, in accordance with their vision of the world, always seem to have devoted a lot of attention to *mirabilia*, to *portenta*, to any event that differed from the norm; and a few collections that have survived give the impression that they kept records of them.

Moreover, it seems that such observations must have led them quickly to wonder to what extent the following events could not have been *not only preceded, but also announced* by the antecedent ones, precisely because of the idea that they had of both the role of the gods and of the mysteries of their writing system. It goes without saying that we do not know how and when they became aware of that, but to the extent that we can take as historical the following passage of another Treatise on hepatoscopy, also from the Old Babylonian period, we can formulate some idea on it by way of hypothesis: *If in the liver, on the right hand side of the gall bladder two clearly marked perforations* (Akkadian *pilšu*) *are pierced* (*palšu*): *this is the omen of the inhabitants of Apišal whom Narâm-Sîn* (fourth king of the Akkad dynasty: between 2254 and 2218) *made prisoner by means of a breach in the wall* (*pilšu*). Once more, if the fact is authentic, we would have a double reason to relate the two oracular elements, the omen and the prediction, to each other. Not only had the observation of a strange liver perforated in this way preceded the capture of the southern city of Apišal by a breach in the wall, but the wording of the omen and that of the oracle were tied by characteristic similarities in sound: the perforations (*pilšu*) pierced (*palšu*) in the liver evoked not only the breach (*pilšu*) but the name of the conquered city (*Apišal*), by a slight consonantal metathesis. Besides, we have to know that in the eyes of the Mesopotamians—we have numerous examples of this—names were not simple *flatus vocis* arbitrarily attached to objects in order

6. See below, chap. 8, n. 13.
7. A. Goetze, *Old Babylonian Omen Texts*, pl. 6, no. 9: 21f.

to indicate them, *they were the objects themselves*, given a sound. The names emanated from the objects they represented, and hence any similarity in sound was highly significant. Whatever its value may be, historical or not, the oracle in question at least helps us to understand how the sequence of two empirically observed events could evolve into a much closer relationship between the two, one *signifying* the other, which constitutes its recording in writing, i.e. pictography.* It is such a modification of the relationship between omen and oracle that has raised divination to an entirely different level. It is not any more purely empirical and pure registration, but deductive and *scientific*. Because, henceforth one could entirely abandon the attention paid to the material succession of events, in order to concentrate on the decipherment of these that presented themselves as being significant and as bearers of written messages, by their bizarre aspect itself. That which was announced by unusual events was legible in the events that announced them.

Such a reading certainly had its code, which escapes us now to a great extent, because at the moment Assyriologists have paid too little attention to those difficult and abstruse problems, and especially because we know the obscurities and the possibilities of the extraordinary cuneiform writing system much less than did its original users. Thus there is little chance that we will succeed in using the cuneiform script with as much clarity and result as the ancient scholars. We know at least that the decipherment had to operate on a double level, which also exists in the writing system in question: the pictographic (or, if you prefer, ideographic) and the phonetic. We know in fact that each cuneiform sign could be read either as the name of a thing, of a certain number of things or of notions that are more or less connected to each other, or as the expression of one (or often several) syllabic sound(s). On the first level we can cite as an example almost all the omens where a lion appears, which is always echoed in the corresponding prediction by the idea of power, of brutal force, of carnage, or of tyranny. The lion was in some way the ideogram of those ideas. Or, in a slightly different way, the oracle cited above can be recalled, where the attempted coition between a horse and a cow, which was in any case a sterile one, could not announce anything but a resulting sterility: a decrease in the harvest. With regard to the phonetic value of signs, the oracle of Narâm-Sîn and Apišal, quoted earlier, is also instructive with its assonances. But there are several other examples of this: *If a gall bladder is lying (kuṣṣa) in fat: it will be cold (kuṣṣu)*,[8] or *If it rains (zunnu) on the day of the festival of the city god: the latter will be angry (zêni) at the city*,[9] etc.

8. A. Goetze, *Old Babylonian Omen Texts*, pl. 43, no. 31, iii: 32–35.
9. *Revue d'Assyriologie* 19 (1922): 144: obv. 20.

The indisputable existence of a code and of rules succeeds in showing to us the truly *scientific* character of divination in the eyes of the ancient Mesopotamians. These rules were not any less rigorous and were not less foundations for the possibility of progress in a sector of knowledge, by deduction and assured conclusions that were certified, necessary, and universally valid, just because they were never explained as such. Certainly, the Mesopotamians, in compliance with their habits and with their own genius, never formulated these rules and this code in their pure and naked form. Mesopotamians did not believe in abstractions, they were casuists. All their sciences were structured not according to axioms that were revealed and demonstrated, according to laws that were deduced and articulated, but they were based on the accumulations of concrete and individual cases that were enumerated in the way of Lists. When the contents of these Lists were sufficiently varied, the result could be duly assimilated by inculcating and by impressing upon the mind the principles of the solution by means of models and by references to analogy. That is the meaning of the Treatises, on the divinatory domain as well as in any other area ever approached in that ancient country: they were didactic works that taught how to reason and how to draw conclusions by using reasoning and the faculty of inferring from a large number of cases, whose sequence and order were informative by themselves. If you wish, they were the equivalents of our tables of multiplication and of our paradigms, by means of which we were in our youth initiated into arithmetic and into grammar, without the least recourse to principles and to laws. Thus, it would be wrong to allege, based on the uniform and tedious presentation both of the Treatises and of the Lists, that they are nothing but boring and empty enumerations, as has been done implicitly up to now. It would be wrong to neglect these very precious documents that allow us to take hold of the "birth" and the ancient progress of science and of the scientific spirit, so to speak.

Only a narrow, superficial, univocal, and biased viewpoint can obscure the evidence for us. This evidence is given to us by the careful and detailed examination of the cuneiform archives and shows that these ancient scholars, from the first half of the second millennium or somewhat later on, had discovered abstract thought, analysis, deduction, the research and the establishment of principles and of laws, *in their own way* and according to their rationality and their world vision. In short, they had discovered the essentials of the methods and the spirit of science, even if they saw them and formulated them in their own way, very removed from ours, and even if they also applied them to objects that are in our opinion inconsistent, such as divination. This is not to diminish the merits of the Greeks but to put forth the truths of history, i.e. the facts. This will allow us only to circumscribe the Greeks better and to define and to understand them better, by putting them in their place in a lengthy genealogy that started long before them.

Good historians are always aware that history as well as life knows only developments, and that absolute origins escape them. There is always something earlier!

3

A Century of Assyriology

PROFESSIONAL HISTORIANS DO NOT LIKE TO BE QUESTIONED ABOUT "origins," as these escape us and as we find in history nothing but progress or decadence.

Who can say when, exactly, Assyriology was born? Was it when the old Benjamin of Tudela, who traveled through Upper Mesopotamia around 1165, found Nineveh, the ancient capital of the Assyrians, "separated from Mosul only by a bridge over the Tigris and completely in ruin"? Was it when, about half a millennium later Pietro della Valle, "a Roman gentleman" returning from his travels to Persia and to Baghdad, brought with him to Europe the first "bricks inscribed with unknown characters" which he had collected in the ruins of Babylon? Was it in late 1802 when the young Georg Friedrich Grotefend informed the Royal Society of Sciences of the University of Göttingen that he thought he had discovered the key to the "Persepolis inscriptions said to be in cuneiform"? Because it was indeed he who, twenty years *before* the famous *Précis du système hiéroglyphique* by Jean-François Champollion, and without a bilingual text or any help but his own shrewdness and thinking, was the first to make progress on the long road that lasted half a century, at the end of which one could finally unravel the triple and formidable secrets that had for two thousand years protected the "Assyrian and Babylonian inscriptions."

Whatever may be the uncertainty, in 1857 Assyriology could walk by itself and could begin its progress and its discoveries. At that time the Royal Asiatic Society of London submitted to Henry Rawlinson, Edward Hincks,

This chapter first appeared in *Histoire et Archéologie—Les Dossiers* 51 (1981): 16–25.

William Talbot, and Jules Oppert, four of the most prominent historians who flattered themselves as knowing "Assyrian cuneiform," a long inscription that had just been excavated. The society asked each of them to study the inscription without communicating with anyone. When the translations were compared, it was realized that there was sufficient agreement to be certain that an objectivity and a "scientific" certainty in the matter had been attained.

It is remarkable that the progress of Assyriology was in the beginning the work of philologists, sedentary people who hate agitation and noise and avoid it in order to ruminate, their noses in illegible scribbles. All that the authors of those mysterious inscriptions and their contemporaries could have left behind after an occupation of several millennia in a country that was exposed to entirely new adventures for twenty centuries, was "completely ruined," like the Nineveh of Benjamin of Tudela. In this region of clay and reeds the ruins were shapeless, with nothing to catch the eye or excite the admiration and the curiosity of archeologists.

But from the moment that the small world of decipherers started to feel it was at the verge of finally breaking the secret of these "unknown characters," around 1840, a great passion to find other remains of those shrouded people arose. An era of archeological excavations started, inaugurated in 1842 in the north of the country by Paul-Émile Botta, the consular agent of France in Mosul. The excavations have not ceased ever since and, fortunately, do not seem to want to stop. Thus it would be useful to draw up a quick account of these finds, and of the accomplishments of Assyriology which today is more than a century old but still young, active, and full of initiatives and projects.

Assyriology shares with a few other fields of ancient history the inestimable privilege that in its quest for the past it can rely both on monumental remains, the field of the archeologists, and on written documents, reserved for the philologists.

As historians we can join our ancestors in this ancient world, who are removed from us in various degrees and whose lives and thoughts we attempt to reconstruct, only by discovering the things they left behind: the objects they made and, in the few cases when they could record their thoughts, their written compositions. In any given civilization, remains of material life and of works put down in writing go back to the people themselves. Each in its own way, these remains preserve something of those people in a more or less eloquent, more or less lively, way, and when properly analyzed, they better acquaint us with the people.

The archeologist who has just excavated a statue looks upon it somewhat in the same way as did those who sculptured it, who erected it, who admired it or honored it in the past. He trembles before it as they did. He becomes aware of their art, their perception of faces, of bodies, of poses, of the spirit they wanted to catch in the work. He finds out their feelings about clothes and about appearance. He may even know to what more or less remote place they went to find the stone from which the statue was made. However, without written words that are precise and detailed, he will never know the name of the man or of the god that the statue represents. He will never know the reason why the man or the god was represented, the role he played in his day, what moment in history, what point of view, he represented to his contemporaries; nor even on what basis the interchange was made that placed the material in the artist's hands. He will never know how the artist lived and what place he and his art had in the society of the time. All this they could explain to us, if their voices had not been silenced for so many centuries.

The archeologist finds a three-dimensional reality that is tangible, that has body, reality, and emotion, but is at the same time speechless and intellectually vague. The philologist derives from his documents an image that is in some ways abstract, disincarnate, and unreal, but that is of an irreplaceable eloquence with regard to its dense and precise meaning. Using that image, he can, in the end, without *seeing* anything, *know* everything. Both the archeologist and the philologist have access to only half of the total object of historical research: the complete human of the past. Only the historian who has at his disposal both streams of information that derive from the same faraway source, and who mixes the two sources together, can reconstruct that human being, as far as the latter remains recognizable to us.

Assyriologists have the ability to claim such a total historical vision, restored on the basis of the archeological evidence and of the details provided by the written documentation. Of course, their historical reconstructions are necessarily limited and imperfect. They are limited in time as they do not go beyond the beginning of the third millennium at the earliest. It was then, undoubtedly for the first time in world history, that the means to record thoughts analytically and, somewhat later, speech were established in Mesopotamia. Before that, we depend on archeological research and we have nothing but material remains that are speechless. The reconstruction is imperfect, because in ancient Mesopotamia as elsewhere, people never bothered to recall everything of their lives and of their ways of sensing and of feeling things. And whatever they reveal to us, both in the material remains of their lives and in the transcriptions of their thoughts, is badly presented to us, scattered in various degrees of obscurity depending on the time and the place in their vast empire and their endless history. We have recovered and explored only a fraction, one that is perhaps numerically enormous but proportionally minute.

If we compare, however, even superficially, what we knew of ancient Mesopotamia at the beginning of this "century of Assyriology" with what we know today, how could we not be dumbfounded by the enormous progress?

In the collection "L'Univers: Histoire et description de tous les peuples," the part devoted to *La Babylonie: Assyrie, Chaldée, Mésopotamie*, by the hand of Ferdinand Hoefer, appeared in 1852, ten years after the beginning of the first excavations and five years before the definitive recovery of the Babylonian cuneiform system. It comprises almost three hundred pages. Besides commentaries and syntheses by the author, almost the entire book consists of translations of all passages devoted to the ancient country, on the one hand from the Bible, on the other hand from the different "classical" authors: Herodotus, Ctesias, Xenophon, Berossus, Diodorus Siculus, Strabo, Arrian, Pliny the Elder, Velleius Paterculus, Justinian, Ammianus Marcellinus, Paulus Orosus, Agathias, and others. It also includes descriptions by more recent travelers, from the time of Benjamin of Tudela to the middle of the nineteenth century. The well-informed author added to this long extracts from the reports of the first excavations undertaken "in the region of Mosul" a few years earlier, both those by Paul-Émile Botta and those by Henry Layard.

The historical results of this long secondhand inquiry are summed up at the end of the volume in only thirty pages, not one more. There are four pages on "the religion of the Chaldeans," eight on their "astrology" ("based on a paper submitted to the Academy of Berlin in 1815"), and the rest on their "history." All told, the last part consists only of a series of some one hundred names of rulers, most of them strange and of a hybrid appearance, deformed and disfigured by their transcriptions in Greek or in Latin. Only the last of them are recognizable to us as they are attested in Biblical Hebrew, and less altered: Teglatphalassar, Sennacherib, Asarhaddon, Nabuchodonozor, Nabopolassar. Although the real history is extremely reduced and limited to a few details of their reigns, it really starts only with them, spanning the period from the first third of the first millennium before Christ to 539, when Babylon was captured by Cyrus. Only two centuries!—just enough time to see the collapse of an "Assyrian kingdom" followed by that of a "Babylonian kingdom"!

If the honorable Ferdinand Hoefer would return to earth today, he would get hopelessly lost in the enormous flood of information that has risen from the tiny trickle of water that he had so laboriously diluted in his thirty pages.

First of all, an uninterrupted series of excavations, starting with the ones by Botta, was undertaken in the entire country. To them alone the historical account would have to devote several large volumes. The *Bibliography of Mesopotamian Archeological Sites* by R. Ellis (1972), which records all sites that have been explored to date, at least on the surface, if not excavated, lists more than five hundred names for the territory of ancient Iraq alone. Of these, some sixty, at least, are names of centers of great importance, ones that are better excavated and have very often yielded incomparable riches: Nineveh, Khorsabad, Kuyundjik,* Uruk,* Ur,* Eridu,* Tello, Nippur,* Sippar, Babylon, Borsippa, Fara,* Assur,* Kiš, Nimrud, el-Obeid, Djemdet-Nasr, Larsa, Tell Asmar, Khafadjah, Ishchali, Tell Agrab, Aqarquf, Uqair, Tell Harmal, Nuzi, Tell Billa, Tepe Gawra, Arpachiya, Jarmo, Shanidar, Abu Salabikh, etc. This does not include the large and the small peripheral excavations, such as those of Susa* in Iran, Boghazkoy in Anatolia, and Carchemish, Ras Shamra,* Mari,* and most recently Ebla,* all in Syria. Although these sites are outside the political boundaries of the ancient Mesopotamian kingdoms and of modern-day Iraq, all of them depend to various degrees on the Sumero-Akkadian cultural traditions and have provided us with invaluable pieces of evidence.

This dogged enterprise undertaken by teams from France, Britain, Germany, the United States, Italy, and ten other countries (among them Iraq itself has taken a prominent place) was barely interrupted by the two world wars. It has revealed to us, through hundreds of thousands of pieces, intact or fragmentary, large or small, all the material aspects of life in ancient Mesopotamia: living conditions; architecture; urbanism; fortifications; waterworks; agriculture and date cultivation; animal husbandry and domestication; hunting and fishing; feeding and the preparation of food and drink; economy and trade, both local and international; travel over land, over rivers, and over sea; the technology of clay, of reed, of animal and vegetable fibers, of leather, of wood, of bitumen, of stone, of metal; "fashions" and ornaments; various manifestations of plastic arts: ceramics, both painted and incised; etching; glyptics; sculpture; mosaic; jewelry; painting; monumental art; music, etc.—to end an infinite list that one can illustrate without difficulty by reference to the articles in the two volumes of the *Dictionnaire archéologique des techniques,* for instance.

More particularly, the religious domain, to which Mr. Hoefer had devoted four short pages almost entirely filled with rhetoric, is now abundantly documented by the recovery of temples, sanctuaries, cult instruments, sacred images, reliefs representing liturgical ceremonies, and by numerous burials, that are most often as modest as were their occupants, but that are sometimes very rich and that betray by their accumulated treasures and by the profusion of bodies of animals and of servants slaughtered near the corpse of the ruler, a sinister and grandiose mythology of death.

These innumerable speechless objects, these sites and buildings, this gigantic archeological apparatus was originally investigated for its own sake, driven by the type of curiosity of collectors that haunts archeologists. But, little by little, one learned to question the objects at length with the help of technologies and analyses, in order to extract from them every possible aspect of their intelligible contents: all that by its material, its form, its construction, its placement, its setting, and its finality is preserved to us of the life and the thoughts of its creators. The enormous documentation of parched bones that has rediscovered its life and its speech, is supplemented by the immense treasure of written pieces, that span the three millennia before the Christian era.

No one has yet made a detailed count of the plaques or objects in stone or metal, of the bricks and especially of the clay tablets, sun-dried or baked, that served as "papers" in local usage, and on which were engraved or impressed with a stylus the countless cuneiform signs. Because of the nationalities of the excavators and the accidents of distribution, all these documents are scattered among the great museums of the world: the Iraq Museum in Baghdad, the British Museum, the Berlin Museum, the Louvre, the great American collections, especially in Philadelphia and at Yale, the Istanbul Museum, the Musée du Cinquantenaire in Brussels, the Hermitage in Leningrad, and many others. In total there must be more than half a million documents. Several times they have been found together by the thousands, having formed archives and libraries before the abandonment and the destruction of the buildings that housed them: forty thousand in Tello, thirty thousand both in Nippur and in Kuyundjik, fifteen thousand in Mari and most recently in Ebla, several thousands in Assur, in Ur, in Uruk, in Susa, in Sultantepe, in Fara and Abu Salabikh, in Kiš, in Sippar, etc., and hundreds and tens in some fifty or one hundred sites.

The number, the variety, and the precision of the details of the three-millennium history of Mesopotamia that are revealed by this enormous dossier recovered over the last one hundred and thirty years, is inconceivable. It is not only that a mass of people from the past have reappeared before our eyes with their names, their relations, their origin, their place of dwelling, their adventures, their family affairs, their love affairs or their affairs in general, their businesses, their capital and their debts, their routines and their special deeds, their acts of goodness and their crimes; not only do we know today annals of their political organizations but also the almost four hundred names of their rulers. The first of these rulers were seemingly legendary and "antediluvian," but the later ones are all real, and we have found authentic inscriptions for the majority and we can establish the lengths of their reigns and their place in time, sometimes with an accuracy of one or two years. We are familiar with their dynasties and with their political and ethnic changes.

Instead of the simplistic picture drawn up a hundred and thirty years ago of an "Assyrian kingdom" followed by a "Babylonian kingdom," both disappearing in two centuries, we have established a real history of several millennia. This history is complicated, difficult to understand, and full of unforeseen events, as are all histories. It is based partly on documentation, and partly on reconstructions that cover periods of various lengths of time, using techniques developed for the study of prehistory. We have now learned that the Land-between-Two-Rivers appeared only little by little around the sixth millennium as a result of the general drying of the climate after the glacial periods in Europe. We know that it was then populated progressively by the inhabitants of the piedmonts of Kurdistan and of the Zagros Mountains, themselves possibly descendants of the cave-dwellers, whose oldest remains go back more than a hundred centuries. We know that in this new, muddy, and fertile territory people seem to have devoted themselves to the growing of grains, besides the husbandry of small animals and cattle. Due to the extreme climate and the lack of rain, it was indispensable to establish a tight network of canals that would connect the two rivers and give the earth an exceptional fertility. This collective enterprise not only enriched the inhabitants enormously but permitted the grouping of workers, first in villages and soon afterwards in larger agglomerations that became centers of administration and redistribution.

During the fourth millennium the Sumerians,* who probably came from the southeast, seemingly came to mingle with the first population of "natives" about whom we know almost nothing, and with Semites* who had left the seminomadic groups that led their flocks of sheep and goats on the northern and eastern borders of the great Syro-Arabian desert, and that never ceased to infiltrate among the sedentary people. We do not know the roots of the Sumerians or their earlier habitat, with which they seem to have cut all contacts and from which they never received any new blood, in contrast to the Semites, who were perpetually reinforced by the arrival of new relatives. It is especially due to this Sumero-Semitic symbiosis with the probable but to us unrecognizable participation of the ill-known earlier occupants and of their cultural heritage, that from the fourth millennium on what we can call an urban *high civilization* flourished. It was complex and original, and it was the first in world history. Numerous elements were gathered in this civilization: social and political organization; the creation of institutions, of obligations, and of laws; the production of all goods of use and of exchange, procured overabundantly by a planned effort, and their circulation in the interior of the country as well as abroad; the appearance of superior and monumental art forms; the basis of a scientific spirit, characterized first of all by a constant urge to rank, to classify, and to clarify the universe. And finally, around the year 3000, came the last great innovation, doubtless the most decisive discovery of an importance that can barely be measured: the establishment of a system of writing. It was at first a simple mnemonic device, but in a few centuries it enabled the recording of all that is expressed by the spoken language, and in the way it is expressed by it. This ability of the script allowed people to objectivize knowledge, to organize it in an entirely different way, and to propagate it. Hence knowledge became rapidly more extensive and more profound.

The original Sumero-Akkadian civilization was not only going to animate Mesopotamia and its inhabitants and condition all its progress for three millennia, which is admirable in itself, but it was also going to spread into distant lands and profoundly influence the entire Near East. Its essentials were transmitted to us when, around the beginning of the Christian era, the foundations of our Western civilization were laid. In this way Mesopotamia is our oldest known ancestor by a direct line of descent.

For three thousand years we can follow the history and the political changes as well as the cultural progress of these astonishing people. At first they were divided in small "states," each with a monarchical government and centered around an independent city. Their alliances, their struggles for influence, and their conquests regrouped them into successive kingdoms of greater or lesser importance, whose capital cities changed with the military victories. It seems to us that these struggles never had an ethnic or cultural motive. If a political or economic interest did not set one city against the other, Semites and Sumerians lived in good understanding. The first were mainly found in the center of the country in the "land of Akkad,*" the latter were dominant in the south in the "land of Sumer."

In the last third of the third millennium the Semites took the upper hand for the first time, and created a vast empire that seems for a while to have controlled the entire area from the Mediterranean Sea in the northwest to the Persian Gulf. But this creation soon collapsed and was replaced between the years 2100 and 2000 by a less imposing kingdom governed by southerners. The latter were completely overrun and absorbed—on the ethnic level—by new Semites who had come to the country, in increasing numbers, in successive waves. The Sumerians disappeared forever, leaving behind only their language besides their enormous earlier contributions to the ways of life and thinking and to every type of progress. As far as Chinese is removed from French, their language was removed from the Semitic Akkadian language, which became commonly used in the country. But Sumerian remained, until the very end, the scholarly and liturgical language, as Latin was to us in the Middle Ages. That is undoubtedly the best proof of the intellectual preponderance of the Sumerians in the Sumero-Akkadian cultural complex.

Thus the division of the country into Sumer and Akkad was practically abolished in the beginning of the second millennium, and the history was centered around the city of Babylon, from about 1760 on. The great Ḫammurabi* had promoted Babylon to the capital city of a kingdom whose existence ended definitively the system of city-states. First Babylon prospered, then it was plunged for several centuries into a dormant period, not on the cultural level but on the political level, because of the strange invasion by the Kassites* (ca. 1600). Around 1100 Babylon saw the rise, in the north of Mesopotamia, of its most formidable competitor: Assyria, first around Assur,* then around Kalḫu*-Nimrud, and then around Nineveh. The preponderance oscillated between these two poles of Mesopotamia, until Babylonia took it away definitively from its rival around 610. But less than a century later (539) Babylon itself fell to Cyrus and, with its entire territory, was annexed by the Persian empire.

Of this long adventure only two moments, the two last, were recorded by Hoefer, in less than thirty pages: the succession and the disappearance of what he called an "Assyrian kingdom" and a "Babylonian kingdom." Today a thick volume would scarcely suffice to sum up all that we know of this history. How many pages would we need for the three millennia of history that came earlier, and for the endless earlier prehistoric period, none of which was even suspected in 1852? Does this not point to the incredible recovery by the spade of the archeologists and by the decipherment of the philologists, both groups working hand in hand?

This triumph greatly surpasses, however, the history of events, the simple framework of the millennia-long life of the people. The Mesopotamians were original and intelligent and did not cease to improve their existence, to enlarge their horizon, and to deepen their thinking. In a sense they prepared for us from faraway our own attitude towards life and the universe. In order to give an idea of their creativity, their refinement, and their riches, let us at least glance at the entirety of their monumental literary production, which has come down to us to this day. Certainly this is the most transparent and brilliant reflection of their genius.

Approximately four-fifths of the almost half a million records are "business documents" which betray an extraordinary passion both for formalism (most of the pieces in this dossier are drawn up according to rigid and recurring formulations, somewhat like our notarized acts and our judicial decisions) and for accounting that deals in the most meticulous way with the circulation of goods: stock inventories; accounts of receipts and of issues; contracts of selling and of buying of landed property and of people, of loans, of marriages, of dowries, of adoptions, of wet-nursing, of service; wills; litigations and court protocols, etc. Business letters often accompany these administrative records. They are sometimes written between individuals, but most often between superiors and their subordinates. A rather large number center around the ruler and are written by him or to him, and they often touch upon internal or international political issues. What were called "law codes" after the discovery of Ḫammurabi's "code" in 1902 (our collection now consists of some ten pieces of various lengths), are collections of royal decisions intended in their totality to show the wisdom and judicial sense of the ruler, to preserve jurisprudence, and to serve as models to teach those in charge how to judge.

If there were groups of real "intellectuals" and "scholars" from the very beginning in Mesopotamia, they had their own ways of knowing and of learning. Still unable to accommodate themselves to abstract concepts, to general ideas, or to universal law, their knowledge was made up of concrete cases, duly drawn from reality. These cases were stripped of their singular characteristics and compared in mutual variations, in the manner of the paradigms and the tables of multiplication that replaced the laws of grammar and the principles of calculus in our youth, and allowed us perhaps to grasp the laws so much better and with more certainty. The numerous treatises on "science" which they created and expanded, sometimes very early in their history, reflect this point of view, be it treatises on lexicography or on grammar, on jurisprudence, on mathematics (geometry and algebra), on medicine, on deductive divination that was to some degree rational, or later, on astronomy. We have recovered a really enormous collection of them, that are much more developed than the few collections devoted to technical matters. Only a small number of the latter were seemingly considered worthy of being put down in writing instead of being left to the oral tradition: hippiatry, perfumery, glasswork, dyeing, pharmacology, brewing, and cooking.

They do not seem to have appreciated either art for art's sake or literature for literature's sake, or the unique pleasure of listening or of reading. The last skill was moreover accessible only to a very few. The imposing difficulties of the system of writing made reading as well as writing real *professions*. On the other hand, there were those who devoted themselves to it without any qualms from the moment they saw a theoretical or practical use for it. We have, for instance, an entire series of short competitions between two persons, two animals, or two objects, that in reality attempt to analyze and to evaluate the nature and the advantages of both, in the vein of academic disputes (see above, pp. 30f.). And we also have found an entire system of aphorisms, even of rhetoric, contained in the vast collections of "proverbs" or of instructions towards the leading of an "intelligent" life, i.e. a successful life.

They were persuaded that the world had been organized and was directed by a supernatural body of divine personalities. Therefore, they associated most of the problems that are raised by our own nature and our existence, our destiny, the absurdities and the sufferings of our lives, to what we would call "theology." These issues were treated by them in a mythological manner, that is by allowing the intervention, not so much of concepts and of conflicts of ideas, but of imaginary persons and events. The origin and the appearance of the gods, of the universe, of mankind; the avatars of their existence before the actual, the "definitive" world so to speak, was able to function; the happiness and the accidents of human life, our destiny after death, all form the subject of an entire literature that is neither the poorest nor the least revealing of intelligence, of imagination, of logic and of the heights in thinking to which these ancient people could rise, so long ago. They even attempted to explain thus the great events of their past. And it is perhaps in this double field of the theology of nature and of history that they created several times real masterpieces of world literature: Atraḫasîs* (*The Supersage*) and the great *Poem of Creation** in one field, the *Poem of Erra** and the *Epic of Gilgameš** in the other.

We cannot leave belles-lettres without mentioning a number of songs, of hymns, and of prayers that were sometimes quite admirable, and the flood of "exorcisms," a type of procedure where incantations and sacramental gestures alternate, that were considered to be mutually suitable for obtaining from the gods the withdrawal of the evils of life, whose causes were readily imagined to be the acts of an entire litany of "demons." We should also not forget the pious almanacs of daily life indicating the supernatural risks and the chances, the devotions, the religious prohibitions and the obligations of every day of each month. Nor the great liturgical ceremonials the masterpiece of which is undoubtedly the one that describes the eleven days of the great Festival and the procession inaugurating the New Year.

It would be wrong to take a cavalier attitude towards the riches accumulated by Assyriologists during their first century as some type of diploma of self-satisfaction. These people are historians, and honest historians are too much aware of the extreme disproportion between the little that is preserved from the past and the infinite density of the past itself, to ever feel satisfied. What is the use of these two or three million pieces of archeological debris and nick-knacks and of written pieces in reconstructing the history of three millennia and of a prehistory that is even more enormous, involving the lives of hundreds of thousands of people? The balance-sheet that I have drawn up here, for only one of these "stages," is something that must be done from time to time, in a good system of accounting, in order to know where one is, before one goes on in a better way.

Numerous questions remain on all the levels and in all the areas of the discipline described above. Vast reaches of space and time are not documented by the least bit of information, and about numerous sectors of life, about the economic, social, or political organization, about the religious practices and thoughts, about the "scientific" views, we know practically nothing. A large number of documents in our dossier are incomplete! Thus, we have to pursue this work indefatigably. First of all we must pursue the excavations because they feed us, both the archeologists and the philologists; but we must also pursue the questioning of the objects on the one hand, and the decipherment of the texts on the other, and finally this historical synthesis as the result of the two, which is the only thing that can reconstruct, even imperfectly, a total image of our subject of research: the past of a wonderful ancient population to which we owe infinitely more than we realize.

Perhaps a century from now—I certainly hope so!—our descendants will consider our "balance-sheet" to be as weak and lacking as we judge the meager catalogue drawn up in 1852 by the scholar Ferdinand Hoefer to be.

II

WRITING

4

The "Avalanche" of Decipherments in the Ancient Near East between 1800 and 1930

RECENTLY THE VENERABLE TEXT OF THE COMMUNICATIONS DELIVered from October 3, 1802, to May 20, 1803, by the young Latin teacher G. F. Grotefend (1775–1853), announcing to the Royal Society of Sciences of the University of Göttingen that he thought he had succeeded in "reading and explaining the Persepolis inscriptions, said to be in cuneiform," was re-edited in Germany: *Praevia de cuneatis, quas dicunt, inscriptionibus persepolitanis legendis et explicandis relatio.*

These modest forty pages are useful for reminding us that in the beginning of the nineteenth century, when certain long-deferred or unimaginable inventions were suddenly "in the air" and in our reach, it was not only Ancient Egypt that was the subject of a sensational discovery, of a wonderful decipherment that was to overturn and enrich infinitely its and our history, but also the Ancient Near East. The Ancient Near East had kept its secrets for many centuries, and its documents remained inaccessible to all efforts of analysis and to all understanding, until the find by someone "who was less than thirty years old," and who was not even a specialist, but who was appropriately inspired by genius.

Matters were actually much more complicated in the Ancient Near East than in Egypt. This is perhaps why the discovery by Grotefend was received with indifference, even if it preceded the *Précis du système hiéroglyphique* of J.-F. Champollion by twenty years. It required another twenty years after the appearance of Champollion's immortal work before Grotefend's discovery, meanwhile taken up by others and further devel-

This chapter first appeared in *Archeologia* 52 (1972): 37–45.

oped, was accepted and greeted by everyone, as if first the security of an amazing success in a related field had been needed.

However—and this will be better understood further on—the subtle Grotefend and his successors did nothing but lift a section of the heavy cloak of darkness that had fallen on the documents that had been found and noticed for several centuries in the Near East, especially in southwest Iran and in Iraq, and of which originals and copies had been brought back. All of these were covered with a bizarre and grim confusion of marks that were each comparable to a "wedge" or a "nail,"[1] hence the qualification that was given to them of *cuneatus*, "cuneiform," or in German *Keilschriftlich*. Some people even wondered whether these were not simply decorative zigzags. But many wagered that it was a writing system. Nothing more was known, and, except by recourse to divination, it could not be seen how anyone could "enter" this hermetically sealed blockhouse.

THE "FIRST SCRIPT" AND OLD PERSIAN

C. Niebuhr was the first to have closely examined these obscure scribbles, around 1775, and especially to have roughly counted the different "signs" that they contained. He suggested that we had to assume three distinct writing systems. One of them consisted of only some forty characters, which made it similar to our alphabets and therefore made it less formidable. It is this script that Grotefend started attacking, in order to win the bet he had made with a friend, so he tells us, to "find the meaning of written documents whose alphabet and language were at the start entirely unknown."

As the title of Grotefend's presentation indicates, he had taken as the subject of his study the inscriptions of Persepolis which were better known and better preserved. They appeared on the facades of the ruined palaces and the majestic rock tombs of Persepolis, the ancient capital of the Achaemenids. Thus he devoted his attention entirely to the shortest among them, where the same sequence of identical signs was found. Taking into account the intuitions and the discussions of his predecessors, Niebuhr, O. G. Tychsen, and especially K. H. Münter, he compared the inscriptions, and he established first of all that one could find three different scripts in them. These were, moreover, sometimes attested in parallel columns on the same monument, seemingly to translate the same text, which presupposed the existence of three different languages. To distinguish the scripts, he called them provisionally *Prima scriptura* (I), *Secunda scriptura*

1. Later on it was understood that they owe their particular appearance to the fact that they were impressed with a stylus in unbaked clay, instead of being traced with a sharp object in stone, as had been the original idea. See below, p. 73.

(II), and *Tertia scriptura* (III). The first of them represented the script that Niebuhr had recognized to be "alphabetical."

Then Grotefend posited that in such a graphic system each sign had to represent a different sound, and not "as in China or in Japan" a word or a syllable. This "alphabet" had to be read like ours, from left to right, if one took into account the way in which it appeared on the monuments. The position itself of these monuments implied that the language underlying them had a good chance to be the oldest known language of the Persians, the "Zend" as it was called in those days. It also implied that they had to be accredited to Darius and Xerxes, the greatest Achaemenid kings, the successors of Cyrus the Great, who had made Persepolis the capital of their empire, as we particularly know from Herodotus.

Once Grotefend had limited, and in a sense specified, the field of his research as the result of fortunate intuition and of shrewd reasoning, he compared the shortest inscriptions with each other. He found identical groups of signs, repeated in the same phrases in various situations, but sometimes with different endings. These were *words*, as they were clearly separated from each other by single wedges. He concluded that they had to be proper names, which were probably declinable—as happens in Zend—and royal titles and genealogies, considering the assumed character of the inscriptions.

In reading them he attacked first of all the proper names, as decipherers usually do. These change only very little from one language to another, and can offer a quite certain "entry" into a text's cipher. It seemed to him that these proper names were represented by groups of signs interspersed between the "royal titles" and reappearing from one inscription to another, sometimes in different places, as if for a genealogical line. As it indeed involved royal names and as they contained the same letters, it was easy to recognize them and at the same time to know the value of the signs used to write them: *D*a*R*ius, *X*e*RX*es. Some of the signs were also found in the presumed "royal titles," whose reading could then be discovered by using the Zend vocabulary.

Thus Grotefend succeeded in reading, with enough exactitude and with some luck, two or three inscriptions: *Darius, mighty king, son of Hystaspes; Xerxes, mighty king, king of kings, son of Darius,* and so on. He succeeded in determining the value of almost a third of the alphabetic signs used in the "first script," and hence he had found the key to the script.

If the scholarly society to which he submitted his finds would have encouraged him just a little, instead of remaining aloof, undoubtedly he would have pursued his discoveries further, not only in the area of the "first script," but also in that of the other scripts.

In order to achieve the identification of the entire alphabet and to acquire a more substantial knowledge of the underlying language (which we now call "Old Persian") others took up the torch that the rebuffed Grotefend had dropped: R. C. Rask, F. Burnouf, C. Lassen, and especially the extraordinary H. C. Rawlinson (1819–95). Rawlinson was a simple officer of the East India Company by profession, but his intelligence, his tenacity, and his genius must make him, after Grotefend, the greatest name in the budding history of the Ancient Near East. It was Rawlinson who discovered on the western border of Iran, not far from Kermanshah, the majestic and long trilingual inscription on the rocks of Behistun. The abundant proper names in it allowed him to achieve the decipherment of the alphabet and the reconstruction of "Old Persian."

Today this language is well known and it has been given its place in the group of Indo-European languages. Today there are, however, not many new documents in addition to the Achaemenid royal inscriptions that were already known to the original decipherers. The extraordinary importance of their success does not lie in the historical and cultural resonance of the language. It lies in the fact that after half a century of genius and of prodigious efforts they obtained an "entry" into the block of the cuneiform scripts, until then without a crack, and that they were hence in the same position—but at what price!—as was J.-F. Champollion with his Rosetta Stone. Of the three columns of the Persepolis inscriptions the first one was perfectly well understood, and consequently one could force the other two.

THE "SECOND SCRIPT" AND ELAMITE

The less imposing script was the second, which contained only about 110 signs of script. Between 1838 and 1851 the examination of the proper names allowed E. Norris rather quickly to notice that it involved a mainly syllabic script. That is to say, each sign indicated a syllable, most often a simple syllable (of the type *a*, *ba* or *ab*), but sometimes a complex one (of the type *bab*, *kab*, or *bak*). Where the Old Persian column wrote *D-a-r-i-w-u-s*, we find *Da-ri-ia-wu-u-is* in the second column. The large number and the great variety of these proper names, especially in the gigantic inscription of Behistun (containing more than 260 long lines), permitted a fast mastering of the "syllabary" and the spelling of the second script.

The language written in this script, which one could understand and reconstruct through the already intelligible Old Persian text, was entirely unknown and unrelated. After having been named "Scythian," "Median," and "Sacian," it was finally called "Elamite" because, later, quite a lot of documents were found in the southwestern part of Iran in the area called Elam, where the second script seems to have been the oldest language. Considering the small variety of these documents—they were chiefly royal dedications and administrative texts—and the confirmed impossibility of relating Elamite to another known language family, the understanding of this language has essentially not progressed since Norris, and it is only known and "studied" by half a dozen specialists today. However we can count on the fact that a systematic exploration of ancient Elam will some day reawaken interest in this obscure language, by bringing to light more numerous and especially more varied documents. It will increase the number of people who devote themselves to it, and it will allow us to reconstruct, in some way, large segments of a forgotten ancient history, of which we have found only some scraps.

THE "THIRD SCRIPT" AND AKKADIAN

While the Elamite language was being deciphered, other scholars, among them L. Lowenstern, E. Hincks, W. H. F. Talbot, J. Oppert, and the untiring Rawlinson, devoted themselves to the analysis of the third script. This was much more formidable, with its four or five hundred different characters that excluded the possibility of a simple syllabary, as for Elamite, and many idiosyncrasies and complications were foreseen. Moreover, the stakes were much higher, as the scholars recognized that the third script of the Persepolis monuments was identical to the only script encountered on a number of pieces found outside the Iranian area and especially, in increasing numbers, inside the borders of ancient Mesopotamia, present-day Iraq.

The identification of the proper names soon made it apparent that this script involved a very complex graphic system. It used a syllabary, as did Elamite, but with rather striking variants: *Da-ri-ia-a-wu-us, Da-a-ri-ia-a-wu-us, Da-ri-ia-wu-us,* etc. Moreover, it contained a certain number of signs that seemed to be purely "indicators" or "classifiers*", indicating the general value of the word which they preceded or followed. For example, a vertical wedge was placed systematically before all proper names of persons; a different, more complex, sign before toponyms, and another immediately after them; and still another sign before the names of divinities, etc. Finally, as there were common terms that were spelled with more than one alphabetic or syllabic sign in scripts I and II, but appeared here with a single character, it was necessary to attribute to the latter an ideographic value, where a character indicated immediately an *object* and not the *phonetic pronunciation of the name of the object.* For instance, after the name of the Achaemenid rulers a single sign appeared to indicate his function as "king." Moreover, the use of this "ideography*" seemed to be extremely frequent in the third script, which accounted partly for the extravagant number of characters that made up that script. The fact that from one inscription to the other, or from one passage to the other in the same inscription, sometimes a single ideographic sign was found for the same word, and sometimes a certain number of signs could be used to spell it syllabically, allowed the recovery of the phonetic content of the ideograms, whose meanings only had been known, stressing the difficulty of the system. Thus the sign for "king" had to be spelled *šar-ru*, that for "great, mighty" *ra-bu*, and that for "father" *a-bu*, etc.

These parallels and this variety helped to master the structure of the third script, with time, with patience, and doubtless with some headaches, even if it was unusually complicated, as we have seen. The language that was revealed in this way was related to Hebrew, Aramaic, Arabic, and to the other Semitic languages, although it had a rather particular position among them. First it was called "Assyrian"—hence the name "Assyriologist" which still survives for the specialists devoted to it—as a reminder of the terrible monarchs whose exploits were denounced in the Bible; or it was called "Babylonian," because it was closer in time to the rulers of Babylon who had defeated and replaced those of Nineveh. Today it is called Akkadian.[2]

In 1851 Rawlinson had been able in this way to finish the translation of the third column of the Behistun inscription (containing 112 very long lines). With what he himself and his followers had learned both of the script and of the language of "Assyrian," it was possible from that moment on to read and to interpret the unilingual inscriptions (i.e. those not accompanied by an Old Persian version). These had now begun to be found in abundance in Mesopotamia. In fact, it seems that the tour de force of the decipherers and their resounding philological successes aroused a strong interest in the ancient Near East, and set off an entire epidemic of excavations in the homeland of the cuneiform inscriptions, particularly in Iraq.

One of these inscriptions, freshly taken from the soil and still "virgin," was submitted in 1857 by the Royal Asiatic Society of London to the four "Assyriologists" who were most famous at that time: Rawlinson, Hincks, Talbot, and Oppert. They each had to study it alone, without communicating with the others. When less than a month later they sent the results of their work to the illustrious society under seal, the four translations coincided sufficiently for the unbiased mind to conclude without doubt that the mystery of the third and last Persepolis language had been solved indeed. This result had required more than half a century of obstinacy, of exhaustion, of patience, of ingenious intuition and shrewd deductions by at least ten great scholars and great minds. As we stated in the beginning, the situation had been much more difficult than that of the Egyptian language.

In a certain sense, the results had to be comparable. Through repeated excavations, in one century, in the entirety of Mesopotamia and its sur-

2. "Babylonian" and "Assyrian" are nothing but the two main dialects of the Akkadian language; the first for the south, the second for the north.

roundings, hundreds of thousands of documents in this third script of the trilingual Persepolis inscriptions began to be unearthed. It became clear that they opened up not only large parts of long-past millennia that had almost completely escaped human memory but also the secrets of the oldest history of mankind, and of its first steps in civilization, in the formal and most complete sense of that word. What an incomparable treasure that can be credited, in the end, to the genius of Grotefend!

But in contrast to Egypt, whose ancient history has not known any special turns of fortune in the linguistic field once a prefatory decipherment of the script had been ascertained, Assyriologists have not reached the end of the surprises of this diabolical cuneiform writing system. The "chain reaction" set off by Grotefend from Old Persian to Elamite, and from those two to Akkadian, continued.

THE DISCOVERY OF SUMERIAN

It did not take long before questions were being asked about the functioning and the composition itself of this "Assyro-Babylonian" script that was so complicated and so strange. The mixture of ideograms* and syllabograms* suggested that the script had been originally entirely ideographic, each character designating first of all an object. Afterwards would have come the idea of using the signs to indicate, not the *things* whose ideograms they were, but the entirety of the *sounds* by which the things were named in the spoken language.

It was, in fact, noticed that in this system the same signs could be used freely either as ideograms or as syllabograms. Thus one of them indicated sometimes the "bovine," and at other times the syllable *gud*. Another ideogram indicated in some contexts "cutting," "separation," in others the syllable *tar*, and yet another indicated in some places "mouth," in other places the syllable *ka*. Under these circumstances it was difficult to attribute to the Semites,* who used the Assyro-Babylonian script, the invention of that script, because none of the words corresponded to the Semitic lexicon in general, and the Assyro-Babylonian in particular. There "bovine" was pronounced *alp*, "separation," "cutting" *paras*, and "mouth" *pû*. Would not one have to assume at the origin of this way of writing a population in whose language "ox" was pronounced *gud*, "to cut" *tar*, and "mouth" *ka*?

There were heated and long discussions about this original language. More than one scholar refused to admit its existence and preferred to see in the cuneiform writing a system that was invented in all its elements, an "allography" as they said. Assyriological folklore reports that in this debate two honorable French Academicians exchanged blows with their umbrellas in the hallways of the Institute. Those were epic times! The most obstinate proponents of "allography" did not give an inch when in the

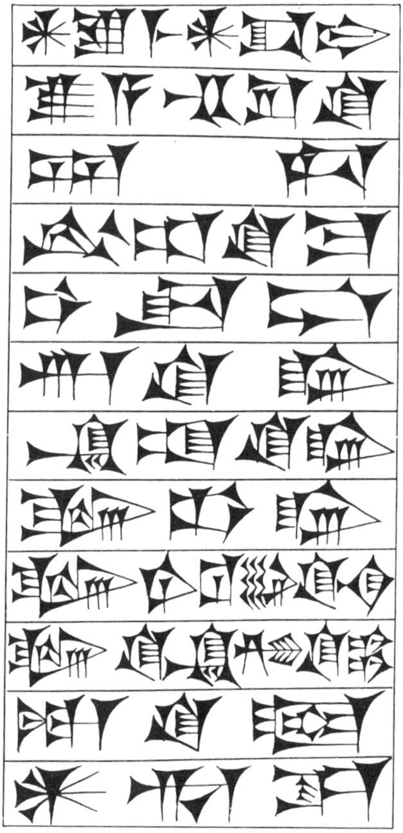

^{d}Iš-me-^{d}Da-gan
ú.a Nibru^{ki}
sag.uš
Urim^{ki}.ma
u_4. da gub
Eridu^{ki}.ga
en Unug^{ki}.ga
lugal kalag.ga
lugal Ì.si.in^{ki}.na
lugal Ki.en.gi Ki.uri
dam.ki.ága
^{d}Inanna.ka

Išme-Dagan,
provider of Nippur,
support
of Ur,
who daily stands for
Eridu,
priest of Uruk,
mighty king,
king of Isin,
king of Sumer and Akkad,
beloved "spouse"
of Inanna.

FIGURE 1 REPRODUCTION OF A ROYAL INSCRIPTION

One of the earliest cuneiform documents published after the decipherment of the script. An inscription, in Sumerian, on a brick by King Išme-Dagan of Isin (1953–1935), from a copper engraving in H. C. Rawlinson-E. Norris, *The Cuneiform Inscriptions of Western Asia* (London, 1861), 1: plate 2, no. V.

south of Iraq, where excavators had started to work shortly before 1880, documents that were written from beginning to end in pure "ideography" started to come out of deeper and more ancient levels. A strict linguistic study of the texts had to convince the less prejudiced scholars that the "ideograms" surrounded by prefixes, infixes, and suffixes, were in fact *words* of a language. This language was correctly characterized as being of the "agglutinative" type. It was isolated from all other known languages and language families, as was Elamite, and was also as different from Akkadian as Tibetan is from French. After various attributions to "Scyths," to "Touranians," and to others, it was finally recognized as being the language of the Sumerians,* the ancient inhabitants of southern Mesopotamia, who had promoted a high civilization starting from the end of the fourth millennium, who had invented writing around the year 3000, and who disappeared afterwards, absorbed by the longer-lived and more numerous Semites, at the latest during the transition from the third to the second millennium.

The existence and the autonomy of this language—and hence of its real place in the ancient history of Mesopotamia—was irrefutably proved by the great François Thureau-Dangin (1872–1944) when in 1905 he presented in his famous work *Les inscriptions de Sumer et d'Akkad* the "ideographic" royal inscriptions, i.e. those in Sumerian, in a coherent and exact translation, which implied a substantial reconstruction of the Sumerian grammar.

In the latter field enormous progress has been made, and the language which is attested in a good third, if not more, of our collection of cuneiform documents, opens the door to the ancient history of Mesopotamia. This history is the most imposing as it has seen the establishment of a civilization that was perhaps the first in mankind's past to really deserve that name. In any case, for three millennia it has illuminated, inspired, and instructed all the people of the ancient Near East and has radiated into the Greek world, and through that civilization, to us.

HITTITE AND ITS DIALECTS

The final step of this "avalanche," a new, unexpected decipherment in the first decades of this century, allowed us to reconstruct an intermediate stage in the spread of Mesopotamian civilization to the Greek world. In 1906 German archeologists under the direction of H. Winckler dug the first trench in the Anatolian site of Boghazkoy, some 100 kilometers east of Ankara. Soon they found an abundant number of texts redacted there in a cuneiform writing system identical to that in use in Mesopotamia. Moreover, they found documents written in a strange script, which was said to be "hieroglyphic" because of its very vague similarities to the Egyptian script and had already vexed a number of scholars who had not been able to master it.

A part of these archives was written in the Akkadian language. These texts could be understood without difficulty, and thus immediately allowed the rediscovery of a powerful empire that had entirely disappeared from human memory after it had developed a high civilization in Anatolia during the second millennium; a civilization that had transmitted to the West a number of treasures from the ancient and still active Mesopotamian civilization: the Hittite empire.

The cuneiform signs of the other part of the documents were certainly easy to read for the Assyriologists, but the underlying idiom, apparently the indigenous language, "Hittite" as it was called, remained entirely unknown and unintelligible. Two pieces of it had already been found in the cuneiform archives at el-Amarna in Egypt (1887 and following) and, as it involved diplomatic messages, scholars were able to reveal and understand in them some recognizable stereotypical formulas, especially thanks to the presence of ideograms. Thus: "*I am well,* my *house,* my *wives,* my *children,* my *officers,* my *soldiers and* my *horses . . . are well! May you be well in* your *house, may* your *wives,* [etc.] *be well!*" From this a number of observations were drawn dealing, for instance, with the possessive pronouns, which seemed to relate this language to the Indo-European ones. Such a hypothesis still had to be proven before anyone could embark on an analysis and a translation.

It was in 1915 that among the documents of Boghazkoy the Assyriologist B. Hrozný came upon the following phrase, in which he could at least understand one of the terms as it had been written with the ideogram for *bread: nu* BREAD *ezzateni watarma ekuteni.* Moreover, the word *bread* was followed by a word that recalled the Indo-European root *ed-/ess-* for *to eat: EZZA-te-ni.* Then the *-te* could be compared to the verbal designation for the second person plural in these languages. The second part of the sentence called to mind the words *water: WATAR-ma* and *to drink,* another Indo-European root that is found in *aqwa: EKU-te-ni.* Except for some particles, he could understand: *you eat bread and you drink water,* and he could consequently explain this sentence as being Indo-European. After that it seemed practically impossible that the "Hittite" language could not be associated to the Indo-European ones (it even revealed itself as the oldest representative of this language family). Thus its reconstruction, based on its character and on its lexicographical and grammatical associations with other languages of that group, was only a matter of time. The understanding of the texts was moreover greatly facilitated by the abundance of ideograms known to Assyriologists.

Today the "Hittite" language has its grammar and its dictionaries. Several adjacent dialects have even been distinguished and, as one of them is hidden behind the enigmatic "hieroglyphic" script, scholars have been able to pierce the secrets of an isolated pre-Hittite language, Hattic, which is also attested in the cuneiform documents of Anatolia—new stages in this "avalanche." "Hittite" has its numerous specialists who, each working on a number of documents, have been able to reveal several centuries of the history and the culture of the great Anatolian empire that up to that moment had been entirely erased from mankind's memory.

URARTIAN AND HURRIAN

For the sake of completeness, we must mention two other languages written in cuneiform and similarly deciphered. It was possible to read them and even, in part, to understand them, thanks to the use of certain ideograms or the existence of short passages that were almost bilingual, having a parallel text in Hittite or in Akkadian. These two are Urartian, spoken and written in the first millennium in ancient Urartu (Armenia), and Hurrian, its ancestor (the two are closely related), the language of a people who descended since the end of the third millennium from the mountains of the north and who played an important role in the history, the politics, and the culture of the Near East in the second millennium. Considering the isolation of these languages, and the restricted number and variety of the documents of both, they were only partly understood, somewhat like Elamite. But a breach has been made and here again are two large reconquered areas of history. In the end this is due to the decipherment of cuneiform and the genius of Grotefend.

THE ALPHABET AND THE LANGUAGE OF UGARIT

A last important discovery must be mentioned here, since it is of interest for the ancient Near East and since it belongs in its own way to the cuneiform area, somewhat like Old Persian.

As in the case of the latter language, it involves in fact an alphabet, impressed on clay tablets and with elements in the shape of "wedges" or "nails." These elements have nothing else in common with the cuneiform scripts of Mesopotamia, properly speaking. On the other hand, the language is almost a millennium older than Old Persian and some scholars have even wondered whether it is not the oldest alphabet in the world.

The first documents in this script were found in 1929 in Ras Shamra, ancient Ugarit, on the Mediterranean coast, a dozen kilometers north of Latakia in Syria. As in Mesopotamia, these were inscribed clay tablets, but not one of the characters on them resembled those familiar to Assyriologists. How do we read them? And what do they conceal?

The learned Orientalist Ch. Virolleaud quickly recognized that it had to be an alphabetic script, considering the small number of signs (some thirty at the most). H. Bauer, taking into account the location of the finds and the small number of characters used to write each word (the words were separated by a vertical wedge), suggested that we were dealing with a Semitic language. Under these conditions, the two scholars, joined by E. Dhorme, worked in concert and communicated their finds to each other. They soon managed to identify certain signs (in Semitic languages words composed of a single letter—as occurred on the tablets of Ras

Shamra—are rare and easy to recognize; moreover, only a small number can serve as prefix or suffix, at the beginning or at the end of a word: *l, b, k, m, n, t, . . .*). Some lucky guesses or deductions permitted them, then, to reconstruct the entire alphabet in a few months. For instance, they used the hypothesis—which proved to be correct—that the four characters on a bronze axe preceding a group of characters, which was found by itself on other axes and which clearly contained the name of the owner, could indicate the name of the object: *axe of so-and-so*. Besides, in Semitic languages there just happens to be a word of four letters (four *consonants* which were the only letters written in the oldest alphabets, as is well known) that can have the meaning "axe": *GaRZeN*.

In this way the Ugaritic alphabet was soon deciphered—by 1931 it had been accomplished! It was clear that it involved a Semitic language that could be related to the group called "Canaanite,*" and thus the grammar and the lexicon were drawn up quickly, and the few thousand documents were translated. Thus the veil that covered the history, the daily life, and the thoughts of a population in the northwest of Syria-Palestine in the middle of the fifteenth century B.C. was pulled aside in one sweep.

In the entire history of historical research there is perhaps not a single adventure that is more remarkable than this one. In one century it has led scholars from a first spark, to which no one paid attention originally, to an explosion of discoveries and decipherments, all of which were difficult, ingenious, and unimaginable. It brought to light enormous and important segments of our past, that until then had been mislaid in time.

In reality, if the minds of our contemporaries were somewhat less clouded with worries about the useful and the profitable, with earthly things and with numbers, if they were somewhat more aware of the real grandeur of mankind, which on the intellectual level lies in the knowing, and the real knowing, of pure knowledge that has not the least practical application, they would have to celebrate this glorious epic as being equal to the most memorable episodes of the history of our progress.

5

From Mnemonic Device to Script

THIS CHAPTER DEALS WITH THE DISCOVERY AND THE DEVELOPMENT in lower Mesopotamia, near the end of the fourth millennium B.C., of a writing system called "cuneiform" (because of its elements which created the effect of "wedges" or of "nails"; see above, p. 56 n. 1). The system was used in that country until approximately the beginning of the Christian era, and spread throughout the different regions of the Ancient Near East. It is probably the first writing system known, and it is not impossible that it influenced, from afar, the other archaic writing systems: in the west (Egypt, shortly after 3000) and in the east (India, around 2500, and China, around 2000/1500). That is why it is interesting to consider it for a moment.

THE SETTING

The geographical setting of this "invention" is the lower part of Iraq, more or less between Baghdad and the Persian Gulf.

We cannot talk in more than a general sense about its historical setting, because history, properly speaking, cannot be written if not based on documentary evidence and is thus impracticable before the existence of writing. However, from the situation in more recent periods that are better known, we can make a certain number of deductions and transpositions which are reinforced by their accumulation and by their convergence with archeological information.

This chapter first appeared in the Actes du Colloque international de l'université Paris 7: *Écritures. Systèmes idéographiques et practiques expressives* (1982): 13–26.

In the geographical area of southern Iraq in the middle of the fourth millennium a complex and original urban civilization was born, which was perhaps also the first in the world to have surpassed simple "culture" by the accumulation of progress. There was a social and political organization, and the creation of institutions, of rights and duties. There was the production and the circulation—on an internal level as well as with "the outside"—of all goods of use and exchange, plentifully procured by a planned labor of agriculture, animal husbandry, and of transformation. Also there was the appearance of superior and monumental forms of art, and the rudiments of a "scientific" spirit, characterized foremost by an extreme concern to rank, classify, and clarify the universe. The invention of writing is undoubtedly one of the most recent accomplishments—and the most unexpected and remarkable one—of the prehistoric civilization that we can call "Sumero-Akkadian" in its ethnic setting.

The ethnic setting. Setting aside the intervention of other people, whether natives or immigrants (such an intervention very likely took place but we know almost nothing about it, and, in any case, it was marginal and secondary), the ethnic setting is in fact the result of the symbiosis between two populations, two cultures: the first Sumerian, the other Semitic and conventionally named Akkadian.

The Sumerians* must have arrived in Mesopotamia during the fourth millennium, apparently from the southeast. But we do not know anything of their earlier ties, and they seem to have burned all bridges with their country of origin, from which they never received any new blood, as far as we know. They were originally predominant in the southern part of the country, later called Sumer.*

The Semites* are much better known since their descendants still inhabit a large part of the Near East and its surroundings. They were prevalent in the area more to the north: in Akkad.* They were members of seminomadic sheep-herding tribes, living on the northern and eastern fringes of the Syro-Arabian desert, who came to settle between the Euphrates and the Tigris. Such an immigration movement continued during the entirety of history in successive "waves" or "layers." Over time these people became differentiated from their original stock in various degrees.

The linguistic setting. The language of the Semites (still widely spoken today under various families of dialects: Hebrew, Aramaic, Arabic, South Arabian, Ethiopian) is inflected. This means that it expresses the grammatical correspondences by internal phonetic modifications of the words (declension and conjugation), and the words are mostly polysyllabic.

The Sumerian language is entirely isolated and is of a type that is called "agglutinative." This means that it translates the same grammatical correspondences by juxtaposing with the essential words ("full words*"—those that remain phonetically unchanged) equally invariable prefixes, suffixes, and affixes, isolated or in a chain ("hollow words*"). On the other hand, a considerable pat of its vocabulary seems to have been monosyllabic (consonant + vowel; vowel + consonant; consonant + vowel + consonant) and it must have contained a surprising number of "homophones," which were phonetically more or less identical, but of different meanings: for example, *du* was used for "to go," "to build," "to butt," "to free," etc. The majority of these homophones were undoubtedly sufficiently distinguished in the spoken language, but we do not know how.

The cultural setting. Sumerians and Semites lived in communities assembled around a "city-state.*" These city-states were agglomerations that served as the governmental, administrative, economic, intellectual, and religious center of a usually not very extensive territory (a third or a quarter of one of the *départements* of France). They were occupied mainly by peasants and herdsmen. Power of a monarchical type was recognized on two levels. The temporal power was in the hands of a sovereign whose title varied from city to city and who resided in a palace in the capital. And the supernatural power, superimposed on the temporal one (with a probable tendency to a certain theocracy, at least in the earliest period?), was in the hands of one of the principal gods. He resided in a temple, surrounded by his entire "family" and by his "court" of minor deities, paralleling the image of the royal family and court.

These Semitic and Sumerian urban communities seem to have existed side by side, sharing the same civilization, and were separated only on the political level, with no more hostilities or aversions than those that could be caused by territorial or economic disputes. For the rest, over time, more and more Semites lived in Sumerian "states" and vice versa.

The Sumerians seem to have played the role of pacemaker in the establishment, the promotion, and the development of the cultural complex that was inspired by both Sumerians and Semites. The Sumerians were more inventive, more open, more daring than the Semites—which does not mean that the latter did not contribute anything of their own culture and mentality. A proof of this eminent role of the Sumerians is that after their disappearance as an autonomous ethnic group, "swallowed" by the Semites (at least by 2000, and probably much earlier), their language remained until the end of the history of the country, shortly before the Christian era, the liturgical and scholarly language, as Latin was for us until the Renaissance.

It was in this milieu and in this setting that writing was "invented" around the year 3000.

THE CONDITIONS OF THIS DISCOVERY

The oldest written archives in Mesopotamia found to this day consist roughly of four principal collections of those clay tablets that served as the "papers" of the country. The oldest come not only from the soil of Sumer, at Uruk* (whence the name *Uruk tablets*), but also from Akkad, at Kiš. They date to the period around 3000, and we have good reason to believe that they are very near to the "invention" of writing.[1]

Of the second group, dating about a century later, deposits have been found in Uruk, but also in the north, near Kiš, at a site that has given them their name: *Djemdet-nasr tablets*.[2]

The group excavated at Ur* in the south, and called *Ur tablets*, dates from around 2700.[3] Those discovered in Fara* (and in Abu Salabikh), in the land of Akkad, are from around 2600.[4] Those groups of tablets represent the stages of the first evolution of cuneiform writing.

The fact that the Uruk tablets were located in the enclosure of the great temple of that city, and that the pieces clearly constitute accounts of the movements of goods, listing numbers first in detail and then totalled, makes us think that this script was established mainly in order to memorize the numerous and complicated economic operations centered in that temple. The temple was the exclusive or principal owner or redistributor of the products of the labor of the land. The finds from Djemdet-nasr and Ur are almost exclusively composed of analogous pieces, with the single exception of a small number of sign lists evidently prepared especially for the teaching, the training, and the use of the scribes.[5] It is only starting with 2600 (the first royal inscription and the "literary" archives of Fara) that the use of the script was extended into other areas. In other words, Mesopotamian writing did apparently grow from the needs and necessities of the economy and the administration, and therefore any kind of religious, or purely "intellectual" preoccupation seems to have been excluded from its origins.

FORM AND PRESENTATION OF THE CHARACTERS

First we have to note that on the morphological, or if you will paleographic, level, the script in question was not at first "cuneiform" but *linear*. It was made of lines engraved in stone or marked with a pointed instrument on a small slab of soft clay (in the end sun-dried, or later, and only in some cases, baked with fire).

These linear traces make up generally rather simple entities of which a

1. A. Falkenstein, *Archaische Texte aus Uruk*.

2. S. Langdon, *Pictographic Inscriptions from Jemdet Nasr*.

3. E. Burrows, *Ur Excavations. Texts*, 2: *Archaic Texts*.

4. A. Deimel, *Die Inschriften von Fara*, 1–3: R. D. Biggs, *Inscriptions from Tell Abū Ṣalābīkh*.

5. The text was edited in B. Landsberger, *Materials for the Sumerian Lexicon*, 12: pp. 3–21 and pls. I–II.

large number are real sketches of easily recognizable objects, such as heads or parts of the human body or of various animals, plants, utensils, and profiles of mountains (see fig. 2, cols. I and II). Their abbreviation and their stylization is of the type of those practiced in Mesopotamia since the end of the fifth millennium both on painted pottery and on engraved seals.

Another group of signs that are more or less geometrical or arbitrary, and in which we cannot discern any model *in re,* perhaps reproduces types of tokens in stone or in clay of which we have archeological collections and which were made according to some convention and used to facilitate calculations.[6] For instance, a type of pellet whose surface was incised with a cross was used to indicate units or groups of sheep. One could sketch the token as a circle divided by two lines intersecting at right angles. That drawing in effect came to designate "the sheep": (no. 761 of the *Zeichenliste* by Falkenstein, cited below).

Finally, a last group of characters, possibly more important numerically, remains entirely enigmatic to us with regard to its origins. This fact is not at all surprising considering the five millennia that separate us from its period of origin. Thus no. 631 of the *Zeichenliste:*

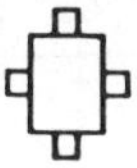

Approximately a fifth of these characters, even among the two last groups, has been identified by various comparisons and cross-checking, and has been related to the more recent stylized representations, which are familiar to the Assyriologist. These comparisons allow us at least to "understand" the characters individually, even in the most ancient documents.

A catalogue of the "primitive" characters of the "cuneiform" script was drawn up by A. Falkenstein in 1936, in his fundamental work *Archaische Texte aus Uruk.* In his *Zeichenliste* he listed 891 characters, in addition to 49 for numerals. But he took into account only the tablets found in Uruk, in Djemdet-nasr, and in Fara *before* 1932. One has to add those from Ur, published also in 1935–36, and especially all those that have been discovered since, primarily in Uruk itself where each excavation campaign (some thirty in total) has yielded some tablets, sometimes even hundreds. Their total

6. See M. A. Brandes, *Modelage et Imprimerie aux débuts de l'écriture en Mésopotamie,* pp. 1ff. of *Akkadica* 18 (May–August 1980).

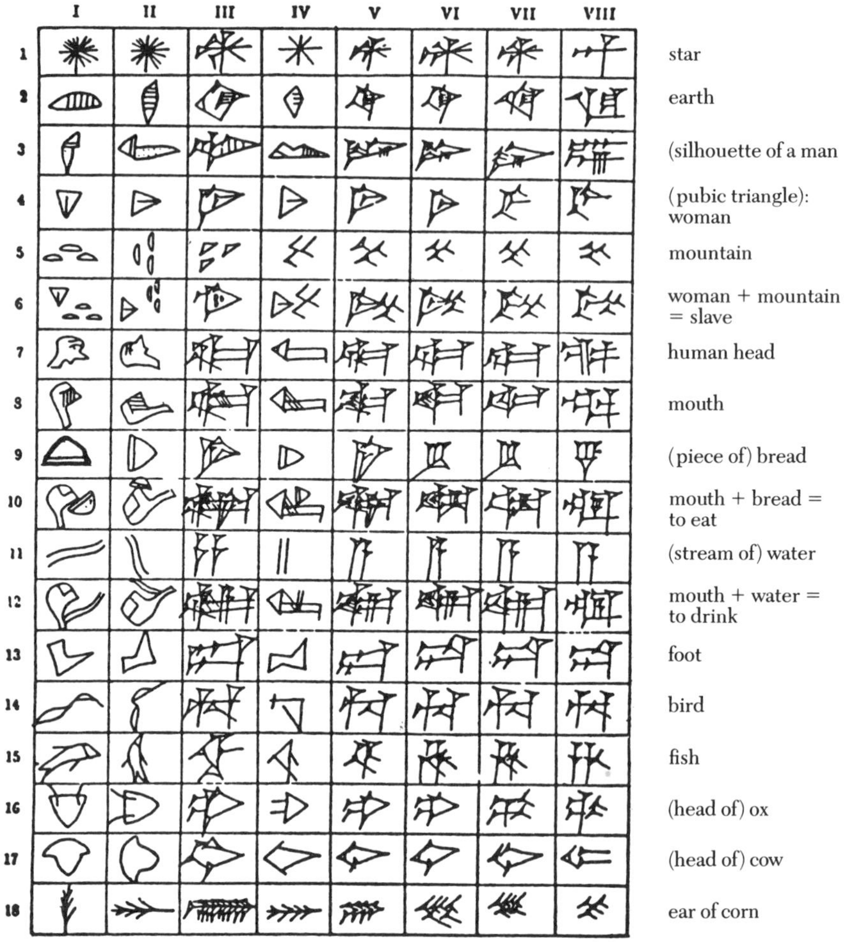
I
II
III
IV
V
VI
VII
VIII
1 star
2 earth
3 (silhouette of a man
4 (pubic triangle): woman
5 mountain
6 woman + mountain = slave
7 human head
8 mouth
9 (piece of) bread
10 mouth + bread = to eat
11 (stream of) water
12 mouth + water = to drink
13 foot
14 bird
15 fish
16 (head of) ox
17 (head of) cow
18 ear of corn

FIGURE 2 PALEOGRAPHIC EVOLUTION OF THE CUNEIFORM SIGNS: FROM LINEAR DRAWINGS TO MORE AND MORE STYLIZED CUNEIFORM SIGNS

In the columns following column I, the clay tablets on which the signs were written are turned 90 degrees. Hence the reorientation of the signs. This table was drawn by S. N. Kramer, *History Begins at Sumer* (New York, Doubleday, 1959), p. xxi.

number has never been calculated to this day, or at least published, much less the number of new signs of the script that one finds on them. I believe that the researchers from Berlin who are undertaking the study of the totality of these documents have counted something like 1,500 characters that can be sufficiently differentiated.

The formal evolution of those signs was determined by the habit adopted early on (since about 2900) of replacing the method of tracing on clay by a method of impressing by means of a reed whose end was cut to form, not a point, but a bevel. Each time the instrument was impressed lightly into the clay, it made a line that was somewhat broader at one end than the other. Thus came the club-shaped or cuneiform aspect.

This technique not only forced the distortion of curves into straight lines, it necessarily led to a more advanced stylization, which without delay abolished all that could have remained "realistic" in the primitive silhouettes of the "pictogram."[7] This stylization was extended to all the characters (easily seen in fig. 2). During this process semantic and other motivations were certainly not lacking, especially including deliberate formal acts of bringing together complex signs that indicate similar realities or those imagined to be similar; for instance the *demon:* udug

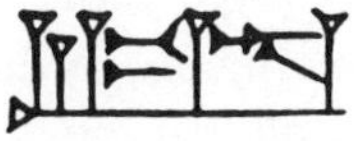

and the *spirit of the dead:* gedim

(see also pp. 271f.). This stylization was pursued until the last third of the third millennium. Afterwards, the graphic material was more or less established, and underwent only inevitable paleographic evolution (fig. 2, cols. V–VIII), at the pleasure of the copying centers and of the scribal schools, especially those in the south (Babylonia) and in the north of Mesopotamia (Assyria).

7. In my opinion there is another difference, on the semantic level this time. While the pictogram refers more immediately to the material reality that it represents, in a direct or indirect manner, the ideogram refers virtually to an entire semantic constellation which was developed around that object. This means that one can say "pictography," when talking about the general type of script, insofar as the characters have nothing to do with phonetics, and that we deal with a script of *things*, not of *words*.

CHAPTER FIVE

THE GRAPHIC SYSTEM

Other ethnic and cultural groups (for instance the Incas) found themselves in similar conditions throughout the course of history: at the same time highly civilized and at prey to the distress of an enveloping and complex economy; taking advantage of a strong tradition of plastic arts; heir to an extensive repertory of themes, signs, and symbols by which they could project and "fix" their internal life. However, none of these other groups ever found or even searched for a real *script*. Thus the Mesopotamians of old took a further step. Which one? And how?

Some historians and archeologists have used the term *script* much too lightly, in my opinion. From the moment that they find sufficiently complex tracings not due to accident, or drawings which are by all indications intentional and thus bearers of messages, they refer to them as script. It is thus that scholars have talked of "the script of the megalithic Bretons." In fact, if words have a *precise* meaning (something that seems to be forgotten or denied more and more these days, at least in practice, if not openly), to have a script it does not suffice that there is a message, an expression of thought or of a sentiment. In the same way, to have *language* it is not sufficient to have a scream. Otherwise all plastic art would be writing, and everything would be jumbled. It is necessary to have a *system* of transmitting and recording *all messages*. In other words, one needs an organized and regulated corpus of signs or of symbols, by means of which their users can materialize and record clearly *all* that they think and feel, or want to express.

In 1928–29 the first tablets were unearthed in Uruk. These, dating to the end of the fourth millennium, bore a great number of "signs," reproduced with regularity, and put in relation to numbers, rendering accounting transactions, by all indications. It was inevitable, then, to think that we had not only some typical examples of intentional suggestions of a thought or of a wish, with only the abridgements of the plastic arts, but also the first evidence of an authentic script.

The difficulty is in knowing to what degree this identification as script was right. How was this writing system established, and how did it function? In its first stage did it totally present the aspects proper to writing, in the true and total sense of the word?

More or less consciously, Assyriologists seem to have given a positive answer to this question, and even when they speak among themselves about the invention of the cuneiform writing system, one has the impression that they present or see it as something exact—something definitive, established all together, at one time, like fire or the internal combustion engine. Even if they accept an evolution, a progress, not only in the paleography but also in the use of signs—the majority among them have a sufficient sense of history not to discard this—they behave as if such a phenomenon (which I have never seen them clearly define, moreover) was only a small detail and did not in the least affect the essentials of what writing is in reality.

I would like to show here that this is not the case. Between the oldest cuneiform documents and those that have been found dated approximately half a millennium later, or even more recently, an entire profound evolution has intervened. I have summed up this evolution under the title "from mnemonic device to script." Thus I have to analyze the three important stages of that progress: (a) pictography, (b) phonetism, and finally (c) writing in the literal sense.

PICTOGRAPHY

Firstly, it is a well-known fact that the Uruk tablets (and to a lesser degree those of Djemdet-nasr, and to an even lesser degree those of Ur, and to a much lesser degree those of Fara) are almost indecipherable to us. An exception to this fact are some more striking documents or passages, which have to be dissected, however, and compared uneasily, with the aid of conjectures and hesitations, in order to derive some modest and uncertain information about the accounting operations found in them. Only the system of numbers is intelligible to us,[8] by the fact that very often their entries, marked at first line by line, are totalled in the end. If I note the presence of ten half-circles spread here and there on the obverse of the tablet, and that of a full circle on the reverse, and if this observation is confirmed by other parallels and sufficiently numerous cross-checkings, I understand that the half-circle designates a unit and the full circle a decimal, and so on. With the signs that appear isolated or grouped together with the numbers, it is another matter. Even if we identify them individually—which is, as I have said before, possible for only a fifth or less of them—and if we derive from them, as a result, some notion of what the copyist could be alluding to by drawing them, their "message" *as a group* almost always escapes us.

The general character of the tablets, summaries of accounting operations and of distributions of goods, makes us think that each number commanded a corresponding quantity of a specific product, distributed to, or collected from, or by, a given individual or group. But which sign played the role of the object, of the person, of the recipient, or of the donor? What is it that indicates whether it is a receipt or a delivery?

Let us take the case of a tablet (from Djemdet-nasr: A. Falkenstein, *Archaische Texte aus Uruk*, no. 595, rev. 2 and 4) where the character that

8. See the work of G. Ifrah, *Histoire universelle des chiffres*, pp. 160ff.

follows the number of unity is the diagram of the pubic triangle which we know to designate "woman" (fig. 2, line 4). This woman, is she the direct or indirect object, or the subject, of the operation? Does the number "one" refer to her or to the product that is transferred? In any case, the tablet does not tell us everything with only these two signs. It supposes that we know both the quality of what it does not mention (direct or indirect object, or subject, of the operation) and the sense of the registered transfer. This is an example of the elementary insoluble problems that nearly all of these archaic tablets present to us. The archaic tablets are thus *illegible* to us. Why?

Because the signs in question are *pictograms*. They are still from a rudimentary stage of writing. Each sign translates first of all *the object that it "depicts,"* that it sketches, that it evokes immediately. Thus, the head of an ox (fig. 2, line 16) represents "the ox," the three half-circles stacked as a triangle (line 5) represents the profile of "the mountain," the ear of grain (line 18) represents "cereals," etc. Such a script is derived immediately from the representations of the plastic arts. It "reproduces," in its own way, material objects or concrete realities.

Things do not end here, however. Just as in the plastic arts a drawing may *suggest* much more than it *represents* (a tree, the forest; a hand, all human labor), a pictogram in this type of writing system not only can evoke other things than those "contained" in the sign that is used, but such a broadening is necessary. To the extent that one has available only sufficiently precise and particularized sketches of objects to express the thought, in principle one needs as many signs as the concrete realities one knows and wants to express (one for the ox, one for the cow, one for the calf; one for the buffalo, etc.). In theory one would need thousands of signs, and in that case the knowledge, and the use, of such a writing system would be beyond, I would not say human capabilities, but the practical usage for which it is needed.

In order to reasonably diminish the number of pictograms (in fact, the maximum number of 1,500 that I have suggested above, is already eloquent in its relative modesty) one has to establish certain procedures, certain tricks, or lift the pictograms out of the uses of the plastic arts. First of all, in addition to the object that it "depicts," a pictogram can relate to other realities, attached to the same object by mental processes that are more or less founded in reality, or downright conventional, and perfectly well known and utilized in the representations of art. The pictogram of a mountain suggests also foreign countries which are bordered by mountain chains to the north and the east of Mesopotamia; the ear of corn represents all agricultural work.

An equally inevitable extension is that a certain number of these realities can scarcely be represented directly. What is the outline of agriculture? How can one draw power, or ferocity, or slaughter, or terror, or tyranny? This can only be done, for instance, by representing a lion in silhouette, or by drawing its head, or its claws. And how better to give the idea of verbs of action, such as "to go," "to walk," "to stand up," than by the sign that represents the essential part of the body involved in all these activities: the foot (fig. 2, line 13)?

In the cases where such associations of images and ideas were considered impracticable, or too obscure, the difficulty could be managed in another way; by having recourse to other practices of figurative art, and by composing, for instance, small *scenes* that bring several signs together. Thus (to mention only the elementary applications of this procedure), by adding the pictogram of water to that of the eye, *tears* could be indicated; by adding the same pictogram to that of the mouth, the verb *to drink* (line 12) could be indicated; and, if water was replaced in the latter case by bread, the verb *to eat* (line 10) was indicated. Also, if one added the sign that indicated wood to the sketch of the plough, that farming tool was directly evoked (ploughs were in fact originally made of wood). If the sign of a man was added to that of the plough, the individual who handled the plough, the ploughman or the farmer, was indicated; and so on. Evidence that such procedures of joining signs in order to obtain a more precise or more complex sense derive originally from the usages of the representational arts is that the order of the pictograms in the entire scene was originally the same as in drawn, engraved, or painted scenes, and remained so for a long time.

Pictography thus has its roots in the practices and the conventions of the plastic arts. There is only one difference, but this difference was radical and sufficient enough to have created "a change of nature" from art to writing. The difference is a deliberate and manifest desire to signify at the same time the more generalized and the more distinct, and thus it is a true systematization. The representations of the signs are made as uniform as possible, and are no longer left to the free will of the artist. Their repertory became organized, as one can see in the lists that the scribes have drawn up for their own use. The different possible meanings of the same pictogram were even codified, it seems, by reducing them to a small, sufficiently defined number. The sign of the foot, which could after all refer to other things besides the bodily part itself, was reserved for the few types of notions listed below (pp. 82 and 90f.); and the use of "scenes made up of signs" became general while their meanings became specific. For instance, the sketch of a woman combined with that of a mountain (fig. 2, line 6) was used to indicate, not "the woman of the mountains," or "the foreign woman," or even "the woman who comes (back) from abroad," but "the woman brought back from abroad" as booty of war, in other words "a slave of the female sex."

However, if they managed in some fashion to construct a real graphic system, designed in the first place to materialize and to fix thoughts, after all they had obtained nothing more than what can be called a *script of things*. The object signified by these pictograms is still always a *thing;* true as it is *thought*, as it fits into a structured body of visions, reflections, and combinations, but still, inevitably, a *thing*, as in the representations of art. That is why such scenes can be immediately understood by anyone who examines them without regard to the articulated language that he hears and speaks, as in artistic representations. When seeing the signs for bread and water in the sign for the mouth, one understands immediately that it concerns "to eat" and "to drink." Just as today when a Frenchman, a German, an Italian, or an Iraqi have even so little as a poster with a finger pointed to the left or to the right, they understand immediately that one has to go "that way." What the concept evokes in the language of each man is: *par là*, *hierdurch*, *da guesta parte*, or *minnâ*.

Such a direct and universal understanding certainly has a great advantage, but the advantage is counteracted by a major inconvenience. The ability of such a system to signify is rudimentary and slight. If only *things*—let us say in Aristotelian language, "substances"—can be represented by immediate representation or by representations mediated for each of them by a sketch as stable and as immobile as the things themselves, how can one indicate "incidents," i.e. the movement of things in their mobility itself; the relationship between things; possession, causality, simultaneity, finality, etc., and the numerous details that surround them and define them concretely, just as we see them *hic et nunc?* For instance, when it is not "the action of walking" in itself that needs to be indicated, a notion which is after all rather vague, but the fact that the person in front of me, to whom I am addressing myself at the moment, is not walking but is preparing himself to do so—"*Will you walk?*"—only *language* is capable, with its words, of rendering entirely the way in which we see the reality. Its "full words" indicate the things, the "substances," and its "hollow words" (or their grammatical equivalents) indicate nuances and "incidents." But pictography is not a *script of words*.

Precisely because pictography is imperfect and rudimentary on the level of meaning and incapable of reconstructing the completeness of a concrete situation, of depicting it, or of communicating it, but is able only to extract from it the material objects and the substantial elements, it can absolutely not play the role of teacher or informer vis-à-vis the "reader." It cannot reveal to him in a precise fashion a truth that he did not know, but only remind him of an event, or a string of events the details of which he was already informed of before. I may very well accumulate pictograms, and use them with all the resources possible from within the system, but I will not arrive at anything more than if I would put forward in speech only "full words" and nothing else—or if I would compose a very nice small picture, in the manner of an Aztec "codex."

To walk, mountain, to purchase, bread, woman is nothing but a quintessential diagram, of which the only unquestionable elements are that it deals with walking, with a mountain, with purchasing, with bread, and with a woman. But *who* walks, and *who* purchases? And *when?* And *how many* realities are at work? Is the mountain the *starting point* or the *goal* of the walk? Is the woman, like the bread, the *object* of the purchase, or is she its *destination*, or its *source?* On the other hand, if I had the experience during a vacation in the mountains of buying a particular loaf of bread, or several of them, in order to take them to my wife, these five words should suffice to make me remember all of it, in the case that I would have forgotten it, or that I would have lost sight of some detail.

This is why and how cuneiform script in its first stage of pictography, was and could not have been more than a *mnemonic device*.

PHONETISM

In order that script would become capable not only of recording memories but also of communicating thoughts; not only of bringing to mind known things but also of teaching the unknown, it was sufficient to relate the script to that which constitutes the most perfect instrument of analysis and of communication available to man: the spoken language. Now, from the time of the Djemdet-nasr tablets, only one century after the establishment of pictography, another discovery enabled the ancient Mesopotamians to take this most decisive step forward.

It is self-evident that we do not know the authors or the circumstances of this discovery. The only certain information that we have with regard to it, and it is an important one, is a very telling sequence of three "pictograms" on one of the tablets in question (A. Falkenstein, *Archaische Texte aus Uruk*, no. 626, 2: 1). We have good reason for interpreting[9] the first two signs as the traditional name of the highest Sumerian god: en.líl* (i.e. *Lord-"atmosphere"*—for this interpretation see p. 233 n. 3) written here líl.en, and this is followed by the sign that represents an *arrow*. Now it is known that in the classical script this last sign in its cuneiform shape, read ti, is often used to designate *life*, its homophone in Sumerian. We also know that in the anthroponymic tradition of Mesopotamia (where the proper names

9. This interpretation has been recently disputed by A. A. Vaiman, "Über die protosumerische Schrift," *Acta antiqua Academiae Scientiarum Hungaricae* 22 (1974):15. But—supposing that his criticism is pertinent and confirmed—he does not question the method and suggests that one can only call its application into use with examples that he considers to be more certain but that he does not specify otherwise.

are most often pious exclamations of the type *This-god-is-my-savior!*, *This-divinity-has-made-me-live*, etc.) the use of the concept of "life" attached to a divine name is extremely common. We thus have reason to conclude that the three signs in question must represent a proper name of a known type, something such as *Enlil-gives-life*.

From this reading, three important conclusions can be drawn:

1. The language underlying the Djemdet-nasr tablets, and thus most probably also those from Uruk (which immediately precede them on the same site, without a cultural break) is Sumerian, because it is only in Sumerian that the homophony between ti: *arrow* and ti: *life* is possible.

2. Consequently we have to credit the Sumerians with the discovery and the establishment of the first writing system—which after all is not surprising, considering what we know of them.

3. Finally, at most a century after the first discovery, the Sumerians made a second one, perhaps even more important that the first, if we consider them in their entirety: that of *phonetism*.

It is probable that phonetism was at first nothing but a new procedure intended to bring a remedy to the semantic restrictions which are inseparable from pictography. Homophony, which is common in the Sumerian language, could have given the idea of using a pictogram to designate not only the object that it represented directly or indirectly, but also another object whose name was phonetically identical or similar (a common practice, later on).[10] We see this in our rebus, where the drawing of an *eye* followed by one of a *reed*, has nothing to do with the organ and the plant, but has to be read *I read*.

There is nothing to prevent the use of the pictogram of the arrow, ti, in order to indicate another thing that is also pronounced ti: life. One had only to detach the primary connection of the signs to an object (arrow), to arrive at a phoneme (ti), i.e. something that is not a concrete reality but something more universal, and belongs only to the spoken language.

Because, as a pictogram, the sign of the arrow can refer only to the thing that is an arrow, and consequently in its function as an ideogram it can refer only to a more or less extensive group of things that can be evoked by it (let us say: weapon, shooting, hunt, etc.), the sound ti designates with

10. I can cite for this a rather illuminating parallel, one I borrow from the memoirs of T. Ghirshman, *Archéologue malgré moi*, p. 116: "Kassem (the confidential man of business of the excavators at Susa, in Iran) cannot read or write. However, every day he presented me with his accounts, which he had written in a notebook in a very particular way. For example, to indicate meat he would draw an ear. Meat is *goucht* in Persian and cannot be drawn. Ear is *gouch* and is easily represented. For milk: *chir*, one can see the paws of a lion, an animal also called *chir*. Buttermilk: *mâst* becomes the moon, *mâ*, and so on. . . . " In a cultural environment with a written tradition, but of which he was only on the margin, Kassem thus "reinvented" in his way, not only ideography, but also phonetism, even acrophony* (for the last, see p. 90).

precision a phoneme. Hence it can be related to the spoken language, and can be used without the least reference to whatever material object it may be, to indicate some word or some part of a word (for instance, eventually to write ti.gi: a type of *drum*). Thus, the sign is no longer a pictogram or an ideogram. It no longer "depicts" or represents anything. It is a *phonogram:* it evokes and records a phoneme. The graphic system is no longer a script of *things* but a script of *words;* it no longer transmits only thought but also speech and language. And as such, even though one needs henceforth to know the language of the person who has written something in order to understand the writing, on the other hand what is written is able to indicate *everything* that is expressed in the spoken language, and *as* it is expressed there. It is thus no longer reserved to commemorate, to recall, it now informs and instructs. It is not a simple "mnemonic device" anymore but a script in the full and proper sense of the word.

Perhaps, after all, we are proceeding here a bit too rashly, as if the discovery of phonetism in Mesopotamia by itself would have changed pictography into phonography overnight, with all the consequences following right away. The proof that we are not yet there, in the period that one knew how to write *Enlil-makes-live* phonetically, is that the tablets of that time (Djemdet-nasr) remain mostly incomprehensible to us, even if we can decipher here and there some groups of signs analogous to En.líl.ti. Why?

It is probably the case that no one was totally aware of the fact that a discovery capable of revolutionizing writing had been stumbled upon, when for the first time a phonetic rendering had been given to a pictogram. Otherwise, what would they have done? What could they have done, at least according to our logic? First of all pictography in itself would have been eliminated, by keeping only the phonetic values of the signs. Then, among the phonetic values only those that are really useful everywhere, i.e. the monosyllabic ones, would have been preserved. Monosyllabic signs were numerous in Sumerian, we think—because it is easy to find frequent uses for the signs for water, for man, for father, and for companion, which are pronounced a, lú, ad, and tab respectively. It is hard to imagine that frequent use could have been made of the signs for donkey, anše, and for a metalworker, tibira. Even with a little ingenuity—and we know that these people didn't lack that!—they could have gone still further, by rejecting all monosyllabic values that have double uses, by the effects of homophony. They could have preserved, for instance, only one du instead of a dozen or more. With less than one hundred signs, they would have reached the most advanced stage of simplification (as was the case later in Cyprus) with the greatest clarity that could be attained starting from pictography on the one hand, and from the Sumerian language on the other: a script that was entirely syllabic.

If this radical progress did not take place in the very beginning of the third millennium (or even later during the endless history of the cuneiform script),[11] as it could have theoretically, it is because, as I have suggested before, phonetism has been regarded in general as a simple complementary procedure, useful for improving the writing system as it was used at the time, i.e. the pictographic system. The latter has also been preserved, purely and simply, with its signs indicating first of all *things*. The possibility of taking advantage, when needed, of the signs' ability to indicate *phonemes* corresponding to the names of these things, was also maintained.

From this situation came a double result. First, even if the use of phonetic values could have contributed to the reduction of the number of signs, which we see indeed happen little by little (there were only some 800 in Fara; and later there remained around 600 of which some 400 were commonly used),[12] still the script became altogether quite complicated. Each character, while maintaining its objective meanings (*to go, to stand, to be well founded, to transport, to carry*—for the pictogram of a foot), assumed corresponding phonetic values (the same sign for the foot could be read du—*to walk;* gub—*to stand;* gin—*to be well founded;* and túm—*to transport, to carry*) and as a result doubled its semantic capacity.

To introduce some order and certainty within the irresolutions of such a multiplicity, the context was certainly decisive. But one could also resort to a number of auxiliary procedures. For instance, aside from the use of "classifiers" (p. 89), when a character had to be read not as the sign of an object but phonetically, and it was known to have more than one value among which one had to choose the correct one, the scribe had the freedom to add to the character another sign, also phonetic, that would specify that value. The same drawing of a foot, followed by the sign to be read in, had to be spelled gin; preceded by the sign to be read gu, it had to be pronounced gub, etc.

In consequence of this state of affairs the writing system remained fundamentally what it had been at the time of the first Uruk tablets: a simple mnemonic device. And that is why, ignorant as we still are of the precise circumstances of the various operations registered on the Djemdet-nasr and Ur tablets, we remain still unable to *read* and comprehend them completely. At most we perceive the content somewhat better than with the Uruk tablets.

11. Only once was a type of syllabary developed of somewhat less than 120 signs, all of them phonetic, and with very few ideograms, in the nineteenth century in Assyria. But this system was used as far as we know only in the area of "business documents," survived for less than a century, and does not seem to have had any echoes.

12. R. Labat lists 598 signs, including those for numerals, in his *Manuel d'épigraphie akkadienne*.

For various reasons this progress will become more noticeable in the Fara period. First of all, around 2600, the conformation of the signs had become close to the one that would become familiar to us henceforth. We understand the largest majority of the signs from then on directly and, thus, at least the content and the *details* of each document can be sufficiently clear to us, even if occasionally the entire and the precise sense escapes us.

On the other hand, the documentation expanded at that time. Henceforth we do not have only administrative and economic texts, but also dedicatory royal inscriptions, and especially the first outlines of a real literature: hymns and prayers, myths, and wisdom counsels,[13] etc. These inscriptions and this "literature" can be compared to pieces of more recent date of the same type or with the same subject matter, or that are in the same vein, and sometimes have the same tenor. This allows us at least to guess at or foresee the sense, and even, upon occasion, to understand the sense rather well. With regard to "business documents," the repetitive formulas, the almost unchangeable order that presides over their redaction, and the small amount of "grammar" they involve, greatly facilitate their understanding.

And this is the maximum of comprehension that can be procured from a script that was still so fundamentally pictographic: an overall grasp of the content of the text, with, here and there, a clearer perception of some details.

The recourse to phonetic writing is still limited to a minimum in these texts, and the recording of only the "full words" with some rare prefixes and affixes (MU.si.le; IM.dé.E) is kept as much as possible. Nothing but "full words" are found: Enki Isimu gù.dé: *Enki-Isimu-shout,* while later all the grammatical nuances will be reproduced: Enki.ke Isimu.ra gù.mu.un.na.dé.e: *Enki** (subject), *to Isimu* (dative) *spoke* (literally: *shouted* = verb in the third person singular, in the preterit, and with the usual repetition of the complement which is also in the third person singular by an infix). The only indication of the role of each of the two persons in the earlier script is their position, the subject first and, as always, the verb last, with nothing to indicate to us the tense and the various modes. It is still fundamentally of the order of the mnemonic device. Not only do the contracts and the "business documents" register solely the essential elements of the affairs in question, to preserve their memory and their value, with the complete unfolding of the affairs not

13. We find also the use of a very strange system of notation that seems to us more or less cryptographic in comparison with the usual system. In any case it betrays an intense effort to establish the supply of characters, by way of choices that were more or less thought out and learned, or that varied from one "school" to the other.

being recognizable except to the parties involved. But the royal inscriptions also constituted reports recalling a dedication or an offering, *ad perpetuam rei memoriam*. And the rough drafts of the literary pieces were, according to all indications, also destined to evoke the pronunciation of a text of which one or more versions circulated in their entirety in the oral tradition.

Such was, in fact, the radical defect of the cuneiform writing system at that time. It could not establish and communicate *all* that the spoken language expressed of things, and *how* it expressed them, because it remained too badly and too loosely connected to the spoken language.

REAL SCRIPT IN THE FULL AND COMPLETE SENSE OF THE TERM

What was needed in order to arrive at the stage of a real script was the coupling of the script to speech by the development of phonetic writing. What finally encouraged such a step forward was the existence and the use of the Semitic language, besides the Sumerian one, in Mesopotamia during the first half of the third millennium, and the consequent obligation to transcribe and record the Semitic language with picto-phonograms that were invented by the Sumerians for their own language. The proximity, and often even the mixing of the two populations, placed in front of the scribes persons with Semitic proper names who also had to appear in the accounts of the movements of goods or in contracts. Moreover, the mental osmosis of the cultures was, as can be expected, evidenced by linguistic borrowings. The foreign products usually kept their names in the new environment in which they were adopted. Semitic words which passed into Sumerian had to be phonetized, such as *rakkâbu*, written rá-gaba, *messenger* (literally, *horseman*); *šumu*, written su.me. or reversed me.su in Ur, *garlic*, and sa.ḫi.li for *saḫlû*, *cress*(?). Or in the Ur I* and Fara periods, and somewhat later—around 2400—*tamḫaru*, written dam.ḫa.ra, *confrontation;* and the proper names of the Semites, such as *I-lum-qur-ad; Qì-šum; I-pù-úr?-Il;* and *Pù-abi*, which we erroneously read *Šub.ad* for a long time. Here, only the first part of the word was phonetically rendered, and the sign-for-a-thing was maintained in the second part, a procedure that became common.

Therefore, the Semitic language infringed more and more in daily use, upon the Sumerian. It even became the official and state language at the time of the Akkadian empire (ca. 2340–2160) and, even though we do not have more than trifling and shapeless remains, it is possible to think that a Semitic literature started at least to see the light of day at that time. If the always unchangeable character of Sumerian words (both "full" and "hollow" ones) was well suited to the use of the ancient pictograms, it was difficult to render clearly a Semitic text, of which at least the "full words," the most important ones, change constantly in aspect according to the role they have in the sentence. It was difficult to represent these words always and everywhere with the same unchangeable profile.

Due to this, it became necessary to "attach" the script more and more to the spoken language, first of all to Semitic, but equally to Sumerian. By the end of the third millennium—and perhaps precisely because, due to its death or its passing away, the language had to be recorded in the absence of an oral tradition—we see progressively the writing down of all the prefixes, affixes, and suffixes that are indispensable to the clarity of the spoken language, in addition to the recording of the "full words."

In the same way, the cuneiform script became capable, not only of commemorating the known, but also of teaching the new. The long literary and religious works known as "The Cylinders of Gudea"* (dating to around 2130), that were respectively close to 800 lines (Cylinder A) and 550 (Cylinder B), are perfectly understandable in themselves without the least appeal to an oral tradition, and without the need for more explicit duplicates (which do not exist in any case).

Henceforth, it can be said that the script, after more than half a millennium in existence, plus some additional centuries to accommodate itself entirely, had arrived at its most accomplished state in Mesopotamia. The writing system was based on the language, or even on several languages (at that time Sumerian and Akkadian, but also "Eblaite"* and Elamite*; soon afterwards Hurrian,* Hittite,* and the other tongues of Asia Minor, Urartean,* etc.). Due to its phonetic capabilities, which came into full use from that moment on, the script rendered very distinctly all that the spoken language could express, and as clearly and perfectly as the spoken language did it. This was a real *script* in the full and formal sense of the word; it was no longer a simple mnemonic device.

However, the script was always to keep profound traces of its primitive and imperfect stage. This is not the place to describe these traces in detail, because, to do that, we would have to take apart the terribly complicated mechanism of the "classical" cuneiform script.[14]

It suffices to indicate two points. First, the script never did attain the logical conclusion of its evolution, which we have already described as perfect syllabism. It never rid itself of its antique pictograms (which one can better call *ideograms*, as we have seen, from the moment that the stylization of the characters does not permit seeing in them the "drawings" of any-

14. The complete system and the functioning of the usual cuneiform script are explained in *Manuel d'épigraphie akkadienne* by R. Labat, pp. 1–28, and on pp. xv–xli of *Akkadisches Syllabar* by W. Von Soden and W. Röllig. In this book a very summary idea of the fully developed cuneiform script can be found on pp. 88–91.

thing at all)[15] is to the benefit of phonograms* only. Almost every one of these 400 or so cuneiform signs in common use has one or more double values: ideographic (i.e. it indicates a thing, a word or a concept, if you will), and phonetic. Thus the sign of the mountain can designate *the land* (*mâtu* in Akkadian), *the mountain* (*šadû*) and also the idea of *conquest*, of *reaching* (*kašâdu*); and it can be read phonetically—*kur, mad, lad, šad*—and have other values which are more unusual.

In the end, it is the context that permits the reader to choose the right reading: this is why in our foreign and removed eye a cuneiform text can never be simply read, it has to be deciphered. According to periods and usages, the variation of the phonograms and of the ideograms changes; but it is rare that some ideographic readings do not occur in even the best phonetized text. And sometimes ideograms replace phonograms, especially in the learned literature.

In short, not only does a text always have to be deciphered, but to fulfill that task in the best fashion it is indispensable to know well both the language and the general context of the documents that one is studying. Hence comes the extreme difficulty and the uncertainties of the translation of entirely new pieces, which are without duplicates and without parallels. In order to understand well one has to *know already,* or at least to a certain degree, at least for *us*. The native literate ancients knew perfectly well what to think of, because of the living tradition in which they grew up. Thus the cuneiform script has preserved some of the disadvantages that were inherent in it when it served only to recall to memory.

Second, let us go further in time. Around the fifteenth century (at the latest?) the alphabet was established in Phoenicia, perhaps at first under the more or less evident influence of the cuneiform script. This ultimate perfection, by which the script was reduced to the smallest possible number of univocal signs that correspond exactly to the fundamental (and the virtual) sounds of the language, refrained from reserving characters to indicate anything but the *consonants*, therefore leaving to the reader, who is supposed to know the language and its mechanism, to supply the vowels.[16] Thus even then the written text did not express everything and acted still, in that regard, as a mnemonic device. We have to wait until the beginning of the first millennium before our era, until the intervention of the Greeks, who added the signs for vowels to the alphabet borrowed from the Phoenicians, to complete once and for all, thanks to them, the trajectory of writing, henceforth arrived at its full maturity and perfection.

15. Assyriologists prefer to talk of *sumerograms** to the extent that these ideograms cover in fact Sumerian words of the "classical" period.

16. The vowels in fact normally played a secondary role in the lexicographic and grammatical system of the Semitic languages, where all the significant elements are essentially composed of consonants. Cf. J.-C. Février, *Histoire de l'écriture*, p. 208.

6

Writing and Dialectics, or the Progress of Knowledge

THERE ARE VERY STRONG INDICATIONS, AS WE HAVE SEEN, THAT the first writing system known in our history, the cuneiform system, was invented and developed around the year 3000 in Lower Mesopotamia by the Sumerians. We do not have apodictic proof of the priority of this discovery, only a solid mass of indications. Apodictic proof is in any case impossible in the study of history, where only "indirect observations" play a role, using testimonies which become less revealing and meaningful the farther back in time they originated. To all the probabilities that have already been collected and that are well known, there is one that must be added of which not a great deal seems to have been made up to now: it is the astonishing and powerful impact of this script, *precisely in its so-called native shape*, on the point of view, the mentality, and what one may call the "logic" or the "dialectic" and the rules that commanded the progress of knowledge among the inhabitants of Ancient Mesopotamia. It is as if their spirit had been profoundly marked by the discovery itself.

A certain number of documents that are more or less well known or studied inform us of such an influence. One of these is particularly informative. It is worth the trouble to pause over it for a moment, even if we have to forgo exploring it here in depth,[1] due to the lack of space and the intrinsic difficulties for the non-Assyriologist. However, in explaining it even slightly, one cannot avoid discussing Sumerian and Akkadian, even if we steer clear of heavy erudition. The document under study involves nothing

1. As I have attempted to do in the article "Les noms de Marduk, l'écriture et la 'logique' en Mésopotamie ancienne," pp. 5–28 of the *Essays on the Ancient Near East in Memory of J. J. Finkelstein*, which I am summarizing and adapting here for nonprofessionals.

less than the final section of the famous *Epic of Creation** (here cited *Ep.*; from the end of tablet VI starting with verse 123, and especially the entirety of tablet VII). This epic justifies and celebrates the accession of the god *Marduk** to supreme sovereignty over the universe of heaven and earth. After his coronation the entire chorus of the gods was thought to confer "fifty names" upon him. The majority of the names are in Sumerian and represent such a large number of prerogatives that their accumulation makes him an exceptional personality among his equals (*Ep.* VII: *143*f.).

Each of these names is followed by a sort of gloss that explains their bearing in a few verses. Now, it is perfectly clear that in the opinion of the ancient scholars of the faith, these paraphrases were entirely *included*, and as if actually *contained*, in the few syllables of the corresponding "name." To take an example: we read in *Ep.* VII: *1–2* that by the "name" of *Asari**[2] Marduk was defined as:

giver of agriculture	*šârik mêrešti*
founder of the grid (of fields)	*ša eṣrate ukinnu*
creator of cereals and flax	*bânu šeʾam u qê*
producer of (all) *greenery*	*mušeṣṣu urqîti*

These scholars have shown us in one of their "treatises" of which a good number of fragments are preserved and which we will use here as an example, that this entire theological phraseology, can be *drawn out* of the three syllables of *Asari.* In order to understand how, and to penetrate at once into one of the rules of their logic, of their knowledge, it is indispensable to recall first, in a few words, what their writing system was, and how it functioned.

THE SYSTEM OF THE SCRIPT

Cuneiform writing started as *pictography:** this means that, on the basis of the simplified and stylized representations of decorative arts and glyptics, the script at first represented objects by their outlines: profiles of the whole object (the *fish;* the profile of *mountains,* etc.) or of an important part (the pubic triangle of the *woman;* the star in the *sky,* etc.). (See fig. 2, lines 15, 5, 4, and 1, p. 72 above.)

Such a procedure could not lead far. Too few realities can be represented in that way and, in any case, too large a number of character-images would have been required to make the system suitably useful. It has thus been improved upon by using different tricks.

2. We do not know the meaning of this archaic name. See also p. 234, where it appears in an equally enigmatic composite name of an ancient divinity of the entourage of *Enki/Ea,** who was ultimately absorbed by *Marduk.*

First of all, still according to the usages of the figurative arts, small scenes were composed that said more than each of the elements used in their composition: bread or water in the mouth for *to eat* or *to drink;* a woman associated with mountains for *the foreign woman*[3] because the valley of the Two Rivers was separated from the other inhabited countries by mountain ranges in the north and the east.

Some of the small scenes allowed the use of recurring themes that could, in some way, act as indicators, as "determinatives" or "classifiers," and they could relate the object with which they dealt to a determined semantic category: *man* to indicate that it dealt with an agent, or a state; *wood* to indicate the objects usually made out of that material, etc. The former sign placed in front of a plough indicated the *farmer;* the second placed in front of the same tool indicated the *farming instrument.*

But one could also (and this is a vein that was even more exploited) enrich the semantic contents of the characters by recourse to the natural ties that the objects have among each other (a foot also evoked *walking, standing up, solid foundation on its base,* the *ground,* the *earth,* and even the *underworld,* and also the *site,* the *place,* etc.). Such connections could have even been entirely arbitrary, like the circle divided by a cross to indicate *sheep,* which had been copied from the old clay pellets marked in that way to keep account of herds.

By these various shifts, each character could thus be enriched by an entire constellation of meanings, actual or potential, used or usable. This process worked so well that even when the field was limited by the assignment of a definite and reduced number of usual meanings to each character (apparently very early in time), the users of the original ideography* kept open the possibility of overstepping the boundaries and of concentrating in one and the same sign an entire aspect of reality, an entire network of meanings that were more or less connected, till the very end of the history of the script. The sign of the star, for instance, which in the common script only referred to heaven and to the god(s), could also be taken to signify everything that was "on high," "superior," or "sovereign." The scholars* of the country never forgot this original and deep-seated capability of their script, even if the redactors and the copyists* did not take it into account at all.

This awareness was so strong that the original ideography remained integrated in the script and inseparable from it, even after the phonetic values of signs had been discovered; that is, after the realization that each sign did not only attach itself to the objective universe, to the *things,* the *objects* of which it was the image or the symbol, but also, forcibly, to the spoken language, to the *names* of these objects, to *words,* each of which

3. Or more precisely "woman brought back from abroad as war booty," "slave of the female sex" (see above, p. 77).

was expressed by an ensemble of phonemes. It is possible, even probable, that in the language of the script's origin, Sumerian, words had been mostly monosyllabic (but we do not have evidence for it). That is why the phonetic value of the signs is almost always monosyllabic: single vowel; vowel + consonant; consonant + vowel; or vowel between two consonants. Even though the original monosyllabism of the Sumerian language might be an illusion, it is still imaginable that the "inventors" of this phonetism could have maintained only the first syllable of each word, to confer to the corresponding sign its phonetic range. This is elsewhere called *acrophony.** But this problem is of little importance. The only thing that counts is the essential result of such a process: the cuneiform characters (known among Assyriologists as "sumerograms") from that moment on were each given one or more syllabic values. Each represented first of all the name (or the beginning of the name?) in Sumerian of what it immediately designated, as an ideogram, and continued to designate this name, because in this highly conservative country, phonetism was always taken and preserved as nothing more than a reinforcement and a help, even a double, of ideography instead of revolutionizing the writing system by simplifying it considerably into a syllabary. The character of the fish no longer evoked only this animal but *also* the phonetic entity *ku* which designated "fish" in Sumerian. The foot was read at times du when it indicated *walking*, at times gub, *standing up;* gin, *the solid foundation on its base;* and túm, *to transport*. The use of these phonetic values presented an assured way to transcribe polysyllabic and even monosyllabic vocables not only in Sumerian, but especially also those of foreign origin. Instead of writing gin one could coin the word gi.in; instead of adaman, "disputation, discussion," one could spell clearly a.da.man, and dam.gar could render the name of non-Sumerian origin of the "merchant": damkar. But due to the fact that ideography was identified with the idea of the graphic expression itself, it never occurred to the ancient inventors and organizers of the script that henceforth one could ignore this basic ideography.

With this new and supplementary register of meanings, it followed that each character first of all obtained a certain *polyphony,* in the sense that as an ideogram it referred to a "constellation" of objects and thus acquired, on the phonetic level, a proportional multitude of syllabic values—as we have seen above for the sign of the foot: du, gub, gin, túm. On the other hand, a certain *homophony* among the totality of characters was unavoidable, because a great number of the names of the realities to which these characters referred originally, and to which they always kept on referring, coincided phonetically (or their first syllables did, separated according to the acrophonic principle). The phoneme du, for instance, corresponded to a good dozen of signs which were different, but which referred to objects that were in their designations more or less homophonous, if not homonymous.

"Foot," production, ruins, blow, goodness, to speak, and still others were all pronounced more or less like du. Distinguished by their ideographic meanings, these characters were all confused in the phonetic register. But in practice, varying according to regions and time periods, a defined number of values was reserved to certain signs, and the copyists used these values almost exclusively. The scholars could always resort to any value and freely replace one by another in their speculations, without any restrictions.

BILINGUALISM AND ITS CONSEQUENCES

In the establishment and the elaboration of the writing system another main element played a role, whose importance we have to stress now: the thorough bilingualism of the civilization that used this writing system. This civilization was derived from the confluence and symbiosis of two original cultures, whose representatives found themselves reunited in Lower Mesopotamia from the fourth millennium on: on the one hand Sumerians, on the other the Semites that we conventionally call Akkadians.

Their respective languages were as far removed from each other as Chinese is from French, even if their users did not seem to have kept track of the differences, treating them apparently less like two irreducible linguistic systems than like simple coherent variants of one and the same language. The phonetic material of Sumerian was less rich than the Semitic material. And while a large number of the Sumerian words could have been monosyllabic and remained unchanged whatever their grammatical role, the Semitic vocables were usually polysyllabic, and changed their outlook according to their function within the sentence, as in all languages that have nominal and verbal inflection. The Sumerian language, which was originally the only official language of the administration, religion, and culture, soon competed with Akkadian, and was then replaced by it. Sumerian did not survive except as the learned language among scholars, somewhat like Latin among us in the Middle Ages. It remained the scholarly language until the very end of the history of Mesopotamia, shortly before the Christian era.

These linguistic divergences and avatars had their repercussions on the script. Created for Sumerian, the script underwent important changes when it had to be adapted for Akkadian.

First of all, in the ideographic register, each of the signs was enriched by references corresponding to the Akkadian nouns, on top of its references to Sumerian nouns. In addition to du, gub, gin and túm, the use of the sign of the foot was extended to indicate also the verbs *alâku, izuzzu, kênu,* and *w/tabâlu* (and all their multiple inflected forms which were required by the context: *izzaz* for "he stands up," *tukân* for "you fix," "you establish";

ušatbalu "they make transport," etc.) which in the Akkadian language indicate "to walk," "to stand up," "to be solidly fixed on its foundation," and "to carry/transport/bring."

On the phonetic level, the first readings (du, gub, gin, túm to use the same example again) naturally remained in use, not only to transcribe Sumerian, but also Akkadian. Certain signs, however, could also receive new values, drawn this time from their correspondents in the Akkadian language, just like the older ones were drawn from their Sumerian correspondents. Thus the sign for head, which was pronounced sag in Sumerian and was syllabically read *sag,* took on the new syllabic value *rêš,* derived from the Akkadian noun for "head": *rêš.*

When one wanted to transcribe an Akkadian term, one could always resort to ideography, as long as it mostly involved current and well-known realities: the man, the king, the house, etc.; otherwise (but even in these cases according to the circumstances) one necessarily had to spell in some fashion the successive syllables of the Akkadian word by representing it with syllabic signs. One of the oldest Akkadian personal names inscribed in our texts is *Ilum-qurâd* (which is translated as *The god is a valiant warrior!*). It was rendered by the ideogram of the star to indicate *the god, ilum;* and two signs with phonetic values, *qur* + *ad,* were used, to spell the epithet. However, as the division of the syllables remained in theory arbitrary (even if it became sufficiently regulated in time for the use of the copyists), one could also coin *I-lum/Ilum-qu-ra-ad, I-lum/Ilum-qu-rad.* Even *I-lum/Ilum-qu-ra-a-ad,* etc. could be written in order to stress the length of the last syllable by repeating the vocalic sign, according to a usual convention. The scholars also used this theoretical freedom in the division of the syllables of the words with the utmost liberty in their "dialectical" use of the script.

On the other hand, the characters which were devised for Sumerian phonetics could not express the subtleties of Akkadian phonetics. The latter, as in other Semitic languages, contained a number of particular phonemes unknown in Sumerian: an entire range of laryngeals and of sibilants, as well as the "emphatics," pronounced with a particular stress. With the material of Sumerian, such phonemes could be rendered only very approximately and in an ambiguous way. Moreover, written Akkadian seems to have contained only two largyngeals; a weak one and a strong one. The same signs recur, especially to indicate the voiced, the voiceless, or the emphatic consonants: bi for *bi* and *pi;* ad for *ad, at,* or *aṭ* (emphatic); ku for *ku, gu,* and *qu* (emphatic); sa for *sa, śa, za,* and *ṣa* (emphatic), etc. In this way, if we want to introduce here a theoretical example, the same signs *ka* + *pa* + *du* could, at least in principle, refer to Akkadian terms which are as phonetically and semantically different as *kapâdu* "to plan," *kabâtu* "to be heavy," and *kapâtu* "to succeed." For a spelling such as *ḫa* + *zu* + *u,* only the context could distinguish between *ḫasû* "to cover," and *ḫazû*, "to object." In such cases the context generally enabled the exclusion of certain possibilities which sufficed to compensate for such a graphic ambiguity; not to mention the customs of the copyists, which varied according to period and place, but which more or less regulated the use of the characters and their phonetic specifications.

If Sumerian was responsible for the imprecise way in which many Akkadian consonants were rendered, one perhaps has to attribute to the latter language a certain limited but real ambiguity in the expression of the vowels. In fact, as explained above, the Semitic languages in general assign only a semantic and grammatical role of secondary level to vowels. Furthermore, during the evolution of the language certain vowels were deformed or muted, especially those at the ends of words. This led the copyists, who in this syllabic script could not separate vowels from consonants, to use signs where the place of the muted vowel was taken by whatever vowel they chose. These phenomena were able to introduce a certain vocalic fluidity in the phonetic values of the signs in Akkadian. There was confusion not only between *i* and *e*, whose pronunciations seem to have been very close, perhaps already also in Sumerian, but between other vowels as well. This does not happen when the vowel precedes the consonant; but when it follows the consonant one finds signs that refer to *su* as well as to *sa*, to *ku* as well as to *ki*, to *ta* as well as to *tu*. And this is even more frequently the case with the interconsonantal vowels: *bal* can be read as *bul; lum* as *lim; nak* as *nik;* and *mad* as *mid* and *mud*, etc.

However, one does not have to conclude from the preceding that in this hellish script *every* sign was uncertain with regard to the consonant or indifferent with regard to the vowel. That would at once have taken away any coherence or precision whatsoever from the system, rendering it then, if not impracticable, at least almost useless. In reality the users of this script made the maximum effort to avert any ambiguity. This effort coincided with the gradual evolution of the system from its original state as a simple "mnemonic device" to that of a script in the full and accomplished sense of the term, capable not only of recalling the known to its readers, but also of teaching them the unknown. Varying according to location, period, and even literary genre of a text, the choice of signs and their values was restricted. Classifiers, about which I said a few words before, were used and phonetic indicators were placed before or after a sign with several ideographic or syllabic values, in order to point to the value that the copyist had in mind, not to mention the clarification that was necessarily provided by the context. All of these elements together eliminated almost all ambiguity from the text, and conferred upon it an exactitude and coherence without which it could not have fulfilled its role.

Because of the origins, the formation, and the development of the script, it always remained true that a certain number of permutations and side-steps *could* intervene, on the level of the *things* indicated as well as on that of the *signifying* words. Certainly, when writing and recopying the texts, the scribes and the copyists avoided these ambiguities as a rule; but scholars could return to them at their leisure. And that is precisely what they did. Even better, they derived an entire "logic" and a "dialectic" from them, as we are going to show by returning to the document that is the subject of this chapter.

THE "DIALECTICS" OF WRITING

First of all, in the light of such principles, we can understand without difficulty how one could, in some way, extract from the name *Asari* the contents of the two verses cited above which comment on it.

A copyist spelling this name phonetically to write it would never have divided it otherwise than a + sa + ri. But a scholar, who had to analyze it on an entirely different level, not that of script, but that, as he thought, of reality (because he thought that the name was *identical* with the thing), was not bound by the rules of orthography. What counted in his mind was the actual or potential phonetic contents of the name, *of which each syllabic element represented a Sumerian word*—like all the syllabic values of the characters of the script—*and beyond that word, a reality.* Thus he divided *Asari* into a, sar, and ri.

The sign sar was represented in the pictographic sketch by two ears of grain along a furrow:

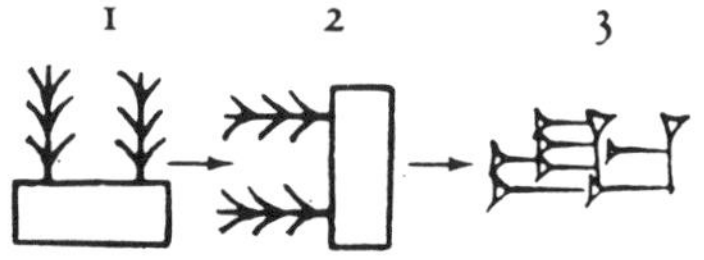

1—upright, 2—turned 90° (see fig. 2 above), 3—cuneiform

In the daily script the sign was reserved for the meanings of *greenery* and *garden* (orchard or vegetable garden). Therefore, it is to be expected that one would find *greenery* at the end of the two verses cited above. But it also preserved, in its primary semantic constellation, the capacity to evoke all that touched upon the labor producing useful plants: all agricultural and arboricultural work, by itself (*the agriculture* of the first of the two verses) and by its results (*the cereals* and *the flax* of the second verse). By virtue of the polyphony of the signs, the same sar could also be read ma_4[4], a Sumerian word that corresponded to the Akkadian verb *aṣû, to (make) leave* (possibly from the idea of the "sprouting" of the plants, of their "leaving" the earth), which figures at the end of the second verse in its "causative" form: *who makes shoot up, who produces.*

The fundamental and central value of the character *a* is "water." It seems that the scholars referred to this "water," by an indirect way of reasoning, when they mentioned the *grid* (of the fields), of the fields' *outlines*, i.e. their delineation and distribution on the ground. Such a delineation was done automatically by the use of canals and ditches, without which all agricultural work would have failed in the country, for want of irrigation. This is why the a in a + sa + ri referred to the *grid* (of fields) mentioned in the first verse.

Ri, as such, was not useful in the context of the commentary on *Asari*. But by virtue of the secondary character of the vowels, explained above, one could substitute the sign by rá or ru. The latter had as equivalent the Akkadian verb *šarâku*, which means *to give* (as a present) and is used here in the beginning of the first verse. The sign rá corresponded by homophony to another sign, ordinarily read dù. The latter sign translated the idea of *to create*, and appeared at the beginning of the second verse.

Thus all the "full words," all these notions included in the gloss in two verses on *Asari*, were found *in* the name in the form of Sumerian words evoked by the phonetic breakdown: *to give* (ru for ri); *agriculture* (sar); *to found* (rá, for ri); *tracing/grid* (hydrography of the agricultural fields) (a); *creation* (rá in its reading dù); *cereals* (sar); *flax* (sar); *production* (sar, in its value ma_4) and *greenery* (sar). These notions composed the name; they were an integral part of it: it is thus not surprising that one could extract from the name *Asari* the details of the prerogatives that it accorded to *Marduk:*

> Giver of agriculture, founder of the grid [of fields], Creator of cereals and flax, producer of [all] greenery.

Only the "full words,"* those that refer to realities, were taken into account here. The "hollow words" which indicate the relationship between them, those relationships that in Akkadian were indicated by the nominal

4. To avoid the confusion caused by the homophony of the cuneiform signs in their transcription into our script, Assyriologists have chosen to attach a conventional mark to the transcription of each sign, in order to indicate exactly to what character the transcription refers. Either a "mark zero" (the simple and pure transcription, ma to refer to the character of the *fig*); or an acute accent (má for the character of the *boat*), or a grave accent (mà for the sign of a *box*), or a numerical index placed in small type below and to the right of the transcription (ma_4 for *to leave;* ma_5 for *to grind*, etc.). These diacritics* have no relationship at all to the pronunciation.

or verbal inflection and by the use of prepositions, conjunctions, and even of pronouns, were entirely left aside. This concept is in perfect accordance with the archaic state of the cuneiform script described above.

Some one hundred lines are fragmentarily preserved to us of a type of explanatory analysis that must have covered in its complete form at least the entirety of the seventh tablet of the *Epic of Creation.* It demonstrates very well to what extent the scholars, authors, or readers of the work (which can be dated in broad terms, at the earliest, to the end of the second millennium or to the beginning of the first) were convinced of the total, real, and substantial identity between the prerogatives and the powers of *Marduk* detailed by his epithets, and the corresponding "names" which had been conferred upon him by the council of the gods at his accession. It shows to what extent the conferring of the "names" and the granting of the realities implied by the names were in their minds one and the same. For each of the twenty names that are extant in the fragments, one can find a syllabic breakdown. This was done, not according to the usages of the copyists, in actual and juxtaposed syllables, but in potential syllables for which it was sufficient that they could be found in one form or another in the name. Each of these syllables was understood in its ideographic value, thus corresponding to a Sumerian word. It was either understood by itself, as it was found traditionally specified on the semantic level (just as, above, sar was understood as *greenery*). Or one could pass on to one of its phonetic equivalents which referred to another Sumerian word (with the vowels as well as the consonants eventually interchangeable according to the rules indicated above: sar read ma_4 for *to produce;* and ri read rá or ru for *to found* and *to create*). Finally, the syllable could be understood by a more or less oblique or subtle reasoning (a starting from "*water*" to end up with the *grid* of the fields, which was created by the distribution of the irrigation water in canals). Each of these values corresponded to the syllabic contents of one of the terms whose sequence constituted the theological paraphrase of the "name" in question. Such equivalencies show very clearly that in the eyes of these ancient scholars the multiple attributes identified by the various "names" of *Marduk* were really and materially *included* in those names.

There is thus no need to multiply the examples of the dialectical mechanism whose functioning we have shown. Nor is it necessary to cite other works, or simple pieces of principally religious documents, such as myths, hymns, and some others, not to mention "commentaries," where the same procedures are clearly visible—and there are many of them.

The system is not formally attested until the seventeenth century before the Christian era. A famous passage of the *Supersage,** a long mythological account that describes the creation of mankind and the establishment of its condition until after the Flood and the beginning of "historical times," is incomprehensible if one does not study it according to this same vision of things.[5] The creatures in the story are entirely identified with their written names, to such a degree that in analyzing the names it is possible to discover and to know their entire nature—somewhat like taking apart an instrument or dissecting an animal. It is possible that such hermeneutics were as old as the script and thus attached to it in its original state, more or less explicitly and consciously.

PRESUPPOSITIONS OF THIS SYSTEM OF HERMENEUTICS

If one thinks about it, this type of "dialectics" which consisted of analyzing the written words to advance the knowledge of things, was founded on a double postulate that is also far removed from our own vision of things: a *realistic* conception, both of the *name,* i.e. of the word insofar as it names and designates, and of the *writing.*

The first point is known to all who work with the civilization of ancient Mesopotamia—or with some neighboring and tributary civilizations. We have known for a long time that the *name* in ancient Mesopotamia was not, as in our own view, an epiphenomenon, a pure accident extrinsic to the object, a *flatus vocis,* a simple, arbitrary conjunction of a relationship of signification with a group of phonemes. On the contrary, the ancient people were convinced that the name has its source, not in the person who names, but in the object that is named; that it is an inseparable emanation from the object, like a projected shadow, a copy, or a translation of its nature. They believed this to such an extent that in their eyes "to receive a name" and to exist (evidently according to the qualities and the representations put forward in the name) was one and the same. The first couplet of the *Poem of Creation** (I: 1f.) states:

> When, on high, the heaven had not (yet) been named (and), below,
> the earth had not been called by name

to indicate the nonbeing, the nonexistence of Heaven and Earth; of Above and Below. This passage is always quoted in order to illustrate this manner of viewing things. It is but one piece of an enormous dossier, one that does not have to be discussed here. This realistic conception of the onomasticon and of the vocabulary is especially clear in the list of names of *Marduk* with their paraphrases, because each designation of that god contained, in some way materially, all the powers, the merits, and the attributes that identified

5. See J. Bottéro, "La création de l'homme et sa nature dans le poème d'*Atraḫasîs,*" pp. 24–32 of *Societies and Languages of the Ancient Near East.*

him. The fabulous total of fifty titles for him alone thus forces one not only to recognize in him an extraordinary personality, even on the divine level, but allows one to acquire a profound and detailed knowledge of this personality.

The context of the list of names in the same epic allows a better perception of where each name derived its value in the end—its *realistic* value, of course. Each name, in the opinion of the authors, was the expression of a will and of a particular decision of the gods concerning that which was the subject of naming. To put it according to the local terminology, each name precisely stated that *destiny* of the named object. The text places *destiny* and *name* in a relationship of quasi-identity when it shows the gods taking the decision to *name the destinies of Marduk, in order that one could invoke him with* (as many) *different names* (*Ep.* VI: 165f.). This notion of destiny, so important in the Mesopotamian view of things, defined the very *nature* of beings, but according to the calculations and the desires of the gods. It is the nature of beings in the sense understood in this good old scholastic word, i.e. their constitution insofar as in it their behavior and their specific activity were programmed—something comparable, if you will, to the genetic code, but on an entirely different level. And it is such a nature that allowed one to find and to bring forth the analysis of the name, because the name was nothing but the translation of the destiny, in other words, the proper and authentic expression of the nature.

Undoubtedly this is why in the mythological tradition of faith the destinies of creatures, resulting similarly from the deliberate decisions of the gods, were often presented as being consigned to a famous *Tablet-of-destinies* whose keeper was the highest god himself. Thus in Mesopotamia the name or the word had its full value only to the extent that it was established in writing, as a result of this realistic way of seeing.

The *realism of the written,* this other postulate of Mesopotamian "logic," has been discussed less. Perhaps it has even been misunderstood or misjudged up till now. However, it was equally important and well documented, and we have to think about it as carefully as we did for the dialectic method described above.

For *us,* the entirely alphabetized script (i.e. founded on the phonetic analysis of the word, which is broken down to irreducible elements) has as a primary function to *fix* materially that which has but a transitory existence as a pronounceable word, and but a mental and incorporeal reality as a signified concept. The script thus serves, first of all, to bestow an objective, independent, and lasting existence upon speech, which translates our thoughts and our vision of things. Script keeps itself in the background of speech and of that which is represented by speech. It is nothing without speech and does not add anything to the spoken, if not materiality and duration.

It was not at all like that with the ancient Mesopotamians. As there are so many differences between us and them on this point, as on many others, it is necessary to remember not only that they had created their own script (and perhaps, at the same time, script in general), but also that the first stage of the latter, the first form that it took when it appeared, was *pictography.** Moreover, pictography was not a script of words, because it did not recognize any phonetism, but a script of things. It transcribed the things directly by sketches or conventional drawings, which were things in themselves because, directly or indirectly, material objects were recognizable in them. Even after the invention of phonetism (that is, of the possibility of stripping these sketches of their objective specifications in order to attach them only to a group of phonemes which constituted the pronunciation of the object in the language in use) the cuneiform writing system never abandoned its original, deep-seated habits of immediate reference to things. Even with regard to phonograms* the Mesopotamians never lost sight of the fact that these were, after all, pictograms stripped of their objective contents, for the benefit of their phonetic value. And they could in any case find the objective contents immediately, as is eloquently shown by the "logical analysis" of the "names," illustrated above.

This is why in the opinion of the ancient scholars of Mesopotamia the script was fundamentally *concrete and realistic.* One did not write first of all the word, the pronounced name of the thing, but the thing itself, furnished with a name. The name was inseparable from the thing, confused with it, as I have just restated. And this written name, equal to the thing, constituted a material given, which was concrete, solid, and comparable to a substance of which each portion, even the smallest one, contained all the faculties of the total, just as the smallest grain of salt has all the characteristics of the heaviest block. One could also make use of the word, just as much as one could use the thing itself. One could scrutinize the word like the thing, analyze it, reduce it to its elements and thus take out of it all that it contained of the reality and the intelligibility of the thing.

Mental processes were being utilized in order to do these analyses, these examinations, these advances in knowledge, these "reasonings" (as one could call it). They allowed the passage from one and the same *written* sumerogram* by intermediate terms to various adjacent terms whose accumulation enriched the knowledge of the subject of the name. One cannot acknowledge these mental processes, understand them, judge them as not being absurd, nor perceive their rationality, if one does not place them in the realistic perspective of the script. As I have recalled above, the multivalence of the signs, their polysemy as linguists would say, goes back in effect to the original pictography and to the obligation of organizing around each of them a "semantic constellation" based on the things themselves and on their real or imaginary interrelations.

The script detached itself sufficiently from this realism later on and, hooked up to the language, it could have become a more abstract instrument of communication for common use by the scribes and the copyists, without reference to the original pictography. However, the scholars always kept, if not the archaic vision, at least the memory and the consciousness of a script of things, and of the possibility of having recourse to its first realism, to its concrete and polysemic character (fueled even more by the catalogues and the lists of which we have large sections). This character permitted the passage from one thing to another in one and the same sign, the extraction of one reality from another, and the resulting enrichment of the knowledge of an object derived from the analysis of its written name only, as we have seen it practiced above by the authors of the list of "names" of *Marduk* and by the exegetes.

THE IMPORTANCE OF THIS SYSTEM FOR THE MESOPOTAMIAN MENTALITY

This is quite an irksome and dry subject. It is however necessary to deal with it, if only to reconcile our point of view with a cardinal point of the ancient Mesopotamian *Weltanschauung.* A professional historian is always ill at ease and suspicious when someone thinks or claims to have found in a civilization so far removed, cultural phenomena that can be taken exactly in the sense of our cultural phenomena and that can be superimposed upon ours. After all these pages, the demonstration seems at least to have indicated that the conceptions and practices of Babylonia were far removed from our own. They differ like night and day concerning the script and its bearing, as well as in the relationship between the words and their contents, and the possible use of names to increase and improve the knowledge of the named things. It is one thing that we cannot accept this type of dialectic and its presuppositions, but with regard to qualities the historian cannot make value judgments on the past that he recovers. He must only ascertain and try to understand it, not according to his own parameters, but by placing the ancient concepts in their own time and milieu. However strange, even aberrant, such a vision of things, such a treatment of the signifying and the signified, and such a realistic and simple agreement between written signs and words and things may seem to us, they are nothing less than rooted in the very origins of the script. These concepts have ruled the country to the same extent as the script, and they were integrated in the rationality and the culture of the country. They may have provoked in their own way a real progress of thought in spite of all their fantasy, and they were spread all around in the ancient Near East,[6] where perhaps their meaning would have escaped us if we had not understood it at its source.

In its country of origin, this vision provided us with the clues to a number of phenomena that, without the clues, were unintelligible and even absurd. Let us not talk about the entire mythology of the contacts between gods and men, of the profoundness of the gods' creative powers and the mysteries of their behavior towards their creatures. Let us simply take the very ample sector of thought and practice which I have called deductive divination.* It was most probably typical of ancient Mesopotamia and carefully developed there, and it is widely attested in thousands of documents. According to the opinion of their devotees, the gods had to determine and to decide first of all the *destinies* of all things, in order to produce and govern the world and the people from day to day. Their orders had to be *written down* in order to give them substantiality, publicity, and force. Utilizing as pictograms and ideograms the *things* to come, which they created as needed, they impressed in them the "individual words" of their decrees by anomalies and surprises in their presentation or their evolution. Whoever understood the code used by the gods (a real transposition of the code of cuneiform writing), in other words, the significant value of their "ideographic signs" materialized in the objects of the universe, could decipher the signs and read in them the irrevocable will of their authors. They would understand, for instance, that one had to prepare oneself for violence, for brutality, for something all-powerful, or for carnage each time a "lion" appeared—as in cuneiform every "star" made reference to the heavenly, the elevated. It is for all these coordinated and related reasons that deductive divination had become rational and possible, and that one could develop logical and strict ties between "divinatory ideograms" and their "real contents" by devoting oneself to this divination intensively and with

6. Especially in the rabbinical exegesis of the Bible, where a type of hermeneutic reasoning called *noṭarîkôn* figures which is nothing more than the adaptation of the procedures of the ancient scholars of Babylonia, studied here, to the Hebrew writing system. Conforming to the alphabetic character of the Hebrew script, one did not proceed from syllables, but only from the consonants that appear in the written text. Consider verse 21 of Psalm 77, where this is said to God:

> You have led your people like a flock
> by the hand of Moses and Aaron!

To understand all that was concealed in this doublet, one took apart the written elements of the first verb, NâHITâ, i.e. the consonants: *N* recalled the word *Nâsîm, miracles; H, Haiim, life; I, Iam, sea,* and *Ť, Tôrâ, the Law.* In other words, to "lead his people like a flock by the hand of Moses and Aaron" God had to perform *miracles* on behalf of his people, the moment that he made them leave Egypt in order to make them acceptable to him: he gave them *life*, going so far as to part *the sea* before them, in order to deliver them and to give them finally *the Laws* that constituted his charter, his rules, and his prerogatives in the Sinai. See, further, J. Koenig, *L'Herméneutique analogique du judaïsme antique*, pp. 392f.

perseverance. These ties were constant, universal, and necessary. We can thus discern, in a discipline that seems frivolous to us, the first outlines of a rigorous mechanism of systematic inquiry, of analysis and deduction of the intelligible connections between materially distant realities that, at a cursory view, seem unrelated to each other. Moreover, this entire divinatory system was a simple projection of the "graphic dialectic" studied above, which was extended to an area of reflection as extensive as the entire earthly realm.

It was thus worth taking apart such a mechanism, however strange and grim it may seem at first glance. Starting from a situation as far removed from our own point of view as possible, a development oriented to what had to become our own notion of *knowing* was inaugurated.

III

"REASONING" INSTITUTIONS AND MENTALITY

7

Oneiromancy

IN CONTRAST WITH OTHER CULTURES, SUCH AS THE CULTURE OF pharaonic Egypt, the recognition, the practice, and the study of the divinatory value of dreams in Ancient Mesopotamia did not occupy more than a small sector of a much larger enterprise, the object of which was virtually the entire earth. In the eyes of the Mesopotamians, *everything* in the world was divinatory; and dreams were just like the rest. Therefore, it seems useful to me to start with a presentation in broad outlines of this universal divination. It will be easier, and certainly more fruitful, to place oneiromancy in this context.[1]

DIVINATION

It is impossible, however, really to gain access to the Mesopotamian way of viewing the subject without recalling a few fundamental parameters of their system of thought. They were convinced that the world around them did not have a raison d'être within itself. It depended entirely on supreme forces that had created it and that governed it primarily for their own advantage. The images of these gods were based on a human model; they were greatly superior, however, by their endless life, by their intelligence, and by their power that was infinitely above our own. Everything on earth, all objects and events, came forth from the gods' actions and their will, and

1. See *Divination et rationalité*, pp. 70–197.

This chapter first appeared in *Ktema* 7 (1982): 5–18, under the title "L'oniromancie en Mésopotamie ancienne."

fitted into some kind of general plan that *they* had in mind. This plan was impenetrable, as such, to humans, who discovered its unfolding from day to day. Nothing that we are ignorant of in the past, the present, and, of course, the future, escaped the gods' knowledge and their decisions. But they could report on it to mankind at their pleasure: this was the entire meaning of divination.

Such notification could take place in a direct and an indirect way. The *direct way* consisted of the gods *revealing* frankly what they had to say. There are only one or two examples of such public revelations (once to the army—M. Streck, *Assurbanipal,* 2: 48f., 95ff.). The gods preferred clearly to take a single intermediary, a "medium," and to communicate to him their secret, by ordering him to broadcast it. It seems that anyone could be chosen and could receive a message from a supernatural being by means of an auditory or visual signal, but preferably by means of the two together. This message could pertain to the past, the present, or especially to the future. The content of such revelations was sometimes clear and immediately intelligible, but it could also be obscure, and a certain indispensable exegesis of it was reserved for specialists. This first type of mantic, modeled on direct discourse—"from mouth to ear"—we can call *inspired divination,* taking into account its supernatural context. To our knowledge, this form of divination does not seem to have been very widespread—and it was even less valued, by the literate in any case—in Mesopotamia proper, with the exception of certain periods and certain milieus.

The other type of mantic, the *indirect* one, which I call *deductive divination,* was far more usual, to judge by the innumerable texts that are left to us. This method of divination was based on the model of written discourse: the gods did not communicate what they had to say "by word of mouth," but coded it graphically, and put it in writing to offer it for reading to its addressees.

One must not forget that the ancient Mesopotamians, probably the inventors of the oldest known system of writing, created around the year 3000, were profoundly impressed and influenced by this innovation. Not only because this transformation placed them in the written tradition,[2] but also because the writing system in a certain way inspired and shaped their way of thinking. This writing system was fundamentally pictographic in origin (and always remained partly so): i.e., the script called to mind the things that it had to express by signs that represented these things either directly (an ear of grain for *cereals,* the pubic triangle for *woman*) or indirectly (the profile of mountains for *the land, abroad,* the foot for *to stand, to walk, to bring,* etc.). In fact, one represented concepts or actions by other things that were drawings, which themselves referred to objects. This

2. See the *Catalogue de l'exposition Naissance de L'Écriture,* p. 29.

method struck the imagination of the ancient Mesopotamians, and, as we have seen, gave their "logic" a certain number of patterns, among them, the one that in a certain way rationalized a type of divination.

The "objective" foundation of deductive divination was without doubt the repeated observation of sequences of events. One event that drew attention because of its unnatural character preceded the other which was equally accidental and unexpected. The first event was imagined as the harbinger of the second, regardless of whether their mutual bond was real or imaginary. For example, some unusual meteorological event could inaugurate an agricultural catastrophe; the appearance of a monstrosity might cause the fear of an accident; some unusual behavior of an animal or a man might prefigure a change in life. It is here that the mechanism of the script intervened, in the sense that the premonitory phenomena were taken as things intended by their authors (the gods) to signify other events. Thus, types of "divine pictograms" transmitted a message from above, conveying what had to happen next.

Once the framework of this type of "pre-diction" was established (perhaps because it was best adapted to the classifying and rational spirit of the ancient Mesopotamians), they at once developed it to an extraordinary degree, and systematized it. Thus they established a type of "code" which was entirely parallel, even here and there identical, to that of the script, from which the experts, informed about the values of the "divine pictograms," could decipher exactly and univocally their message concerning the future (in contrast to the haziness and uncertainties inseparable from intuitive divination). They could *extract* it from the divine pictograms, *deduce* it from them; hence the name *deductive divination*. And as the entire universe was at the mercy of the gods, who regulated its functioning and progress, the Mesopotamians logically considered the sublunary world in its totality as the supporter of their "script" understood in this fashion, and also as the bearer of their messages to be deciphered. Through this shift, the whole of nature assumed a divinatory value: the movements of the stars and the production of meteorites; changes in the weather; the curiosities of the mineral and the vegetable world; the appearance (especially at birth or at the moment of dying) and the behavior of animals, and even more so of men; the particular aspects of their physiognomy and their conduct; and, finally, their dream life.

DREAMS

To grasp better how this last aspect could integrate itself into such a universal divinatory system, it is useful to recall the little we know of the idea the ancient Mesopotamians had of the world of dreams. Supposing that such an idea was entirely clear in their eyes, which is greatly to be doubted, they never took the trouble to explain it to us, and we ourselves have to extract it from their vocabulary and from the way in which they talk to us about their dreams.

The names that they gave to dreams show clearly that they attached them essentially to *the night* (ma.mú(d), after A. Falkenstein, and máš.gi$_6$, *product(?) of the night,* in Sumerian;[3] in Akkadian, *tabrît mûši, nocturnal vision*), and to *sleep* (in Akkadian, *šuttu, dream,* is of the same "root" *wšn*—Hebrew *yšn* and Arabic *wsn, to sleep*—as *šittu, sleep*). The dream was thus an essentially nocturnal phenomenon, and especially proper to sleep (even if it was accidental, as there was also sleep without dreams). However, "to dream" did not constitute a specific action or state. No verb expressed it in Sumerian or Akkadian. One said only *to see* a dream (Akkadian, *amâru,* and *naṭâlu;* sometimes *naplusu* and *šubrû*), and the dream was first of all a *vision* (as is shown by the Akkadian *tabrît mûši* above), a spectacle.

Not every vision, not even every unnatural one, was a dream, however. For instance, the cases are well distinguished where one dreamed the death of people and where one saw them appear in full daylight.[4] It is clear that one was perfectly aware, as elsewhere, that the objects of the oneiric visions had a consistency, a particular appearance that set them apart from objects that one saw around oneself, as well as from supernatural "appearances." This is without doubt the reason why one imagined a god to preside over dreams. The god himself was called *Dream* (*^{d}Ma.mú* in Sumerian—see above), and especially *Light Breath, ^{d}Ziqîqu,* in Akkadian, a term known and also used here and there to indicate the immateriality of the "ghost" of the dead, a kind of "double," evanescent, untouchable, and disincarnate, to which people are reduced after death. Thus the oneiric world in Mesopotamia has to be regarded as a universe in some ways airy, hazy, ungraspable, and immaterial.

Another difference with the three-dimensional world that surrounds us when we are awake, is that the dream gave rise to experiences that were completely unknown, indeed unimaginable in conscious life, not only by their illogical character (one dreamed of being decapitated, or of eating one's own penis, etc.—see below), but also by other unusual conditions, such as the extreme mobility that made the author of a letter address his faraway correspondent as follows: *Whatever you do, down there, my dreams will bring to me* (*Textes cunéiformes du Louvre,* 1, no. 53: 27f.). But, as different as they are, dream life and daily life still have one and

3. *La Divination en Mésopotamie ancienne . . . ,* p. 56 and n. 3f.

4. While in the Treatise on oneiromancy, the dead are seen in a dream (Oppenheim, *Dreams,* pp. 327: 66 and 72ff.), in the Treatise "on the accidents of daily life" it dealt with the appearance of ghosts (*eṭemmu*) or of *the dead as if* (they were still) *alive,* (*mîtu kîma balṭi*). One saw them, they frightened, they cried out, they stood at the end of the bed, entered and left, etc.: see *Cuneiform Texts . . . in the British Museum* 38, pl. 25f.: 23ff; and pl. 30f.: 1ff.

the same individual as a subject, who passes from one state to the other, sometimes in an instant (as when he "woke up with a start" following a nightmare—*negeltû; tebû*), while perfectly aware that he has left the dream world to return to earth.

In short, the dream world was only a possibility, a modality and a moment of life, a mysterious pursuit. In special circumstances (that seem not to have been further analyzed) it was a part of conscious life, with a felt difference, but without the slightest opposition between the dream world and conscious life. That is why this dream life could be integrated in the divinatory system along with conscious life.

INTUITIVE ONEIROMANCY

The first subject to be dealt with in intuitive divination is *intuitive oneiromancy.* We have said that it is founded on the belief that the gods are free to communicate directly what they alone know to whomever they want, and that they can choose at their pleasure for that purpose the dream as setting and vehicle. In the Flood story (*Gilgameš, Ninevite version,* XI: *187*) the god *Ea* wants to ward off the annihilation of mankind, and for that purpose reveals the imminence of the catastrophe to the Babylonian Noah. He says: *I have revealed to Atraḫasîs a dream, and it is thus that he has learned the secret of the gods.*

Such a belief in divine revelations through dreams is archaic in ancient Mesopotamia. The oldest example appears in the famous Stele of Vultures where the author, the king of Lagaš Eanatum I (ca. 2450), engaged in battle against Umma, tells how the god *Ningirsu** appeared to him during his sleep to reassure him of the happy outcome of the war: *Even Kiš will not support Umma! The god Utu will side with you!* (VI: *17*ff; E. Sollberger-J. R. Kupper, *Inscriptions royales sumériennes et akkadiennes,* p. 49). And we know other analogous manifestations from the Old Babylonian king Ammiditana (1683–1647), who was warned in a dream that he had to offer a statue of himself to the gods (*Reallexikon der Assyriologie,* 2, p. 187b: 223), to the time of the Neo-Assyrian Assurbanipal* (668–627), and to the last Neo-Babylonian ruler, Nabonidus (555–539; for instance S. Langdon, *Die neubabylonischen Königsinschriften,* pp. 218f., i: *16*ff.). However, perhaps because our preserved documentation concerns mainly public affairs, such private "revelations-in-dreams" are exceptional (*Archives royales de Mari,* 10, no. 100; S. D. Walters, *Waters for Larsa,* p. 93, no. 69: *4–10,* R. F. Harper, *Assyrian and Babylonian Letters,* no. 1021 = S. Parpola, *Letters from Assyrian Scholars,* no. 294: *13*f.).

Yet, even when their message was addressed to the ruler, the gods seemed to prefer to resort to simple subjects as intermediaries. Here is a very detailed example through which it will be easier to imagine the functioning of the system. In a letter addressed around the year 1770 to the king of Mari, Zimri-Lim, the governor of a province of the north explains to him:

> On the very day that I sent this tablet to my Lord, an inhabitant of Šakkâ, a certain Malik-Dagan, arrived here to tell me: "In a dream I intended to go with a companion from Sagarâtum to Mari. . . . Arriving in Terqa I immediately entered the temple of Dagan to prostrate myself. When I was thus prostrated, Dagan addressed me: "The Sheikhs of the Iaminites and their men, he told me, are they on good terms with the people of Zimri-Lim who come up here?" I answered: "They are not on good terms!" And just before I left the temple, he talked again: "Why then do the emissaries of Zimri-Lim not reside here with me all the time to show me in detail this affair? If they had done it, it would have been a long time ago that I would have delivered the Sheikhs of the Iaminites to Zimri-Lim. I commission you thus now to go say this to Zimri-Lim: "Order your emissaries to come and reveal this affair in detail to me!" This is what this man told me to have seen in a dream. I send thus today this message to my Lord, so that he can think about it. And if my Lord wants it, may my Lord have his affair explained before Dagan, and that, for this purpose, the emissaries of my Lord may be sent regularly to Dagan. The man who told me this dream must make an animal sacrifice to Dagan, and therefore I have not sent him to you. On the other hand, as this man is (already) worthy of trust, I have taken no piece of his hair or of the fringe of his coat. (*Revue d'Assyriologie*, 42 [1948]: 128f.)

The entire mechanism is taken apart here: a certain individual receives in a dream from a god a revelation bearing on a public matter. He reports it immediately to his superior, who quickly transmits it to the ruler, so that the latter, being warned, can draw his own conclusions. We understand that according to the rules he should have verified, if not the veracity of the account—an impossible thing—at least the good faith of its author: either by presenting the man himself to the king for interrogation or inquest, or by sending something personal such as a piece of hair or fringe of a coat, for a verification whose procedures escape us.[5] But, as the dreamer was known to be *worthy of trust,* such an examination was unnecessary. In other words, such dreams lend themselves easily to a certain imposture, and one can even discern "pressure groups" behind the scenes, beginning with the clergy of the temple of Dagan in question!

5. See A. Finet, "Les symboles du cheveu, du bord du vêtement et de l'ongle en Mésopotamie," *Annales du Centre des anciennes religions*, 3, pp. 101–30.

On the other hand, if in the cited example the message of the god seemed sufficiently clear, at least to its addressees (we know of cases where the dream and the message are repeated several days in a row so that things are even clearer, e.g. *Archives royales de Mari*, 13, no. 112, rev.), we have others where it seems enigmatic, where it is spoken or expressed in more or less figurative gestures or situations. There is an eloquent example of this in another letter addressed to the same Zimri-Lim, this time by a woman who seems to have played an important administrative role in the palace of Mari:

> After the reestablishment of my father's house (= Zimri-Lim, around 1780, after the Assyrian interregnum) in truth I never had a similar dream. . . . In my dream, I had entered the temple of Bêlet-ekallim*: but (the statute of) Bêlet-ekallim was not there! And even the statues (of the other gods) usually placed in front of her, were not there! At that sight I started to cry for a long time. I had this dream in the first part of the night. Later I had another: Dada, the priest of Ištar-bišrâ was standing at the gate of the temple of Bêlet-ekallim, while a hostile voice did not stop crying: "Return! Dagan![6] Return! Dagan!" (*Archives royales de Mari*, 10, no. 50: 3ff.)

In this case not only the situation is unclear, but even the shouts of the *hostile voice* are ambiguous, because *Return! Dagan!* in Akkadian is said *Tûra-Dagan*, which is also the proper name of several contemporary individuals, some known to us, some not. Such dreams could thus necessitate an interpretation.

That is the reason for the existence of the *šâ'ilu*, literally *examiners*, *questioners*, or *investigators*, but in reality often specialists in the exegesis of these dreams. We do not know their techniques but there are cases where, by a sort of counter-proof, they had to appeal to the "objective" information of deductive divination. But it seems clear that their profession was based above all upon personal gifts, a certain temperament and a particular wisdom and "inspiration"—something like our modern fortune-tellers, one might say. This is apparently the reason why, by preference, the profession was often exercised by women (*šâ'iltu*), more or less related to pythonesses and sorcerers. A famous passage of the Old Babylonian epic of *Gilgameš** may at least give us some idea of this mode of exegesis. This is the account of the first dream of the hero. Before meeting Enkidu, who will become his friend and companion, Gilgameš has his first premonitory dream, which he *tells* (*pašâru*, *to explain* in the sense of *to detail*) to his

6. Dagan was a god.

mother, who then interprets it for him (the same verb *pašâru, to explain,* in the sense of *to give meaning; Gilg. Pennsylvania: 1–23*):

When he woke up, Gilgameš, "explaining" his dream,
said to his mother:
"Mother, during the night,
with all my dignity, I was walking around
among the men
under the celestial stars,
when a "block" from heaven fell in front of me.
I wanted to lift it, but it was too heavy for me;
I wanted to move it, but I couldn't stir it!
The population of Uruk* was standing around it
and the men were paying homage to it ("kissed its feet")!
I pushed it in front of me, while they helped me
so that I ended up by lifting it and bringing it to you!"
The mother of Gilgameš, who knows all,
said to Gilgameš:
"It could well be someone who resembles you, Gilgameš!
After he was set on earth in the steppe,
the desert saw him grow.
When you will have met him, you will rejoice
and the men will pay homage to him!
You will embrace him, and bring him to me!"

And in fact, Enkidu, born and raised wild in the steppe, as strong and powerful as Gilgameš (this is a *block*), and sent by the gods (he *fell from heaven*) will arrive in Uruk, surrounded by the *curiosity of the population* and *admired by the men.* At first Gilgameš will measure himself against him, to *lift him* and to defeat him, then he will become friends with him and *lead* him to his mother so that she will bless this brotherhood. In reality, to interpret the dream, the mother of Gilgameš has proceeded with a sort of intuition mixed with foreknowing. There is nothing rigorous and "technical" about that, nothing comparable to what we see of deductive oneiromancy. The other dreams of Gilgameš and Enkidu—there are many, some of which are frankly incubatory*—insofar as the pertinent passages of the *Epic* are preserved, are all interpreted by analogous procedures, essentially by intuition. There was even, seemingly, a case of "clairvoyance" in a dream, with Enkidu participating in the council of the gods where his death is decided (Hittite fragment corresponding to the beginning of tablet VII). That dream is very clear; but one could say that Gilgameš (*Ninevite version* VII/ii), dismayed at this nightmare, tries to reassure his friend and suggest to him that to understand the message he should proceed by inverting the values, and that, consequently, this terrible dream can only be reassuring.

DEDUCTIVE ONEIROMANCY

To pass on to *deductive oneiromancy* now, we are going to see that, if we set apart the common supernatural character of their source and the remedies that are brought to their inconveniences, deductive oneiromancy is diametrically different from intuitive oneiromancy.

First, it was valid for everybody. There was no longer a question about extraordinary dreams and explicitly supernatural messages, which were perhaps more easily reserved for the great of this world(?), but of ordinary, current, daily dreams of "the man on the street" and valuable for all. Whoever dreamed, and whatever his dream was, that individual was the recipient of the message that the dream bore. Only, the message was "written" and "coded," and to "read" it one needed a real technician, a specialist initiated in this "writing": a *bârû*, i.e. an *examiner;* someone who looked closely at and studied the "pictograms" incorporated in the dream, who deciphered them and translated them for the interested party who came to consult him. And as if to emphasize the small place held in this technique by temperament, natural disposition, and inspiration, we find it practiced only rarely by women (as with writing itself).

The oldest example of these "oneiric pictograms" is interesting because of its notably late date (around 1700), and because of its context and its form. It appears in a small collection of some sixty oracles, drawn from physiognomy as well as from human behavior by night and by day—a combination that underlines to what degree dream life was considered but a particular moment in life, in everything and for everything. The dream in question is what we could call a nightmare. It is presented to us in two antithetic propositions; each starts by depicting the dream in the form of a hypothesis and ends with a laconic indication about the future that will ensue:

> If a man, while he sleeps, dreams that the entire town falls upon him (in the material sense of the collapse of buildings, or figuratively, the hostility of the citizens?) and that he cries out and no one hears him: this man will have good luck attached to him.
>
> If a man, while he sleeps, dreams that the entire town falls upon him and he cries out and someone hears him: this man will have bad luck attached to him. (*VAT* 7525, iii: 28f., in *Archiv für Orientforschung* 18 (1957–58): 67)

A similar presentation is found for *all* other oracles, not only from the cited tablet, but from *all* divinatory collections, already numerous (some one hundred) and varied at this time (especially oracles of extispicy;* also physiognomy,* tocomancy* and teratomancy* at birth, even astrology,* and from other sectors of deductive divination). Already at that moment it had been customary for a certain period of time to formulate the universal deductive divination in a particular way, and the odds are strong that the nightmare cited above was only a short extract from a "Dream Book" already developed and later enriched.

Our documentation is too scattered and weak to put us in a position to follow its subsequent history. Only remnants are available to us that can be considered as an intermediary stage (a collection of some one hundred dreams, very mutilated, found in Susa* and to be dated probably in the second half of the second millennium) and the final result: the classical Treatise on deductive oneiromancy, the canonical Babylonian "Dream Book," of which the principal manuscripts are from the first part of the first millennium, but of which we have fragments that go back a few centuries earlier.

This work, called—as usual—by its *incipit: ^{d}Ziqîqu, ^{d}Ziqîqu, "O, Dream God! O, Dream God . . . ,"* in its entirety must have consisted of eleven tablets. We will come back to the first tablet and the last two, which are not immediately divinatory, but exorcistic. The body of the work in eight tablets (II–IX) with about 400 to 500 oracles each, had to yield a respectable total of at least three or four thousand dream situations. Unfortunately, only a paltry amount of that total has come down to us, approximately a fifth, interrupted by many lacunae. But if such sparse remnants do not provide us with enough to even reconstruct the general plan of the Treatise, at least we can form a rather good idea of it, and perceive its principles and methods.[7]

This Treatise was composed of elements exactly modeled in their formal presentation on the "nightmare" cited above. Each entry is introduced by a hypothesis (which grammarians call "protasis*"), to underline the theme of the dream taken as omen, and ended with an "apodosis*" to draw from it the pertinent prediction. As in all other divinatory collections and treatises, these omens were carefully classified by their principal elements. Thus we have categories of chapters devoted to dreams of movements and

7. See L. Oppenheim, *Dreams*, where the Treatise is published in its actual form, and studied. Add, from the same author, "New Fragments of the Assyrian Dream Book," *Iraq*, 31, (1969), pp. 153ff. For the Susa text, see V. Scheil, *Mémoires de la Délégation en Perse*, 14, pp. 49ff. and pl. 6. Consult as well pp. 90–108 of *Annuaire 1969–1970 de l'École pratique des Hautes Études*. The roman numerals and the capital letters that are used in the citations here refer to the order established by L. Oppenheim in *Dreams*.

voyages (tablet I), others to consumption of different foods, then of drinks (A); the making and production of multiple merchandises (III/i, etc.); the transfer of objects, received or taken by the dreamer (B), and a number of other affairs: for instance, a long paragraph on the emission of urine (VII, rev. *1*–end). Here are two sufficiently long extracts:

> 3′ If (a man dreams that he eats) the meat of a dog: rebellion, desire not realized.
> If . . . of a beaver(?) (in Akkadian: dog-mortar): rebellion
> 5′ If . . . of a gazelle: skin rash (?).
> If . . . of a wild bull: his days will be long.
> If . . . of a fox . . . : skin rash; for the ill, this is a good sign.
> 10′ If . . . of a monkey: he will succeed.
> If . . . of (some animal, otherwise) known: peace of mind.
> If . . . of (some animal, otherwise) unknown: no peace of mind.
> If . . . from a man: he will acquire great wealth.
> If . . . from a dead man: someone will take away all that he owns.
> 15′ If . . . from a corpse: (same oracle) . . .

and so on; after which he eats himself; he eats the flesh of his neighbor (*companion*); then of different parts of his own body—hands, feet, penis, etc. Then follow a number of dishes that form an impressive "menu," then various meats; all sorts of fruits and vegetables; then animal food—food for bovines and for wild animals (once *after having sniffed it*); straw; cut straw; wood; reed . . . , baked brick; unbaked clay; earth; leather; excrement (A obv. ii: *3*′–rev. i: *27*′).

And this is the fragmentary passage (reference above) where the emission of urine is studied:

> 4′ If his urine, directed by his penis, [inundates] a wall: he will have children.
> 10′ If . . . a wall and the (adjacent) street: he will have children.
> If . . . several streets: his belongings will be stolen or distributed to his fellow citizens.
> 15′ If, once his urine has left his penis, he prostrates before it: the son that he will engender will become king.[8]
> 20′ If . . . he moistens a wall and that [ ]: he will have children.

8. One has to recall here the story of Astyages, told by Herodotus, I, 107f.: his daughter dreamt that "*she urinated so much that the city was inundated, even the entirety of Asia was submerged.*" The Magi interpreters of dreams told him that the child would become king in his place.

If with his urine he moistens "small reeds(?)": he will have children. [. . . : lacuna] . . .

If . . . he washes his hands: several people will devour the goods of his children(?).

If, he soaks himself with his urine and wipes himself: (the disease called) Intervention of Ištar.*

If he directs his urine towards the air: the son whom this man will beget will become famous, but his own days will be short.

If he urinates into a river: his harvest will ⟨not⟩ be bountiful.

If . . . in a well: he will lose all his goods.

If . . . in an irrigated field: the god of rain will flood his harvest.

If . . . on (the image of) a god: [he will not recover] his lost property.

Then, after a certain number of hypotheses, one reads, at the end of the tablet:

If he lets his urine run when he is sitting: sorrow.
If he urinates upwards: he will forget what he has said.
If he drinks the urine of his wife: this man will live in great prosperity.

THE ONEIROMANTIC SYSTEM

What is most striking in these examples is the *system*. The subjects that are considered and classified include, if not all existing hypotheses (which would be an impossible task!), at least the largest possible number of them. The classification is arranged according to a system which is often impenetrable to our minds, but which exhibits a logic that is clear to us now and then: dog → badger; straw → cut straw → baked brick, in which cut straw was mixed → clay; urine inundating a single wall, then a street, then several streets, etc. The entire system composes a type of casuistry which, by resorting to analogy, permits the extension of the conclusions drawn from what is established into those areas not explicitly mentioned. This was the universal procedure in ancient Mesopotamia used at the same time for pedagogy and scientific explanation.

The Dreams

On the other hand, each *oneiric situation* that was collected and catalogued is never presented by more than its essence; i.e. the element which was considered to play the role of a "pictogram" and to carry the "message." The concrete factual circumstances of the dream, those which made the dream particular and associated with a specific person, are set aside. That is why, based upon the evidence of the Treatise it is impossible for us to seek an "entry" into the daily life of the dreamer, past or present (i.e. the psyche of the dreamer), as one likes to do these days. One does not find anything "alive." The erotic dreams, for instance,[9] are only defined by their object without mention of anything else. The concerned party dreamed that he slept with the goddess of love (*Ištar*), with a god, with the king, with the wife of another man, with the son of another man, with a young woman, with a young man, with a young boy, with his own daughter, with his own sister, and even with a corpse. Nothing is added, however, about the *Sitz im Leben* of the dream. There is no indication about the precise way in which the incidents took place, about the sensations and about the released emotions, and so on. Clearly, the only thing that counts is the central theme of the situation dreamed, as only that in its abstraction is considered to be significant. In the pictographic script it is any ear of corn, any foot, any mountain, any woman that is significant in itself and not a particular ear of corn, a particular foot, a particular mountain, a particular woman. In passing, it has to be said that the acknowledgment of this care for *abstraction* convinces us to speak here of research, not of the individual and the accidental, but of the universal and the essential. In other words: of "science."

The Oracles

These characteristics of abstraction also apply to the "messages" deciphered in the pictograms. The oracles are presented only in a generalized form and are stripped of even the smallest concrete and individual features: desire not realized; rebellion; skin rash; long and short life; success; (great) wealth; peace of mind or no peace of mind; he will have children; one of his children will become a person of importance, or king, etc. The divinatory collections seem originally to have been filled with particularized and detailed oracles taken from daily life. They were recorded because of an original attention to sequences of events, even if with time they tended to narrow the expression of these "apodoses" down as much as possible to a *yes* or a *no*. In other words these apodoses became merely a favorable or an unfavorable answer to the question asked, which is essentially what one expected when questioning a diviner. More than one of these original "fragments of daily life" were preserved until a very late date. For instance, in a Neo-Babylonian treatise on extispicy, dating to the middle of the first mil-

9. In *Dreams* p. 334 (n. 1), x + 3ff. For the value *ṭeḫû*, *to approach* someone, *to sleep with* someone, of the sumerogram UM/DUB used here, and not translated by Oppenheim, see R. Borger, *Zeichenliste*, p. 95, no. 134.

lennium, real morality tales are still found: If (the surface of the liver appears in such and such condition), this woman, pregnant by another man, will constantly pray to the goddess Ištar, saying: "May my child look like my husband!" In every known part of the Treatise on oneiromancy the ancient Mesopotamians seem to have cut out such realistic or fantastic "visions of the future," to the benefit of generalities that tend towards a *yes* or a *no* answer to the most precise question that the dreamer could ask when consulting the diviner.

Perhaps we have to consider the fact that the "predicted" future in the same Treatise is more than once presented as depending on the peculiar condition of the dreamer, that it is the result of a certain resistance to such an increasing universalization of the oracles, somewhat like the fact that, in writing, the precise sense of a pictogram depends on its context (e.g. *home* or *abroad* for the profile of mountains, *to walk, to stand up,* or *to carry* for the foot, etc.).

> If he dreams that he eats the meat of a fox: skin rash; but for him who is (already) ill, it is a good omen. (A obv. ii: x + 7).

> If . . . that he received a seal marked [. . .]: if it is an important man he will become poor; if it is a poor man, he will become wealthy. (B obv. i: 25).

> If . . . that he has wings and that he flies to and fro: his foundation is not solid[10] (and) if he is poor, his bad luck will leave him; if he is rich, his good luck will leave him. (C rev. ii: *21*).

and almost immediately following:

> If . . . that he has wings and that he takes off and flies away: if he is poor, his bad luck will leave him; if he is rich his good luck will leave him; if he is in jail he will leave the jail, he will become free; if he is sick, he will get well. (C rev. ii: 25).

Perhaps we have to reason in the same fashion when the situation arises of one and the same dream predicting various futures (and this is not unusual). According to the same hypothesis, different oracles, when presented one after the other, are to be regarded as variants:

> If . . . he eats mandrake (in Akkadian: "plant-of-destiny"): catastrophe; he will prevail over his enemy (in court); conscription (in the armed forces); alarming news. (A rev. II: x + 8ff.)

10. Note that this proposition is in some sense a general one, which would indicate the global sense of the omen before its concrete applications. Compare it to the document studied in *Divination et rationalité*, pp. 185ff.

Of the four "conclusions" to the dream foreseen here, at least two are of evil portent, and one is favorable! Such multiplicities, even contradictions, possibly preserve the memory of the empirical origins of deductive divination. The same unusual event could have been followed by different situations according to the circumstances. As a result one can imagine, as well, different "schools" of interpretation. But as in the preceding case, such variants could also betray the awareness of a certain ambiguity and multivalence of the pictograms, in divination as in the script.

The Code of Decipherment

What remains to be discussed is the problem of the "code" used for the reading of these "oneiromantic pictograms." What was it that determined their value and that allowed the *bârû* who examined them to "decipher" these pictograms in a way that was sufficiently univocal and assured, and to pass thus, without the least arbitrary element or the least fantasy, from the omen to the oracle—from the protasis to the apodosis? When we consider the millennia and the profound ideological differences that separate us from the ancient users of the Babylonian dream interpretation, we have to expect that it will not be easy, often not even possible, to understand in the pictographic script, the usual one as well as the divinatory, the reason for the connection between the signs and the signified.

In the divinatory and oneiromantic messages, as in the script, this semantic connection often seems to have been based on a real, imaginary, analogical, or purely conventional relationship, that made one the sign or the symbol of the other. To him who dreams that he is eating the fruits of a vineyard, it is natural that one can promise either joy, or—a frequent drawback of such gluttony—*stomach pains* (A obv. iv: *10*). In dreams, as in everyday life, if water assures health and *prolongs life* (B rev. ii: x + *14*), abuse of wine *shortens it* (ibid. 1: 9 and ii: x + *16*), while too much beer makes one lose one's head. That is why he who dreams that someone has given beer to him *will no longer know what he said* (ibid. i: *10* and ii: x + *15*). We find this pathological loss of consciousness in another area: in daily life to wet oneself implies a lack of control over oneself, if not senile decay. It is thus not surprising that a similar accident, dreamed, promises the same decline (VII, end: 2′f.). In all these cases, aspects and effects of things of the conscious universe were simply transposed in the world of dreams. The modern-day "dream books" do not proceed in a different way, when they explain to us, for instance, with regard to the sea seen in a dream: "if it is black and wild, that is a bad omen; if we sail on it in a beautiful boat, then it is an omen of a subdued, controlled future, of victory over the obscure forces of the unconscious."

For us at least, things are, at times, somewhat more complicated, and in order to explain the transition from the protasis to the apodosis, we have to appeal to a way of seeing or a habit which was indigenous but which has become foreign to us. For instance, why is it that someone who dreams *he fell in a river, and came up again*, feels assured that *he will stand up* (in court) *to his adversary* (C rev. ii: 45)? It is the effect of a reference to the procedure of the river ordeal practiced in Mesopotamia. When the aspects of a court case did not allow the judge to decide, he subjected the parties to the judgment of the gods, in this case to the river as a supernatural force commissioned by the gods. If the accused sank into the river, he was shown to have been guilty by this fact. If the river let him "come up again," it declared him to be innocent and made him win the court case.[11] In the same way, he who dreamed that he slept with his daughter (still under his authority, and thus before her marriage was effective) had to expect a *decline in his financial gains* (Susa, iii: 9). This means that the marriage has become less "profitable" because of the defloration of the girl and her subsequent depreciation. The interested party will thus not receive as high a compensation (what one called the *terḫatum*) as was customarily expected to be granted by the in-laws to the family of the bride.

In these transpositions of elements of conscious life to the world of dreams, a reversal of values intervened, for reasons that escape us. In the nightmare cited above, he who did not get help in the dream received good luck, and vice versa. *Whoever dreams that he is sitting on the ground: he will receive honors* (III obv. II: 6) and L. Oppenheim, (*Dreams*, p. 266a) observed that, totally against the grain of reality, the dreamed infractions against inhibitions and "taboos" regularly produce happy results. To him who eats his own excrement in a dream, *an increase of his goods* is promised (A rev. i: 23), and *a great prosperity* is promised to him who drinks the urine of his wife under the same conditions (VII rev ii: end).

Symbolism also plays an important role in the mechanism of the decipherment of omens. Here also our "dream books" know that very well ("The way of the dream symbolizes destiny, the 'road of our life' . . . the mountain represents an insurmountable difficulty"). It is thus that almost everywhere, as we have seen above, the emission of urine promises *children*—by assimilation of urine to sperm. In the same way, he who *dreams himself to be eating his penis*—i.e. to suppress it—has to expect the death of one of his children (A obv. ii: x + 30). The semantics of the penis are not univocal, however (and this is also the case for more than one pictogram in the script), and it can be taken not only as an instrument of procreation but also as a sign of virility. Thus, he who dreams his penis *to be very*

11. See "L'ordalie en Mésopotamie ancienne," *Annali della Scuola Normale Superiore di Pisa, Classe di Lettere e Filosofia*, ser. 3, vol. 11, pp. 1005–67.

long: he will have no rival (Susa, iii: *18*). Another interesting symbol is the cylinder seal. As a usual mark and substitute for a person, it often represents that other mark and extension of each of us: our offspring. When we find the seal *given* in a dream, the apodoses are multiple: the dreamer *will have a son as his oldest child* (B obv i: *11*); *he will have sons and daughters* (*13*f.; *17; 18; 20;* etc.); and if he dreams that his seal is taken away from him, *either his son or his daughter will die* (ibid.: *23*).

In certain cases the connection between the omen and the oracle is created by a simple resemblance of sounds, what we would call a "play on words." For instance, to him who *meets a donkey* (in Akkadian: *imêru*) in a dream, the *vision* (*imertu*) *of children* is promised (A rev. iii: z + *6*). This strange image, an hapax as far as I know, to indicate simply that the dreamer will see children around him, that he will have them, was seemingly chosen because of the quasi-homophony with *imêru.* In a partly lost protasis, where the main verb at least is preserved, the dreamer sees himself *eating* (*akâlu*) [something], and the apodosis promises, first of all, that he *will eat* (*akâlu*) *sweet things* (word for word, sweet bread—*akalu;* the general sense is that he will be well fed = at ease); then, as a variant or a consequence, that *he will be wasting away* (*etkulu*) (VII obv. i: *19*f.). He who goes to the land of *Laban* (= Lebanon?) in a dream, *will build himself a house* (IX: Sm *29*+: *10*). This conclusion was drawn because the name of the country evokes the verb *labânu,* "to fashion bricks." And the term *ḫat[tu], terror, panic,* figures in the damaged apodosis of a dream of a voyage to the land of *Hatti* (to the Hittites*) (IX rev. i: *6*–*7*). But these are not simply plays on words, as we would think. In Mesopotamia, where nouns were not considered to be arbitrary epiphenomena and consequently subjective elements, but were thought to be the real objective expression of the proper essence of things, each phonetic similarity was considered to be serious and very significant: two realities whose names coincided were bound as closely together as their designations.

Another possible technique for "reading" dream pictograms appears in the interpretation of a travel dream to the (unknown) land of *Itrân:* it is promised to the interested party that *he will free himself from a crime* (IX rev. ii: *21*). This latter concept is expressed in Akkadian as *aran;* and the name of the country in question is written with a first sign *IT* that can also be read *Á:* from *It-ra-an* (under the assumption that it was spelled that way) one can thus easily pass to *Á-ra-an,* homophonous to *aran.* Here it cannot be forgotten that in cuneiform writing the rather frequent homophony of signs, and the regular multiplicity of their phonetic as well as ideographic values, both in Sumerian and in Akkadian, was the foundation of an entire system of "dialectics" and of a heuristic method. To us, this system seems frivolous, but the Mesopotamians considered such substitutions most seriously. It is very likely that among the numerous "readings" of divinatory pictograms that we cannot understand or explain, some played on such subtleties, which are difficult for us to discern. Due to lack of information, it will most often be foolhardy to speculate on these interpretations. This is why an ample portion of the "code" for the reading of omens is beyond our reach. Here is an example of a double oracle, which is unusual in that the protasis and the apodosis are identical and identically expressed. One oracle deals with a *fox,* the other with a supernatural *lucky charm,* called a *Lamassu* in Akkadian: he who *takes a fox* in a dream, *will take*—i.e. *will obtain—a Lamassu;* in other words, he will have good luck. But if *the fox escapes* after *it has been caught,* the *Lamassu* also *will escape,* after *it has been caught* (B rev. iii: 9f.). There is thus a total assimilation between the fox (in Akkadian *šêlibu;* in Sumerian ka_5-a) and the *Lamassu* in (Sumerian, Lamma; written *AN.KAL*). But what is the intermediary term, what is the relationship between them, what is the symbolism, what is the phonetic or graphic—even iconographic—"pun"? No one, at the moment, is in a position to know; and this is very often the case.

Despite these uncertainties, it still remains a fact that divinatory apodoses, and those of oneiromancy, were not all arbitrary, and that there existed an entire system mastered by the technicians, the *bârû.* They would *deduce* from the protases, and read, as such, in events of oneiric life, that which the gods had written in it concerning the future.

RECOURSE AGAINST AN EVIL FATE PREDICTED BY DREAMS

A last question: what future is concerned? An absolute, unavoidable future? The entire basic sense of oneiromancy—and of divination—depends on the answer. We have to return here to tablets I and X–XI, which frame the body of the dream treatise. Not much more than fragments are left to us, but we can partly restore them by means of better-preserved parallels. What do we see in these fragments? They are exclusively devoted to what we call "incantations," or better yet, in my opinion, *prayers* of a "sacramental" type. These prayers were addressed to the gods in order to obtain from them the dispelling of a threat, of bad luck, or of an evil, and they are made up from a mixture of oral rituals and manual rituals, which support each other mutually. Here are one or two of the shortest examples:

> If a man had a dream of evil portent, he must in order that its evil consequences may not affect him, say to himself before he sets his feet upon the floor (in the morning): "The dream is good, good, verily good before Sîn* and Šamaš*!" In this way he makes a good omen for himself (instead of an evil one), and the evil fate promised by his

> dream will not come near him! (Sm 1069 rev: 3ff. // KAR 252, i: 7ff; *Dreams*, p. 300a).

or:

> "O [the name of the god invoked is no longer legible] dispel and remove the curse (that threatens me)! May the wind carry off the evil fate promised by the dream I had!" This is the prayer to remove the evil consequences of the dream in question. To be accompanied by the following manual ritual: when he has such a dream he shall make a libation of vinegar before he sets his feet upon the floor (in the morning while reciting the above prayer), and only then he will set his feet on the floor. Then the evil fate to be expected from his dream will be removed from him! (K13330 // KAR 252 iii: 47f.; *Dreams*, p. 300b).

The presence of such exorcisms in the canonical* Treatise of deductive oneiromancy itself suggests that it can only apply to dreams that are recorded in the Treatise. The exorcisms apply evidently to those dreams that are bad omens and that promised an unfavorable fate. The very existence of the exorcistic rituals shows that fate, even if communicated by the gods and decided beforehand by them—as was everything that involved the way of the world and its occupants—could be fought, even annulled, by having recourse to the authors of the decision themselves and of its "written" communication. And keeping in mind that the way of communicating—which was after all the only difference between deductive oneiromancy and intuitive oneiromancy—is totally secondary to the value of the communicated decision itself, we can assume without hesitation that the same recourse was applicable to the content of "supernatural" dreams. Thus the future revealed by oneiromancy, deductive as well as intuitive oneiromancy—and in more general terms of deductive as well as inspired divination—was not the absolute future, that which would unavoidably and really happen, but a *conditional* future. I have called it *judicial future* because its decisions and consequences seem to have been taken directly from the decisions of justice. When the judge has to decide the fate of a defendant, he has before him a certain number of factors on which he bases his decision. Similarly, the gods—whose entire doctrine in ancient Mesopotamia was based upon a transposition of the powers exercised here on earth—when they decide the fate of a man, do so based on the given elements of a certain number of circumstances and, once such a decision is arrived at, they announce it, either immediately or "in writing," specifically by means of dreams. Whether these dreams are immediate and "intuitive" communications, or "written messages" that are "to be deciphered and deduced," their content is, all in all, nothing but a legal decision. This decision does not indicate what will infallibly happen to the concerned party, but what is, at that moment, promised to him and what he has to expect. The contents, as that of all legal decisions, is thus circumstantial, and may be the subject of an appeal to the clemency of the judge.

This is why the "exorcisms" of tablets I and X–XI of the dream Treatise were established and propagated, as well as numerous others for all the sectors of divination, for all the communications of divine decisions relating to the future. They were called *namburbû*,* procedures of "dissolution" of the evil fate promised by the oracles,[12] and they give the real meaning of Mesopotamian divination. Divination did not exist on the level of the unavoidable and did not appeal to forces which were in some way metaphysical and immovable. It did not relate to decisions that were arrived at for all eternity and that were infallibly realized. Such gods are unknown in Mesopotamian theology. In that theology the role of the representatives of the supernatural world was to administer the world. The gods functioned like the kings on earth but on a superior level, with a power and an intelligence infinitely larger, and with immortality in addition. They governed and regulated the role and the fate of their subjects. But, as with kings, their decisions were always tied to circumstances, and were perfectly modifiable on condition that one knew how to deal with them. These are the decisions that the gods communicated, directly or "in writing," in the revelations or dream omens; and these are the decisions that the people involved had to avoid, and could change by prayers and the proper rituals.

In this way, divination in general, and oneiromancy in particular, are intelligible in ancient Mesopotamia only when reintegrated into the system of thought of the inhabitants of that ancient country, only when placed into the global vision that the Mesopotamians had of the universe.

12. See *Mythes et rites de Babylone*, pp. 29–64. For more general information on exorcism (which is too often confused with magic), see the article (in French) *Magie* in *Reallexikon der Assyriologie*, 7.

8

Divination and the Scientific Spirit

IN THE HISTORY OF SCIENTIFIC THOUGHT IT HAS BEEN SUGGESTED more than once that the Greek science of astronomy had its origins in one of Mesopotamia's divinatory practices: that of astrology. But the proof for that has never been given, and perhaps it is impossible to do so, as there are so many basic differences between the two.

I wonder whether the question formulated in this way is not badly put, and whether we cannot take it up again in a different way than from this rectilinear and simplistic point of view. I would like to show influence by discussing—from a great distance, of course—connections between divination and science in Mesopotamia; in other words by suggesting that it is wrong to reserve divination for Mesopotamia and science for Greece, but that in Mesopotamia itself, from very early and long before the Greeks, divination had become a scientific type of knowledge and was, essentially, already a science. What may have been passed on to the Greeks was this scientific point of view, scientific treatment, and the scientific spirit. Consequently the Greeks did not develop their conceptions of science, which we inherited, out of nothing; in this important point, as well as in others, they owe a debt to the ancient Mesopotamians.

DIVINATION IN MESOPOTAMIA

As we have seen, two types of divination are attested in Mesopotamia: one by the revelation of the gods, *inspired divination,** the other by a mental activity of the people, by a type of deduction, *deductive divination.**

This chapter was originally written for *Sciences et Avenir*, 313 (1975), pp. 284–89.

Inspired divination is rather badly known and is confined to a few areas that are chronologically and geographically restricted. It does not seem to be typical for Mesopotamian civilization, and we will not discuss it further.

Deductive divination, on the other hand, is attested, without interruption, from the beginning of the second millennium to the Seleucid period shortly before the Christian era. It must have been the subject of an enormous mass of works and documents, if we judge by the considerable amount that is preserved to us. Not counting the numerous pieces dealing with practice, we have found more than thirty thousand oracles divided over some one hundred Treatises at the very least. It is doubtless the best known, at the same time as being one of the most characteristic, intellectual activities of Mesopotamian culture.

This gigantic mine of information does not seem to have been sufficiently explored yet by Assyriologists. There are today only a few specialists in divinatory texts and they behave like Talmudists. One of the reasons for this neglect is perhaps the extraordinary monotony of the Treatises on divination that make up the principal pieces of the dossier. But I wonder whether the main reason is not that divination is considered, consciously or unconsciously, to be a simple superstition, trivial, outdated, and not really deserving of attention. Such a point of view implies an attitude that we could call "egocentric," and is particularly harmful in the discipline of history. The proper vocation of a historian is not only to rediscover the past through the witnesses that remain to us, but to discover it as it was; not as we see, feel, and judge it from our point of view, but the way it was seen, judged, and lived by its actors. If he really knows the meaning of his profession, the historian will always leave himself and his time behind and put himself in the place and time of the characters whose deeds and works he studies. To consider, even subconsciously, Mesopotamian divination as a superstition is to judge in our terms. Such a judgment will prevent us from ever understanding it, and this means that we will fail one of the essential rules of our discipline. Hence, let us try to consider and judge the mantic techniques* by putting ourselves, as much as possible, in the position of their ancient users. Of course, we will deal here only with deductive divination as an intellectual activity and a type of knowledge.

THE APPEARANCE OF DIVINATORY TEXTS

The essential, the most original and most typical documents, are those that we call Treatises, collections of oracles (sometimes several thousand). In each Treatise all oracles are drawn from the same material object considered in its particular and abnormal appearances: for instance, such and such position of a star, or the more or less monstrous aspects of a newborn or of the liver of a sheep.

If we count the objects whose appearance was considered to be ominous*—to use this latinized synonym of the term "divinatory"—and that were listed in the Treatises, we see that they cover almost the entire material universe: stars and meteorites; the weather and the calendar; the configuration of the earth, of waterways, and of inhabited areas; the outlook of inanimate and vegetal elements; the birth and the conformation of animals and their behavior, especially of man himself—his physical aspects, his behavior, his conscious and sleeping life, and so on. In addition to these phenomena which present themselves to observation, a number of others were latent and had to be revealed, such as the internal anatomy of sacrificed animals. Or they could be virtual and needed to be provoked, such as the shape taken by oil or flour thrown on water.

Of course, we should not say that the multiple ominous areas always and everywhere had the same interest in the eyes of the practitioners of divination. But what is important here is that everything could be considered as the possible object for examination and divinatory deduction, that the entire material universe was taken as the evidence from which the future could in some way be extracted after a careful study. There was already an encyclopedic curiosity that was very remarkable, and that is the first thing to notice.

The irreducible elements of the Treatises, from the stylistic as well as from the logical point of view, are the oracles, each of which indicates and explains an ominous appearance of an object from the Treatise, and then deduces what it allows us to foresee about the future. All of the oracles, from the first to the last, are constructed exactly on the same grammatical and logical pattern: the first part of the sentence, the "protasis"* as the grammarians say, is followed by a second part, the "apodosis."* The protasis is introduced (at least virtually) by the indication of a hypothesis—*if, supposing that* (in Akkadian: *šumma*)—and then gives the special appearance of the object—the omen. The apodosis shows the part of the future that can be derived from the omen: it is the prognosis, or the prediction. For instance:

> If a man's chest-hair curls upwards: he will become a slave.[1]
>
> If a man has a flushed face and his right eye sticks out: he will be devoured by dogs far from his house.[2]
>
> If the gallbladder (of the sacrificial sheep) is stripped of the

1. *VAT* 7525, i: 19f., in *Archiv für Orientforschung* 18 (1957f.): 63.
2. *Cuneiform Texts . . . in the British Museum*, 28, pl. 28: *12b*.

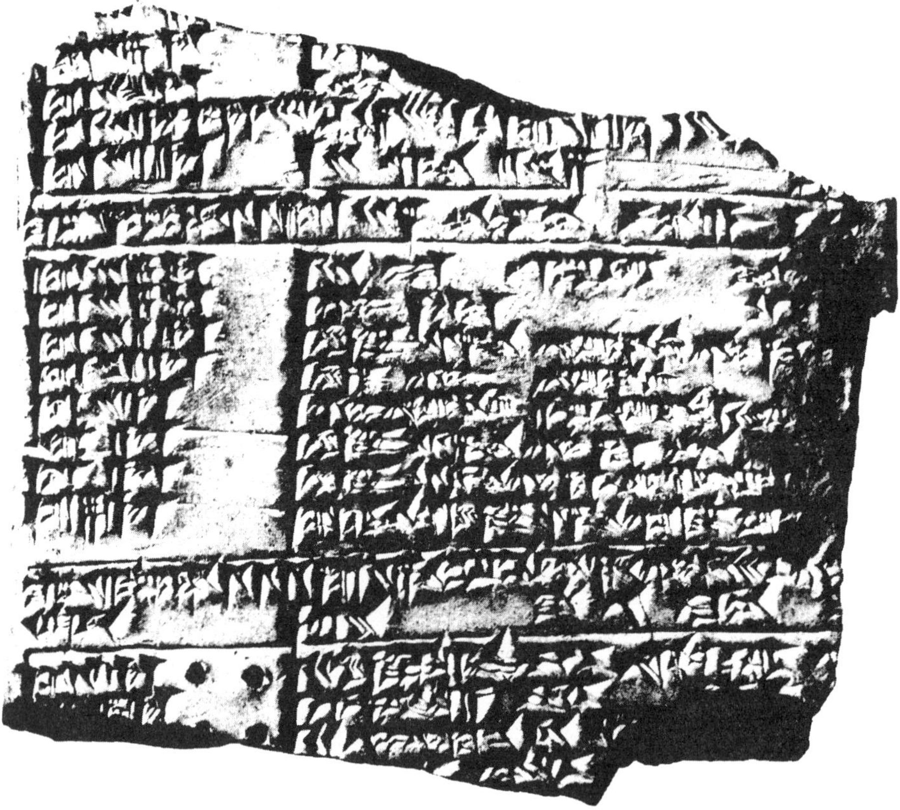

FIGURE 3 FRAGMENT OF THE TABLE OF CONTENTS FROM THE GREAT TREATISE ON ASTROLOGY

(The seven chapters dealing with the eclipses of the moon)

Nisan is the first month of the Mesopotamian year (March–April) and *Tešrît* is the seventh (September–October) in a total of twelve months.

On lines 15f. the copyist first indicates the total of all the tablets enumerated up to then in his table of contents: 22 in all. The preceding chapter, on the eclipses of the Moon, only contained 8 tablets. He then summarizes the essential contents of the 8 last tablets. He ends by stressing that, after counting and verifying, he guarantees his copy to be correct.

In line 12 the exclamation point indicates a correction. The text gives the number 1,200 which is clearly mistaken.

Photo: Musée du Louvre, Paris.
Apography: François Thureau-Dangin, *Tablettes d'Uruk* (Paris, 1922), plate 29.

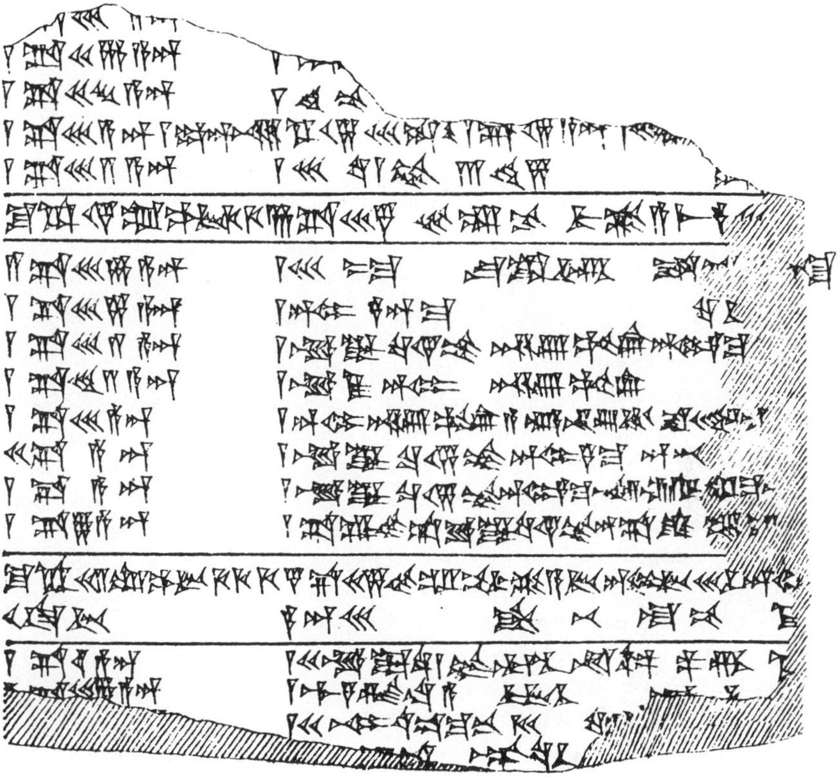

APOGRAPHY

156 (hypotheses, under the title): If the Moon be[omes dar]k fast in the evening

85 (under the title): If the sky becomes overcast during an eclipse

82 (under the title): If on the 14th of Nisan an eclipse happens in the evening, [. . .]

82 (under the title): If an eclipse happens in Tešrît

80 (under the title): If an eclipse happens in the evening and lasts till the end of the vigil, and the north wind (then) comes up

120! (under the title): If, when an eclipse happens on the 15th of Nisan, Venus [. . .]

60 (under the title): If, when an eclipse happens on the 15th of Nisan, the sky becomes overcast in the south and that [. . .]

68 (under the title): If in the beginning of the year, on the 15th of Nisan, the eclipse of the M[oon takes place]

In total (up to now) 122 tablets including 2,065 lines. Observations of eclipses and oracles (taken) from (these) eclipses, as well as predictions (based on the movements) of the Moon. (The total) is complete.

hepatic duct: the army of the king will suffer of thirst during a military campaign.[3]

If the north wind sweeps the face of heaven until the appearance of the new moon: the harvest will be abundant.[4]

MEANING AND ORIGIN OF DEDUCTIVE DIVINATION

What is most important for an understanding of divination as an intellectual activity, as a way of knowing, is contained much less in the protases or apodoses themselves than in the transition from the first to the second. How could someone decide to base the conclusion that a man would become a slave on the fact that his chest-hair curled upwards?

To answer this fundamental question we have to understand how deductive divination originated in Mesopotamia. We know enough of it at least to make conjectures, with a high degree of probability, based on converging elements. Often all we have to be satisfied with are such conjectures when we write the history of a world so old and so cut off from us.

Divination seems to have been at first entirely empirical, i.e. based on simple a-posteriori observation. A certain number of specific oracles from the enormous collection that we have allows us to think this, and at the same time explains this original stage. They have been called "historical" oracles because their prognosis, instead of dealing with the future, mentions the past and refers to an ancient event in the history of Mesopotamia that the Mesopotamians thought would repeat itself. For example:

> If on the right side of the liver (of the sacrificial sheep) there are two finger-shaped outgrowths (probably what anatomists would call "pyramidal process") it is the omen of a period of Anarchy (in other words the period between 2198 and 2195, approximately, that preceded by some thirty years the fall of the dynasty of Akkad).[5]

And also this passage already cited on p. 37:

> If in the liver, the part called "The Gate of the Palace" (the "umbilical incision" of the anatomists, it seems) is double, if there are three "kidneys," and if on the right-hand side of the gall bladder two clearly marked perforations (Akkadian *pilšu*) are pierced (*palšu*): this is the omen of the inhabitants of Apišal whom Narâm-Sîn (fourth king of the Akkad dynasty: approx. 2260 and 2223) made prisoner by means of a breach in the wall (*pilšu*).[6]

3. A. Goetze, *Old Babylonian Omen Texts*, pl. 43, no. 31 iii: 6ff.
4. *Zeitschrift für Assyriologie* 48 (1936): 309: 6f.
5. *Textes cunéiformes du musée du Louvre*, 6, pl. 3, no. 1. rev.: 23.
6. A. Goetze, *Old Babylonian Omen Texts*, pl. 29, no. 24: 9.

Another formulation, found among the oldest documents that can be formally associated with deductive divination, i.e. the famous "liver models" found at Mari,* is perhaps even more telling:

> When my country rebelled against Ibbî-Sîn (last king of the Third Dynasty of Ur: approx. 2027-2003) it is thus that the liver appeared.[7]

It should be noticed that these "models" were only half a century later than the revolt, which stresses that a close connection had been observed between the particular appearance of the liver of a sacrificial animal on a certain day and the revolt against the last king of the Ur III dynasty.

Moreover, we have to take into account that almost all the events recorded in the historical oracles are from the half-millennium between the period of the Akkad dynasty and the first years of the second millennium. We have good reason to assume that it was just in that period that deductive divination was developed, matured, and established in Mesopotamia.

What we know from other sources about the events recorded in the historical oracles seems to indicate that at least some of those events have a good chance of being authentic. From its closeness in time, the last example cited above, the liver model from Mari, is particularly impressive in this regard. On the other hand, as there is by all indications not the least intrinsic and necessary connection between any of the events and the aspect of the omen with which they are related, it has to be true that these oracles were based on the observation of the coincidence of the two phenomena.

In this country where we know that from very early on there was an interest in what the Romans called the *portenta*—unusual events that allow the prediction of something—sacrificers, when dissecting their victims, would have noticed if a liver had an unusual appearance. And somewhat later a special event must have taken place, a "turning point" in the history of the country. The coincidence must have been first noticed, then stressed. Perhaps because of other similar appearances, multiplied in the eyes of the people who "believed" in them, and who expected them, the coincidence was later considered to be something entirely different than an accidental encounter. *Post hoc, ergo propter hoc.* The first phenomenon would thus have been regarded as the announcement of the second, and the two together were recorded as an oracle of universal value, so that one could expect to see a repetition of an analogous event in the destiny of the land or of the king, whenever the anomaly was noticed again.

These conclusions should certainly not be reserved only for historical oracles properly speaking. Many others that deal with the country, the king, or with simple individuals seemingly must have had their origins in

7. *Revue d'Assyriologie* 35 (1938): 42f., no. 7.

similar observations: the only difference is that it was considered necessary to keep a mention of the names and of the individualized circumstances which are preserved in the historical oracles. Prognoses such as:

> Omen that the (entire) country will be covered by snow[8] or
> Omen of retreat (i.e.) when the army beats a retreat[9]

maintain in their presentation itself the indications of historical omens. These indications are especially numerous in the oldest Treatises, but we find them still here and there in a fossilized form in more recent periods. Many other omens that do not maintain these indications have preserved enough particular elements for us to recognize easily a concrete and particular event or an anecdote, a *fait divers,* taken from the daily routine. Here are some examples taken from the thousands available:

> A lion, after having killed someone before the city-gate, will be killed himself.[10]
>
> A small boy will fall from the roof.[11]
>
> When you will be in front of the city that you came to besiege, its garrison will break through the barricades put up to lay siege to it, and will attack you.[12]

And finally this gem, already cited:

> The wife of that man, pregnant by another man, will not cease to implore the goddess Ištar, and say to her while looking at her husband: "May my child look like my husband!".[13]

The oldest layers of oracles have thus a very good chance of having been formed in this way: from an observation of a sequence of events that do not have any apparent link between them, but were noticed to have followed each other once, it was thought that such events would always follow one another. That is what we would call empiricism.

It seems that from very early there was a desire to go further by looking beyond the appearances for an internal connection between the two events which formed an oracle. Let us look again more closely at the first historical prognoses mentioned above. In one of them the *two* finger-shaped outgrowths evoke the rivalry between *competitors* for the throne, a rivalry that

8. *Revue d'Assyriologie* 38 (1941): 82 (and 40 [1945f.]: 82): *AO* 7029 obv.: *10*f.
9. *Revue d'Assyriologie,* 35 (1938): 46 no. 16 (corrected translation).
10. A. Goetze, *Old Babylonian Omen Texts,* pl. 26, no. 21: 5f. and 8.
11. Ibid., pl. 17, no. 17: 53.
12. Ibid., pl. 74, no. 41: *41*.
13. A. T. Clay, *Epics, Hymns, Omens and Other Texts,* pl. 14, no. 12: 36f.

causes a "Time of Anarchy." In the second, the perforations (*pilšu*) pierced (*palšu*) in the liver correspond in the prognosis not only to the breach (*pilšu*) in the wall that causes the collapse of the besieged city, but also to the name of that city, *Apišal,* with a slight metathesis (and we have many other examples in the religious hermeneutics of these phonetic similarities).

In our eyes such "connections" do not exist. They are pure coincidences without importance. We have to believe (and we know it from other sources as well) that such was not the case with the ancient Mesopotamians, especially with their well-known doctrine of the world's government by the gods, and hence the preliminary fixing of the destinies, that is, the names, of all things by these gods.

In Mesopotamia, where writing was invented in the beginning of the third millennium, and where this invention played an important role in the material and intellectual life, it was imagined that the fates thus decided were inscribed by the gods on the *Tablet of Destinies.* The gods were even thought to have *written* these decisions in things whenever they created them or directed their movements. A certain number of texts, such as this one speak in this way:

O Šamaš . . . , you who write down the oracles and indicate the divinatory decisions in the entrails of the sheep!.[14] And even if the manuscripts in which we find these statements are from the first millennium, they must record a much older tradition.

On the other hand, the original and basic nature itself of the cuneiform script required that it was first of all a writing of things, and it always remained more or less so. It used pictograms that are after all things that indicate other things: the sketch of a foot for "to walk," or "to stand up"; the figure of the pubic triangle for "woman," "womanhood." Hence the idea could originate that the *two* finger-shaped outgrowths, instead of the expected single one, written by the gods on the livers of their victims indicated, beyond doubt, duality, opposition, and conflict, and played in a sense the role of the "pictogram" of rivalry and competition in the "divine writing system," just like the *perforations* expressed the *breach.*

This way of seeing things became a norm, unexpressed but always applied, based on the rule that governed the writing system: whenever the same sign appeared in an omen, one could "read" in it the same future event. In fact, whenever one finds in the description of an oracular object a duality (it has to be abnormal and unexpected, because what is common, usual, and according to the rule has no value at all as an omen), one has in the prognosis an idea of opposition, of rivalry, of misunderstanding, of battle.

14. E. Ebeling, *Die akkadische Gebetsserie "Handerhebung,"* p. 48: *110.*

We could compile numerous examples to show to what degree divination really functioned as a writing system in Mesopotamia: *by deciphering the "pictograms."* Of course there are numerous cases, both in the divination and in the script, where the connection between the signifier and the signified is not clear, not even intelligible sometimes, or imaginable for us. However that was certainly not the case for the ancient Mesopotamians, and this is important.

It is thus that divination passed from its primitive state of simple empirical observation to that of knowledge a priori, to "deductive" knowledge. From the moment they discovered that a lion is the sign, the ideogram, of violence or of power, it became useless to "wait for the events," which would have been indispensable in an empirical system. They could foresee without fail brutality, carnage, or domination from the moment that they noticed the presence of a lion in an ominous circumstance. This was a capital transformation and of considerable importance: because, in fact, a knowledge a priori, deductive knowledge, is already the essential element of science.

DIVINATORY SCIENCE AND ITS RECORDING IN TREATISES

Such a "scientific" character explains well the elements that are revealed from the oldest Treatises on. Notably this wish to analyze and systematize which strikes the readers of these documents so much. In each treatise the oracular object is taken apart in a sometimes surprising number of ominous appearances. For instance, the configuration of the head of a man and especially of his hair, takes up not less than sixty-six paragraphs in the Treatise on physiognomy.* These analyses and classifications are usually done according to a certain number of recurring categories: the presence of an object or its absence; its quantity and its dimensions; its internal disposition and its relative position; its coloring, which is sometimes extended to some ten different hues around the principal colors, which in those days were red, white, black, and yellow-green; then the addition or the lack of nonessential elements; and so on. All these eventualities are ranked in an order that is quite rigorous and constant.

It is very clear that at least in a certain number of cases not all of these hypotheses could have been observed in reality. There are even some that are entirely impossible. Thus in the liver of the sacrificial animal *two* gallbladders are foreseen, which is an imaginable though rare phenomenon (and that is why it is ominous). But then, driven by his wish to systematize, the author of the Treatise talks about *three*, *five*, and up to *seven* gallbladders, numbers that are entirely fantastic. In the same way, after the mention of twins delivered by a woman, the possibility of triplets is envisioned, then quadruplets, quintuplets, and then sextuplets, septuplets, octuplets, and finally nonuplets!

In a systematization that rejects all empiricism, all appeal to experience, all reference to a controllable reality, and ends up with eventualities that are entirely impossible, there is in the end a wish to record not only all that has been observed but also all that could be observed in theory, all that could exist, without ever having existed. And, in fact, for someone who does not have our biological evidence, if there can be two gallbladders, why couldn't there be more, even up to seven, if the gods wanted it?

Thus the scientific character of divination has led them beyond the observed reality to the possible: in other words, in logical terms Mesopotamian divination has attempted to study its subject as being universal, and in a certain sense *in abstracto*, which is also one of the characteristics of scientific knowledge.

It is because divination because in its own way, and certainly from the end of the third millennium on, a real "science" that the need was felt to put it down in Treatises. The Treatises were manuals of a science that they wanted to make available to those who wanted to learn it—and this definition is also valid for other disciplines common among the Mesopotamians: jurisprudence, medicine, and, in its own way, mathematics. They did not teach the same way we do, by extracting and formulating principles and laws: it is well known that the Mesopotamians of the past never formulated any such abstractions, as their minds did not at all tend towards them, and in their vocabulary there is not a single word to indicate "principle," "law," or "concept" in any field. In conformity with their type of intelligence they ignored such statements, which were universal and abstract in form. Instead they preferred concrete and individualized cases that they accumulated and changed to show the general idea from a particular angle.

The Treatises are manuals of casuistry: by surveying the variable elements of the same object, whether they were real or imaginary, observed or posited a priori, he who assimilated them acquired the sense of laws and principles, without having to learn them in abstract terms. Nowhere is it said that a lion announced tyranny, carnage, violence, or supreme power. But by the fact that the reader found in the cases where a lion appeared in the protasis a prognosis of either empire, or massacre, or oppression, or brutal force, he became aware of this constant element, of this law, without ever having seen it formulated. We were taught in this way when we were children and our minds could not yet grasp the abstract formulation of some principle of arithmetic or of grammar. We were made to learn by heart the tables of addition and of multiplication, and the nominal and verbal paradigms, which are also lists of varying cases, as are the Mesopotamian Treatises. Therefore the existence of such works stresses the scientific character of divination.

THE "DISCOVERY" OF THE SCIENTIFIC SPIRIT

From a knowledge based on pure observation a posteriori, starting from individual cases that were fortuitous and unforeseeable, divination became thus an a-priori knowledge, even before the period of our earliest Treatises, i.e. before the end of the third millennium at least. That knowledge was deductive, systematic, capable of foreseeing, and had a necessary, universal and, in its own way, abstract object, and even had its own "manuals."

That is what we call a science, in the proper and formal sense of the word, as it has been taught to us by the ancient Greek teachers, after Plato and Aristotle, and as it still in essence governs our own modern idea of science—at least for those among us who keep our minds sufficiently sharp and open not to reserve the term only for the mathematical disciplines, as if the universe was nothing but numbers and quantities, and as if logic, abstraction, and certainty were confined to that mocking field alone.

In this divinatory "science" we have to distinguish carefully between the object and the method, or spirit. The object is the possible future as it can be known through the present, as it can be deduced from the present. It could keep some type of consistency only in a mentality such as that of the ancient Mesopotamians, as in their eyes the world was directed by superior forces, who decided at their pleasure its fate to come, and also knew the details of it. This they could communicate, and they communicated it in fact by "inscribing" it in objects. Such an object would lose any value in a different world vision. Thus the Greeks already—I am talking about the philosophers and the scholars—repudiated this object, and we even more strongly find it empty of all meaning, outdated and "superstitious."

But the method, the spirit, once it had been established, did not depend on the primary object, and kept its value even when the object was ignored. The encyclopedic curiosity; the way to approach the universal reality by looking for a knowledge that is analytical, necessary, deductive, and a priori; the "abstract" and scientific attitude before things: these were definitive acquisitions of the human mind. They represented an enrichment and a considerable progress that could not be lost once they had been discovered, like fire or the technique of making pottery. I do not have to repeat how the Greeks learned and assimilated this "scientific spirit," born before them and in another country. I am only looking for the origin and I find that it appeared in Mesopotamia more than fifteen centuries before Socrates, Plato, and Aristotle. Its birth and establishment cannot be observed better outside divination, a science which constitutes one of the most essential and typical characteristics of the ancient Mesopotamian civilization.

We have to acknowledge that this constitutes a great moment in the history of mankind. Just like the discovery of fire, the domestication of plants and animals, the invention of metallurgy and of writing, this invention of abstraction and of universal and rational knowledge, in a word, of what we call the scientific spirit, at least in its roots, represents remarkable progress, judged from our point of view, i.e. in relationship to what we have become and to what still makes us live.

Does that not justify in itself the existence of Assyriologists and of all their labors?

9

The Substitute King and His Fate

It happened sometimes in Mesopotamia that the situation required a single individual to take the place of the king for a while. For instance, we have preserved to us a fragment of a ritual for the preparation for war,[1] and, of course, for a victorious war. In order to imitate and thus "make real" the battle from which the king, and the country with him, had to emerge victoriously, they fashioned from tallow a figurine representing the enemy, whose head was turned backwards (as a sign of fleeing after the defeat); and they confronted the figurine not with the commander of the army himself, i.e. the king, but with one of his officers *who had the same name as the king* and was dressed with his sash. In this fictional combat, which was supernaturally dangerous because it was "sacramental," there was some risk for the ruler, and this is why he was replaced. His replacement, however, did not have the title of *substitute king*, literally *king* or *image of substitution, of replacement* (*šar*/*ṣalam pûḫi*/*andunâni;* in Sumerian níg.sag.íla).

That designation seems to have been reserved for the central character in a real institution, which was at the same time religious and political, and was intended to save the king's life when it had been condemned by supernatural forces. It is this substitute king that I would like to discuss here.

Our documentation on this institution is very scarce, but it allows us at least to formulate an idea about it. An idea that is very imperfect, I have to

1. H. Zimmern, *Beiträge zur Kenntnis der babylonischen Religion*, 2, pp. 172f., no. 57.

This chapter first appeared in *Akkadica* 9 (1978):2–24, under the title "Le substitut royal et son sort en Mésopotamie ancienne."

admit, because our documents are almost all in a fragmentary state, and extraordinarily badly distributed in time and space. The oldest known example appears in the *Chronicle of Ancient Kings*[2] which we have some reason to think preserves a number of historical aspects. It reports that the ninth ruler of the First Dynasty of Isin, Erra-imitti (1868–1861) *died* prematurely *in his palace after having sipped a "broth" that was too hot* (A: 3ff.). He had as successor a simple gardener named Enlil-bâni (1860 1937) whom he had taken as a replacement, in other words as a substitu king, and who after his death simply remained on the throne.

After that, if we disregard a Hittite ritual from around the thirteenth century[3] which unveils to us an analogous institution in Anatolia, probably borrowed from Mesopotamia, we must go to the time of the Neo-Assyrian rulers to find our substitute again, and it is almost exclusively for this period that we can grasp the situation more or less clearly. The *šar pûḫi* is mentioned once, erratically, in an administrative document of the last year of Adad-nirâri III (810–783; ND 3483 in *Iraq* 15, 1953, p. 148 and pl. 15). But he reappears more than once, principally in the correspondence of Esarhaddon (680–669) and also in that of his son and successor, Assurbanipal* (668–627). Directly or indirectly, in clear statements or with oblique allusions, some thirty letters of the royal correspondence of that time deal with the substitute king.[4] These references are often broken in important parts or difficult to understand, as is the usual case in this type of document. We have also found in the library of Assurbanipal some fragments of a ritual that seems to have been devoted to the substitute king.[5]

Later it is only for Alexander the Great that we can read accounts of one and the same method, only differing in details, in the works of three Greek historians (Plutarch, *Life of Alexander*, LXXIIIf.; Arrian, *Anabasis*, VII, 24; Diodorus Siculus, *Bibliotheca*, XVII, 116). They undoubtedly reveal the same institution as that of the time of Esarhaddon and his son. I am not entirely certain that we should associate with this, without reservations, a passage by Berossos,*[6] which would complement a short note from *De Regno* by Dio Chrysostom (IV, 6f.) where there is mention of the festival of

2. A. K. Grayson, *Assyrian and Babylonian Chronicles*, no. 20, pp. 45ff. and 152ff.

3. E. Laroche, *Catalogue des textes hittites*, nos. 419–21.

4. These letters, which were published in cuneiform by R. F. Harper between 1892 and 1914 in the fourteen volumes of his *Assyrian and Babylonian Letters (ABL)*, were at least partly transcribed, translated, and commented upon by S. Parpola in his *Letters from Assyrian Scholars to the Kings Esarhaddon and Assurbanipal*, 1 (1970) and 2 (1983). I am citing them here only with two numbers: the first from the collection by Harper, the second from the translation by Parpola.

5. W. G. Lambert in *Archiv für Orientforschung* 18 (1957f.): 109f. + 19 (1959f.): 119. Cited here as *Ritual*.

6. *Babyloniaka* in P. Schnabel, *Berossos*, p. 256, 1: 15.

the "Sacae" and of their ephemeral ruler. But we find, almost certainly, a reflection of the ideology that explains the Mesopotamian substitute king, on the one hand in Persia, if we believe Herodotus (VII, 15), and on the other hand in Rome at the beginning of the Christian era, according to Suetonius (*Life of Claudius*, XXIX, 3) who, moreover, does not seem to have understood well the real importance of what he tells us.

Even if this dossier is incomplete, fragmentary, and scattered, we see throughout it such sinister glimmerings around the central character, related to the final fate reserved for the substitute, that for a long time the Assyriologists, good-natured people who have little feeling for sadism, have refused to see the worst in it. But now it proves to be true that we must accept the worst. On the other hand the phenomenon is characteristic of a certain way of seeing and feeling that is not at all like ours, but whose contemplation should help us to discover and to understand better, through it, these ancient Mesopotamians, so far removed from us. That is why I have told myself that it might be fruitful to reopen and look through the dossier, even if I have nothing essential to add to it.

Instead of exhibiting first the facts regarding the substitute king and his fate in order to comment upon them and to explain them later, it seemed to me more enlightening to turn this logical order around and to begin by giving what I think to be the key elements of this institution. The institution stands, in fact, at the crossroads of three axioms, each of them in its way particular to the mentality of the ancient Babylonians and Assyrians: faith in the prediction of the future, the "doctrine" of substitution, and the political hierarchy.

THE PREDICTION OF THE FUTURE

We know that in the eyes of the ancient Mesopotamians unexpected events, abnormal conjunctures, and unusual encounters constituted warnings, "signs" through which the gods, organizers of the world and directors of the way things evolve, let their decisions regarding the fate of mankind be foreseen, according to a definite code. The birth in a stable of a lamb with two heads attached to each other and with eight legs, but with one spine, predicted internal strife in the country and a period of trouble.[7] Someone who laughed while fast asleep had to expect a serious illness.[8] If the planet Venus seemed to be stationary at its zenith, it would announce the stopping of the rains.[9] When a horse tried to couple with a cow it prom-

7. E. Leichty, *The Omen Series* šumma izbu, p. 86, vi: *20*.
8. *VAT* 7525 (in *Archiv für Orientforschung* 18, pp. 62f.), i: 39f.
9. Ch. Virolleaud, *L'Astrologie chaldéenne, Ištar*, p. 3, no. 2: *16*.

ised a decrease in the growth of the cattle.[10] If one discovered bright red splotches on the lungs of a sacrificial sheep, one had to dread a coming fire.[11] These "omens" taken from all aspects of nature had been studied and scrutinized over the centuries with an incredible zeal, and then classified in lists, each accompanied, as we just saw, by its predicted outcome: the part of the future that it was thought to announce.

Among the countless Treatises made up of these lists, some concern mostly the life of the individual and the joys and sorrows to be expected by him, others concern mostly the future of the entire country, and consequently that of its political leader: the king.

In the earlier periods it seems that the role of forecasting for public life was played by the haruspex*. Beginning in the second half of the second millennium, and even more in the first millennium, this role was paralleled, reinforced, and perhaps even partly supplanted by astrology, whose manifest omens from heaven encompassed the entire world. Among the *signs in the heavens* one of the most revealing, most dramatic, and consequently most infallible, in the opinion of the time, was the eclipse. The occultation of the light of a star was a transparent omen of another occultation here on earth: the disappearance of him who played the role of illuminator and pride of his people—the king. Things were not that simple, however, at least when important oracular decisions were involved, as was doubtless the case with the future of the ruler. They were complicated by the fact that people had noticed during the development of the divinatory "science" that *the signs on earth do (not) give us* (assured) *warnings* (regarding the future) *(if not) in agreement with these from heaven. The omens have to be the product both of heaven and of earth: even if they seem (to us) to be* (materially) *separated, they are inseparable* (in divinatory terms) *because heaven and earth constitute one whole.*[12] In other words, every important divinatory inquiry required the examination of omens drawn from various areas of nature, compared, criticized, weighed, and calculated as the result of a "parallelogram of forces," even if one of them, readily taken from astrology, gave an alarming signal.

Considering what we have just seen, the future predicted by the omens was, seemingly, the object of a total and unreserved faith. But we have to specify that in the eyes of those faithful the future was not what we would call "absolute": that which had to happen unavoidably. It was a conditional future, one that I have called "judicial," because the decision of the gods who determined the future predicted by the omens was somewhat like the

10. F. Nötscher, *Die Omen-Serie* šumma âlu, *Orientalia* 51-54, p. 162, Taf. 72f.: 25.

11. A. Goetze, *Old Babylonian Omen Texts,* pl. 64, no. 36: 25f.

12. L. Oppenheim, "A Diviner's Manual," in *Journal of Near Eastern Studies* 33 (1974): 200: 38ff.

sentence handed down by a judge. Each oracle was like a verdict against the interested parties on the basis of the elements of the omen, just as each sentence by a tribunal established the future of the guilty person based upon the dossier submitted to its judgment. The divinatory future, the predicted future, was what had to be expected at the moment that the gods publicized their decision by means of and in the omen. But there was possible recourse against the decision, as there is recourse against that of judges here on earth. Each verdict could be commuted by the gods, as is often the case among men. Thus a certain number of procedures were established to urge the gods to "give pardon," to reverse their decrees that condemned—in other words, an avoidance of the evil predicted by the omens, by those to whom it had been promised. This was accomplished by exorcistic rituals, named *namburbû** and composed, as are all analogous procedures, by a "sacramental" intertwining of ritual acts and addresses to the gods, i.e. of prayers, or, as is said improperly, of "incantations."

THE "DOCTRINE" OF SUBSTITUTION

This was precisely one of the essential postulates of exorcism: it was thought, in fact, that evil, either actual or promised and predicted, could be transferred from one individual to another, and could in some way shift its weight—as with a burden. Among the innumerable exorcisms that have been preserved, and that evidence a universal and continuous practice, and a profound belief, whether they are very short ceremonies or long and solemn liturgies, this *transfer* of evil played a major role.

The sine qua non of its success seems to have been a close bond between the starting and finishing points of the "evil" in question, between the first bearer and the one on whom the evil was loaded. This bond could be either by contact, or by resemblance, with a frequent combination of the two. Often it was possible to be satisfied with some material object that was considered "to take" the evil (like a contagious disease). In a letter from Mari* dating to around 1770 we have the oldest evidence of the knowledge of such an infection, of *disease that is caught* after the immediate contact with the "sick person."[13] Very often figurines (*ṣalmu*) in clay, in dough, in wax, in tallow, or in wood were used for that purpose. This had the advantage of being able to represent, more or less accurately, either an enemy to whom one wanted to pass on the evil one suffered, or another carrier who could even be the bearer of the evil himself, if needed. An example of the

13. L. G. Dossin and A. Finet, *Les Médecins au royaume de Mari*, Annales de l'Institut de Philologie et d'Histoire orientales et slaves, 14 (1954f.), p. 129 and n. 1; and J. Bottéro, "La magie et la médecine règnent à Babylone," *L'Histoire*, 74 (1984), p. 19.

latter is the fetus which promised bad fate and which was thrown in the water according to a certain *namburbû*.[14]

When the threat was especially serious, for instance when it involved the life itself of the interested party, an animal could serve as substitute. We have a fragment of a ritual intended to ward off the death promised to someone, and entitled: *In order to* (procure) *for Ereškigal** (the queen of the dead) *a substitute (pûḫu) of the interested party.*[15] It should be said in passing that we know that this ritual had been performed several times in the circle of Esarhaddon and Assurbanipal (*ABL* 439/140: *14;* and 1397/299 rev.: 5). Here is a summary of the text; it is instructive and suitable for making us understand clearly both its functioning and especially the spirit that inspired it. The sick person had to take with him to bed at night a small "virgin" goat. The next day a ditch with the outlines of a tomb was dug, and in it the sick person had to stretch out, still with his small goat. After that, the gestures of cutting the throat of both of them were made, with the difference that for the man a wooden blade was used, which did not hurt him, while for the animal a metal blade was used to cut its throat. Then the small corpse was treated as the human remains would have been. It was washed and perfumed, it was dressed in pieces of the clothes taken from the "diseased" person, and the officiating priest started the period of mourning by reciting a prayer and by proclaiming, as if it involved the "diseased": *Behold the dead one!* Then he organized a triple sacrificial funerary meal (*kispu*) in honor of *Ereškigal,* who had to be appeased, and for the commemoration of the spirits of the family of the person involved, as if a new deceased had joined their ranks. All that remained was to place the corpse ceremoniously in a shroud and to hold mourning for a decent period of time. The ill person had nothing to fear anymore because a living creature, identified with him both by contact (the night spent together) and by assimilation (the simultaneous cutting of the throat, the clothes of one placed on the other, the treatment of the corpse, the proclamation of death, etc.), had lost its life in his place.

Such a substitution was not an evasion or a way of leading the gods astray. The person just wanted to enable the gods to realize their wish, to accomplish their decision, under the same conditions but on another "basis" as close as possible to the one they originally had in mind, even if it was materially different. Similarly in law it was acceptable that a member of the immediate family of the debtor settle the debt in his place, and work as his substitute in the service of the creditor. That was the idea that the ancient Mesopotamians had about substitution and its role.

14. Translated and explained in *Mythes et rites de Babylone*, pp. 44ff.

15. E. Ebeling, *Keilschrifttexte aus Assur religiösen Inhalts,* no. 245, and E. Ebeling-F. Köcher, *Literarische Keilschrifttexte aus Assur,* nos. 79 and 80.

THE POLITICAL HIERARCHY

It is not necessary to split hairs about this principle, which implied the absolute primacy of the ruler. We have perhaps the same idea from another point of view; it suffices to think about all the excesses and the crimes that we have seen and that are still committed in the sacrosanct name of "state reasons." The only clear difference is that today we ascribe, in sentimental and ideological terms, a greater, theoretically even absolute value to the existence of the individual, and to the rights of the people, even with regard to power—though it has never prevented anyone in political power from scorning those rights for the least reason, real or imaginary.

It is probable that the Mesopotamians of yore—and this is still the case for several contemporary civilizations—regarded an individual and his death in an entirely different manner, even if their way of thinking may have undergone some evolution on that point. After the first dynasty of Ur* in the middle of the third millennium, we seemingly do not find any more traces of those terrible hecatombs of an entire royal court being ceremoniously immolated to accompany its master in the hereafter. But it is quite certain that the rituals were in the first place made to preserve for the country him who was its head, master, director, shepherd, and father. It is enough to reread the prologue and the epilogue of the "Code" of Ḫammurabi to be informed on that point. If danger threatened the life of just the crown prince, the immediate successor of the king, the goods, the interests, and even the lives of the subjects could be sacrificed. The ritual for preparation for war, summarized above, shows to what degree they were careful in protecting the existence of the bearer of the royal power from absolutely any danger, and perhaps especially from any supernatural danger. We know from at least the eighteenth century (I believe it is in Mari* that we find the oldest example) a revealing formula for expressing one's allegiance, one's loyalty, one's attachment to the king: It was said to him *ana dinâka lullik: May I go in your place* (to danger), as the Iranians still say today: *gorbân-é šôma*. In this way it was expressed to what degree each subject considered it conceivable to offer himself as a victim for the welfare of his master, by substituting for him in order to free him of any possible danger.

It is impossible to understand anything of the facts and the legal aspects of the substitute king if we do not consider together these three axioms of the viewpoints and the feelings of the ancient Mesopotamians: the feeling of the absolute primacy of the king, the practice of substitution, and the firm belief in the predicted future.

THE OCCASIONS AND THE REASONS FOR SUBSTITUTION

Let us meet this substitute king and see what his fate was. He was needed only in case the life of the king or of the crown prince was at risk on the divinatory level. In other words, it seems that only when the "scientifically" observed omens, criticized and studied, indicated that the king's death was certain and near, was one authorized to search for a substitute. A certain number of diverse omens could in that way promise a fatal future, to judge by our "treatises." We have some examples of hepatoscopy[16] and of teratomancy.[17] In fact, regarding Alexander, Plutarch talks about a battle between ravens which gave rise to consultation of haruspices and was followed by another "marvel": one of the king's lions was killed by one of his asses.

It seems, however, that at least in the time of the last Sargonids, in what I have called the "parallelogram of divinatory forces," composed from all the used "-mancies" and illustrated by the expression that sometimes appears, *the signs of heaven and of earth*, the greatest weight was given to the astrological omens and, among them, to the fatal eclipse. It was especially the eclipses, whose appearances were "surveyed" anxiously by the people specialized in the protection of the king, that were the most significant (because they could calculate in advance when they would happen) and almost all the documents in our file mention them directly or indirectly (23/185 rev: *14*ff.; 38/25: *6;* 46/298 rev.: *10;* etc.).

Before these eclipses were regarded as being really threatening to the ruler, they had to be studied according to the month, the day, and the hour of their appearance, according to their place in the sky, and according to the direction of their darkening (*Ritual,* A: *13*, and especially 38/25 rev.: *2*ff., etc.). From such an examination the terrestrial correlative of the phenomenon was first of all derived, i.e. the part of the world that it threatened. That could be *Amurru** (the west), for instance, in other words *either the land of the Hittites*, or that of the Arameans*—only to the ruler of one of those countries was death predicted in that case* (629/279: *16*f.) and one did not have to worry about it in Mesopotamia. Even when it involved Mesopotamia the eclipse could affect the northern part (Assyria) or the southern part (Babylonia). Moreover, *the evil predicted for Assyria and the evil predicted for Babylonia was not all the same thing. When in fact the omen* (the eclipse) *that took place related to Assyria, it was here*[18] *that one had to act* (48/298: *18*f.). The matter was of importance because at that time the king

16. *"If the gall bladder is "taken"* [enclosed by flesh?]: *the king of the land will die,"* in A. Goetze, *Old Babylonian Omen Texts,* pl. 47, no. 31, xi: 22–25.

17. *"If a woman gives birth to a child who already has a skin disease: . . . the king will die in his capital city,"* in E. Leichty, *The Omen Series* šumma izbu, p. 67, 4: *10*.

18. The letter was written at Nineveh.

of Assur and Nineveh was also the king of Babylon. Thus, in the case that the threat was upon Babylonia, it was in the capital city of that country that the procedure of substitution had to be executed (compare, for instance, 437/280, below, pp. 151f.).

This doubling of the threat, no less than the recurrence of the eclipse, must have compelled the Mesopotamians to take recourse to this procedure a certain number of times even in the shortest reign. Everything depended on how the eclipse presented itself, the other omens in the "parallelogram," and the conclusions that the experts drew from them. In certain cases it seems, for instance, that less radical actions were sufficient (1397/299 rev.: 5f. "*Replacement of the person promised to Ereškigal*"—see above). Or some lucky conjuncture intervened unexpectedly to give the evil a providential remedy. Here is one of these cases, described in 46/298 (rev.: *10–14*) by one of the "chaplains" of Esarhaddon, Akkullânu. First of all he recalls the principles which we know from other sources:[19] *If, during an eclipse* (in the month Nisan—March/April), *Jupiter remains visible, it is a good omen for the king, because in his place a high-placed person or an official will die.* And he continues: *Didn't the king notice that before a month had passed after the eclipse his chief judge (sartinnu) passed away?* Such an accidental occurrence must have taken place only exceptionally, however, and thus the use of substitution in case of danger did not have to be, after all, extraordinary. The chief exorcist of Esarhaddon, Adad-šumu-uṣur, reminded him that he had already used the procedure twice (362/166: *15*, and compare perhaps 46/298: *15*), and S. Parpola[20] has calculated that he used the procedure at least four times during his entire reign, as far as we know.[21]

Each time that the totality of the omens, starting with the prime "revealer," the eclipse, presented itself after proper analysis as being fatal to the life of the king, one had to act immediately: in other words install a substitute for the king, either at Assur or at Babylon, according to the case. In fact, only this person could *dispel the evil considered to threaten the king* (674/24 rev.: *5; Ritual,* A: *7*) and *save his life* (23/185 rev.: *20*), by *taking upon himself the evil omens* (223/30: *13*f.), in short by *taking the place of the king* (compare 437/280: *10*), and the texts repeat this very clearly, because that was the whole purpose of the procedure.

19. Ch. Virolleaud, *Astrologie chaldéenne, Šamaš*, p. 11, no. 8: *38;* p. 16, no. 10: *46*, etc.

20. *Letters from Assyrian Scholars to the Kings Esarhaddon and Assurbanipal*, vol. 2: xxiif.

21. Around 26 Ayyar (April/May) 672; around 14 Du'uzu (June/July) of the following year; around 14 Ṭebet (December/January) of the same year; and around 14 Simân (May/June) 669. For Assurbanipal we know of only one example, around 15 Nisan (March/April) 666.

THE CHOICE OF A SUBSTITUTE

This was certainly done by experts: diviners and astrologers, exorcists and various "priests," who in a sense made up the defense council of the king, his protection team in matters that were at the same time religious and political. The criteria and the formalities of this choice escape us. Only *someone (memêni)* to replace the king is mentioned (23/185 rev. *18*, and compare 674/28 rev. *4*). In the case of Alexander, Plutarch presents us with a common criminal who was already in prison, a tradition that Arrian mentions after having suggested that, in his opinion, it had to be a *man of the street*. As we have seen, it was an *ordinary subject: a gardener*, for Erra-imitti. A famous letter by the governor of Babylon, Mâr-Ištar, to which we will return, has probably the same meaning, when he stresses the necessity to select, *as before, a saklu* (437/280 rev. *15*f.), a term that indicates, in general, a man who was simple, naïve, perhaps even somewhat "retarded." But, in the context, Mâr-Ištar had to stress the insignificance of the individual, who was without importance on the social level and whose fate really could not be of interest to anyone. However, the same Mâr-Ištar seems to imply that, before he could choose this individual as a substitute, he had to give him the office of *šatammu:* someone who was simultaneously an administrator and a cult official in the temple. Thus, at least in this period, it was considered necessary that the substitute had to be of a high social standing in order to be worthy of the man he was going to replace, even if the social promotion were fictitious. The same letter shows that a person really of the upper class could be chosen, when it describes the scandal caused by the choice of a son of a real *šatammu*. I will return to that later.

In any case it is possible that, spontaneously or on demand, the gods had their say in the choice: the intervention of a *prophetess*, of a *soothsayer* as they were known in Assyria at that time (*ragimtu*) (149/317: *7*ff.; 437/280 rev.: *1*) could have played a determining role in it, at least by contributing the supernatural warning.

Be that as it may, once chosen, the substitute seems to have been properly warned, at least, that he had to take evil omens upon himself. But it is not certain that this was always done clearly and explicitly. The wording of 629/279: *11*f. is purposely obscure (the substitute is *made to recite the* [usual] *formulae of the scribes—naqbîtu ša tupšarrûte*). It even seems that they might have taken care to put these words down in writing on some medium. Then, they either attached the words to the fringe of his dress(?) (676/26 obv.: *6′*ff.) in order to identify them more closely with his person, or made him ingest them, mixed in one fashion or another in his food and drink, in order to better ensure that he had them well assimilated and integrated into his body (223/30: 6f.). *Thus*, continues the same document, *wanting to be better informed, he cried: "Because of what bad sign have you enthroned* (me as) *a substitute king?" And he appealed to the king* (15f.).

The substitute in question had to be put in place as soon as the eclipse appeared—because from that moment on the eclipse started to threaten the king—perhaps even a little earlier, as a precaution. And he could continue in this function for the entire period that the eclipse remained harmful. In theory, it seems that the period was *three months and ten days*[22] long, whence the number of *one hundred days* that we sometimes see (594/249 rev.: *7*f.; 1014/292: 2′f.). But such a long period could have its disadvantages, considering that the king was, at least relatively, removed, as we will stress presently. It sufficed that the substitute had accomplished his role to the very end, even before the end of the theoretical harmful period of the eclipse, in order to have the promised "evil" annulled by the substitute. Thus, it seems that they gladly waited less time (twenty days, for instance, from the 14th of Du'uzu (June/July)—the date of the eclipse—to the 4th of the month Ab: (July/August) which immediately followed: 46/298: 6f.). Sometimes it was even preferable to end the substitution right away; on the day after the eclipse (359/135: *13*f.; 362/166: 6f.).

THE BEHAVIOR OF THE "REPLACED" RULER

During that time, what happened to the king? Not much about it is revealed to us. Certainly he had to keep himself aloof and withdrawn, even if he were somewhere other than where the substitute exercised his functions. For instance, he could be in Nineveh when the substitute was in Babylon: *During the period of an eclipse of the moon, or of the approach of the (two) "gods"* (Sun and Moon), (the king) *cannot go out in his territory* (427/280 rev.: *11*f.): in other words, he should not show himself in public. And at another moment the same defense technique seems to have been used for the two princes, Assurbanipal and Šamaššumukîn, on the occasion of an analogous, even identical, supernatural "danger" (594/649: 6′f.).

Because the *Ritual* recommended at the end a general purification of the palace before its reoccupation, it is likely that during the "reign" of the substitute, the king granted to the latter his own dwelling, or at least one of palaces. In the case of Adad-nirâri III, however, we can ask ourselves, whether the substitute was not installed in a secondary residence, outside the capital; ND 3483 (cited above, p. 139) mentions the town, or the borough, or Ḫariḫumba.

The letters seem to allude to a particular building into which the king

22. R. C. Thompson, *The Reports of the Magicians and Astrologers of Nineveh and Babylon,* 2: 100, no. 270, rev.: 10.

withdrew, and where he perhaps resided while his replacement paraded around in full daylight. It was called the *qersu*, seemingly isolated from the profane areas by one of the reed enclosures so often used in the rituals of exorcism in order to keep evil influences away (4/137: 7f. and 183/138: 6ff.). The same letter suggests a certain number of purifying ceremonies and practices (ibid. and 361/167: 9ff.), either "by the river" (thus 53/205: *11*f.), or in the *qersu*, and these possibly took place every day for as long as the retreat of the king lasted. These rituals were doubtless an additional precaution, in order to guard the king from any possible supernatural danger.

Another prudent measure of deception consisted of changing the "official name," the "title" of the king. He was called *the farmer* (*ikkaru*) perhaps in opposition to *the shepherd*, which was a common royal epithet in ancient Mesopotamia. Many letters are addressed to him under that title (4/137; 183/138; 15/139; 38/25; etc.). However, such a designation must have been either subject to rules that escape us or optional, as there are a certain number of messages sent to the king during the period of substitution in which he is addressed under his usual title: *My Lord the king* (46/298; 149/317; 359/135; etc.).

At least there was no question that the real government of the country was taken away from the king. It is enough to go through the material in question to be convinced to what degree the king was informed about everything as usual, took all the necessary decisions, and firmly held in his hands the reins of political and administrative life, while his substitute presented all the appearances of power. That was probably a very wise decision.

THE ROLE OF THE SUBSTITUTE KING

All in all this role was but a facade. Residing in the capital city (compare 46/298: 8f. Babylon), and *having entered the palace* (629/279: 6f.), the substitute king was enthroned and, in fact, *sat on the throne* (23/185 rev.: *18;* 46/298: 8f.; 53/205: *9;* etc.; the three historians of Alexander agree with each other by representing the "substitute" as *sitting on the throne*). That was seemingly even the proper "technical term" to indicate the taking up of his functions (*ašâbu, šûšubu: to sit, to seat*). Also used was the expression *to take the rule (bêlu) over the country* (437/280: *8;* 629/279: *14*f.), which did not necessarily imply the real exercise of power.

The presence of the substitute on the throne was nothing but a pure fiction, a play: he held the role of the king, he was put in the place of the king, and he was dressed like the king. In fact, he received the royal clothes, and in particular the large red—or white—ceremonial robe called *kuzippu*, the necklace, the crown, the weapon, and the scepter (compare

653/134: *10*f.; Plutarch and Diodorus of Sicily also mention the royal clothes and the diadem in the case of Alexander; Herodotus mentions in the case of his Persian king, together with the clothes, the accession to the throne and the sleeping in the bed of the king himself). Perhaps, even undoubtedly, the dressing and the conferring of the royal insignia were accompanied by a ceremony, during which a *prophetess,* apparently charged with informing the candidate of his fate, played a role (149/317: 7ff.). Was it also then that he was *informed* about the evil omens that were *attached* to him or that he was *made to consume?*

In order to preserve appearances even more, he was given a queen (437/280: 9, perhaps the *young girl, batultu* of 15/139: 6f.), who, according to the *Ritual* (A: 20) was supposed to be a virgin (*ardatu*), as she had *to become a woman* by him. This unfortunate woman, moreover, shared his fate to the very end, as we know especially from 437/280 (see below). Insofar as it is not wrong to identify the "rule" of the substitute with the ceremony of the Sacae about which Berossos* and Dio Chrysostom speak (see p. 139f.), we could thus imagine a type of parody of kingship, taking place like a "carnival" where the entire social hierarchy is turned upside down. But I am not certain that we can identify the Sacean ceremony with royal substitution; it is something that needs to be studied in more detail.

Besides this "play" we do not have the slightest trace of any effective exercise of power by the substitute; if he had exercised it, he would have been really in opposition to the ruler who, as we have seen, pulled all the strings from behind the scene. The real office of a *šar pûḫi* was not to rule in the place of the king but to play publicly the role of the person of the latter, and thus to serve as a lightning rod in a way, in order *to take upon himself* and to draw upon himself the evil fate that threatened his master. This he did precisely by ending his ephemeral rule and by suffering his fate.

THE FATE OF THE SUBSTITUTE KING

In the end, what was his fate? It is indicated more than once in our letters by the expression *he has to go to his fate* (359/135 rev.: 2f.; 362/166: 8f.; 594/249: end). It is true that this phrase often means in Akkadian *to die a natural death, to die of natural causes.* And it was long thought that we had to adhere to this original meaning in this context, as we found it repugnant to imagine a cold-blooded murder of an innocent person. However, such a *pia interpretatio* is not tenable in view of all the elements of the dossier. This dossier, when considered without prejudices, forces us clearly to glimpse underneath the hypocritical euphemism, borrowed in fact from a natural death, and see a real killing not only of the substitute king but also of the "queen" who had been given to him. The *Ritual* (A: 6) states this clearly:

The man who was given as the king's substitute, shall die (imât) in order that . . . the evil omens will not affect that king. And somewhat further, in a passage that is broken but still clear enough, they seem to beseech his ghost(?; see below) *to take down with you . . . all his evils and to make them thus disappear into the Land-of-No-Return* (B: 4). All the accounts of the case of Alexander also agree on the point that the "substitute" was *put to death*. The most revealing among our letters is perhaps 437/280, an important document that we have to read from beginning to end, not only because it sheds light upon this rather frightful and ominous point, but also because it adds perhaps the even more sinister colors of a real political assassination.

This letter is a report made to King Esarhaddon by his representative in Babylon, Mâr-Ištar. On the occasion of an eclipse threatening the life of the ruler as king of Babylon, this high official had taken it upon himself to start the procedure of substitution in that city, as was his duty. But, apparently in order to terrify the Babylonians, who were tired of the Assyrian yoke, or in order to stop any impulse to revolt among the most influential of them, he had chosen as substitute Damqî. He was the son of the chief administrator (*šatammu*) of the temple in Babylon, one of the highest personalities of the old capital, whom B. Landsberger referred to as the "bishop" of the Esagil*: Šûm-iddina. Mâr-Ištar is thus making his report to the king, and perhaps the drama that he had initiated had left some bad memories, due to the personality of his victim. He seems more than once, if not to excuse himself, at least to justify himself, and especially to swear that he will not repeat what he has done, at least not in the same circumstances. Here is this letter that is beyond doubt the most revealing document related to our subject matter:

> [Damqî], the son of the chief administrator of the temples of Bab[ylon], who had ruled the land of Assur, Babylonia, and all (other) territories (of the kingdom), he and his queen died on the night of [the date is lost] instead of the king, my lord, and [to save the life of (the prince)] Šamaš-šumu-ukîn. He "went to his destiny" in order to save them.
>
> (Afterwards) we have prepared their burial chamber. He ⟨and⟩ his queen have been decorated, treated, displayed with funereal pomp, they have been buried and wailed over (according to the usual funerary ceremonies). The burnt-offering has been burnt, all the evil omens have been cancelled, by the execution of numerous namburbû rituals of the (ceremony called) "The house of washing," of the (ceremony called) "The house of sprinkling (the lustral water)", of (various) exorcistic rituals, (and) (of the recitation) of the

"Penitential Psalms" and of (other) traditional formulae. The king, my lord, should know this!

(The king, my lord, should also know that) I have heard that before these facts and deeds (=the choice and the killing of Damqî) a prophetess had prophesied saying to Damqî: "You will take over the power of kingship!" The (same?) prophetess also had declared to him in the assembly of the country: "I have revealed the hypocritical polecat of my lord, (also) I am going to put you into the hands (of your destiny?)."

These namburbû that were performed should have a favorable outcome; the mind of the king, my lord, should be entirely at ease!

(Certainly,) the Babylonians were terrified (by the death of Damqî), but we have "given them courage," and they calmed down. I have even learned that the temple administrators and (others) granted power (by the king in the sanctuaries) of Babylon had been (also) terrified (for the same reason). (But we have shown them that after all it was) Marduk* and Nabû* and all (their) other gods (who) through these means (have wanted) to prolong the life of the king, my lord.

(Still) because the king cannot appear in public in his territory (according to the rules) during the period of an eclipse of the moon or the approach of the "gods," if it pleases the king, my lord, a common man (saklu): should be invested with the office of temple administrator as (was done in any case) before. He will present (in that function) the daily offerings before the "altar" and, on monthly festival days he will pour the incense in honor of the Lady of Akkad* on the censer. Thus, when an eclipse affecting Babylonia takes place, he may serve as a substitute for the king, my lord. Consequently, the life of the king, my lord, will be saved, while the people will remain calm. It is one of these people that the king, my lord, should install as replacement, if that is acceptable to him.

Among other things this impressive document teaches us very well how the curtain fell over this tragedy in the end: on the set day and hour the substitute king and his companion were executed (we are not told how), treated as dead of the high class, and solemnly buried, always with the idea that even in death they replaced the king, taking upon themselves what was his destiny. Another allusion to this funeral pomp (*taklimtu*) is perhaps also found in 670/4: *18* and rev. *2*. It was doubtless at the moment when the corpse of the substitute king disappeared into the grave, i.e. the entrance to the kingdom of the dead where he would reside from then on, that they ordered his ghost (?) to "*Take down with you in the Land of No Return the evils that you* (have taken upon yourself)," according to the *Ritual* (B: *4*).

Thus the essential mission that had been the replacement's, that of substitute, of double, was restated for the last time.

THE RETURN TO NORMAL

Almost all exorcistic rituals have the characteristic that, after the ceremony reached its highest point for suppressing or transferring the present evil, it was ended by a sometimes substantial number of supplementary acts "as precaution," or, as M. Mauss said, "as a way out."[23] They had to assure in some way by their cumulative effectiveness the total eradication, the absolute annihilation of any trace of the abolished evil, and any enticement of a hostile return of the eliminated calamity that could have survived. The procedure for the substitution of the king was not exempt from that rule. As soon as the substitute was buried, they started by cutting all ties with the "carrier of evil" that he had been, by destroying with fire (*Ritual* B: 5f.) all the clothes and royal insignia that he had worn and thus could have contaminated (compare perhaps also 361/167 rev.: 5f., etc.).

After that, a *general purification (têbibtu) of the country and of the king* took place (*Ritual* B: 8), doubtless during public or private ceremonies the details of which are not revealed to us but may have been echoed in 361/167 just quoted. Finally, a profound "cleaning" of the palace had to be undertaken, since it had been apparently "soiled" by the presence of the dead substitute. This operation was done in six phases (and possibly in as many days if we understand correctly 361/167 rev.: *13*), each consecrated to one of the nerve centers of the building: four for its principal points of access (B: *13:* Gate of [. . .]; *16:* Gate of the chapel; *20:* Great gate; *34:* Gate of the foreigners or guests), one for "the courtyard" (*tarbaṣu;* B: 29) where perhaps the public ceremony throne was located; and one for *the Bedchamber (bît maiâli;* B: *24)* where the king held his audiences during the daytime, where he received his subordinates and dictated and announced his decisions. Before each of these points figurines of zoomorphic demons were burnt in pairs. On the left hip of each of them this order was inscribed: "*Go away evil!* (And you,) *well-being of the palace, come back!*" Perhaps 361/167, already mentioned, and also 22/179: 5f. make a reference to these ritual prescriptions; perhaps also K. 1526/136: 9f., which assumes the use of similar ceremonies "of recall" even after only one month, or even earlier.

Then the king could reenter his palace, reassume his official role, and take up again his public life. Thanks to the death of his substitute all danger had been henceforth averted from his person and therefore from his people and his country, until the next alert would set in motion the same security measures.

23. *Sociologie et anthropologie*, p. 42.

CHAPTER NINE

THE INSTITUTIONAL CHARACTER OF THE PROCEDURE

This very recurrence stresses the character of the royal substitution, not only as a religious and political institution, but as a real ceremony. The existence of a ritual, recalling the "Ceremonial Tablets" characteristic of the great liturgies of exorcism, confirms this. For anyone who is familiar with these "measures for the elimination of the evil promised by the omens" that are the *namburbû* there is not the slightest doubt. The procedure of substitution of the king is a genuine example of *namburbû*. Moreover, it seems, once or twice, to have been designated by that title (46/298 rev.: *15*) or in that context (818/334: *1*f. and 437/280: *17*). The essential fact that it involves here the avoidance of a danger promised by the oracles, forces us to accept this comparison, even this identification.

In the beginning I recalled the three axioms on which a practice was founded that in our eyes seems to have been so extraordinary, if not aberrant: the belief, the *religious* belief, in the truth of the omens and in the efficiency of substitution as an infallible means of turning away evil, and the conviction, both religious and political, that the ruler had some kind of superhuman character, and that it was necessary to sacrifice everything in order to save his life and his position at the head of his people. With such convictions the use of the substitute king became a formality that was as logical, as irreproachable, and as "normal" as was, on the one hand, the sacrifice of a goat or any cultic act intended to protect people, or, on the other hand, the execution of a criminal, the suppression of an enemy, or any other way assuring the well-being of the country and the people.

However, some type of reservation, of discretion, perhaps even of uneasiness seems to show up here and there in our letters when allusion is made to the crucial moment in the procedure, i.e. the death of the substitute. We have noted it in passing in the letter of Mâr-Ištar, that we have just quoted at great length. But these reservations have their origin not in some bad conscience with regard to what may have been envisioned as a real crime, as *we* would think of it, but in the memory of the danger from which the kingdom had escaped. The southern part of it could very well have started a revolt over the fearless use of "reasons of state" due to which a high dignitary had been chosen as victim. The proof of this is that Mâr-Ištar recommends the return to an old practice. Who would worry about the killing of a common man, a *saklu,* for the king?

Another passage could be used by those who want to reveal at all costs the scruples, the embarrassment, and the remorse in the mind of the authors of something that seems to *us* a heinous crime. In 362/166 another high official, the royal exorcist in his area, Adad-šumu-uṣur, seems to be looking for good reasons to urge himself on, at the moment that he has to execute the substitute king. After all, he says (13ff.) *our fathers*—the exorcists of old—*did the same for their masters. The present king has done it twice up till now, Marduk and Nabû have given the order. Like that we will do now! And why should we hesitate as if it were not a good thing?* . . . But if we read closely the entire text, its purport and the way it uses the terms *good/not good (ṭâb/ lâ ṭâb: 12*, rev.: *11*f., and cf. *magir* = *favorable:* rev. 6) show that it does not involve anything more than an embarrassment over the question of knowing whether or not the sixteenth of the month is favorable for the killing. It is nothing more or less than the scruple of a liturgist and an officiating priest who is worried about succeeding in his work, and performing it according to the rules!

Thus, we find here a mentality governed by convictions that are not at all our own, providing that we are honest citizens, evidently. By its character, which seems scandalous in our eyes, the procedure of substitution for safeguarding the life of the king is one of the features that betrays, perhaps most clearly, a vision of the world, a state of mind, and a sensibility that are diametrically opposed to ours. It is perhaps because of that opposition that it is most profitable for us to study it, to penetrate it, and to comprehend it. Because as long as we enter in its own logic and rationality, and we accept them, we leave ourselves in order to take on the personality of these ancient people. We would fail to attain this familiarity as historians (like travelers who never learn the language of the peoples among whom they move), if we would allow ourselves to be led by our natural inclination, which is to bring others closer to ourselves, rather than to allow ourselves to be taken and educated by them.

10

The "Code" of Ḫammurabi

HISTORIANS, ESPECIALLY THOSE THAT OCCUPY THEMSELVES WITH faraway regions and bygone times, should never forget to what degree the content of words is elastic. Each word can evoke realities that are doubtless more or less comparable from one period to another, from one cultural milieu to another, but that are profoundly different. Even if one does not study them closely, they are clearly different, in their extent as well as in their comprehension, to use the logicians' terms. If the real goal of history is to rediscover the past, not as *we* see it, but as closely as possible to the way it was seen, lived, and understood by those who were present at the time, then it is a healthy exercise to question our own understanding of what we have excavated from the ancient soil.

If I have chosen the "Code" of Ḫammurabi[1] for such a review, it is because that monument constitutes a striking example of this more or less implicit naïve belief in the homogeneity of words, which is so dangerous in the study of history. When Ḫammurabi's monument was discovered and deciphered, eighty years ago now, it was baptized in the field as a law "Code." This title was applied certainly not because the monument presented itself as such, but simply by the disposition and the appearance of the monu-

1. The last and the best translation of the "Code" in French, with a short but excellent introduction, is by A. Finet, *Le Code de Ḫammurapi.* I remain faithful to the transcription Ḫammurabi (not -rapi) for reasons that need not to be pointed out here, much less discussed. On the other hand I have considered it preferable to give my own translation of the passages that I quote *in extenso.*

This chapter first appeared in 1982, in *Annali della Scuola normale superiore di Pisa,* Classe di Lettere e Filosofia III/xii: 4, pp. 409–44.

ment. And, consciously or not, since then no one has given up that viewpoint despite some reservations by authorities;[2] it was a viewpoint immediately gobbled down and embedded in a "universal consensus."

Let us try to form an idea of what Ḫammurabi's "Code" could have represented in the eyes of its author and of his fellow citizens and contemporaries at the time it was composed, somewhat before 1750. Such a critical consideration would have the advantage of reminding us, *in actu exercito*, of one of the fundamental demands of our job as historian. Taking into account the extraordinary riches of this famous monument, we have some possibility of finding in it some essential features of the ancient and high Mesopotamian civilization, of which the "Code" in question is beyond doubt one of the richest, most suggestive, and best-preserved monuments.

THE "CODE"

The "Code" is engraved on a tall stele of dark stone that has formed one of the treasures of the ancient Near Eastern collection of the Louvre Museum ever since the discovery of the stone by the team of J. de Morgan in 1902 at the site of Susa* in the southwest of Iran. On the top of the monument, on what is known as its front, a relief represents the author, King Ḫammurabi of Babylon (ca. 1792–1750), receiving the insignia of royal power from the god *Marduk*.* Underneath this representation a first group of twenty-three vertical columns of writing were originally arranged and engraved, divided into cases. The last seven of these columns were later erased by Šutruk-Naḫḫunte, the Elamite king who transported this heavy stele as war booty to Susa around the year 1200. On the back of the stele, twenty-eight additional columns complete the monument. Thus more than 3,500 inscribed lines are preserved.

This long text is not all the same style of writing; prose and "poetry" alternate in it. Five columns at the beginning and five more at the end (they are called respectively prologue and epilogue) are a piece of bravura from the mouth of Ḫammurabi. They are written in the elevated style typical for heroic and lyric literature in ancient Mesopotamia. These ten columns serve as the introduction and the conclusion of the main body of the work.

In the prologue the king declares himself to have been appointed by the gods for the military glory and the political success of his country, which he proclaims to have secured by a series of conquests, recited at length. He also claims to have been dedicated to the government and the prosperity of

2. See, especially, F. R. Kraus, "Ein zentrales Problem des altmesopotamischen Rechts: Was ist der Codex Ḫammurabi? in *Aspects du contact suméro-akkadien*, *Genava*, 8 (1960), pp. 283ff. I have to add here, however, that after I had written the present article, this so-called universal recognition seems to have crumbled somewhat here and there; so that my article seems not to have been entirely useless.

his people by these same gods. He presents the "legislative" aspect of these appointments in a group of measures taken by him as an experienced and just monarch in order to accomplish this grandiose divine wish. In the epilogue he pursues the same train of thought. By underlining the wisdom and the fairness of the decisions recorded in detail in the body of the text, he offers them as a perpetual model for rulers to come. The prologue and epilogue clearly are not farfetched and superfluous pieces; they are essential for the entire work, whose profound meaning they indicate in their own way. We will have to return to this point.

The "Code" itself is written in prose and in the language commonly used in the legal profession of that time. It is presented as a succession of propositions apparently prescribed in order to regulate the social conduct of the inhabitants of the kingdom, at least in a certain fashion and to an extent that we will have to determine. Since the *editio princeps* of the text by P. Scheil, at the end of 1902,[3] scholars have maintained the habit of considering each of these propositions as an "article" and of giving each of them a number. Thus there are a total of two hundred and eighty-two "articles," taking into account the lacuna in the middle. All of those are rigorously structured according to the grammatical order of the conditional proposition: they begin (as do the clauses in the divinatory Treatises, with a "protasis,"* introduced by the conjunction "if," and describing a concrete situation, a state of circumstantial elements, in the past or in the present tense. The "apodosis" which follows, in the future tense, indicates what should be, on the judicial level so to say, the result of such a situation. Here is, for example, the text of the first "article":

> If a man has brought an accusation of murder against another man, without providing proof: the accuser shall be put to death.

And here are a few others:

> If a man, distrained by a debt, sold or handed over for service his wife, his son or his daughter (in order to pay off the debt): the latter shall work for three years (at the most) in the service of their purchaser or their distrainer. But, after these three years they will be released to freedom. (§117)
>
> If a woman is not discreet but a gadabout, thus neglecting her house and discrediting her husband: they shall throw this woman in the water. (§143)
>
> If a physician has set the broken bone of a man of importance, or has healed one of his sprained "tendons": the patient shall give the physician the sum of five shekels (= ca. 40 grams) of silver. (§221)

3. *Mémoires de la Délégation en Perse*, 4, pp. 11–162 and plates 3–15.

And here is the last one:

> If a male slave has said to his master "You are not my master anymore": when his master shall prove him to be his slave, he will have the right to cut off his ear. (§282)

The "articles" have been grouped according to different sectors of communal life. Thus we find the following sequence: five paragraphs devoted to *false testimony* (§§1–5); twenty devoted to *theft* (§§6–25); sixteen to *tenure of royal fiefs*, a common practice in Mesopotamia, especially in this period (§§26–41); twenty-five to *agricultural work* (§§42–66); approximately ten at least to *places of dwelling* (§§76– . . . the great lacuna due to the erasing of the seven last columns on the obverse prevents us from establishing exactly how many); at least twenty-four to *commerce* (§§. . .–111); fifteen to *deposits and debts* (§§112–26); sixty-seven to *wives* and *the family* (§§127–94); twenty to *assault and battery* (§§195–214); sixty-one to various *free professions* followed by *subordinate professions* (§§215–77), and finally five to *slaves* (§§278–82).

According to our logic, such an order of subject matters, and the distribution of the different "articles" inside these divisions, is not always easy to justify: they evidently presuppose a way of viewing and evaluating things quite removed from our own (we will return to this later), and we do not always have the means to penetrate this approach.

And now, what must we think of this work, and how can we characterize it? It has to be understood that we are always talking of what the work had to represent in the eyes of its author and of its addressees.

First of all, contrary to what is perhaps still thought here and there, even if the "Code" of Ḫammurabi is in effect the longest and best preserved of this genre of documents, it is not the only one, nor even the oldest one of its kind. To date, we have found in bits and pieces of varying size—unfortunately sometimes very tiny—a dozen analogous "codes" scattered over the entirety of Mesopotamian history from the end of the third millennium onward. The first in date goes as far back as Ur-Nammu (ca. 2111–2046), the founder of the Third Dynasty of Ur*; the most recent dates to the middle of the first millennium.[4] One among them, associated with the city of Ešnunna some 110 kilometers northeast of Babylon and 40 kilometers northeast of Baghdad in the Diyala River valley, must have preceded the publication of the "Code" of Ḫammurabi by only a few decades. And if luck is on our side, we have the chance of finding more of them. There are a

4. Collected and translated by R. Haase, *Die keilschriftlichen Rechtssammlungen in deutscher Ubersetzung*. For some of them there are more recent introductions and more complete translations: see for the "Code" of Ur-Nammu, J. J. Finkelstein, "The Laws of Ur-Nammu," *Journal of Cuneiform Studies* 22 (1969): 66ff.

certain number of indications which suggest that more than one ruler of ancient Mesopotamia could have had occasion in the course of his rule to publish documents whose contents at least, if not also their form, coincided more or less with that of our "Code".[5] We do not have to imagine therefore that because of the "Code" of Ḫammurabi, a situation arose in Mesopotamia analogous to that in France, for instance, where the Code Napoléon, promulgated more than 150 years ago, still maintains its universal value, simply reshaped, augmented, or reduced according to the development of social problems and the reactions to them of the legislature.

On the other hand, the famous stele in the Louvre is without doubt the most complete and best-preserved copy left to us of the text of our "Code," but it is not the only one.[6] Up till now we have found some forty manuscripts, most of them very fragmentary. There are even some remains of monuments similar to the one in the Louvre. They must also have been engraved at the order of Ḫammurabi, perhaps in order to exhibit them in cities other than Sippar whence the looting king Šutruk-Naḫḫunte seems to have taken the stele which he had transported to Susa. But three quarters of the known manuscripts are copies from a later date than the period of origin of the "code" (the Old Babylonian period which ended around 1600). Some of them date even from shortly before the end of the independent history of the country: from the Neo-Babylonian period in the middle of the first millennium. Considering the situation in Mesopotamia that we just described, i.e. the absence of a lasting legislation promulgated at once for everyone until it would have been revoked, it is certain that the prescriptions of the "Code" of Ḫammurabi had become outdated at the latest from the moment that the political and administrative situation of the country changed, if they ever did have some legislative value. This change occurred at the moment of the fall of the Ḫammurabi dynasty, at the start of the Kassite* period, around the year 1600, if not at the death of Ḫammurabi himself. Therefore, if the Mesopotamians indefinitely recopied this work word for word after these events and at least for a millennium later, we have to adjust to the idea that it was because they saw in it something other than a text that was, so to say, normative and legislative.

This twofold consideration should suffice to awaken our suspicion about the very term that has been applied to the document under study here since its discovery; a term which is still in widespread use to designate it: "Code" or

5. See the references on pp. 364b–65a of the article *narû* ("stele") in the *Chicago Assyrian Dictionary,* N/1.

6. The list in G. R. Driver—J. M. Miles, *The Babylonian Laws,* 2: 1ff. has to be updated. See, for instance, J. J. Finkelstein, "A Late Old-Babylonian Copy of the Laws of Ḫammurapi," *Journal of Cuneiform Studies* 21 (1967): 39ff.

"law code." In short, is the "Code" of Ḫammurabi really a "Code"? It is not, and this is why.

The law code of a land is first of all a complete collection of the laws and prescriptions that govern that land: "the totality of its legislation" (*Trésor de la langue française*, V, 975, A: 3). From this point of view, it is enough to have a glance at the above list of the "chapters" of our "Code," to notice in it disturbing lacunae in legislative matters. For instance, we find no trace of the organization of justice itself, nor the repression of delicts and of crimes. There is no trace of criminal law properly speaking; there is no trace of a codification of the social hierarchy, or political obligations, of administration, or of fiscal policy. Even the side of the local economy which stood abreast with agriculture, namely animal husbandry, is barely mentioned and then only in a very cursory way.

Even among the subjects treated in some detail in the text, many important points are left in the dark, or are even dodged. Such an omission would be difficult to justify in an authentic code. Thus, in the chapter on "battery and assault" (§§195–214), blows given by a son to his father are foreseen, but patricide or infanticide are not. The case of assault and battery leading to death is only considered when involving brawls (§§207f.) on the one hand, and in the case of pregnant women whose deaths resulted from abortions seemingly caused by beatings (§§209f.). And I could continue in the same vein, seizing on the minutiae of the text.

These numerous omissions are even more surprising if we see that in the administrative and legal literature of the period, of which several tens of thousands of tablets are preserved, we encounter at every turn problems and conflicts of which the "Code" does not breathe a word. By all accounts the document should not be considered more than a type of anthology at best. It is certainly not a code in the true sense of the word—even if, for the sake of convenience and by convention I have no difficulty in preserving this almost century-old designation, being careful, however, to place it in quotation marks.

Can one at least continue to maintain, as many still do, that this "anthology," if it really is an anthology, contains real "laws"? To this question we must also answer in the negative.

It is clearly not the grammatical form or the stylistic presentation of the "articles" that would urge us to deny any legislative character to the text. We can very well express the same universal obligation, the same "law," by saying: *if a man has brought an accusation of murder against another man, without providing proof: the accuser shall be put to death* (§1), as by writing, as does the French penal code (art. 361): "whoever is guilty of false testimony in a criminal case, whether against the accused or in his favor, shall be punished with a penalty of imprisonment." There is no question here of form, but of essence. What makes the assimilation of the "articles" of the "code" with laws inexcusable is first their content, then their illogicality, and finally their manifest inefficiency.

According to the dictionaries a law is an imperative rule of social conduct, laid down and enforced by the legitimate authorities. Hence, it is first of all something general, something universal. But, if we look at our "Code" closely and without any preconceived ideas, what we find most often are situations, about which the least one can say is that they are very particularized, in spite of the universal situations that they express. In §1, cited above, there is no question of false testimony in general, even in criminal matters, but only of a most specific case of the false accusation of murder. In the article about blows given by children to their parents, we find only an *expressis verbis* mention of a son who has beaten his father: *"If a son has struck his father: they shall cut off his hand"* (§195). There are no provisions for the mother, the daughter, or for other children. Paragraphs 229f., which determine the responsibilities of the master-builder in the case of the collapse of a house built by him, presupposes that the house in question is inhabited by its owner, that the man has a son, that it is just that son who dies, and that the master-builder also has a son, who will be chosen as the redeeming victim:

> If a master-builder did not secure the solidity of a house that he was asked to build, and if the house that he built in that way collapsed and so has caused the death of the owner of the house: this master-builder shall be put to death. If the collapse caused the death of the son of the owner of the house: they shall put the son of the master-builder to death.

If we look candidly at the "Code," a number of problems brought up by it have this appearance of concrete cases much more than of conjunctures voluntarily deprived of any trace of singularity, and raised to the real absolute of the "law."

Doubtless this phenomenon is what can account for another fact that is unacceptable when it involves the law, namely the illogicality that we see here and there among the decisions taken to resolve these cases. Here is a rather striking example: in paragraph 8 the theft of some personal property is punished with tenfold restitution:

If a man stole either an ox or a sheep or an ass or a pig or a boat . . . belonging to a private citizen: he shall make good ten times the value of what he had stolen. And added to this as a subsidiary punishment is even the death penalty: *If the thief does not have sufficient means to make restitution: he shall be put to death.* While in paragraphs 259f. the theft of an agricultural instrument seems only to have been punished by a payment of a sum that does not seem to have exceeded the value of the object by much:

If a man has stolen a plough from a field: he shall give five shekels (40 grams) *of silver to the owner of the plough. If he has stolen a hoe or a harrow: he shall give him three shekels* (24 grams) *of silver.*

In paragraph 7 the agent, who has received the personal property of someone without a written title or without witnesses, is considered to be the thief of that property and, as such, he is condemned to death: *If a man has bought, or has received for safekeeping without witnesses or contracts, from the hand of another man or of a slave, either silver or gold or a male or a female slave, or an ox or a sheep, or anything whatsoever: that man is a thief: he shall be put to death.*

Here is, however, the text of another paragraph (123); *If a man gave for safekeeping* (gold, silver or whatsoever), *without witnesses or contracts, and the agent denied it: that case is not subject to claim.* In other words, even if this case is materially the same as the previous one, the "Code" is satisfied to nonsuit both parties involved, rather than having one of them executed. Even though such inconsistencies are rare in Ḫammurabi's collection, they are so fundamental that they suffice to deny the document any character of a code or an anthology of laws.

Finally, it has long been recognized that among the numerous pieces of procedures and protocols of judgments, or the "dossiers" of the administrative and judiciary practice of the time of Ḫammurabi, no verdict was given, no official decision was taken, nor any agreement signed that made a reference to any article of the so-called "Code," even if the latter contains explicit references to subjects upon which they are based or dependent. Some rare documents make reference to *the Stele* which could refer at times to the stele that contained the text of the "Code." But these references are made more to give an idea of the way one should behave than really to indicate some kind of an obligation that would have been exactly defined in the "Code." When one wanted to give authority to a decision or to a claim of a contract by referring to some explicit regulation, one only appealed to the *decisions of the king (ṣimdât šarrim).* We will return to that term, which designates in effect all that expresses the compelling will of the ruler. Let it suffice for the moment to stress that the "Code" of Ḫammurabi can be confused neither with these royal decisions nor with a selection that would have been made from them. At least twice the "Code" cites the *ṣimdat šarrim* and refers to them as its own normative authority. In paragraphs 51 and '89'-M where in different circumstances the borrower, or the debtor, has to reimburse the capital and the interest, he will do it, the text says, *in compliance with the rates established by the royal decision (ṣimdât šarrim* §51: *64*f. and §'89': *16).* It is thus not the content of the "Code" as such that had authority. Besides, what law is it if it is not compelling in itself, nor compelling for everyone?

Even better: what law is it if one could break it officially and easily in practice? We have cases where public documents contemporary with the "Code" settle a difficulty in an entirely different way than the "Code" would, as if the latter did not exist. In the area of the costs of labor, for instance, whereas the "Code" anticipates between five and ten liters of grain, depending on the case, as the daily salary for paid employees (boatmen §239; agricultural workers §257; cowherds §258; herdsmen §261; day laborers §273; artisans §274), the contracts regularly state sums that are two times higher on the average.

Undoubtedly it is possible to resolve these contradictions by taking each of them apart and perhaps sometimes by changing the prices. But what has importance for a historian is their accumulation. In the end this does not permit us to consider with any likelihood the "Code" of Ḫammurabi as an authentic law code.

On the other hand, everything that denies this definition to the "Code" by the same token confers upon it at least the appearance of a type of collection of jurisprudence. If we reconsider one by one the formulated criticisms and the reservations made, they vanish the moment that we regard each of these "articles" not as a *law* intended to regulate uniformly all the matters involved, but as a *verdict* given to decide a particular case. If paragraph 195 talks only about a son hitting his father, it is because a family tragedy involving only these two actors had been presented, *not to the legislature*, but to the *judge*. And if paragraphs 259f. are much less harsh than paragraph 8 in the matter of the punishment for theft, it is because of particular circumstances that are not described to us but that are implied therein. The judge had considered it necessary to condemn the thief in paragraphs 259f. to the fate of having to pay a simple reimbursement (more or less), and to double the indemnity to be paid by the one in paragraph 8. All of that happens as if the compiler of the "Code" had, in fact, collected here decisions of justice by omitting only the circumstances that were too particular and too concrete (starting with the names of the parties involved).

Furthermore, this is exactly what Ḫammurabi himself declares to us when in the beginning of his epilogue he wants to give a name to the elements of his collection: *These are*, he says, *the just verdicts (dînât mêšarim) that Ḫammurabi, the experienced king, has imposed in order to establish firm discipline and good governance in his country* (Rev. xxiv: 1f.). The word *dînât*, the plural form of *dînu*, indicates in Akkadian exactly the act of the judge who, by the virtue of a universal law, decides *hic et nunc* how a particular conflict that had arisen in the order of social behavior must be resolved. Who better than the old king could know what that had to mean? If he defines the prescriptions that he has collected in his "Code" as *verdicts*, it is because he wanted to compile there, not laws, but decisions taken by virtue of those laws.

We know that in Mesopotamia the rendering of justice was a royal prerogative, starting long before the second millennium. The ruler often delegated the duty to his representatives, even to professional judges, but it belonged to him in his own right. The procedural accounts, as well as the royal correspondence, that have survived, show more than once how lower authorities refer certain difficult or unusual cases to the royal tribunal. They also show how simple subjects brought their cases freely before the monarch whom they went to find—as did the Parisians with Saint Louis under the oak of Vincennes—or to whom they wrote, without any intermediary or without going through a hierarchy. It was thus up to the king to make a decision or to indicate to his representative in what way he meant for him to decide.

What Ḫammurabi wanted to collect in his "Code," as he tells us in so many words when he talks of *verdicts*, was a selection of the principal decisions of law, the most just decisions, the wisest, the most sagacious, the most worthy of an experienced ruler. These decisions he must have taken himself, or ratified, imposed, or even dictated to his delegates during his forty years of rule. We say so because we know that in its actual form the "Code" could not have appeared before his thirty-eighth regnal year, since Ḫammurabi alludes in the prologue to the capture of the city of Ešnunna (implied in obv. iv: 37f.), a feat that had not been accomplished until that very year.[7]

Perhaps there is at least a trace of the transfer of a single decision taken by Ḫammurabi into the "Code." Here is the text of a letter which he wrote to two officials and which has survived: "*Please buy back Sîn-ana-Damru-lippalis, son of Maninum, whom the enemy has captured: for this purpose deliver to the business agent who has brought him back from his captors* (after having paid the ransom!) *the sum of ten shekels silver* (ca. 80 grams, the usual price to buy a slave at that time) *taken from the treasury of the temple* (his town's temple, that is) *of the god Sîn*" (M. Stol, *Altbabylonische Briefe*, 9, pp. 22f., no. 32). This decision seems really to have found a place in the "Code." Here is what "article" 32 says:

> If a traveling business agent has ransomed abroad a soldier who had been taken prisoner during a royal campaign, and has brought him back to his city, and if in the household of that soldier there is enough to pay the ransom, he himself will pay it; if there is not enough to pay it, it is by taking from the treasury of the temple of his city that he will be bought back; and if in the temple of the city there is not enough to buy him back, the palace will buy him back.

7. *Reallexikon der Assyriologie*, 2, s.v. *Datenlisten*, p. 181, no. 140.

If all the archives of the long reign of Ḫammurabi would have been preserved, it is beyond doubt that we could have found in them the origin and source of a number of verdicts compiled in his "Code."

If we want to understand what the "Code" really represented in the mind of its author, the reasons why Ḫammurabi compiled these verdicts have to be found.

We could first of all suggest that Ḫammurabi, as all other writers, had to say something that had not been said before. As the founder of a new regime, he must have been a great reformer in all areas, including that of law. And in fact, compared to what has been left to us from before his reign, the "Code" offers us numerous examples of a spirit unknown up to then in juridical matters. Sometimes they are more lenient measures taken in favor of the poor; I have cited above §117, which establishes the automatic release after three years of family members sold or given into servitude by an insolvent debtor in order to compensate for his debt. Other verdicts of the "Code," on the other hand, show an increasing severity. It is thus, for instance, that paragraphs 196f. deal with the application of the law of retaliation—until then unknown in the land—for wounds: *If a man has destroyed the eye of a member of the aristocracy: they shall destroy his eye. If he has broken his limb: they shall break the* (same) *limb*. The somewhat older "Code" of Ešnunna only prescribes a heavy financial penalty for the same offenses: *If a man has bitten the nose of a member of the aristocracy, he shall pay him one mina of silver* [almost 500 grams, a very large sum!]; *for an eye: one mina; for* (broken) *teeth: one mina* . . . (A. Goetze, *The Laws of Eshnunna*, p. 117, §42). This is not the place to discuss the reasons for these alleviations or these increased severities. Neither is it the place to wonder about other changes made in the former "legislation," nor even whether or not there had been in fact a correction of the ancient traditional regime or only a modification of a state of affairs, attributable to one or more earlier rulers. However, it is beyond doubt that in more than one domain the "Code" of Ḫammurabi represents a real reform. The question is whether it was precisely in order to proclaim the reform as such that the king compiled and published his "Code."

If we examine the prologue and the epilogue of the so-called "Code" even slightly, the answer does not seem to be necessarily in the affirmative. We see there in fact that, far from emphasizing the novelties that he could have introduced and the "reforms" that he would have wanted to impose, Ḫammurabi saw things in an entirely different way.

When he wants to indicate in his epilogue what he considers to be the purpose of the monument he refers to as his *stele*, he declares: *Let the oppressed citizen who has a legal case . . . have the inscription on my stele read out . . . The stele will explain to him* (the literal translation is even more eloquent: *will show him*) *his case. And as he will understand then what verdict* (literally: his verdict—*dînû*, as above) *he will have to expect, his heart will be set at ease* . . . (Rev. xxv: 3–19). In conclusion, the ruler would have written his work in order to make his subjects understand what their rights were, and in order to show them how they could resolve their judicial difficulties.

A little further into the epilogue he directs his attention to the future, and he adds: *If one* (of my successors) *is sufficiently wise to be capable of maintaining order in the land, may he heed the words that I have written on this stele: that the monument may explain to him* (= *show to him*) *the way and the behavior to follow* . . . (ibid.: 75–82). In other words: my successors will learn to give justice and practice fairness by studying in detail, in my work, how I myself have exercised judicial power.

All this is very clear: in the eyes of its author the "Code" was not at all intended to exercise by itself a univocal normative value in the legislative order. But it did have value as a model; it was instructive and educative in the judicial order. A law applies to details; a model inspires—which is entirely different. In conclusion, we have here not a law code, nor the charter of a legal reform, but above all, in its own way, a treatise, with examples, on the exercise of judicial power.

And that is not all. Because by composing and publishing the treatise, Ḫammurabi saw in it certainly more than just usefulness: he thought of his own glory. This is an excusable weakness, after forty years of rule which the old monarch clearly must have felt to have been one of the high points in the history of his country. If he had only wanted to play the role of teacher and professor, why would he have added to his collection the solemn lyrical framework where there is no question of scientific merit and literary fame, but only of achievements and glory by themselves?

However, while studying closely the entire work, we see that the long sequence of *just verdicts* that form the "Code" is balanced by another list that almost fills up the entire prologue: that of cities and territories annexed and conquered, little by little, and grouped together in the end in a large, lasting kingdom—for the first time in the history of this ancient country. The king certainly claims the merits of such a military and political success with pride. But if he counterbalances it in some way by the even longer details of judgments that prove his wisdom as administrator, as judge, and as ruler, it shows that he considers his achievements in that area at least as important as those that he had accomplished in the area of power, or perhaps even more so.

Almost at the end of the list of old capitals annexed to his empire he makes a curious mention of Akkad* (obv. iv: 51), the ancient capital which was probably almost deserted at the time or at any rate well in decline. This was the city around which Sargon I and his successors had assembled the first and the largest Mesopotamian empire (ca. 2340–2150); an empire which joined into one entity the territory between the two seas: the Persian Gulf and the Mediterranean. An ambiguous memory had been preserved about this old adventure in Mesopotamia: people knew that such an exceptional political rise had been paid for with unending sufferings, violence, revolts, wars, misery, and bad luck. I wonder if Ḫammurabi did not want to subtly contrast his own achievements and his own glory to that of the most famous of his predecessors by evoking Akkad, which undoubtedly had not the least importance at the time, unless as a symbol. This he did perhaps by suggesting that, if in the time of Ḫammurabi the country had become again almost as powerful and extensive as before, it had however remained in prosperity and well-being. Why? Because Ḫammurabi knew how *to keep the country in order.* He provides the proof by enumerating at length the entire list of his activities as ruler: as an administrator and as a judge. Here is how he introduces the list of the *just verdicts* that make up the "Code" itself at the end of the prologue: *when* (my god) *Marduk* had given me the mission to keep my people in order and to make my country take the right road, I installed in this country justice and fairness in order to bring well-being to my people.* (That is why) *in those days* (I rendered the following verdicts) . . . (obv. v: *14–25*).

And he returns to it once the catalogue is finished:

> The great gods have called me, and I am indeed the good shepherd who brings peace, with the just scepter. My benevolent shade covered my city. I have carried in my bosom the people of Sumer and Akkad. Thanks to my good fortune (literally: the divine protection of which I am the object) they have prospered. I have not ceased to administer them in peace. By my wisdom I have harbored them. In order to prevent the powerful from oppressing the weak, in order to give justice to the orphans and the widows. . . . , in order to give verdicts in my land, in order to give my land fair decisions and to give rights to the oppressed, I have inscribed on the stele my precious words and I have placed them before the statue (that I had made) of myself (with the name): (Here is) the righteous king." (Rev. xxiv: *40–78*)

We know in fact that in the twenty-second year of his reign Ḫammurabi had erected such a statue of himself.[8] Thus he had already a good idea both of his mission and of his success. It is the same idea that he wanted to stress in his "Code." By drawing from his long experience as judge and administrator a "treatise on the exercise of judiciary power" which was addressed to everyone—to those seeking justice and even more so to judges par excel-

8. *Reallexikon der Assyriologie*, 2, p. 179, no. 124, s.v. *Datenlisten.*

lence, i.e. kings; and by presenting to them and for posterity this most solid monument of his glory and of his merits, he wanted to indicate that, in his eyes, there was no more precious and, perhaps, rarer value for a rule worthy of that title than the feeling for justice and the efficient will to make justice govern.

This is why, if the "Code" of Ḫammurabi is a scientific work devoted to justice, it is at the same time the expression of a political ideal in which justice had to occupy the first place. Still with the aim at understanding better how it would have appeared to the eyes of its contemporaries, it will be useful to study the "Code" under this double aspect: we will judge it by the idea that the Mesopotamians had both of science and of justice.

THE "CODE" OF ḪAMMURABI AND MESOPOTAMIAN SCIENCE

By presenting the "Code" as a scientific work, I am not making some foolhardy connection with the unknown. I am simply associating this work with a literary genre which is rather well represented in the cuneiform documentation: that of the scientific treatises we have already encountered.

Since the invention of writing around the year 3000, the Mesopotamians were given not only an admirable instrument for verbal memory, for precision and conceptual analysis, which revolutionized the type of culture itself, but also a class of scholars. These scholars were simultaneously specialized in the difficult art and the *profession* of reading and writing as well as in a way of viewing things: the intellectual treatment of reality to which writing gave access. The "mandarins," who assembled in schools or academies around the palace and the temples, started very soon to be interested in a number of phenomena, and to study them and to compose reports about them that we cannot refer to as anything but "scientific." These reports were copied, studied without respite, revised, enriched, and re-edited until the very end of Mesopotamian history, shortly before the Christian era. Thus we have from at least the first third of the second millennium a certain number of *treatises* dealing with subject matters that were of most interest to the "wise men" of the land: lexicography and grammar, divination, mathematics, medicine—not to mention jurisprudence. These treatises are preserved in fragments of various sizes, some of which are almost complete. It is to this type of research and literature that the "Code" of Ḫammurabi also belongs. We have to compare the "Code" to works such as these in order to convince ourselves of its "scientific" character, and in order to better understand what we must comprehend by evoking the "scientific way of thinking" of the "Code's" contemporaries.

For the sake of being concise I have chosen only one work as point of comparison for this purpose, keeping in mind that all these treatises were uniformly developed according to the same framework of thought and expression. This work is at the same time rather extensive, well preserved, and typical, and it bears on a discipline that is not, epistemologically speaking, so far removed from jurisprudence: diagnostic medicine. It is a work of about five to six thousand lines which R. Labat reconstructed and published in a most commendable way, some thirty years ago, under the title *Traité akkadien de diagnostics et de pronostics médicaux*. In fact, it is not the art of healing that the ancient authors have analyzed and organized in this work, but the "scientific judgment of physicians" on the nature of illness and its predictable evolution.

Two elements especially have to be considered here: *the component parts of the report* and *the order in which they are presented*. We will study them one by one and compare them successively with the "Code" in order to better understand why and how the latter was developed as it was. We will also take advantage of this comparison, which broadens our inquiry, by considering if we can speak of "science" in ancient Mesopotamia.[9]

The Component Parts

The entirety of the treatise, from the first to the last line, is composed of an unending succession of conditional phrases introduced by "if" and made up of a protasis and an apodosis in the same way that has already been pointed out for our "Code." Here are some examples of it:

> If, in the beginning of the illness, the sick man shows profuse transpiration and salivation, without the sweat of the legs reaching the ankles and the soles of the feet: this man will be sick for two or three days, after which he has to recover his health. (pp. 156f., XVII: *1*f.)
>
> If a man who is feverish has a burning abdomen, so that at the same time he feels neither pleasure nor dislike for food and drink, and also his body is yellow: this man has a venereal disease. (pp. 78f., XXIII: *12*f.)
>
> If a man, while walking, suddenly falls forward with dilated eyes and is unable to restore them to their normal condition, and if he is himself incapable, at the same time, of moving his arms and legs: an attacks of "epilepsy" has started. (pp. 190f., XXVI: *16*f.)

This use of protasis and apodosis is something that might have seemed to us a special characteristic of the "Code," but in fact is not. This "conditional scheme" could very well have represented to the ancient Mesopota-

9. See above, pp. 125ff., where the matter has been considered from another point of view.

mians the proper canvas for their rational thought, the fundamental logical framework for their discourse—something like the syllogism provides for us. We posit premises to draw out of them a conclusion that becomes apparent to us through them. The Mesopotamians put forward a hypothesis and then, by a judgment based upon the elements of that hypothesis, they draw a conclusion that they have found in it. Fever, burning abdomen, no appetite, a yellow color of the skin—these are the elements given in the hypothesis; venereal disease—this is the judgment that the symptoms conceal and that the diagnostician can draw out of them in some way. Blows given by a son to his father—this is a hypothesis of an article of the "Code"; amputation of the guilty hand—that is the verdict that the judge draws out of it; that is the jurisprudential context of the elements of the hypothesis. Now we can better understand how in the Mesopotamian mind the "Code" also had to be considered as a scientific treatise. When writing the "Code," Ḫammurabi formulated it in such a way that he gave the indispensable logical form of scientific thought (in his way of thinking) to the *just verdicts* that had been pronounced, ratified or inspired by him, and that formed the material of the "Code."

Let us now analyze the two components of the scheme somewhat more closely: the hypothesis (protasis) and the conclusion (apodosis).

The protasis does not contain individual elements as such, it is not a news item that is recounted in the "Code": a man, of this name, this age, this appearance, of this social class or of this profession, passes, on a certain day, a certain hour, through a certain street of a certain town, and from a certain height falls suddenly forward in a certain way and remains there, paralyzed and with dilated eyes. A similar accident, even a repetition of similar scenes, is evidently the basis of the hypothesis. But the doctors that observed it were able to isolate and extract only the typical and essential elements from a medical point of view; by ignoring everything that is individual, casual, and without medical significance *they were able to transform the scene in the street into symptoms.*

The same task has been accomplished in the "Code." Starting from the collection of the activities of his tribunal and of the cases judged there, as he tells us himself, Ḫammurabi has suppressed all the individual, contingent, and insignificant elements from the juridical point of view, in order to insert these cases into his "Code." Let us recall a single example: the person in the letter cited above who was named Mister *Sîn-ana-Damru-lippalis,* son of Mister *Maninum, whom the enemy had captured.* In the corresponding "article" of the "Code" this man became a *soldier captured during a royal campaign.* The only thing that counts here is the subject whom the king has taken care of, because he was in the king's service and because he suffered a loss of freedom in consequence of that service. And it is like this throughout. In the entire "Code" there is not a single detail that is not important in its way for the determination of the verdict. Just as there is not a single element in the entire treatise that is not medically significant and of consequence for the diagnosis and prognosis to be made.

Therefore, we can already propose, with the texts in hand, that the ancient Mesopotamians had been able to acquire this selective way of viewing that sets the "scholar" apart from the simple spectator of the same event. They had found the manner of abstraction that such a point of view imposes, by eliminating from a concrete event all that does not properly fit such a defined intellectual preoccupation. They had, at least de facto, uncovered this essential prerogative of science; i.e., knowing that it does not bear upon the individual, the casual, or the run-of-the-mill, but on the universal and the necessary.

The conclusion drawn in the apodosis is naturally as general and permanent as the elements in the hypothesis on which it is based: venereal disease or "epilepsy" in the medical treatise, and amputation of the hand, the fine, or the imprisonment in the "Code." They are all terms that are entirely depersonalized.

But on what did they base themselves in order to derive this conclusion from the elements of the protasis? What was it that enabled them to decide that, if there had been a bad fall during a walk, followed by paralysis and dilated eyes, an attack of "epilepsy" had to begin? Evidently, even though the authors of the treatise do not breathe a word of it, it was in the end also empiricism: observation, repeated observation, and undoubtedly the discussion and criticism of these observations led to such a judgment. They had observed for a long time, and with an attention so great that they could be certain about the connection between the two, that a hard fall forwards during a walk, accompanied by a fixed stare and paralysis of the limbs, was regularly followed by a crisis of a "great pain." They had learned to derive the necessary diagnosis from these premonitory symptoms: it was a case of "epilepsy." Also here we are faced with the same necessity, which is inseparable from scientific thought and which the ancient Babylonians had already understood, that two phenomena which constantly succeed each other are necessarily connected one to the other: *post hoc, ergo propter hoc*. This is the entire meaning of *causality.* I use "the meaning" because *the law* of causality had not yet been formulated by these people.

It goes without saying that in the "Code" it is not entirely the same objective necessity, so to speak, that connects the hypothesis to the conclusion: the amputation of the hand does not seem to follow immediately, as if by a natural and intrinsic obligation, from the blows given by a son to his father. What connects the first fact to the second is either custom, traditional social coercion, or the explicit will of the authorities. We will return later to this double source of obligation in the domain of the "Code." But whatever the differences may be between justice on the one hand and, for instance, medicine on the other hand, they do not affect the only important fact from the epistemological point of view. This fact is that in the "Code," as in the medical and other treatises, a perception of necessity intervenes. We are forced to acknowledge that the ancient Mesopotamians had been able to become aware of this necessity.

The Order

A distinctive characteristic of the scientific treatises is that the elements that are brought together in them, often in enormous numbers, are not accumulated in a haphazard fashion, as if they were the details of a tale of daily life or of a street scene, but were ordered and formulated in the treatises according to a definite order and a real system. In the medical treatise, which serves us here as a model, the elements are grouped around the different parts of the body which provide the ingredients of the hypothesis: the skull, the temples, the forehead, the eye and its different parts: sclera, iris, muscles, eyelids, etc.; then the nose—and so on according to their natural position going from the top to the bottom, from head to toes. We may find this arrangement superficial, but at least it attempts to follow nature and is thus objective rather than arbitrary.

This undoubtedly also applies for the ordering of the principal "chapters" in our "Code" enumerated above. *We* certainly do not understand the reasons for the plan that controls their placement. That is, however, due more to our ignorance, both of the mentality of the times and of the bias by which they associated one thing with another, than to any whims of the compiler in strewing them around randomly. The proof for that is that the logic of their placement is still clear to us here and there. For instance, if the "chapter" on battery and assault follows immediately after the one on the family, it is precisely because of the last problem discussed in the first chapter: the son who revolts against his father and raises his hand against him, leads naturally to the topic of blows. And if the "chapter" on battery and assault is immediately followed by the "title" on free professions, it is because the latter begins with the physician. The placement is entirely appropriate because there is question of the treatment of wounds and bruises in the previous chapter. The general appearance suggested by this observation—and a better understanding of the cuneiform documentation confirms it amply—is that these people preferred a *linear* arrangement, so to speak. Each point raises the next one, while we tend more to establish a *hierarchy* around a principal essential object.

The same layout is found within the "chapters", where it involves the ranking of the various arrangements of the object under study. But here a constant procedure shows up which is seemingly of great consequence: the *variation*. One starts with an object that one wants to dissect systematically, in other words of which one wants to get a global knowledge, i.e. objective and scientific. This procedure makes the aspects of the object change, as many hypotheses are used in order to produce different conclusions, somewhat in the way one would turn a toy around in one's fingers in order to examine it from different angles. Here are, for instance, the beginnings of the protases drawn from the observation of the nose of a sick man in the medical treatise:

> If blood drops from the nose of the sick . . .
> If humor drops from his nose . . .
> If the tip of his nose is wet . . .
> If the tip of his nose is successively hot and cold . . .
> If the tip of his nose is yellow . . .
> If the tip of his nose has a red rash . . .
> If the tip of his nose has a white rash . . .
> If the tip of his nose has a red and white rash . . .
> If the tip of his nose has a black rash . . . (pp. 56ff., VI: 19ff.)

—and so on. In short, they have collected and classified the greatest possible number of observations of different states of the object. These possibilities are chosen here exclusively for their medical importance, of course, and each is followed by its consequence expected on the scientific level. This treatise deals with the diagnosis and prognosis to be made when these symptoms are confronted. The different cases are all medically significant and are taken from the nature and characteristics themselves of the object considered in its formal aspect. In the case of medicine the characteristics include cold and heat, dryness and humidity, the different possible colorations of the nose itself, etc. In order to know in depth all that the nasal appendage can hide of medical diagnoses and prognoses, it is sufficient to enumerate all these appearances and to group the observations that were made from them. And if these same aspects are found in other parts of the body, they will lead to the same hypotheses. These hypotheses will increase in number by still other observations which are as recurrent, according to the appearance or the disposition of the organs involved. For instance, the situations on the right and on the left side of the body appear in pairs.

It seems that through this invariable system the authors of the treatises had devised the nomenclature and the framework of all the essential presentations—according to the scientific point of view of their examinations. These they used again and again and enumerated, constantly in the same order, according to need. Hence, when reading the medical treatise, one finds throughout the document the protases considering the different colors of the part of the body under study: white, yellow, red, black (and always in this order!), sometimes mixtures of colors, or nuances, listed in the same order, for the forehead (pp. 44f.), the face (pp. 72f.), the hands (pp. 90f.), the breasts (pp. 100f.), etc. This is what clarifies the will to make a really complete review of each object under consideration, the will not to forget anything that might be symptomatic, even to foresee *all possibilities* involving the object. In my opinion this is an element of great importance.

If this examination bears upon phenomena common in medical matters in general, certain protases sum up observations that seem to be much more unusual. Here is an example: *If the sick man is deeply absorbed by what must take place after his death, and he orders his share of his own funerary meal* (which should be organized after his death!)[10] *and he eats it: he will die* (pp. 182f., XIII: 43). If the author of the treatise has recorded it, it is because he did not want to leave *anything* in the dark, but wanted to make known, so far as he could, everything about the object that he was analyzing. For him it was thus a matter of including in his work not only the common and commonly observable reality, but also the exceptional, the aberrant; in the end, everything *possible*.

If I attach great importance to this phenomenon it is because, in my opinion, it shows that the ancient Mesopotamians had not only arrived at a certain scientific abstraction, and at a feeling that science deals only with the necessary. But they also know that scientific knowledge is, in itself, universal and much broader than a single observation or the simple passive contemplation of what goes on before our eyes. That is why a scientific work had to foresee everything that related to its object. There are even cases where such a principle has led the authors of the treatises to state hypotheses that are in our opinion entirely fantastic and unrealistic. They considered it necessary to include these fantastic hypotheses in their work in order to treat the object thoroughly, in order to foresee everything. They were conscious of the fact that they played not only the role of a memorizer who reports what he sees but also of a scholar who has to take into account even that which might happen. Possibly because of my ignorance of medical matters I have been unable to reveal such cases in our treatise; but I know of others. For instance, in the treatise on tocomancy* (divination based on the features of newborns, premature births, or miscarriages; we have to remember that in Mesopotamia divination was considered and treated as a science)[11] the births, not only of twins, triplets and quadruplets, etc. are taken into consideration, but also those of eight or nine children in one and the same delivery! This type of extrapolation, aberrant to us, is guided by the conviction that the type of knowledge recorded in the

10. This refers to the *kispu;* see below, p. 282.
11. See *Divination et rationalité,* passim, and above, pp. 34f. and 125ff.

treatises does not have to be satisfied with what one can ascertain in fact, but has to go as far as what one might ascertain one day in order to foresee everything—there is always the same concern for the universal!

We find this also in the "Code" (I am not insisting upon the ordering of the "articles" within one chapter). The "Code's" essential procedure is seemingly to make the elements of the hypothesis vary as much as possible, by considering successively all possible situations of similar juridical importance. While some hypotheses offer simple and recurring conditions, it can also happen here that we find the same framework of variations applied to various objects that are materially different. This is, for instance, the case with the "social classes" (there were three principal classes: aristocrats, common citizens, and slaves), which we find in like order both in the chapter on battery and assault and in that on tariffs for surgical care:

> If a man has destroyed the eye of a member of the aristocracy . . .
> If a man has destroyed the eye of a commoner . . .
> If a man has destroyed the eye of a slave . . . (§§196–99)
> If a physician has operated successfully on the eye of a member of the aristocracy . . .
> If a physician has operated successfully on the eye of a commoner . . .
> If a physician has operated successfully on the eye of a slave . . . (§§215–17).

The tariffs (in the "conclusion") vary in effect from one class to the other: ten shekels (ca. 80 grams) for the healing of an aristocrat, five for a commoner, and two for a slave. When an eye is destroyed, if it is the eye of an aristocrat the eye of the assailant will be destroyed; one mine (ca. 500 grams, a very large sum!) was demanded for the eye of a common citizen, and half the price of a slave for the eye of a slave. Other comparable sequences are found elsewhere: father, son, slave, for instance. And sometimes the compiler has combined several of them in one and the same paragraph:

If a man has bought or received for safekeeping, without witnesses or a contract, *from another man,* free or enslaved, either silver, or gold, or a male or a female slave, or an ox, or a sheep, or an ass, or finally any sort of thing: *this man is a thief and* (as such) *he shall be put to death* (§7).

It can happen, finally, that this same desire to cover everything (the usual, the exceptional, and what is simply possible) leads in the "Code," as well as in the treatises, to hypotheses that are, it not unimaginable, at least entirely unusual but considered worthy of mention by the author, who wanted to foresee everything and to go round his subject. I have to admit that this is very rarely the case. With a lot of reservations, I will cite the rates for the hire of animals used to trample the grain on the threshing-floor. The "Code" gives first of all the "wages" for an ox, than for an ass—both of them, as we can see elsewhere, normally assigned to that task; but then for a goat (§§268–70)! We cannot easily imagine (perhaps mistakenly) that one would ever, or in any case not frequently, have used this stubborn animal, so unmanageable, and too light for such a task. Thus it undoubtedly involved an expansion of the perspective, in order to give an idea of the possible conditions when substitute animals would be used in exceptional cases.

The Purpose and Use of the Treatises

This is a last thing to be considered. As different as these scientific works are from ours, they all seem to have been composed for the same purpose: they are essentially *practical* and *didactic.* For the authors it was not a question of speculating about knowledge for its own sake and of theorizing, but of putting the knowledge within the reach and at the disposal of the practitioner. The medical treatise, for instance, has only one prefatory rubric before the endless list of symptoms and of diagnoses and prognoses. This rubric gives the meaning of the entire work: *When the practitioner*[12] *will go to the patient* (pp. 2f.: *1*)—in other words: *when the practitioner will be called for consultation*—(here is the list of symptoms that he will have to look for and observe in order to derive knowledge of the type of disease that the ill person has and of its anticipated development . . .). —To return to the "Code," it may suffice to recall how Ḫammurabi claimed in his prologue and his epilogue that he wanted to teach the practice of justice by writing the "Code."

It is here that a new characteristic of "science" in Mesopotamia shows up most clearly. In a specific scientific area that we want to study in itself or teach, we first worry about deducing and establishing, on the basis of the facts, the principles and the laws that govern that scientific area. Nowhere in any of the numerous treatises, nor anywhere else in the enormous cuneiform literature, do we encounter an utterance of such a *principle* or of such a *law,* taken by itself in abstraction and with formal universality. We see in them nothing but an enumeration of indefinite litanies of *cases:* hypotheses followed each by an exact judgment that one has to express based on them. Neither the hypotheses nor the conclusions ever rise to the level

12. Literally: the *exorcist.* The *physician* is not presented here. This is due to the fact that the medical treatise was attached to another type of therapeutics which was equally traditional in the country, and whose views and means were not of the natural (medicine) but of the supernatural order (exorcism) after a secular history of which we do not know the details and which I have ignored in my remarks. On these two methods, their coexistence and their interactions, one can consult the article in *L'Histoire,* no. 74, cited above, p. 142 n. 13.

of our absolute principles and laws, in which all the cases of interest are subsumed in a simple statement that represents the cases by their most common and most pertinent aspects.

It has often been suggested that these shortcomings in Mesopotamian science are only apparent. In reality, it is sometimes said, these treatises were only manuals of instruction. The master who explained them evidently had to transmit aloud what was not represented in the catalogues of examples, namely the real laws of the science in question. It is always dangerous in history to launch into hypotheses that will never be confirmed by anything, whether directly or not, and whose use will lead soon to abuse and to the absurd. If the ancient Mesopotamians knew and passed on by word of mouth such propositions, why would they have persistently abstained from *ever* recording them in writing? It is much more likely that they had no idea of such laws, that they did not know them—at least not with this clear and immediate knowledge that is always easy to formulate. An indirect but solid proof is that there is not a single word, neither in Akkadian nor in Sumerian, to render what we understand by *principle* or by *law* in the scientific or in the juridical sense: thus the ancient Babylonians had not the slightest distinct notion of these quintessential formulations.

In reality they learned and furthered the sciences in the same way that all of us learn grammar and arithmetic at a young age: by memorizing examples of conjugated verbs or declined words, and of multiplied or divided numbers. By means of these *rosa, rosae* or these litanies of increasing or diminishing numbers, by means of these sequences of concrete and varied cases chosen as examples, and by taking advantage of the instinctive recourse to analogy, we have assimilated all the essentials of grammar and of the science of numbers, of which we probably would not have understood anything at all if we had been presented at first with the laws and principles.

The cuneiform treatises are nothing else but types of paradigms or tables. It was by the repetition and the variation of particular cases, of models to be considered in a spirit of analogy, that the substance of the discipline in question was assimilated, that the habit of scientific judgment was formed, that the sense of correct reasoning was acquired at the same time as the capacity to extend these same judgments and reasoning to all the material objects of the science in question, according to their eventual presentation. The Mesopotamians of old never crossed this threshold which many people in our days do not cross and to which, moreover, most people perhaps do not even get access. It was the Greeks who have taken us further, to the universal concepts, the absolute formulations, that allow us the clear perception and the distinct expression of the principles and the laws in all their abstraction. May they be honored for that forever! But this honor should not tarnish that of their ancient predecessors in Mesopotamia. The Mesopotamians, who probably started from nothing, or from very little, had already, by themselves, made a long journey towards the acquisition of science, in the definitive sense of the word. They had recognized the importance of multiple and critical observation, and of the natural and objective ordering of things. They had derived from them already a scientific point of view that knows how to eliminate from an object what is singular and contingent, in order to preserve nothing but the typical and the symptomatic. In the material succession of repeated events, they had discerned the causality that connects one event to another, and the analogy that presides over parallel series. And this double awareness of analogy and causality had made them take an enormous step forward to the scientific universe that surpasses the verifiable realities and extends into the prediction and the deduction of the possible.

Thus readjusted in its original perspective as a scientific work, the "Code," as it will be seen and understood henceforth, has some chance to escape the anachronisms with which it has been obscured since its discovery.

It is a "work of science devoted to the exercise of *justice.*" What remains is to consider one more point.

THE "CODE" AND THE MESOPOTAMIAN SENSE OF JUSTICE

Although this topic is of importance, I will hardly deal with it. First of all because this is an area that is at least more accessible, if not better explored. Secondly, because what we have just discussed should greatly clarify it.

A first element that shows very convincingly that the ancient inhabitants of Mesopotamia did not understand justice in entirely the same way as we do, is that "they never knew laws," in the juridical area as well as in the scientific one. As I have pointed out above, the word, "law," does not exist in their language. And laws are not found in their writings, because we have to admit that their so-called "codes" are not that, and that they record in fact not laws but decisions of justice. Such a statement could at first contain something disturbing. I myself was perplexed when I was forced to accept this negative conclusion, without being able to perceive clearly at that time with what to balance it, after I had read and thought over the fundamental article by B. Landsberger, "Die babylonischen Termini für Gesetz und Recht" (*Symbolae . . . P. Koschaker . . .*, pp. 219ff.). If we believe our dictionaries, justice is in our eyes that "which conforms to the law." Once the law is eliminated, does not everything else become unstable?

Clearly not! Let us not lose sight of the "Code" itself. If it collects in fact *verdicts of justice,* it establishes by that very fact the existence of a system of justice. It is only that the people did not have the same point of view as we have—just as they did not have the same idea of science as we do.

Each "article" of the "Code," as we have said repeatedly recalls a verdict, stripped from the form in which it was given, in order to be incorporated in a "manual of jurisprudential science." A verdict is an action by a judge who, by virtue of a universal law, decides *hic et nunc* how a particular conflict in the order of communal life has to be resolved. How then did this universal law, this foundation of social life, present itself to the minds of the ancient Mesopotamians?

First of all, it was presented in the form of interventions of the royal authority, of actions by the ruler, in order to regulate one or another aspect of communal life: the *decisions of the king (ṣimdât šarrim).* We know some of these decisions indirectly, through texts of legal practice that sometimes refer to them. For example, the contracts for the hiring of day-workers for certain important seasonal activities, such as the harvest, include the mention of an advance payment of silver agreed upon for such undertakings, that is paid several months beforehand. Then a clause is inserted: *if they do not appear at the appointed time, they will be punished according to the decisions of the king.*[13] We have good reason to believe that it involved in fact royal ordinances imposing a heavy penalty or fine upon the people failing to appear.

Also preserved are the texts of some "decrees" in which are consigned what we can consider to be such royal decisions. Here are two that appear in an edict of the fourth successor of Ḫammurabi, Ammiṣaduqa of Babylon (1646–1626):

> The wholesale and retail merchants [who have used] a false seal (in order to certify their "documents"), will be put to death.
>
> The representative of the king or the local governor who has forced upon the family of a worker attached to the king, grain, silver, or wool, in order to make him harvest or perform work for his own profit, will be put to death. His victim will keep everything that was given to him. (*Edict of Ammiṣaduqa* §§18 and 22)[14]

It is possible that in one form or another these royal decisions had been in the end incorporated into the "Code," or even that the latter, just as it expresses in its own way the will and the authority of the ruler, could have been regarded as a collection of his decisions. There is a copy of his "Code" which has been entitled a *ṣimdât šarrim,* dating from the end of the Old Babylonian period, i.e. a century or somewhat more after Ḫammurabi

13. References in *Chicago Assyrian Dictionary,* Ṣ: pp. 195bf.

14. F. R. Kraus, *Königliche Verfügungen in altbabylonischer Zeit,* pp. 180f. and 182f. With regard to this edict, see also "Désordre économique et annulation des dettes en Mésopotamie à l'époque paléo-babylonienne," *Journal of the Economic and Social History of the Orient* 4 (1961), pp. 113–64, a study based on the first edition (1958) of the work in question, by the same F. R. Kraus, and of its context.

(*Journal of Cuneiform Studies* 21 [1967]:42a). Enforced by the royal authority, these *dînâtu*-verdicts could thus be retrospectively regarded as a type of *ṣimdâtu*-decisions!

The *ṣimdât šarrim* was an act of the man in power regulating particular aspects of communal life which up till then either had not caused any problems or had been regulated differently (we can imagine, for instance, that the severe condemnation by Ammiṣaduqa of the use of forgeries in business documents or the abuse of power at the expense of royal personnel, and in consequence to the detriment of the king himself, was caused by an enormous increase in these crimes at that time). The decisions of the king innovated or reformed; that was their only role.

But this particular character of the decisions as innovations and as reforms had necessarily only a secondary role in the regulation of social life. Even by maintaining all those decisions taken by the predecessors of the ruling monarch (supposing that they had not lost their value when their author died), and by adding them to those taken by the ruler himself, one would certainly still be far from having achieved the equivalent of an exhaustive legislation.

What then maintained such legislation, indispensable to all social life? There were undoubtedly "laws," but they were *unformulated*, just as the principles of sciences remained unformulated. Mesopotamian law was essentially an unwritten law. Unwritten does not mean nonexistent or unknown, but potential: because it was constantly presented to the people in the form of positive or prohibitive customs, transmitted together with education, or even in the form of traditional solutions to particular problems. It was by receiving these ways of behavior from youth on, and by their presence itself in a society that was unconsciously penetrated by them; by taking notice of concrete solutions through the accidents of daily life, that these people familiarized themselves with the laws. The principles of the laws were not deduced or formulated in explicit terms, but it was as if they were incorporated in a diffuse mass of traditions that generations automatically transmit to each other in any given cultural group, just as with language, or with a world-vision, a feeling about things, different procedures of production or of transformation, and so on. Hence, this is no unusual or extravagant situation. Not to invoke the numerous people who did not know how to write, who among us, without ever having looked at a law code, does not have the infallible, though unreasoned and as if instinctive, sentiment of what the laws allow or prohibit in almost all the events of ordinary life? And who is not able to resolve by himself, in good order, numerous new problems that present themselves to him in that area, taking advantage of the juridical awareness found in this way? The ancient subjects of Ḫammurabi, and of his predecessors and successors, were also at that stage.

The proof that such a situation has in itself nothing that is primitive or barbaric, using these words in a pejorative sense, is that it did not prevent the Mesopotamians from communicating a high idea of social obligation and of justice.

This was the case, first of all, because the law is not a statement, a "letter," but a tendency, a "spirit." When the formulation of social behavior counts much less than this type of impulse that confers upon it its obligatory strength, there is little chance that one would happen upon this irritating oddity that is the prevailing worry to conform to the letter of the law, this rigid and mind-numbing legalism that does not even spare great civilizations and great religions. I have not found any trace of it in Mesopotamia, in spite of the type of rationality that forms there perhaps one of the essential elements of intelligence, and in spite of the formalism that penetrates there a great portion of the literature.

The Babylonians used especially two words that we can associate more or less with our word "justice": *kittu* and *mêšaru*, which they often combined: *kittu u mêšaru*, and always in this order, as if the second complemented and enclosed the first. *Kittu* by its basic meaning (*kânu: to establish firmly*) evokes something firm, immobile, and is best understood as that which derives its solidity from its conformity to the law (abstracting from the law's presentation, written or unwritten). We translate it best by *honesty* or by *justice* in the narrow sense, depending on the context. *Mêšaru*, derived from *ešêru* (*to go straight, in the right way; to be in order*) contains a more dynamic element; one can understand it, depending on the context, as a state or as an activity. As a state it reflects the *good order* of each thing in its place and according to its ways, in other words, its nature and its role (its "destiny" one would have said in Mesopotamia). As a type of activity or of conduct it renders or attributes to each being and to each man that which comes to him by nature or by his place in society: again his "destiny"—*justice* in short. A particular use of the same word is understood as the *repair* and *restoration* of the activities of a society, by this reshuffling of the cards that can be done by the king, usually at least in the beginning of a reign, by "abolishing the debts" of the working part of the population, whose precarious conditions made them increasingly dependent upon the rich elite. Thus the *mêšaru* was an exercise in equity by the king par excellence, and indicated an "act of grace" and a "moratorium on debts."[15]

In my opinion, it is significant that Ḫammurabi only once uses the word *kittu* in his "Code" and then in the expression *kittu u mêšaru: I set forth* (literally: *placed in the mouth:* one says what one has on his mind!) *in the land honesty and justice* (Obv. V: 20f.). Two other times he uses the

15. See the works cited above, n. 14.

plural of the word: *kinâtu*, as if to cut its contents into pieces. But every time he attaches justice—by declaring himself as *he who has proclaimed* (literally: *made shine, revealed*) *the rules-of-justice and the guiding-in-good-order (mušušêr,* of the same verb *ešêru) of the people* (Obv. IV: 53f.) and by presenting himself as a *just king (šar mêšarim) to whom Šamaš has given the rules-of-justice* (Rev. XXV: 95f.).

But the terms *mêšaru* (Obv. I: *32;* Rev. XXIV: *2;* XXV: *65, 96;* XXVI: *13* and *17*) and the corresponding verb *ešêru* (Obv. IV: *54;* V: *16;* Rev. XXIV: *62; 73;* XXV: *38; 77; 87*) appear most often in the prologue and the epilogue. They seem never to make allusion to an "act of grace" which the king must have proclaimed when he ascended the throne: everywhere these words refer to what he considers clearly his essential duty at the same time as his greatest achievement: justice. The contents of his "Code" is made up by *just verdicts (dînât mêšarim:* rev. XXIV: *1*f.) which he has pronounced in the course of his long reign. His *scepter* (we would say *his rule*) *is just (išarat;* ibid.: *45*). The gods have commissioned him *to make appear (to make shine) in the land mêšaru,* i.e. order at the same time as justice (Obv. I: 32f.). And he glorifies himself at that moment because of the knowledge that he has, better than anyone else, responded to this supernatural wish and mission, and he has a statue of himself fashioned with the name *the just king (šar mêšarim;* rev. XXIV: 77 and XXV: 7), a title that he gives himself at least twice more in his epilogue (Rev. XXV: *96* and XXVI: *13*). Of course, we have to take into account the "genre" that forced him to present himself only in a perfect way, as irreproachable, infallible, both in his "Code" and in all his official inscriptions. And it is not important here to know how far he really was like that, or if his people had the same opinion about him. What counts is the definition of his political ideal, if we can use that word, as it is presented to us by the "Code": it is clearly centered upon the establishment, not of a strict and literal justice, but of equity that inspires justice but also surpasses it.

Thus if we attempt to look at this famous and impressive work with the eyes of those who wrote it and who lived with it in its time—even if we do so very imperfectly, as is inevitable—we discover that it is far removed from our own categories. There is no question of reducing it to the simple (and modern) definition of a "collection of laws"! It is too rich, too full of meaning for us to account for it by choosing one simple word in our dictionaries to encompass it.

The "Code" of Ḫammurabi is essentially a self-glorification of the king. But at the same time it is a political charter that synthesizes an entire detailed and organized vision of the "right" exercise of justice. And it is, in that way, a real treatise on jurisprudence. It is after all possible that this "Code" in certain of its propositions could have been used to regulate one or another sector of social conduct, at least in the time of Ḫammurabi and perhaps of his immediate successors, who may have adopted and ratified it. But that is not essential: because this work is absolutely not, in itself, the result of *legislative* action. If posterity in Mesopotamia admired it as an exemplary work, worthy to be distributed and recopied throughout the ages, it was certainly not because of that aspect. It was because the Mesopotamians found in it the memory of a great monarch who, more often and better than others, was able to express, or at least wanted to apply an ideal of the "job of a king." That ideal was at the same time noble, in conformity with the general view on things, and beneficent. He wanted to attain it by improving the greatest virtue of the rule of the land: justice. It was admired because they found in it also the teachings of a great master of jurisprudence, of the science and the art of judging, i.e. of applying justice.

Why, then, would *we* want to find something else in it?

11

"Free Love" and Its Disadvantages

IN ESSENCE, EVEN UNDER THIS CATCHY TITLE, WE ARE STILL DEALING with the same problem of "man and the other."[1] Only this time the other is not "any living being whatsoever"[2] but an individual of the human race. Moreover, it does not deal with a value judgment that can be formulated regarding the individual, but with the inclination that one can feel for him, and especially with the more or less free exercise of an amorous inclination. It is not a question of knowing how in ancient Mesopotamia one assessed fellow creatures according to a certain set of values, but just how and in what spirit one could behave towards some among them, in searching for a complement for oneself, for physical contact, and even for sexual intercourse.

The problem is interesting, not because its answer constitutes "the highest point in time that we can reach in the development of our "philosophy" of mankind,"[3] but, on the contrary, because the answer is entirely different from our traditional one, and it allows us, at least in a sense, to measure the relativity and the frailty of our tradition.

In order to better understand the behavior of the ancient Mesopotamians with regard to matters of love, but also the spirit in which they be-

1. See *Hommes et bêtes. Entretiens sur le racisme*, pp. 103–13.
2. Ibid. p. 103.
3. Ibid.

This chapter first appeared in 1980 under the title "L' "amour libre" à Babylone et ses servitudes," in *Le Couple interdit. Entretiens sur le racisme*, under the direction of Léon Poliakov (Paris-The Hague: Mouton), pp. 27–42.

haved in such matters, I have to recall first of all, in a few words and from a great distance, some fundamental parameters of their world vision.

To begin with, on the *social* level they were perhaps not that far removed from us, in the sense that at least in their opinion, as well as traditionally in ours, the best way to assure the regular and optimal propagation of the species, at the same time as its cultural coherence, was the adherence to a family organization, whose framework and stability had marriage as a guarantee, tying together men and women, usually for life.[4] In this very patriarchal society it was the woman who abandoned her own family in order to live and to die in the family of her husband. By law, at least, he was her "owner" (*bêlu*),[5] and because of that she was entirely dependent on him.

Marriage was first of all a type of contract of association with the aim to procreate and to educate the descendants of the family. This contract was regularly concluded and signed without the knowledge of the parties involved, often even before they were marriageable, by the chiefs of the respective families.[6] The procreating purpose of this union was so essential that the sterility of the woman constituted sufficient reason for the husband to repudiate her,[7] at least if she did not provide him with a replacement who would put into the world children that she would consider her own, without changing her position towards her husband in the least.[8]

Hence the marriage was not necessarily monogamous. To the extent that he could afford it, every man was free to add to his principal wife (*ḫîrtu*)—who remained the female head of the family—an entire harem of concubines (*sekertu?; esertu*). These he could allow, according to his liking, to partake in the essential prerogatives of the first wife by granting them, in addition to the name of *spouse* (*aššatu*), all the privileges and obligations in addition to those assigned by law. He was also entirely free to visit periodically other married or unmarried women outside his household.

It is quite clear that a marriage like this presupposed, or created, and maintained a sexual and emotional life, with all its complications, if it was not intended primarily to "satisfy lust" as our theologians would say, or to resolve problems of the heart. We see this in the "Code" of Ḫammurabi where a cheated husband pardons his wife and does not want her to be chastised,[9] or, on the other hand, in the case of the libertine woman who

4. *Annuaire 1963–1964*, pp. 74ff.

5. A. Finet, *Le Code de Ḫammurapi*, §§129, p. 84 and 161, p. 95 (henceforth referred to as *Code*).

6. *Annuaire 1963–1964*, p. 75.

7. *Code* §138, p. 88.

8. Ibid. §§144ff, p. 90, and §§170f, p. 99.

9. Ibid. §129, p. 84.

ruined her husband,[10] or killed him.[11] These difficulties and these storms of married life readily suggest that neither the man, in spite of his concubines and his mistresses, nor the woman, despite the multiple and varied acts of infidelity that she could commit against a marriage contract that was harsh on her account, were always satisfied by their marriage with regard to love.

To prevent them from going to look elsewhere for what matrimony had denied them, there was no help from either the law, or morality, or religion.

The *law* (in the sense given in the last chapter) sought only to preserve the essential conditions of the institution of matrimony. That is to say, it left the man almost entirely free to exercise his amorous capabilities elsewhere if he felt like it, stipulating only that he support his legal family and that he not violate anybody's rights. The law strictly prohibited the woman from doing the same thing, as her excesses could cause grave disorders.[12] I have to say, moreover, that the legal texts allow us to see that in spite of these prohibitions and harsh penalties, the women followed their own desires as much as they do now.

With regard to *morality* (all that could dictate or animate individual behavior in the areas where law did not interfere), its main rule among the Mesopotamians seems to have been to *succeed,* in a positive or a negative way. Good was regarded by everyone as being that which brought the best conditions in life, or at least did not worsen it by setting in motion a "punishment" inflicted by the human or the supernatural authorities. They did not develop any conception resembling the one given to us by Christianity, i.e. that of *sin,* which would have involved some type of conscience in one's innermost heart.[13] And if we hear some mention of a certain pursuit of justice here and there, or even of goodness towards others,[14] we have not yet found the slightest trace of any ascetic or mystical ideal, or of any "personal law" that would have been more demanding than official law, and that would have urged someone to renounce something profitable that others commonly used.

Religion remains. Not only did it not constitute an obstacle on the road to eudaemonism, but undoubtedly it even encouraged it, at least underhandedly. First of all, there was no credence whatsoever in an afterlife where accounts of behavior on earth would be settled. Secondly, even if there were material constraints, and especially prohibitions in the religious

10. *Cuneiform Texts . . . in the British Museum,* 3, pl. 3: *61.*

11. Ibid., 39, pl. 21: *157.*

12. *Annuaire 1963–1964,* pp. 76f.

13. On this subject one can read "Le péché en Mésopotamie ancienne," *Recherches et documents du Centre Thomas More,* no. 43 (1984): 1–16.

14. *Annuaire 1964–1965,* p. 130.

area, they did not form a moral ideal, nor even a simple hierarchy of values of behavior. For instance, the prohibition on urinating or vomiting in a watercourse[15] was placed on the same level as the prohibition on killing someone after having sworn friendship to him.[16] This is because disobeying any of the commandments did not cause necessarily and a priori a punishment by the offended gods. One only had recourse to the gods after the event, a posteriori, to explain a misfortune or an unexpected mishap, which had no apparent reason. "If I am in trouble, it is because I am punished. If I am punished, it is because I *must* have forgotten some obligation or have violated some divine prohibition . . . "[17] Moreover, in these cases there was a way to escape the matter.[18]

On the other hand the gods themselves were numerous and were portrayed in the human image. Thus they had the same material conditions as mankind: they had wives, concubines, and mistresses, and they used their sexual capacities generously and with great cheerfulness. There was even a goddess whose domain was Love in all the meanings of the term, and she soon became foremost and absorbed all the others in her powerful personality: *Inanna/Ištar.** Her excesses were well known in mythology,[19] and several of them were reflected in her cult.[20] Also known, at least in some places, was an entire liturgy of the sacred marriage, the intercourse between a god and a goddess, which was enacted by the ruler and a priestess, perhaps in order to ascertain the fertility of the earth and the herds, and in any case the prosperity of the land.[21] In this tradition there was something that constantly brought up love and its functions, and preserved it, or gave it a naturalism, an ingenuity, and a candor that is for us difficult to imagine.[22]

Thus nothing withheld the ancient Mesopotamians on this path, and little urging was needed for them to give in to their sexual inclinations, which were certainly not less than ours. This is why with *free love* I want to indicate that which was not dammed up, so to speak, by the institution of matrimony, and could be developed in quite unique ways.

15. E. Reiner, *Šurpu: A Collection of Sumerian and Akkadian Incantations*, p. 21: 63. See also *Mythes et rites de Babylone*, pp. 210f.

16. E. Reiner, *Šurpu*, p. 20: 34.

17. See "Le péché en Mésopotamie ancienne," *Recherches et documents du Centre Thomas More*, no. 43 (1984): 1–16.

18. See J. Bottéro, "La magie et la médicine règnent à Babylone," *L'Histoire* 74 (1984).

19. For instance in tablet VI of the *Epic of Gilgameš*, cf. Labat, *Les Religions*, pp. 181ff.

20. *Erra myth*, tablet IV: 52ff., Labat, *Les Religions*, pp. 131ff., and *Mythes et rites de Babylone*, p. 244.

21. See S. N. Kramer, *The Sacred Marriage Rite* (Bloomington and London, 1969).

22. On the practice of love, see "Tout histoire commence à Babylone," *L'Histoire*, no. 63 ("L'amour et la sexualité") (1984): 8–17.

Their attitude is first of all revealed to us by the proven existence of love's "officiants" of both sexes, who were always numerous and ranked in many categories.

For the prostitutes and courtesans of the female sex, we have at least half a dozen different designations of these groups. Some stress their religious character: the *qadištu* were the *consecrated(?)*, and the *istarîtu, devoted to Ištar,* emphasized the links to their divine patroness. We often find organizations of *kulmašîtu,* whose name means nothing to us. The *kezertu* undoubtedly owed their name to their hair style, which was *curled (kezêru)* and apparently designed in order to make them recognizable, if not to allow them to entice their customers. Likewise the word *šamḫatu* seems to allude to a certain luxury in the dress of the ladies that was somewhat flashy or sluttish. The most common term that seems to have indicated the professionals of free love as a group, is *ḫarimtu,* which stresses the fact that they were *apart* from others (*ḫarâmu: to separate*). It is noteworthy that the term is found regularly in connection with the goddess *Ištar,* indicating that they also had her as a standard-bearer and as a model.

These various associations often appeared together in our texts and regularly side by side with the names of persons of the same sex who were more explicitly devoted to the cult: Beguines or hierodules (*nadîtu*) and servants in the liturgy (*entu, ugbabtu,* etc.), as if there were no real distinction between these groups, all more or less covered by the same banner.

We do not have information on the structure and the functioning of such associations. It is not even certain that the *ḫarimtu, šamḫatu,* and *kezertu* at least, really formed socially organized and closed groups. At least we know that any married woman could abandon her household and her husband to *enter in ḫarimûtu,* i.e. to embrace this new state. This does not mean that the *ḫarimtu* were recruited exclusively from the group of women who were tired of marriage. Others, in particular the *ištarîtu,* were perhaps devoted from their early childhood to *Ištar* and to their vocation, which took them away from union with a single man only in order to offer them to all men. Excepting certain classes of oblates who were more strictly reserved for the gods and their cults, and who were forbidden, if not marriage, at least childbearing, the majority of prostitutes could have children and could even marry, but this forced them to give up their first profession at once. If the "wise" discouraged such unions, it was only because they considered these creatures to be badly prepared by their earlier life for the role of a spouse and a mother. But, in law, there was nothing against it, and we have many examples of it.

It is probable that certain prostitutes, if not all of them, often went to sanctuaries, especially those of their protectress *Ištar.* This would account for the story told by Herodotus (I, 199) who seems to have seen so many of them exercising their profession there, that he mistakenly thought they included all the women of the country. They were also found on the streets and in public places. They were easily recognizable by their outfits as well as by the fact that they were forbidden to wear a veil reserved for married women. We see that in the cities they seem to have been consigned to the area of the walls, at least for their residences, if not for their soliciting, as is said of the courtesan Rahab in the biblical book of Joshua (2: 15). But the place where they were most easily found, and used, was the tavern (*bît sâbî, bît sâbîti*) and especially the hostel (*aštammu, bît aštammi*) which served as an inn but also played the role of a village pub, and almost that of a brothel, where one could drink and enjoy oneself to one's heart content.

Except for one or two scenes such as the famous one in the beginning of the *Epic of Gilgameš* where the courtesan makes love to Enkidu, the professional activities of these officiants of free love are nowhere described, as far as I know. However, allusions to it are not rare. Undoubtedly—if we cannot blame it on the accidents of the archeological recovery—the Mesopotamians, who did not hesitate to call a spade a spade, did not feel much like putting this type of detail in writing—in contrast to our contemporaries. The available documents that are the most explicit on sexual behavior itself are twofold. First, we have the one hundred and fourth tablet of a long divinatory treatise on the accidents of daily life (*šumma âlu*), which deduces the fortunes of the interested party from his sexual practices.[23] Second, we have a group of prayers with "sacramental" procedures ("incantations") that were recited and used by women who wanted to see their sexual partners "hold strong to the very end" in order to obtain from them without "failure" all the pleasure that they had the right to expect from them (*nîš libbi*).[24] In these texts the female partner is usually called *the woman (sinništu)*, not *the wife (aššatu)*, and it is clear that their use was not limited to married couples. Thus we can also get an idea of the work of public women through them. The same has to be said of a certain number of clay figurines where lovers in the midst of sexual intercourse are represented, lying down or standing.[25] Among the latter, at least those figurines where the woman is sodomized while she is drinking beer through a long reed-pipe from a jar, as was the custom in those days, clearly reflect the pleasures of the "hostel" rather than those of the conjugal bed.

Prostitutes, cinedes*, and sexual inverts of the male sex are also known to us, even though some of our bashful or prudish lexicographers have made a habit of seeing in them whatever they wish, including "priests" or "actors,"

23. *Cuneiform Texts . . . in the British Museum*, 39, pl. 44f.
24. R. D. Biggs, *ŠÀ.ZI.GA, Ancient Mesopotamian Potency Incantations.*
25. Catalogued in *Reallexikon der Assyriologie*, 4, pp. 259f. (Heilige Hochzeit).

instead of what they very clearly were. They also seem to have become grouped, if not in organized guilds of which we do not know anything, at least in various categories whose best-known names: *assinnu, kurgarru, kulu'u* do not tell us much.[26] What is very clear on the other hand, is that they were always considered to play a passive role in homosexual love. They were also considered to be *effeminate (sinnišânu),* a qualification to which we will later return. We know of some of them who even had women's names!

Still, there is nothing that shows us that they were necessarily eunuchs, or physically deformed and asexual from birth. That was probably true for a number of them, but others had children who were not necessarily adopted, and they could engage in their careers without any apparent preliminary intervention.

These people were also largely connected to *Ištar,* in whose honor they played the roles of singers, transvestites, mimics, and standard-bearers in certain ceremonies. This allowed them to partake in "abominations" (*asakku*),[27] in other words behavior that is forbidden to common mortals, in order *to delight the heart of the patroness.*

We do not have any more details on their professional activities, but a few reliefs,[28] similar to those mentioned above, contain the image of a sodomized man, who is also busy drinking through a reed-pipe, and doubtless in the same environment of the *aštammu.* Every detail of the posture is moreover described on the divinatory tablet that depicts sexual activities. We see there also that a master of the house could use his servants, who do not seem to have been professional prostitutes, as catamites.* This is somewhat similar to going outside marriage for heterosexual love without having to use a prostitute. The *Middle Assyrian "Laws"*[29] make reference to such interactions between *people of the same milieu.* Hence, it was not necessarily the job of servants.

There is nothing that allows us to think that these homosexual relations were condemned in the least, or even simply considered to be, as such, more ignominious than heterosexual relations, or that they would be discouraged—provided that both types of intercourse did not involve violence. Moreover, this is still the case today in several countries, notably in Africa and Asia. The perfectly natural character is best revealed by the title of certain "incantations," prayers that were addressed to the gods *in order to* (ascertain the success of) *the love of a man for a woman, of a woman for a*

26. See the article "Homosexualität" (in French—only the title is in German) in *Reallexikon* 4, pp. 459ff.

27. *Erra myth,* 4: 55ff.

28. "Homosexualität," p. 460.

29. Tablet A, §20 in G. Cardascia, *Les Lois assyriennes,* pp. 133ff., also "Homosexualität," pp. 461f.

man, and of a man for a man.[30] The omission of the expected parallel *of a woman for a woman* does not indicate that female homosexuality was condemned or unknown. We have at least one record of it,[31] and I have been told that there is a still more explicit one in the Berlin Museum that remains unpublished.

In any case, I have to add that at a cursory view, and if we can appeal at least *grosso modo* to statistics, our documentation seems to make clear that homosexuality held in the lives and especially in the preoccupations of the ancient Mesopotamians a secondary place, much less important in any case than heterosexuality. Some negative signs circumspectly confirm this thesis: pederasty seems never to have had an existence outside homosexuality properly speaking, and I do not know of any explicit examples. Also there does not seem to have been any interest in the androgynous figure, which was unknown, and in mythology and theology we have not the slightest certain example of homosexual relations between gods.

How did the Babylonians judge this free love which they did not consider infamous at all, as we saw, and which they seemingly practiced without remorse or scruples, even with cheerfulness? They seem not only to have tolerated it, nor only to have encouraged it, but to have valued it highly and even to have deemed it to be one of the prerogatives of their life, one of the great conquests of what they considered to be *real* civilization, i.e. their civilization.

This is clearly shown by one of the myths that they developed with regard to the latter. They had thought about their civilization and had even exerted themselves to analyze it in its principal expressions and virtualities, of which they had finally drawn up a list of a little more than one hundred entries. This list appears in a Sumerian myth called *Inanna and Enki,*[32] which was put down in writing in the first third of the second millennium. In it we see that the goddess *Inanna (Ištar),* whose domain was the city of Uruk*, had decided to give to her city the high culture developed by the god Enki.* He had outlined this culture in some one hundred articles, which were carefully listed. Thus she went to *Enki* in his southern city of Eridu*, and as he became slightly drunk during a banquet in her honor, she was able to take his treasure away from him. In the catalogue of this treasure, next to Royal Power, Family Life, Agriculture, Animal Husbandry, "Industry" and its various techniques and products, Arts, Exorcism—to chase away evil, and Writing, not only is Sexual Trade found, but also

30. *Mythes et rites de Babylone,* pp. 104f.

31. "Homosexualität," p. 468.

32. G. Farber-Flügge, *Der Mythos "Inanna und Enki."* For a summary, see below, pp. 237f.

Prostitution, both feminine and masculine, listed in three or four entries. Thus this institution represented in the minds of the authors and the readers of the myth a real acquisition of high culture, an aspect of progress, an improvement, an "invention" developed to make life easier, more enjoyable, and merrier.

A famous episode found on the first two tablets of the *Epic of Gilgameš* reinforces such an impression. In it is explained[33] how Enkidu, the wild man of the steppe, hairy and barbarous, only intimate with animals and living a life like them, *becomes a man* in the full sense of the word (*awîlu*): a civilized man, a city-man who eats bread, drinks beer, and grooms and dresses himself. This transformation is the work of a courtesan from Uruk who came to look for him in the steppe and who introduced him to love; hence, not simple intercourse with a female, but love with a real woman, human and refined love, i.e. *free love.* Once he had discovered it and had acquired a taste for it, Enkidu could only follow his teacher *to the city,* where she taught him to eat, drink, and dress, and where she completed his transformation. Thus free love is presented as being the point of access to a life that is truly cultural and human. It is difficult to better indicate and reveal its worth and its importance.

This importance and worth were doubtless a result of the fact that free love was the only way to express love itself, in its pure and noble form, according to the ancient Babylonians. In marriage, love was seen as being used only for a preset goal, and as subservient to family life in a sense. That is why free love among them was really free. It was practiced without constraints and joyously, promoted by all imaginable "specialists," encouraged by the gods without the least juridical, moral, or religious restriction—provided only that it did not involve any violence or disorder. It was an activity as normal and sane as was eating and drinking. And, as with eating and drinking, when it surpassed simple natural satisfaction in order to strive for the exquisite, the refined, and the artistic, it was a noble activity, worthy of admiration and emulation, and very suitable for being counted among the most advantageous conquests of the civilizing genius.

However, it was not entirely free of what I have called *disadvantages,* let us say counterweights, obstacles, shadows. What is quite unexpected to us is that these inconveniences did not apply at all to its occasional or habitual users, but only to its specialized personnel, both male and female. To give oneself to free love in whatever form was a wholesome, elevated, and enriching activity. But to make a profession of it exposed someone to certain disadvantages. Which ones? And why?

They are explained to us twice, in two different literary works, and in passages that are clearly etiological, i.e. intended to account for a certain

33. *Gilgameš* I/iv: *16ff.*, in R. Labat, *Les Religions*, pp. 152ff.

situation that was considered to be problematic, by recourse to a mythological* explanation. In the two passages the explanation is redacted in terms that are in essence almost identical, as if one of the accounts more or less plagiarized the other. However, we do not know which one was the earlier.

One of them deals with *female prostitutes.* It appears in tablet VII of the *Epic of Gilgameš.*[34] It is still Enkidu who takes center stage. After he had been "civilized" by the courtesan of Uruk, he became the friend of the king of that city, Gilgameš, and the companion of his adventures in the mysterious cedar forest and against the terrifying great Bull sent to destroy the same city. Now he is about to die before his powerless friend. He turns to his past to rail against anything that brought him to this premature end. He curses the woman who had taken him from his steppe and had "civilized" him:

> 6. Come now, courtesan, I am going to decree your destiny . . .
> I will curse you with a great curse . . .
>
> 10. Never will you be able to make a happy household . . .
>
> 12. Never will you dwell in a harem,
> The dregs of beer will stain your beautiful breast,
> With his vomit the drunk will splash your attire . . .
>
> 20. You will live in solitude,
> the recesses of the city wall will be your place to stand,
> thorns and briars will rip your feet,
> drunks and the thirsty will slap your cheeks . . .

The term *destiny* (to which we will come back in a moment) in the beginning of this tirade gives it its entire meaning: it does not involve the individual fate of the girl who has taught Enkidu love, but of *all* courtesans, *all* prostitutes as such, whose way of living is here summarized, and then related to destiny as its cause; in other words to the will of the gods, provoked by the curse of Enkidu. We see that their lives were sad. A woman professionally devoted to free love did not have her own household. She was exposed to the brutality of men. She lived separately, pushed into the fringes of the social space occupied by the city's inhabitants.

Male prostitution was not better treated, as is shown by another passage in the mythological story of *The Descent of Ištar in the Netherworld** in Akkadian.[35] It involves a person who is clearly the prototype of all of them, after *Ea** had "invented" and "programmed" him to go and entertain the ruthless queen of the Netherworld, *Ereškigal**, and thus obtain the

34. *Gilgameš* VII/iii: *6ff.*, R. Labat, *Les Religions*, pp. 190.
35. *103ff.* = rev. *11ff.*, in R. Labat, *Les Religions*, pp. 263ff.

freedom of her prisoner *Ištar,* who had imprudently ventured into the Land-of-No-Return. This sexual invert who bears the programmatic name *Âṣu-šu-namir (Pleasant-is-his-appearance = He-is-good-looking)* succeeds in his mission. But *Ereškigal,* furious to have been fooled by him, curses him:

103. Come now, Âṣušunamir, I am going to decree you an
 unalterable destiny.
 I will curse you with a great curse!
 You will have as allowance nothing but the products of the
 "city-carts"

105. and for drink what comes out of the city's gutters.
 The recesses of the city wall will be your place to stand,
 you will sleep on doorsills,
 drunks and the thirsty will slap your cheeks.

Thus Âṣušunamir and all male professionals of free love whose prototype he is, are devoted to a very painful, uncertain, and isolated life, as are the public women. Like the women, they are marginals; like them, they are the objects of disdain and coolness.

These were for the ancient Mesopotamians the "disadvantages" of free love. As we can see, these disadvantages did not apply to the mass of people who made use of free love without any ignominy or any other inconvenience. They applied exclusively to those who practiced it *ex professo,* in the service of others, and who were condemned to a difficult existence, disgraced and in solitude.

Thus there is a contradiction between the high esteem in which free love was held as an ornament of civilization and the type of disdain that was imposed upon its representatives. Can *we* explain it? The ancient people were very careful not to do so themselves, at least in the abundant literature that remains to us.

It would be wrong to seek recourse in a "moral" appreciation, as we have seen that there is no basis for that. When a "wise man" urges his son not to take a prostitute as a wife, he does not bring up her supposed "immorality," her presumed debased, perverted, or vicious character, but only the fact that her life-style has not prepared her to become a wife, the confidential support of a single man:[36]

72. Do not take a *ḫarimtu* as wife, for whom "husbands" do not
 count,
 nor an *ištarîtu* reserved to the god,
 nor a *kulmašîtu* with numerous hearts(?).

36. W. G. Lambert, *Babylonian Wisdom Literature,* pp. 102f.: *72ff.*

75. In bad times they will not help you,
In adversity they will make fun of you,
They do not know respect and submission.

The low, humiliated, and marginal life of the representatives of free love was not the result of hypocritical reprobation by others but of elements of an entirely different order. It is my opinion that it was entirely dependent on the important notion of *destiny,* in the very center of the theological and theocentric views of the ancient Mesopotamians. They thought that the gods had created the universe as an enormous mechanism whose purpose was to guarantee the production and transformation of goods intended primarily for the gods themselves, in order to assure them an opulent life, without work or worries. The destiny of each of the component parts of the universe organized in this way, starting with the destiny of mankind, the mainspring of the universe, was entirely up to the will of the gods. We would call this destiny nowadays a programming, i.e. a perfect adaptation to a role in a balanced system. That system was complicated but coherent, and in it all wheels were adjusted and fitted to guarantee the good functioning of the entire mechanism.

In this framework the destiny of a woman, as woman, was to bear and raise children according to the chosen model of marriage and the patriarchal family. Thus she was made to become the spouse of a single man, and the mother of his children. On the other hand, a prostitute, as stated literally in the text I have translated above, and by adapting the wording slightly, had *three thousand six hundred "husbands."* In the decimo-sexagesimal system of the Mesopotamians, that is the same as our thirty-six thousand, indicating the countless. She was the woman of all men, and hence she was unable to assure the progeny of any one of them and to take care of his family. Thus in her aspect as prostitute she had missed her destiny. She was not "normal," but inferior to herself. This is why her life could only be debased, separate from that of other women.

With regard to the man who was sexually inverted, not occasionally but as a state and "by nature" in a sense, he also had missed his "duty," as he was essentially made in a masculine form and hence intended to take his place as a male and his role as a procreator. But he was *effeminate,* he played the role of a female, therefore he had gone astray and had become sterile. Thus, he was also inferior to himself, abnormal and devoted to an existence that was different from that of other men, more difficult and less magnificent.

We have some proof that this difference and the inferiority of the life of the officiants of free love was indeed a matter of *destiny.* We should not imagine that for the theologians of Babylon "missing one's destiny" was regarded as a type of revolt, a unilateral withdrawal from the all-powerful will of the directors of the universe. For those who strayed from their path the gods were considered to have taken special decisions, that arose not from their specific fate but from their individual destiny. This is why in the Sumerian myth *Enki and Ninmaḫ*,[37] when allusion is made to the case of sexual inverts by birth—asexuals, neither male nor female—as well as to sterile women, who were unable to put children in the world, the ingenious and engineering Enki could find in the cosmic machine a place for them where they could function in their own way—let us say according to their own destiny: the sterile women among the prostitutes, and the asexual by birth among the transvestites in the royal court. We also know that for those who had lost their virility in an accident, particularly on the battlefield, the misfortune was blamed on the vindicative will of Ištar.[38] Thus it is really on the level of destiny, of the conformity with the will, the plans, and the decisions of the gods, that matters were going on. Moreover, this is the only explanation fitting the Babylonian world-vision.

Under these conditions the rejection and the isolation of prostitutes of both sexes in Mesopotamia was not a condemnation, of whatever kind, by other people, but a conclusion that is in some sense ontological. As they had left their first *destiny* by their deviant life-style, they had placed themselves—or better, they had been placed by the gods who had assigned them this unique fate—in an orbit parallel with and on the periphery of that of others. This fits well with the assigning to male and female prostitutes (as for Rahab, the Canaanite prostitute of Jericho, mentioned above) a residence *in the recesses of the city walls*, i.e. on the borders of the social and civilized space occupied by others, by those who functioned properly according to their initial and "normal" destiny.

There is perhaps another point that has to be taken into account, as nothing is ever simple or straightforward in human affairs. I will mention it in a few words, as conclusion. In this area, on the edge of social and civilized life, public women and sexual inverts were in the company of other marginals, whose names appear several times next to theirs in certain lists: on the one hand sorcerers, and witches in particular,[39] and on the other hand "lunatics" and eccentrics, who were considered to be ecstatics, visionaries, and, in the etymological sense of the word, demoniacs.[40] This entire world has in common that it found itself in regular contact with supernatural forces. Sorcerers held mysteriously to their magic and evil spells, which they could

37. C. A. Benito, *Enki and Ninmaḫ*, summarized below, pp. 232f.

38. See p. 466b of the article "Homosexualität," cited above, n. 27.

39. For instance, G. Meier, *Die assyrische Beschwörungssammlung Maqlû*, p. 23, III, 40ff.

40. For instance, *Cuneiform Texts . . . in the British Museum*, 38, pl. 4: 76–78, etc.

cast upon men, thus bringing them bad luck. The ecstatics were considered to hold divine warnings and messages which they were ordered to publicize. Such powers had their source in some type of superhuman force. They presupposed contact with a force, a vitality, an intensity of being that was far above the possibilities granted to common mortals. One was at the same time fascinated by these people but kept them out of the way as much as possible.

In the same way the officiants of free love, the *ex professo* dispensers of love, were seemingly considered to be holders of the latter, i.e. of a type of paroxysmal life. This is doubtless why they were treated as other marginals and that one could have only an ambiguous and contradictory attitude towards them, as vis-à-vis the superhuman forces that they represented in their own way. All that is paroxysmal is ambivalent. It is admirable and desirable for its riches as well as dangerous, alarming, and to be avoided as much as possible, for its force that is too great.

In this way, in spite of the contempt in which its qualified representatives were held, and in spite of their separation from others, we can rediscover the eminent dignity of free love, in other words of love itself, in the minds of the ancient Babylonians.

IV

"THE GODS": RELIGION

12

The Religious System

THIS ANCIENT COUNTRY, WHOSE OLDEST DECIPHERABLE DOCUments go back in time to the beginning of the third millennium, and whose history continued uninterrupted to just before the Christian era, has the opportunity of revealing to us—as does Egypt of the Pharaohs—the oldest perceptible reactions and reflections of mankind on the supernatural, the oldest identifiable religious structure, that at the same time can be followed for the longest period of time. But, in contrast to ancient Egypt, the indirect but genealogical connections of the ancient Mesopotamian civilization with ours are now recognized, although we are far from paying proper attention to them. Hence, this religion also gives us the oldest verifiable stage of *our* religious thoughts and practices, the first recognizable source of our religiosity in the remoteness of time. For those who have not forgotten that one needs to know whence one comes to understand oneself better, there should be some interest in obtaining at least a summary idea of this religion. Although, taking into account the state of our documentation, many nooks are still dark to us and a number of insoluble problems still remain, we know enough of Mesopotamian religion[1] to discover in it, perhaps to our amazement, a structure that is not only impressive but also coherent and "logical," a real *system* perfectly joined to the other system that was the local civilization.

1. The fad introduced by L. Oppenheim (*Ancient Mesopotamia*, pp. 171ff.) and accepted here and there with some cheers, of asserting that it would be impossible to write a history of ancient Mesopotamian religion, or even to recognize it clearly, did not last long, fortunately. The specific arguments of his feigned agnosticism, which could moreover be logically applied to all other cultural aspects of that country and many others, were too clearly contradicted by his book itself, and by the other works of that learned author.

In order to study with more intelligence and acuteness this vast and confused subject of the religious complex, whatever that may have been, it is indispensable to better define at first both its *nature* and its *state*.

WHAT IS A RELIGION?

What impresses us at first in every religion is its "political" aspect or, as is commonly said today: religion presents itself at first sight to the observer as an ensemble of representations and of collective behavior, that controls an entire social group with regard to its relations to a universe considered to be superimposed on ours. It is also usually approached from this point of view. I am, however, not certain that this is the best way, the way that has some possibility of opening up to us the most far-reaching and profound insights. Even if every religion is by all indications a phenomenon of society; even if as such it models and modifies the reactions of the individuals that make up the society, what remains as the objective and real tools of research are the reactions of the individuals, as is true for anything that we can say about mankind. The ancient scholastics already said very wisely: *Multitudo sine multis non est nisi in ratione*. This is why I prefer to bypass social issues, without, of course denying their existence, to identify religion first of all among the individuals who practice it. It is well understood that each of these individuals realizes in his own way and personal circumstances the definition of religion, whatever that may be, just like each exposes in his own way the nature of mankind, without the latter ever losing its fundamental characteristics. But any ontological analysis has to abide by the essence of things and by what is called the "order of nature," abstracting from its existential and material manifestations and from its evolution in space and time.

It is perhaps easier to understand what religion is in this respect, if we compare it to love. Love is based above all on the feelings that draw us strongly towards another individual of the same species, in whom we imagine, in more or less obscure ways, a complement and an enrichment of our personality and our life. When we are oriented towards the other individual, love urges us first of all (speaking always, as noted above, "according to the order of nature" and not "according to the order of time") to know that individual better, in whatever way such a knowledge can be realized. Thus we adopt towards that individual an attitude that represents the image we have of him as well as the emotions that inspire that image, in terms of what ties us to him and of the image we have made of him.

Religion follows a similar road, although it is oriented differently. It is based on another instinctive and deep sentiment, in a direction that is not "horizontal," if we can use that expression, as for love, but "vertical": not towards something that is around us, but towards something that is above us. We have a confused feeling that there exists an order of things that is entirely superior to us, and to all that surrounds us here on earth. We feel an inclination to submit ourselves to this order, or we feel urged to orient ourselves to it if we want to fulfill ourselves. This "order of things" is what is called, in this context, the supernatural, the sacred, the numinous. And what ties us to it, be it admiration and attraction, or fear and retreat, is the *religious sentiment.* Such an impression of the sacred, however obscure it may be, naturally urges us to seek to identify it better, to define it better. And as it is not of our world, as such, and thus is not directly or indirectly perceptible, we are urged to represent it by constructing an entire association of images and ideas about it, i.e. a *religious ideology.* Religious sentiment and religious ideology, combined, dictate to us a *religious behavior* towards it, to the extent that we experience it and to the extent that we think we know it. These are the three distinct but inseparable elements that define religion and that we can rediscover in any religion.

THE STATE OF MESOPOTAMIAN RELIGION

But when we consider Mesopotamian religion, it is better to first free ourselves of all that would lead us to imagine it to be similar to the great religious systems with which we are nowadays most often confronted: Judaism, Christianity, Islam, and even Buddhism, to mention just the largest ones. Similar to most other religions around the world, from antiquity and from today, Mesopotamian religion was not "historical" but "primitive." It was not founded at some specific moment in its history by a powerful religious mind who was able to impose his religion on those around him, and who could spread and institutionalize his own feelings towards the sacred. Mesopotamian religion was the product of communal reactions towards the same sacred in the darkness of prehistory. The inhabitants of the country had been able to derive religion from the viewpoint, the sensibility, and the mentality peculiar to their traditional culture. In short, their religion only adapted their native habits of thinking, feeling, and living to the supernatural. This is why the religion in reality represents nothing but a vision pointed to the world above of this civilization. Hence, the religion was perfectly joined with the civilization and confused with it, both in its origins and in its developments and changes over time.

A SHORT HISTORY OF THE CULTURAL DEVELOPMENT OF MESOPOTAMIA

Thus, it will be good to draw the outlines both of the history of ancient Mesopotamia and of the formation and the advances of its culture, before entering upon the religious domain properly speaking, in order to clarify the latter better. It involves the country that covered more or less the territory of present-day Iraq. This region "Between-the-Two-Rivers," i.e. the Tigris and the Euphrates, emerged only gradually and rather late, starting in the sixth/fifth millennium. Of the first populations that occupied it we have nothing but archeological remains, and thus we do not know much about them. We can scarcely guess the role that they could have played in the prehistory of the region and in the establishment of its culture. Only one element of these people is known to us from later information: it consists of Semites* who came from the northern and northeastern fringes of the great Syro-Arabian desert, where they seem to have been from the beginning of time seminomadic and raisers of sheep and goats. At the latest, from the early fourth millennium on they infiltrated and settled in Mesopotamia, especially in the north and the center, and they gradually moved further south. We think that another population arrived in the course of the same millennium, either from the east or from the southeast (from along the Iranian coast on the Persian Gulf). These people settled in the very south of the country, and little by little spread out further north, meeting the Semites. We call them Sumerians.* In contrast to the Semites, who always maintained contact with their relatives who had stayed in the area of origin, and who constantly received new blood from throughout their history, the Sumerians, according to all indications, seem to have burned all bridges with their point of departure, and they seem never to have received the least ethnic support from that area.

As far as we know, these two cultural groups formed the principal elements of the population of the country from before the beginning of history, and together they created their common high civilization, by a process of symbiosis and osmosis. Each supplied its own culture and spoke its own language. The language of the Semites (which would later be called "Akkadian"* in Mesopotamia) was related to the more recent Hebrew, Aramaic, and Arabic; that of the Sumerians was as different from Akkadian as Chinese is from French, and we are unable to relate it to any other known language family. The two populations were doubtless originally juxtaposed, each in its own territory, but they met, interacted, and mixed rather quickly, and, so to say, put together their cultural capital. At the latest, from the second half of the fourth millennium on they built together an original civilization. It was rich, refined, and complex, and culminated around the year 3000 in the discovery of writing. We have good reason to think that the script was invented *for* the Sumerian language, and therefore *by* the people who spoke the language. This element together with others, convinces us that in this impressive common cultural construction the Sumerians were at first the most gifted, the most active, and the most inventive.

In a country of mud and clay, almost entirely deprived of wood for construction, of stone, and of metals, such a civilization could economically speaking be based only on the husbandry of sheep and goats, and even better, on the agricultural exploitation of alluvial soil that is potentially rich, especially for cereal production. In any case, in a climate that is so sunny and dry (the rainy season is practically limited to the period from December to February), productivity could be guaranteed and developed only by recourse to artificial irrigation. For that purpose it was decided very soon that more ramified and more numerous canals had to be derived from the two rivers. Soon these canals crisscrossed a large part of the territory, thus ensuring the constant moisture indispensable for the sustained output of fields and gardens. Furnished in this way with voluminous and increasing surpluses that could be exported, the Mesopotamians turned their attention towards the neighboring regions, principally to the east and to the south along the two coastlines of the Persian Gulf,[2] to start an intensive trade and to import the stone, minerals, and all those things for which they felt an increasing need in order to assure an existence that was becoming more and more hard to please.

It is this type of economy that directed the political evolution of the country. Not only did the commercial expeditions abroad, which were easily transformed into raids or even into wars, have to be organized and led, but the large enterprises of digging kilometer-long canals, especially, required the mobilization of the people and of their concerted efforts, as well as the authority of a single chief who was capable of conceiving, imposing, and directing such a concentration. This is why the primitive villages that are revealed to us by the archeological excavations, which were at first isolated and almost autarkic, soon allied themselves into small "states" centered each around a town. There the sole holder of authority resided, with an always growing body of "vicars" and officers around him. This was the administrative apparatus, and it included specialists in works of production and transformation that were less directly related to animal husbandry and to agriculture. Thus was born and soon implanted in the country the fundamental political principle that would rule its entire history, that of monarchy, a "pyramidal" monarchy whose head imparted his power from the top to subalternate authorities of decreasing power.

During a large part of the third millennium these city-states,* as they are usually called, lived side by side and on a basis of collective understanding with their populations, in some places mainly Sumerian, in other places mainly "Akkadian," but becoming more and more mixed, evidently conscious of their profound cultural unity. They were sometimes troubled by hostilities that were usually provoked by conflicts of interest. It happened nevertheless that one or the other of them, more ambitious, more power-

2. It seems that only later, after the middle of the third millennium, they went to the northwest, to Lebanon and to Anatolia.

ful, or more daring because of the personality of its ruler, made itself master of a number of other city-states in the area, and thus formed kingdoms of various importance—even empires, when the conquests extended further and went beyond the traditional limits of the country—but all of them were more or less ephemeral in nature.

Starting from the beginning of the second millennium things changed in at least two ways. First, the Sumerians were definitively absorbed by the Semitic segment of society that was more numerous and more vigorous, and they disappeared forever. Nothing but Semites remained in the country, and the only official and daily language was theirs, Akkadian. But they had been so strongly influenced by the ancient intellectual preponderance of the Sumerians that the Sumerian language, a dead language, remained in use until the very end of their history as the language of culture: for liturgy, literature, and scholarship, somewhat like Latin until the Renaissance in Western Europe.

Another important mutation was that the era of juxtaposed, but more or less confederated, city-states had ended. Starting with Ḫammurabi* (around 1750) the entire country was united in a single kingdom under the authority of the monarch of Babylon, single kingdom under the authority of the monarch of Babylon, this time without returning to the old system. Some centuries later the northern part, Assyria,* cut loose from this kingdom and the center of gravity oscillated between its successive capital cities (Assur,* Kalḫu,* and Nineveh*) and Babylon, until the destruction of Nineveh by the Babylonian king Nabopolassar in the year 609. In 539 Babylon itself was destroyed by the Achaemenid king Cyrus. Henceforth, Babylon became a simple province, first of the Persian empire; then, after Alexander the Great (330), of the Seleucid kingdom.

An eloquent sign of the important changes, not only politically but also ethnically and consequently culturally, which would lead to the ultimate demise of the venerable Mesopotamian civilization, was that around the middle of the first millennium Akkadian lost its role as the language of daily life, as had happened to Sumerian before, and was replaced in that role by another Semitic language that had been imported by more recent invaders: Aramaic. Akkadian is not used anymore, nor its always formidable cuneiform script—which had been replaced everywhere else by the alphabet derived from Phoenician—except in increasingly isolated circles and restricted to literati, priests, and scholars. The last document written in that language and in that script dates from the year 74 of the Christian era, and it is an astronomical text.

This is the historical outline, the cultural and political framework in which Mesopotamian religion appeared and developed, profoundly marked and modeled by that framework.

SOURCES FOR OUR KNOWLEDGE OF THE RELIGION

It is indispensable that we first say a few words about the *sources* that inform us about the religion. Those revealed by archeology—which we refer to in the broader sense as the "monuments" fabricated by man—are countless in number. The ancient soil of Iraq and the Middle East has been dug so much for one hundred and fifty years—and continues to be dug—that we know its riches: cities, temples, statues, images, and a prodigious warehouse of remains and utensils of all types. Whether they are intact or, as is most often the case, in ruin, these "monuments" are precious because they give us the actuality of what they represent. But they are not very talkative, and if we make them speak they are only able to respond to a questionnaire that is very limited in comparison to the matters of the mind that mainly interest us here.

What remains are the "documents," the written sources that are infinitely less equivocal, more detailed, more precise, and much more in a position to satisfy our curiosity as historians. A good half a million at least have been found, and our treasure grows with the smallest excavation. In a period and a society where the supernatural kept close to the world and penetrated it throughout, and where the entirety of life was steeped in religion, much more than in our "disenchanted" and rational (if not rationalistic) minds, we can say that the enormous mass of documentation is almost in its entirety, directly or indirectly, exploitable for a knowledge of the religious universe. A quite substantial portion deals directly with it: hymns and prayers that represent the religious sentiment more immediately; myths and diverse "manuals" of the religious ideology often in a mythological form; rituals that allow us to become familiar with religious behavior and the cult—not counting the numerous works that cut across categories.

The only thing that we have no chance of finding is exactly that which provides the strongest foundation of the "historic" religions: the "sacred writings" derived directly or indirectly from the Founder to which the faithful constantly refer in order to rule and regulate, to define and correct the thoughts and the behavior of each and everyone according to the founder's wishes. Such normative writings and inconceivable in a "primitive religion" which is a simple product of the traditional culture and which stagnates or evolves like this culture, according to the current of events. There is not a single, more or less "dogmatic," collection to define the religion exactly for us. Thus we have to reconstruct this religion from whatever appears about it in our dossier, regardless of whether it is explicitly religious or not. At first glance this dossier with its tens of thousands of documents looks gigantic, and it can indeed supply us generously and reconstruct for us a real portrait of Mesopotamian religion. However, this religion survived for more than three millennia, and precisely because of this extraordinary time-span the dossier is relatively small. We have to rely on it for many details over the sequence of different time-periods and the division in various areas, and even for some major problems, despite lacunae and silences that are of various lengths and without remedy.

When discussing the written documentation, there is another inconvenience that we have to take into account for Mesopotamia. Considering the notorious difficulties and subtleties of the graphic system, and undoubtedly also because of a traditional choice, the related activities of reading and writing were considered a real profession, reserved for a socially very restricted group of people who prepared themselves by long and arduous studies. Hence one could think (and many have done so) that these documents put down in writing and legible only by the literate, reproduce their own religious conceptions and habits but not those of the rest of the population, whether of higher or of lower class, because they were all illiterate. Such a hypothesis, presented in this way, is absurd. It presupposes that the keepers of writing were sequestered in their own circles and were entirely isolated from the rest of their contemporaries. We also have evidence that contradicts this hypothesis. The sanctuaries, for example, were public, even if it was mostly "clergy" who visited them for professional reasons; the common religious spirit is explicitly transparent in the documents that show the life of everyone, not only of the scribes and copyists, as do the letters and many of the administrative "papers." Also, in the sources, the personal names, which in Mesopotamia usually consisted of types of exclamations or theocentric affirmations, confirm for us that the religious sentiments, the ideology, and the behavior did not change substantially from the *majores* to the *minores*, taking into account of course, as everywhere else, the differences of culture, education, preoccupations, and life-styles, which by necessity create distinctions in religious life as they do in spiritual life. It is really the religion common to the ancient Mesopotamians that we find represented in the ancient documents.

THE RELIGIOUS SENTIMENT

Finally, let us begin our topic by examining an idea of the type of religious sentiment that directed the sincere attitudes of men towards the sacred. As with the other elements of religion, we can review this idea only broadly, covering with a panoramic glance both the entire country and its millennia-long history, and taking into account the great events of history only where they are disclosed.

Some extracts from the literature of hymns and prayers will be more useful than long discussions and they will give us a stronger and more deeply felt idea of the religious outlook that inspired these ancient people before a supernatural world that was represented by a certain number of personalities, as we will see later.

Here is a passage from a liturgical poem, composed in Sumerian, at the latest near the end of the third millennium, in honor of the god Enlil,* who was then considered to be the ruler of gods and men:

1. Enlil! his authority is far-reaching
 his word is sublime and holy.
His decisions are unalterable
 he decides fates forever!
His eyes scrutinize the entire world!
5. When the honorable Enlil sits down in majesty
 on his sacred and sublime throne,
when he exercises with perfection
 his power as Lord and King
Spontaneously the other gods prostrate before him
and obey his orders without protest!
10. He is the great and powerful ruler
who dominates Heaven and Earth
Who knows all and understands all![3]

Here is another taken from a prayer whose text in Akkadian could date from the end of the second millennium. This time it is addressed to another god who was ruler in that period: *Marduk*:*

6. Lord Marduk, Supreme god, with
 unsurpassed wisdom. . . .
8. When you leave for battle the Heavens shake,
when you raise your voice, the Sea is wild!
10. When you brandish your sword, the gods turn back.
There is none who can resist your furious blow!
Terrifying lord, in the Assembly of the gods no one equals you!
You proceed in the brilliant blue, entirely glorious. . . .
15. Your weapons flare in the tempest!
Your flame annihilates the steepest mountain.
Your raise the waves of the Sea in fury. . . .[4]

Perhaps somewhat later is the hymn to the sun god Šamaš,* also in Akkadian. Here is a passage from it:

1. Šamaš, illuminator of the entire heaven, who lightens the
 darkness
 shepherd in upper and lower regions! . . . .

3. A. Falkenstein, *Sumerische Götterlieder,* 1, pp. 11ff.
4. E. Ebeling, *Die akkadische Gebetsserie "Handerhebung,"* pp. 94ff.: K. 3351.

5. Your beams like a net cover the earth
you brighten the gloom of the farthest away mountains!
At your appearance the gods and the demons rejoice,
and the Igigi* exult in your presence!
Your rays grasp everything that is hidden,
10. and the behavior of humans is revealed by your light! . . . .
All beings seek out your splendor;
you brighten the universe like an immense fire. . . .
Your glory covers the faraway mountains,
20. Your fierce light fills the lands to their limits!
Perched on the highest mountains you inspect the world
and, from the midst of heaven, you balance the universe. . . .
25. You shepherd all living beings;
to the upper and the lower regions you are the only shepherd.
Regularly and without cease you traverse the heavens.
Every day you pass over the broad earth.
The flood of the sea, the mountain ranges, the earth. . . .
30. Endlessly you pass over the vast sea. . . .
39. You draw in like a cord, you shroud everything like a fog.
Your large canopy covers the universe. . . .[5]

We could cite many more examples; they all reflect the same feelings of admiration, of respect, and of fear—in fact of a certain transcendence. These feelings seem sometimes to be exclusively directed to the god who is addressed *hic et nunc*, as a normal result of the religious psyche. But all of them are considered to be sublime beings, above all dominant and imposing. Before them one bows down, one trembles. Yes, they are merciful, and that is why they are flattered and implored, because it is known that they can do everything. They are especially perceived as being lords and masters: one submits to them. But one is not attracted to them, one does not love them. Religion in Mesopotamia never has anything that is attractive, that one wants to approach, that one has to assimilate as much as possible. In short, one feels before the god the same sentiments that animate the humblest subjects before their ruler, and before the high and mighty persons that participate in his power, with all proportions maintained.

The same image, transposed from the political authority on earth, also directs the religious ideology in Mesopotamia, as we shall see; moreover, it influences all religious behavior.

5. W. G. Lambert, *Babylonian Wisdom Literature*, pp. 126ff; J. Seux, *Hymnes et prières aux dieux de Babylonie et d'Assyrie*, pp. 51ff.

POLYTHEISM AND ANTHROPOMORPHISM

In order to represent the supernatural, the sacred, the object of their religious sentiments, the ancient Mesopotamians could not find anything better than to spread it over a number of personalities—they were bold *polytheists*—which they imagined on the pattern of man—they were also resolute anthropomorphists.

They grouped all the personalities under a common denomination, a species indicator, that we ordinarily translate as *god, divine being.* But this term—dingir in Sumerian, *ilu* in Akkadian—can in neither language be analyzed into otherwise known semantic elements which would give us a basic meaning. In other words, we do not know whence the Sumerians and the Semites could have derived their representation of the "divine." Cuneiform writing gives us, however, an interesting indication: the sign that is used to designate a divinity—the sketch of a star—is the one that also marks what is "on high," what is "elevated," and concretely, the upper level of the "universe," "heaven." Thus the divine world was fundamentally imagined as being "superior" to anything here below, and in some way "celestial."

In fact, we encounter more than once in our documentation declarations that stress the transcendence of the gods, their superiority, and their absolute preponderance over man, because of their power and their intelligence, well above ours, and their lives, freed from our miseries and mishaps, and endless:

> The plans of the gods are as far from us
>   as the center of heaven:
> To understand them properly is impossible,
>   no one can understand them![6]

This is in a passage from the essay on the problem of evil known as the *Theodicy.* The oldest version of the *Epic of Gilgameš** (around 1700) adds:

> When the gods created mankind
> They gave them death.
> But (endless) life they kept for themselves![7]

In conclusion, well before the beginnings of history the ancient Mesopotamians simply transposed the image of what they knew here on earth to be the highest, their "ruling class" as we would say, to portray the gods, who in their opinion represented the sacred; but they placed this aristocracy, so

6. W. G. Lambert, *Babylonian Wisdom Literature,* pp. 76f: 82ff.
7. *Old Babylonian Meissner fragment,* 3: 3ff., R. Labat, *Les Religions . . . ,* p. 205.

to speak, in the superlative. By their function and by the life-style to which they adhered, Mesopotamian monarchs were more powerful and more lucid than their people, and lived a life that was much less worrisome and more opulent. Their subjects suffered to produce this life for them, in order to allow them, in a way, to devote their undivided attention to governing. In the same way they postulated an elite on a higher level that was even more sovereign, even more clairvoyant, and those life was so much more serene and blessed that it was endless—thus stressing its *absolute* superiority.

Other than that, the gods were regarded to be entirely like men, but better. They had a body and a shape identical to ours, but without our imperfections and untouched by our weaknesses and our decrepitudes. Some gods were of the male sex, others of the female sex. And here and there their sexual capabilities and the use they made of these capabilities, sometimes without restraint, were discussed joyously. An attempt to assign to the gods an essence that was less material and heavy than ours was evidently made: a fragment of a legend suggests that one could pierce the body of a god without risk, and that not a single drop of blood would flow out of it. They had children, as we do, and these children were also gods. They formed entire families, and all of the members behaved and acted just as we do: they ate and drank, sometimes even too much, they played with each other, they sometimes fought, they washed themselves, they dressed themselves and decked themselves out, they traveled by chariot or by boat, or they remained quiet in their "houses"—the same word was used for house and for temple. It really seems that people were convinced that the gods lived there, with a real but mysterious presence *in* their cult statues. This did not prevent them from making use of the well-known illogical character of mythological thought, and thinking that the gods resided "on high" in heaven, or "below" in the area symmetric with heaven below the earth.

THE MONARCHICAL PRINCIPLE AND THE ORGANIZATION OF THE DIVINE WORLD

We do not know whether this extremely resolute anthropomorphism was of Sumerian or Akkadian origin: possibly it was of both. What is certain is that it very soon became dominated, and in some way systematized, by the analogy with the political system of the country, and that it thus became organized on the model of a monarchy that undoubtedly existed already on a modest scale in every village, before history. There would already have to be a number of divinities of either sex, that were perhaps already connected by family ties, as among us: fathers, mothers, sons and daughters, brothers and sisters, ancestors and descendants. When these villages became organized into larger political units around a city, the divine personalities must have undergone a mixing analogous to that of the political authorities: the principal god of the city became in a sense the head of the supernatural powers, and grouped around him were the deities of lesser importance, who became in this way assimilated to the high functionaries, in the image of the court and of the royal household. And the same process continued to the benefit of the capital city and its ruler when the cities were organized into kingdoms.

So compelling was the monarchical principle, even among the gods, that we are presented from the beginning of the third millennium on with a phenomenon that is symptomatic and rather surprising. Doubtless because of a common understanding, and in spite of the political crumbling of the territory, the city-states seem to have formed a type of amphictyony by creating above all other cities a unified and organized supernatural power whose residence was placed in Nippur, a sacred city that, as far as we know, had never played the least political role.

At its head was placed what has been called a triad, a term that is misleading insofar as it makes us believe that the supreme power was divided equally among its three members: the gods An* (in Akkadian Anu), Enlil,* and Enki* (called Ea by the Akkadian speakers). An represented the founder of the divine dynasty, the father of the ruling king, Enlil. Such a coexistence could not be imagined among the people, as the crown prince would succeed his father only when the latter had died, but it was perfectly normal among the immortal gods. Thus An was the ancestor, the source, and the guarantee of power. One could rely on his experience in times of crisis, but he left the effective exercise of sovereign authority to his son Enlil. Enki/Ea stood next to the holder of power, the one who had only to order to see himself obeyed by the entire universe. Enki/Ea played the role—well known from its equivalents among the kings of those days—of the intelligent adviser, full of cunning, expert in all procedures, master of all techniques, and hence well-placed to direct in a sense the use of divine power which by itself was nothing but a blind force.

Therefore, the supreme gods, each with a family and an entire pantheon of subordinate divinities that made up their households, were of importance to the entire country. It is as if one wanted, even before a political unification of the country into a single kingdom, to impose on it a unique and universal supernatural power in order to assert better its profound cultural solidarity. This supernatural power duplicated first of all, but on a higher level, the cities' dominions, before absorbing them into a single "pyramid" of power.

The "theological" system paralleled so perfectly the political one that it anticipated, just as on earth, a full assembly of the gods. It was presided over by its king, Enlil, and even by the head of the dynasty, An, in times of great tension. Enki/Ea also assisted in this assembly. Under their authority the gods were considered to stir up and to debate the important questions of their own government and of the world's government. From these deliberations followed the destinies of all beings that established their nature and their behavior. Once the decisions of the assembly were promulgated by the ruling god and even inscribed on the "Tablet of Destinies" (see above, p. 133) which he kept as the sign of his supernatural authority, things happened and evolved. Perhaps nothing shows better than this to what degree the representation of the gods was no more than a sublime projection of the political system.

This "theological" construction survived practically to the end of the history of Mesopotamia. However, after the middle of the second millennium it became, not abolished or replaced (in this country there was no desire to eliminate cultural values or to replace them with others; the superimposition of a new system was preferable), but in a way duplicated by another representation. This was the result of a profound political change, mentioned above, when around the year 1750 Hammurabi made Babylon the capital of a single kingdom that remained intact from then on. Thus Babylon and its ruler took precedence and authority over the other cities. The city-god Marduk, who up to that moment had little importance, had likewise to take precedence over the other cities first of all, and then over the other gods. It must have taken centuries for such a doctrine to become fully developed. Around the year 1200 at the latest, Marduk became recognized, both in popular devotion and by the theologians, as the absolute ruler of the supernatural and the earthly world, as if Enlil in his turn had given the throne to him in order to retire with Anu. Let us say in passing that the famous *Epic of Creation** was written at that time as a charter of this promotion. Later on, the Assyrians of the northern kingdom did the same thing for Assur,* their "national" god, simply by replacing the name of Marduk with that of Assur in the *Epic*. In Babylonia itself during the first half of the first millennium a number of worshipers more or less repeated the process with Marduk to the benefit of his son, the god Nabû.*

A religion that does not have normative texts, or definitions or "dogmas," and that evolves simply with time, without the least internal force to bring it back to the original directions plotted by its founder, accepts very well the plurality of views that in our opinion would be contradictory. Once one view is adopted, it does not have to eliminate others or turn it into a "deviation." These various opinions were in the eyes of the ancient Mesopotamians nothing but cumulative, one enriching the other and hence, so to say, increasing the worship.

Be that as it may, it should become increasingly clear that the system of organization of the pantheon, vis-à-vis the world in itself, was in all aspects nothing but the magnified reflection of the political system. It tended progressively towards an increasingly centralized monarchical power, a process similar to what happened in the political sphere.

THE CHARACTER AND THE ROLE OF THE GODS

Parallel to this evolution of the exercise of authority by the gods, another evolution also transformed their character—and perhaps here we are in a better position to divide the responsibilities between Sumerians and Semites. At first, the Sumerians seem to have tied the supernatural personalities to the functioning of nature and of culture: as if each of the phenomena of both areas presented a problem, in its origin as well as in its functioning, and could be explained only by a supernatural cause that enclosed it and concealed it like a "motor" (in the etymological sense of the word), a "director." Behind heaven there was the god of Heaven: An/Anu; behind the space between heaven and earth, Enlil (literally "Lord-Air/"Atmosphere"); behind the body of sweet water (Apsû*) on which the earthly disk floated, Enki; behind the Moon, Nanna; behind the Sun, Utu; behind rains and storms, Iškur; behind the sprouting of cereals, Ašnan; behind the growth of sheep and goats, Laḫar; behind the transformation of barley into the national drink, beer, Siris; and so on. For these minds that were still "naïve" and far removed from our rational coldness, the entire world in all its aspects, both natural and cultural, would have been arbitrary and absurd if it had not been duplicated in all those aspects by divinities of the male and the female sex, to give it reason. These divinities were then integrated into the political system existing at the moment, each playing his or her own instrument in the universal symphony conducted by the holders of power. For instance, we have found a myth which contains this concept and which was written down in Sumerian at the latest at the end of the third millennium, although it probably reflects an earlier stage of things. In it is related how Enki put in motion the land of Sumer (in other words, the southern part of Lower Mesopotamia), which at that time was thought to be the center of the world. He entrusted to Enbilulu the functioning of the two rivers; to Nanna that of the marshy area filled with fish in the south of the region; to Nanše that of the coastal area; to Iškur the flow of rain; to Enkimdu the work in the fields; to Ašnan the sprouting of plants; to Kulla the making of bricks; to Mušdamma the construction of buildings; to Sumuqan the wild animals; to Dumuzi animal husbandry; to Utu the proper juridical and administrative direction of the land; to Uttu the entire area of textiles; to Aruru all that entailed human reproduction; to Ninmug work with wood; and so on. According to this doctrine the entire cosmos functioned exactly as a kingdom, and was structured according to the "pyramidal" system of authority.

THE PANTHEON

Integrating the gods into a body and organizing them was also a way of justifying the existence of so many gods. And there were many of them; we know between one and two thousand gods at least by name. Moreover, a "canonical" list of gods had been developed, a type of "treatise of divine personnel," which in its classical form contained almost two thousand entries. By far the largest number of gods had Sumerian names. Thus they were beyond doubt imagined and "created" by the Sumerians. It seems that the Semites devoted a more tempered creative imagination to this subject. It appears that this mass derived directly from the archaic period when each independent agglomeration had its own pantheon. The unification as a result of political events caused a certain number of syncretisms*: in the case of two or more analogous gods related by various historical mixing, the strongest personality—in concrete terms the one who appealed most to his worshipers, or whose devotees were triumphant—absorbed the weaker ones, keeping at most their names and their epithets. The most famous case is that of the goddess Inanna, whom the Semites called Ištar. To her were annexed a divinity of the planet Venus (Delebat) and a god or a goddess of quarrels and of war. But she still remained basically what she had been at first, the celestial Courtesan, the divine Prostitute, the patroness of "free" love. Later on she seems to have similarly monopolized a number of goddesses, to such an extent and so successfully that from the beginning of the second millennium on, her Akkadian name, Ištar, was used as a common name for the "divine in the feminine." A female deity as such was an *ištar(t)u,* whatever her own personality and her own lot may have been. In this way the number of gods decreased considerably over time: the *Poem of Creation* from around the year 1200 lists not more than six hundred of them: three hundred in heaven, three hundred below earth (VI: 39f.). But still this round number has to be taken as the rhetorical equivalent of a great number (in the decimo-sexagesimal system of Mesopotamia). In reality, the gods of the first order who were really active and constantly worshiped in general, were much less numerous and seem to have decreased in number over the centuries. At the end we can count not more than some thirty gods of first order—even if quite a few additional ones reappear now and then, somewhat in the way one can even today find worshipers of bizarre saints of antiquity who still have their chapels and images but have almost entirely disappeared from memory.

The majority of the "great gods" that survived, after the middle of the second millennium, were more likely to bear Semitic (or Semiticized) names than their ancient Sumerian appellations. An became Anu; Enlil and some others did not change, as well as Nergal* and Ereškigal,* the ruling god and goddess of the land below, what we would call Hell. But Ea replaced Enki; and Ištar, Šamaš,* Sîn,* and Adad replaced Inanna, Utu, Nanna, and Iškur. Marduk and his "spouse," Ṣarpanîtu, and Nabû and his "spouse," Tašmêtu, are also Semitic. This is a sign that once the Sumerians had disappeared and the Semites became the sole people responsible for the history and the development of the country and its religion, they Semiticized religion more and more but still maintained the ancient structures inherited from the Sumerians.

This change can also be noticed in another area. The gods were detached gradually from the phenomena of nature and of culture to which they had been tied and took a certain distance from them. Certainly they maintained their "human" configuration and their purely anthropomorphic character, but they became increasingly refined, freed from what had been "too human," "too primitive," too rough, too unpolished, too wild and animal-like in their humanity. We know of myths in Sumerian, all from before the second millennium, that tell us, for instance, how Enlil in heat pursued the young and still virgin Ninlil in order to throw himself brutally upon her and to impregnate her, and this he did three times (it is true that she later gave in to him and wanted him). It was so outrageous that his own colleagues were angered at such beastly behavior and exiled him to the Netherworld. We know how Inanna was raped by her father's gardener; or how she had given herself with passion to her "first love," Dumuzi (Tammuz), before betraying him. Certainly the literary tradition has preserved the memory of these excesses, but the myths composed in Akkadian do not have the same coarse tone. Clearly the morals must have improved accordingly. But, in any case, starting from the beginning of the second millennium gods are only portrayed as very high, very dignified, majestic, and honorable personalities. Even when they give in to a passion they remain respectable and imposing—as is proper for this "upper class" invested with power.

Not only the political changes, but also the evolution of morals, in particular under the increasingly powerful, later exclusive, Semitic influence, transformed the divine world little by little, by keeping it always integrated into the cultural system of which it remained the highest reflection.

THE MYTHOLOGY

The "calculated imagination" that the ancient Mesopotamians had used to create an entire supernatural population in order to "establish" in some way their apprehension of the sacred, based on the elements of their physical, aesthetic, emotional, economic, social, and political world, also provided them with a way to answer the great enigmas that the things around them posed to their minds. Perhaps we ourselves, immersed in a milieu of science and technology, and affected by the easily exaggerated confidence that we have in the representatives and prophets of those activities, have got in the habit of letting these representatives question things for us—each of them in his own special field, as everything has been divided up in our type of knowledge—and thus we have destroyed the surprise in the world, the questioning of everything around us and in us, a questioning that is still active in the fresh, open, and rich minds of children, of people that are quite wrongly called "primitives," and of certain poets. This is because these people marvel at the theater of the universe and they have not yet become tired of thinking about it. Let us say that the best minds among this elite of profound and lively spirits that can be found in any time period, in any society, and in any culture, have accumulated their meditations century after century in order to give reason to the universe with the only "intellectual" means available to them: recourse to structures of images, of conjectures, and of events which, though uncontrollable, are able to furnish them with what is sufficient: an explanation of the mysteries among which they feel they live that is at least probable. This is what is called mythology.

The most important, the most pressing of these questions involve the elements that are at the same time the most universal and of the most immediate interest for their own lives: the raison d'être of the world and of themselves. What is peculiar to such a search for the "probable"—in contrast to the search for truth—is the capacity to resolve the same problem materially in different ways, without being detrimental to a profound intuition that is easily the same behind all these solutions and that represents the great parameters of culture. In order to illustrate this double aspect of the mythology of the ancient Mesopotamians, I will first focus on their cosmogonic conceptions and then on their views about anthropogony, the origins and the destiny of mankind.

COSMOGONY

It appears that the authors of myths in the Sumerian language, the most ancient myths put down in writing, did not ask themselves questions about the origin of the world; they seem, for example, to have been satisfied with assigning it to the gods without further details, or they do not seem to have considered it to be their duty to devote any special works to it. Or perhaps our archeologists have not been able to put their hands on one of these special works. We do not have a single cosmogony, which is already significant considering the number and the variety of documents excavated over the last one hundred and fifty years. We have to say that these most ancient writers (before the beginning of the second millennium) had a clear preference for mythological and legendary accounts that were exact, i.e. devoted to a well-defined subject matter in order to answer a precise question. For instance, the "birth" of a certain god; the mechanism that guarantees the prosperity and the glory of the country; the origin—the "etiology" as scholars would say—of certain plants, certain tools, certain techniques, and so on. But none of them, as far as we know, seem to have been devoted to the more general question of knowing how and why the cosmos came into existence. All that we have found is the following, from the prologue of the legend *Gilgameš, Enkidu, and the Netherworld:*

1. In those days, those ancient days,
In those nights, those ancient nights,
In those years, those ancient years. . . .
8. After On-High had been moved away from Below,
After Below had been separated from On-High . . .
11. After An had carried off On-High,
After Enlil had carried off Below
And after he had endowed the Netherworld to
Ereškigal. . . .[8]

Here the "cosmological" conception of the universe in two hemispheres that these people had developed appears in broad outline. Heaven was on-high; below was "Hell," as the anti-Heaven, an immense rounded depression (later we learn that it floated in a fabulous mass of water), through the middle of which extended the expanse of man's earth, centered around Mesopotamia itself. The expanse floated on an immense body of sweet water, which rose up through wells and springs, and was surrounded, like an island, by the "bitter water" of the sea. The myth imagines this state of affairs only as the result of an original "separation" of the mass of the universe that was at first confused and mixed together. The separation was the result of the actions of two great gods: An on the one hand, and Enlil on the other, who were each eager to take one hemisphere. The latter took care to assign the entire underground to the goddess, who became henceforth its queen. This is very little information!

We can compare this laconic information with the ample vision, the variety, and the precision of several more recent accounts (from the second millennium) in Akkadian. It is as if an early period, still little gifted with speculation, was followed by a period of maturity, of urgency and of depth, in which the Mesopotamians expressed themselves easily and well. From the later authors, who were impressive in other respects too, we do not only have here and there a number of allusions to the birth of the world but also works of literature that are sometimes masterpieces, where the theme was treated with a real eminence and dignity.

8. A. Shaffer, *Sumerian Sources of Tablet XII of the Epic of Gilgameš*, p. 99

The most famous, the most complete, and the most detailed treatment of this subject is found in the *Epic of Creation*, even though this work was above all devoted to the justification of the primary position among the gods conferred on Marduk, and not, as is still often thought, to cosmogony. It starts with the theogony, because in the Mesopotamian conception the gods, being part of the cosmos, had to pass also from nonbeing to being, like the rest of the universe. Before the gods existed there was nothing but an immense expanse of water, presented as the unending joining of the female Tiamat,* the salt water of the future sea, and the male Apsû,* the sweet water of the future subterranean sheet of water. At first, deities who were somewhat primitive and roughly made evolved from them. Then pair after pair of the great gods evolved, the oldest of the successful divine dynasty, perfect and ruling forever. Out of two great gods Marduk was born later. From his first appearance he was portrayed as being the most brilliant, perfect and unequalled. We are told then that he will become the supreme ruler of the gods, because he has saved them by heroically battling and defeating the primordial Mother, the enormous and monstrous Tiamat, who wanted to annihilate the gods. He became the absolute sovereign of the world because he himself created, produced, and organized it by using the enormous corpse of his victim. He cut her gigantic body in half, and from its upper part he made the hemisphere of On-high, Heaven, where he placed the various stars, each with its infallible path and role. From the lower part he made the hemisphere of Below, starting with our Earth. The latter was essentially Mesopotamia and its adjacent lands with all its geographical features.[9]

Another myth still assigns the creation of the world to Marduk but presents the events in a somewhat different way. It tells us that in the beginning there was nothing but water, a sea without bottom or shore. To make the terrestrial platform,

> Marduk arranged a raft on the surface of the Water,
> then he made dust and piled it on top![10]

Other accounts, apparently written before the promotion of Marduk and reflecting an earlier ideology, attribute the responsibility of the universe either to three supreme gods, working in concert:

> When Anu, Enlil and Ea, the Great Gods,
> planned heaven and earth. . . .[11]

9. The text is translated in R. Labat, *Les Religions . . .*, pp. 36ff., and J. Bottéro, *L'Épopée de la Création*. It is extensively annotated in *Mythes et rites de Babylone*, pp. 113–62.

10. *Mythes et rites de Babylone*, p. 304: 17f.

11. Ibid., pp. 316f., 8: 5f.

or to the head of the divine dynasty, Anu, for Heaven, and to the superintelligent Ea for the rest:

When Anu had created heaven,
and Ea had established earth. . . .[12]

There is even an account, perhaps very old, that presents creation as a "chain-reaction": the god Anu created only the first and largest element of the chain, heaven, which created in turn the second, somewhat smaller element, earth, and so on:

When Anu had created heaven,
when heaven had created earth,
when earth had created the rivers,
when the rivers had created the streams. . . .[13]

Such variations are not only in accordance with the procedures of mythological thought mentioned above, but they are perfectly in place in a religious system such as that of Mesopotamia, devoid of a "dogma" fixed once and for all, and of "sacred" and normative texts, that in themselves or through the authorized interpretation given by "religious authorities" define a precise and univocal doctrine. However, if none of the answers to the question asked are materially identical in the different cosmological presentations, at the basis of each of them there is still an intuition that is always the same: the world, the entire universe, depends on the gods for its existence, as it depends on the gods for its functioning, whatever the concrete ways imagined for this dependence are in the different accounts.

ANTHROPOGONY

This is also the case for anthropogony. We also have more than one description of it (compare pp. 239ff.). I will not stress this point, and will be satisfied with concentrating only on the most complete and the most remarkable description: that in the *Poem of the Supersage* (in Akkadian: *Atraḫasîs*) composed around the year 1700. In its complete version it contained about 1,200 lines, two-thirds of which are preserved.[14] It is a witness to the taste of the religious thinkers after the beginning of the second millennium, and to their ability to produce large syntheses that were inspired, penetrating, and well constructed, and quite different from the short and concise compositions of older date. It is the oldest known description of the ideas that

12. *Mythes et rites de Babylone*, p. 192: 1f.
13. Ibid., p. 281: 1ff.
14. The text is translated in R. Labat, *Les Religions. . . .*, pp. 26ff.

mankind had developed with regard to its own origins and with regard to the sense of its existence. And it takes matters until after the Flood, which signals the end of mythological times, when things were formed, and inaugurates the beginning of historical times, when these things have only to function according to their eternally established nature. Hence, it is also the first rough draft of the prefatory chapters of our biblical Genesis.

The story begins before the "historical" universe, when only divine society existed. As it was necessary to satisfy its material needs, and as this could happen only through a labor of production, this society was naturally divided into two groups (as is ours!): the leaders, pure consumers, called the Anunnaku* or Anunnaki, and the gods of second rank, devoted to labor, who bore the title of Igigu*/Igigi (I: 1ff.):

1. When the gods (acted[15] like) men,
they did the work and labored.
Their labor was enormous,
The corvée too hard, their work too long,
5. because the great Anunnaku made the Igigu
carry the workload sevenfold. . . .

In the end the Igigu, worn out by their exhausting labor, revolted and went on strike, burning their tools and protesting before their chief employer, Enlil. This caused great commotion among the Anunnaku: without workers there would be misery, famine! A plenary session of the assembly was convened, presided over on the occasion by Anu himself. It was Ea, the shrewd, intelligent, acute, and inventive god, who resolved the crisis by proposing replacements for the worker-gods. These replacements should be devoted enough to work as well as the gods did, but programmed in such a way that they would never complain, like the gods did, in the name of a similarity in nature, a similarity in destiny, and the right not to work, as this would plunge the divine world in the same agonizing danger. This substitute would be man: intelligent, indeed, and capable of fulfilling with perfection his hereditary task, but devoted to a life of limited duration. Accepted with great enthusiasm by the council of the gods, the project was immediately executed and man was created. Clay (to which man will return one day, at this death) was mixed with the blood of a minor deity to give man the qualities needed to accomplish his work as capably as his divine predecessors carried out theirs.

As soon as they were put on earth by the seven original couples derived from the human prototype first fashioned, men started to devote themselves with such alacrity and dash to the needs of the gods that their success was complete. Indeed they multiplied so greatly that their increasing

15. The word has to be understood in the sense of "had the role of."

"noise" literally prevented Enlil from sleeping. In what is probably a satirical element that underlines the degree to which power, even if it is supreme, does not automatically include thorough planning and certainly not intelligence and the gift of foresight, Enlil decided to decimate mankind by inflicting various calamities. He sent first an epidemic, then a drought and a famine, in order to annihilate man and to reverse the course of events so well begun by Ea's "invention." The latter, who knew how to foresee things, intervened quietly every time (since he did not hold supreme authority, he could not go against it). These were all images drawn by the authors of the myth from the crises and changing conditions accompanying the exercise of power by kings.

But in the end Enlil, who was still irritated by mankind, decided to annihilate it purely and simply by the most impressive of calamities: the irresistible inundation of the Flood. Ea this time had to swear with the other gods that he would not speak of the fatal project to anyone. But he arranged to reveal it in a dream (which is not the same as speaking!) to his protégé, "the Supersage." And when he was questioned by him about how to survive, Ea had to explain to him the project of the famous "Ark." He did so not by addressing him directly, in person (in order not to break his oath), but by talking through a reed wall behind which he was sitting. Thus warned, and obeying his master, "the Supersage" will be the Noah of the first Flood, hiding in his boat with his family. Hence he will perpetuate, after the catastrophe that obliterates nature and culture, the human race that is indispensable to the gods. However, when the Supersage stepped upon the empty and deserted earth after the disaster, eager to perform his essential duty of feeding the famished gods, Enlil was foolishly irritated, as in the end he had been frustrated in his plans, stupid as they may have been. It was then that Ea took the right measures to avoid an inconvenient overpopulation in the future. He introduced not only a decrease of the number of births by the natural or voluntary sterility of certain women and by infant mortality, but also a shortening of human life. Men, whose life, as we know from other mythological accounts, was originally much longer, would die before the age of one hundred years. Thus the "final touch" to man's nature, constitution and destiny was given, and the historic period could begin.

It would certainly be worth the trouble to talk more about this document, a balanced and finished work of art. The anthropogenic "synthesis" that appears in it is perfectly clear in its outlines: mankind has been created and put in this world, their constitution craftily calculated and completed, to fulfill the role of servants towards the gods. They are producers who improve the riches of this world in order to provide by their labor *first of all* goods that are needed for the supernatural world: food and drink, clothes and ornaments, furniture and shelter. They also profit from the surplus of things—but only secondarily and as if in addition. Human life has no other sense, raison d'être, or goal than service to the gods—just as the subjects in a state have no other goal than service to the ruler and his household. Also here we find the same transposition, the foundation and the pillar of support for the entire religious ideology of the land.

THE GOVERNMENT OF THE WORLD

Numerous myths extend explicitly or by allusion the same transposition of royal power over the whole of human history "after the Flood." Since the world and mankind were created, the gods could not give up directing them and ruling them, thus assuring the continuous functioning not only of the entire machine but also of its smallest parts. They proceeded with effective decisions—as did the kings with their commands, ordinances, and decrees, which were obeyed by obligation. The divine decisions were called *destinies*. These they *fixed* or *decreed* and "inscribed" in things, as we have seen elsewhere, and communicated in that way to the parties involved according to a known and decipherable "code," thus making possible the divinatory techniques.

The image of royal power, transposed into the supernatural world, was thus not a simple matter of style, a lyrical metaphor, but a real analogy, i.e. a means of knowing: the gods were indeed the authors and the governors of the universe and of each of its elements, as the kings owned and were responsible for their territory and for all of its resources and each of its subjects. This proportional equivalence was at the center and the foundation of cosmogony and anthropogony and, in the end, of the entire Mesopotamian theology about the relations between man and the sacred. It gave a value to the development of the world and the destiny of things and people. And we have to recognize that such an explanation, discovered and elaborated by the ancient scholars and thinkers in the mid-third millennium or even earlier, demands our admiration for its ingenuity, its coherence, and its vigor.

It is this explanation that convinces us to regard their religion as a real system. At first glance these hundreds of gods, this confusion of personalities with complicated names that are foreign to us, this multitude of obscure and bizarre stories of their behavior and their adventures, seem to reflect an immense chaos, a gloomy and enigmatic jumble, almost entirely unintelligible and without the least interest. Yet, at the slightest attempt to get to the bottom of this jumble, we recognize in it a solid, intelligent, and calculated synthesis. Should we not admire its greatness? Even if it is so ancient, so outdated, so far removed from our truths and beliefs, from all that is familiar to us in this field, it still constitutes a coherent structure that is remarkably astute, noble, and worthy of our respect. Hence we understand easily how it could sustain the religious sentiment of millions of people, who succeeded each other for numerous generations over more than three millennia in this ancient world.

RELIGIOUS BEHAVIOR

The same system, the same fundamental analogy of the "ruling gods," also rigorously directed the entire field of *religious behavior*, the third and the last aspect of every religion as such.

Service to the Gods

First of all, the cult properly speaking, the "theocentric" liturgy as we would call it, was entirely identified with the "support of the gods," in other words with the provision to these high personalities of all that was needed or useful to lead an opulent and agreeable life entirely devoted to the government of the universe, a life even better and more blessed than that of the kings and earth.

From the early third millennium on, the Mesopotamian rulers did not cease to praise themselves in their dedicatory or commemorative inscriptions for having undertaken and accomplished building projects or repairs to numerous great sanctuaries that would serve as the "dwellings" of the gods. These temples were built around a central room, the *cella* as the archeologists say, where the usually rich and precious statues and the cult images were placed; both those of the gods to whom the sanctuary was dedicated as well as those of their household and their family. Around this image, which was considered to be the sign and the guarantee of the real presence of the divine being in his residence here on earth, daily ceremonies were organized that were more sumptuous than those in the royal court. Each day the august inhabitants of the place had to be fed. The following is an extract from the cult ritual of Anu in the city of Uruk* that illustrates very well in which ways for many centuries (the rituals were usually very conservative and changed even less than the ideology over long periods of time) the system of what we would call the "sacrifices" for the gods was organized. The worshipers in Mesopotamia considered these "sacrifices" purely and simply as the gods' "meals":

> Each day of the year for the main meal in the morning one will get ready before (the cult image) of Anu in addition to the libation vessels: 18 gold vessels on his table (we would say: his altar): 7 on the right, including 3 for barley-beer and 4 for a beer called labku; 7 on the left, including 3 for barley-beer, 1 for labku-beer, 1 for a beer called nâšu and 1 for a beer in jugs; also milk in an alabaster vase, and 4 gold vessels of "pressed" wine. Items for the secondary meal

> in the morning and also for the main and the secondary meals in the evening: but, in the evening, one will not give milk. . . .[16]

And here is, after the arrangements for drinks, those for meat on the same occasions:

> One will sacrifice (for each meal) a total of 21 sheep of first quality, fattened and "pure," two-year-old ones, fed with grain; 4 . . . of regular offerings, fed with milk, and 25 sheep of lesser quality, not fed with grain. Plus 2 fat-tailed oxen, and 1 suckling calf. . . .[17]

Not to mention the impressive amounts of various breads, cakes, dates, etc., all listed in great detail.

The gods, fed so lavishly, were also dressed, and caskets of jewelry were assembled for them, inventories of which we still have. The gods were groomed, they were bathed and perfumed. They were paraded through the city and in the countryside, transported from one residence to another either in a chariot or in a boat, because they went on visits now and then. The festivities varied according to the days of the months and of the years, following an etiquette and a detailed order, which is well enough known to us to develop an idea of the liturgical year. The year culminated in the eleven or twelve first days of the New Year (celebrated in March), which were entirely devoted to a great celebration, the most important of the year, in which the king and all the people took part. Other feasts of minor importance marked the various months: for instance, a celebration of the "marriage" of the gods, commemorating that union. In the first millennium this was done with divine statues that were adorned before being brought into a "bridal chamber" and left side by side overnight. In the late third millennium and perhaps only in some religious centers, the marriage was represented by the physical union of the king with a priestess. Of all these festivals we have not only detailed rituals but also numerous reflections in the literature.[18]

This ritual was also an imitation—and an elaboration—of the royal etiquette according to the logic of the representation of the gods on the model of the ruling families.

Obedience to the Gods and Their Sanctions

The same representation directed, in another way, the entire life of mankind, and its attitude towards the divine. It was not sufficient to honor the rulers and to serve them with feasts. It was also indispensable to conform to

16. F. Thureau-Dangin, *Rituels accadiens*, p. 80: *1–6*.
17. Ibid., pp. 84f: *24f*.
18. See especially S. N. Kramer, *The Sacred Marriage Rite*.

their wishes, to obey their orders blindly. Thus the religious behavior involved a certain number of obligations, if not "moral" ones in the strict sense of the word (religion in Mesopotamia was far from based on a real ethical code, in contrast to the case of the biblical authors), at least juridical. The religion included a conviction shared by all the Semites, as far as we know: just as all social restrictions came forth from the royal will and received their obligatory strength and, if needed, their sanctions from it, all the imperatives of life, both communal and individual, received their value from the fact that they represented the explicit will of the gods. These obligations or prohibitions were of all sorts. There were some of common law—which reveal also, from another point of view, social sanctions: e.g. one could not harm others or their interests. There are indications here and there that seem to point even further and to preach goodness, generosity, and openhandedness to all. But there existed also an incredible number of positive and especially negative prescriptions, what we would call in the broad sense of the word, "tabus," or prohibitions. Here are a few taken from a famous list:[19] one could not swear an oath without washing the hand that was raised to do so; nor invoke the god's name while brandishing an axe; nor drink from a cup of unbaked clay; nor tear out twigs from the steppe or break reeds in the canebrake; nor urinate or vomit in a waterway; nor take away a clod of earth from a field; and so on. Although they seem arbitrary and devoid of meaning to us, these prohibitions must have had their logic in the minds of their users; in their own world vision and their hierarchy of values. For instance, for them waterways had a supernatural character and one could not soil them. And they believed that there was a real and deep bond between landed property and its legal owners, which first had to be broken in the case of transfer. An ancient prejuridical ritual considered each clod of earth taken from a field to contain that bond, and it was sufficient to throw it in water to dissolve it. Thus these talisman-like symbols could not be handled carelessly. "Logical" or not, such precepts and especially the numerous prohibitions seem to have framed daily existence in every respect, to such a degree that it was difficult not to violate one at every turn.

Moreover, and it is here that a particular aspect of the Mesopotamian view on things shows, *all* these positive or negative prescriptions, whatever their background may have been—juridical, "moral," social, simply convenient, clearly religious, or in the dark area that we call "superstition"—were placed in the religious field on the same level, so to speak. The list mentioned above confers the *same* supernatural risk on such trifles as tearing out a twig in the steppe and on such crimes as killing one's friend. This is because all of them drive from the same source: the will of the gods. Trans-

19. See *Mythes et rites de Babylone*, pp. 209f.

gressors will be exposed to the same avenging reaction of the supernatural rulers offended by the disobedience, just as the transgressors of laws and administrative obligations had to expect a sanction from the king who decreed and guaranteed those laws.

I say deliberately "will be exposed" and "had to expect," because not less than in social life punishment was not unfailing and immediate. Indeed, like the kings, the gods had to punish, but they did not punish always—not because the transgressions escaped their attention, as could happen to authorities on earth, but for a thousand other mysterious reasons that only they could judge, with their sovereign freedom and the depth of their inaccessible designs. What was certain, on the other hand, is that in the face of a suffered accident, a sudden disgrace or illness, or an unexpected catastrophe, which in the theocentric view of those people could derive only from the decisions and the will of the gods, one had to think immediately of the gods as the cause of all evil. And in the belief that such high and irreproachable personalities could not act absurdly, as if they wanted to fool around without reason, it was necessary to consider their sense of justice. Thus one formulated, in a sense, an a-posteriori reasoning: "If I am suffering misfortune without clearly having wished or provoked it myself, it is like this *because* the gods have imposed it on me. And if they have decided to do so, *I must have* offended them by transgressing their wishes, by disobeying one of their commands—even without wanting to or without knowing it." In the above list there are some infractions that are absolutely unconscious, even indiscernible, like the fact of having been in contact at a certain moment with someone who himself is the object of divine displeasure, side by side with knowing infractions such as adultery, and almost involuntary ones such as the breaking of a reed in the marshes.

EVIL AND ITS CAUSES

The same basic vision of the gods in the image of the kings provides a religious and plausible explanation to this other universal and urgent problem of human life: the existence of evil—of "suffered" evil, of course. This baffles our desire for ease and happiness, because in a religion that is indifferent to ethics what we call "moral evil," an evil action as such, does not have any meaning. Most of these evils could be explained by their immediate causes insofar as they were discernible: bad management leads to failure; excessive expenses to ruin; an unhappy marriage to boredom; a sunstroke, a chill, an unsuccessful sexual relation to an illness or a malaise. But such explanations answer only half of the question. What remains is the most pressing part: why did it happen to *me?* The religious ideology provided an answer that was entirely acceptable as well as definitive, even if it was only "likely," as was the entirety of mythological thought. Evil is the punishment ordered by the gods for any transgression of their sovereign will, just as a punishment is the sanction of the authorities on earth for any infraction of the law.

It is true that religious imagination had at first invented a certain number of personalized causes to explain the various evils that prey on human life: supernatural beings of the second rank, those which we would call "demons," who intervened like vicious animals that throw themselves on anyone to bite or to terrify, without any other motive than their own fantasy or their wickedness. The majority of the names of these evildoers come from the Sumerian, which reveals their origin, even if the Semites have added a few others. When the "theology" of sovereignty was universally imposed on belief, the "demons" ceased to act spontaneously. They became like the gendarmes of the gods, charged with the execution of their decisions, and with the bringing of evil and miserable punishments to those who had offended the gods' authority by some "sin," by some transgression of their will.

The "Sacramental" Cult

This mythology of evil, brought in this way into accordance with the royal authority of the gods, also provided a remedy for the evils that were explained by it. Before its adoption (perhaps before the third millennium?) there had been a reliance on "primitive" beliefs related to magic. In the strict sense of the word the latter transposed upon the supernatural and mysterious causes of the inconveniences of life, powers attributed to the actions of man in manipulating things. These actions were thought to create, to change, or to destroy things. Also words spoken over living beings were thought to subdue them, to make them obey or to make them disappear. From these premises an assortment of procedures were imagined, in time, that were considered to be efficient. These procedures made use of manipulations and instruments or materials, as in other technical matters, and of words that were imperative and "conjuring," addressed to those who do the evil. These manual and verbal rituals were preserved, later on, by modifying only their sense and their mechanism: by the use of water to "wash" and to erase the evil, or to swallow it up and make its cause disappear; fire to burn it; such or such plant, mineral, or animal product, considered to be "purifying," to avoid the morbific causes, whether of demoniacal origin or not; and by the utterance of rituals and formulas to make persecutors retreat or flee. These rituals were no longer brought to bear directly on the presumed cause of the evil, but the gods were offered a framework, in a sense, in which *they* could intervene, by infusing it with their efficient powers after having listened to the recited formulas that had evolved from simple conjurations into real prayers. In this way these manual and verbal rituals obtained their effect. They worked because the gods were considered to be merciful, as were the rulers on earth, and capable of reversing their original rigorous decisions and freeing those who had been at first justly condemned, if one could touch a cord in their hearts.

This is the meaning of a very large sector of the ritual behavior, which is not "magic" any longer, as some still persist in calling it; in fact, by its mechanisms, and by the place it occupies in the relations with the gods, it is *theurgy* or *exorcism*. This is the meaning of the "sacramental cults," executed no longer in the gods' honor and for their advantage, but for the benefit of the worshipers. We have at our disposal an enormous collection of specialized formulas against all imaginable evils: physical and "moral" diseases, disgraces, catastrophes, worries and inconveniences of any kind, against which were executed alternatively manual rituals and verbal rituals, manipulations and prayers. Also here, the key, the justification for this entire religious activity was the sovereign power of Heaven imagined on the model of the royal authority.

Death and the Hereafter

To this petitioning of the gods and their efficacious intervention (on condition that they were agreeable to them; just as the kings could refuse their favors, so the gods could persist in their judgment and reject petitions, leaving only resignation to the unfortunates) only one ordeal was immune; this was the worst one, which no one could escape because it had been written in our nature and our destiny: death. It was understood that this meant a normal and natural death at the end of a sufficiently long life, and without atrocious circumstances. There were exorcistic procedures against accidental deaths, premature decease, but not a single one against this expected conclusion of one's life.

However, even after his death man did not escape control and seizure by the gods. What remained of him was, besides a body that returned in stages to its first state of "clay," a type of duplicate that was shady, volatile, and airy, a "phantom" (*eṭemmu**) that entered its new abode through an aperture in the tomb, and rejoined the enormous group of its predecessors on earth in the Netherworld, an immense, dark, silent, and sad cavern where all had to lead a gloomy and torpid existence forever. This did not prevent them, however, from returning once in a while to scare and to torment the forgetful survivors who did not provide them with support for their sorry existence in the form of libations and small food offerings. But if they had changed in shape, they had not changed in condition: although they were passive and useless, they were still the subjects of the ruling gods in their Anti-heaven where everything that was positive on earth in some way assumed a negative aspect. An entire pantheon, different from the celestial one, exercised power under the sovereign authority (still!) of the gloomy goddess Ereškigal, who was joined later by the terrible Nergal, her husband.

THE RELIGIOUS SYSTEM

Thus, from Heaven to the bottom of Hell, ever since the creation of the world, if not even before that, this obstinate and universal analogy with the royal institution flourished and appeared ubiquitously. Thanks to this analogy, which formed an unshaken backbone for the ancient religion of Mesopotamia, it is impossible for us not to see a real system, maturely thought out and constructed little by little, intelligently and solidly. However far removed it may be from our views, it is worthy of our admiration and honorable.

These ancient worshipers had thus formed a "logical" ideal that allowed them to live, not too fearfully, with their sense of a supernatural and sacred world, a world that was sublime, inaccessible, and formidable. They felt that they were led by the gods as they were by their kings. They were used to such subjection. They had even attempted to find in it the means to free themselves of their worries and their sufferings, without which they thought their lives sufficiently tolerable, if not enjoyable, because they did not strive for a superhuman happiness. It was a distant era when man accepted that one never escapes one's ultimate destiny whatever one does, an antiquated period when man had not yet discovered "the contestation of power."

13

Intelligence and the Technical Function of Power: Enki/Ea

To list in detail the names and the particulars of the innumerable divine personalities to which the ancient Mesopotamians addressed their devotion and their cult, would be pedantic, tedious, and almost useless.[1] As this has never been done up till now, it would be better to point out at first that this pantheon, whatever its remote and badly known origin may have been, constituted a perfectly structured *system*, where every element—every divine person—had its place and its original and irreplaceable role, like bones in a skeleton. In order to demonstrate things better from this point of view it is preferable to limit oneself to only one of the elements, chosen from among the most important and the best documented, and to study closely its role and its destiny. In this way the entire hierarchy and the functioning of the whole should become apparent. Thus I will deal here with the god whom Sumerian texts called *Enki*, and those in Akkadian preferred to call *Ea*.[2]

1. For the Mesopotamian pantheon in general, see especially K. Tallqvist, *Akkadische Götterepitheta*, pp. 245–486; D. O. Edzard, in *Wörterbuch der Mythologie* ed. H. W. Haussig, 1: 19–139; Bottéro, *La Religion babylonienne*, pp. 33–45. For a bird's-eye view, see above, pp. 212ff.

2. Enki/Ea has rarely been the subject of a real synthetic study by an Assyriologist. In addition to the works cited in the previous note one should at least see the article *Enki (Ea)* by E. Ebeling in *Reallexikon der Assyriologie*, 2: 374–79; J. Bottéro, *Les divinités sémitiques anciennes en Mésopotamie*, in S. Moscati, *Le antiche divinità semitiche*, pp. 36–39; J. J. M. Roberts, *The Earliest Semitic Pantheon*, pp. 19–21, and more recently H. D. Galter, *Der Gott Ea/Enki in der akkadischen Überlieferung*.

This chapter first appeared in the *Dictionnaire des Mythologies* (Paris: Flammarion, 1981), 2: 102–11, under the title: "L'intelligence et la fonction technique du pouvoir: Enki/Éa—pour donner une idée de la systémique du panthéon."

In order to place this god we should not omit drawing an outline of what we may know regarding the constitution itself of the society of the gods. Its most characteristic feature is that it reflected the society of mankind, but "improved," and even its political evolution. The gods seem to have been imagined to explain the games of nature and of the world, that escape the will of men. Hence there was a god *An,** "the On-high" or "the Heaven," behind the Heaven; *Iškur,* behind "the Storm"; *Nanna,* behind "the Moon"; *Gibil,* behind "Fire"; *Nisaba,* behind "Cereals," and so on. Sometimes such a power over things was registered in the proper name of the corresponding god: *Enlil,** "Lord Air";[3] *Ninḫursag,* "Lady of the Mountain," and so on. The supernatural beings were distinguished from us not only by their supernatural power and knowledge but also by the length of their existence, which could not be terminated by death. Besides that, they were conceived in the image of man: they had a body, that had to be fed, clothed, and sheltered; they came and went, talked, laughed, and cried; they loved and bickered; they created families: fathers, mothers, children.

Such a way of viewing things was natural for the local civilization and was shared by the entire land. Before the last third, or even the middle of the third millennium, that land was politically divided into principalities of sorts where the ancient villages of prehistory had been reorganized around a capital city. These principalities coexisted, sometimes in peace, sometimes in conflicts of interest. Even if the designation of the rulers of these mini-states could differ from one to another, the monarchical principle was accepted by all. On the model of the king at the head of the state apparatus, surrounded in his palace by his close and remote family members, by his assistants and his functionaries, they imagined in the temple a supernatural ruler with this family and his court, made up of personalities regrouped and structured in a hierarchy, doubtless starting with the divinities of the ancient villages and territories before their unification under the control of the capital city, whose major god had become the supernatural king.

It is thus that from the very earliest texts on and continuously in a unanimous tradition of several millennia, Enki is presented as the king of the southern city-state, Eridu,* which at that time was much closer to the lagoon that connects the mouths of the Tigris and the Euphrates rivers with the Persian Gulf. He resided in his temple (*É,* house) the name of which, *É.Engur* or *É.Apsû,* stresses the close ties with "sweet water." Engur and the almost synonymous Apsû indicate in fact the subterranean level of the world that in the opinion of the time formed the enormous reservoir of water on which the ground had to float, because water was discovered wherever one dug and it came up in springs and wells. Whatever may have

3. We have to understand with this term something like the atmosphere, the space that separates heaven from earth.

been the original meaning of the dual name En.ki (it has been suggested moreover that it had been applied originally to more than one god), it was regarded as containing an allusion to that part of the world in which the god was considered to reside: in the Below, the liquid underground of the surface of the Earth. Also the theologians always related his name to that of Water: thus È.a, or more often and regularly É.a, which in fact attempts to render the name *Aia*, or perhaps *Ia/Ia'u* (Ebla), a divine personality of the Semites of Mesopotamia and syncretized with Enki, is the Sumerian expression for "Spouting of Water" or "Residence [in the] Water."

In his kingdom of Eridu, Enki had as a family his wife *Damgalnunna/Damkina*, "The Great Wife of the Prince/The true Wife," and their children. Prominent among the latter was *Asalluḫi**—written at first *Asar(i)-luḫi*—the ancient god of the neighboring town of Ku'ar, which had been annexed by Eridu. As far as we know only later was Marduk* also mentioned, and he absorbed through syncretism the ancient *Asalluḫi*. In his court we also know well his "lieutenant" (*sukkal*), the two-faced god *Isimu/Usmû*. It appears that around these personalities, as around others, a great number of myths were woven, starting in the beginning of time. We cannot say anything about them except for the paltry parts that have survived later in the written tradition and that have reached us.

The political evolution of the land—certain cities became superior to others and became in turn the centers of extended kingdoms—was translated in the reorganization of the divine personnel, who followed the careers of their cities. Some members of the supernatural society, without abandoning at first their local attachments and honors, started to play more universal roles. It seems that in this way, starting at least from the middle of the third millennium, a type of central pantheon was created, which was recognized by the entire country. The divine population was hierarchically structured in this pantheon, with a "triad" at the top of the pyramid that remained preeminent until the very end, despite later avatars. At the head was An (Anu), at first the ruler of the city Uruk,* who was taken under the circumstances as the still-living father and ancestor of the ruling dynasty. The real ruler of the gods and the world was Enlil, whose personal city, Nippur,* seems always to have been only the center of some type of Sumerian amphictiony, without a real political role. The third place was occupied by Enki. What exactly was his role?

Our foremost source for defining his role is the mythology, of which the oldest known documents, from somewhat before the middle of the third millennium, are not yet readily usable because of the difficulties and the imperfections of the cuneiform writing system, which was only three or four centuries old at that time and still too close to its original state as a mnemonic device. It is not before the first half of the second millennium that we have access to a literature, first in Sumerian and then in Akkadian, that is at the same time abundant and understandable. It is clearly highly elaborated and not at all "primitive," but we still find in it many ancient remains. These are good indications for us if we can understand them according to their own code, and if we look in them for Enki/Ea's basic and constant features rather than for his stratified elements.

One of the accounts in Sumerian—we can discuss these first—which seems to preserve very ancient characteristics is perhaps the one that has been titled *Enki and Ninḫursag*, and is some 300 verses long.[4] The god appears in it not yet completely integrated into the great "triad," whose two other members are barely mentioned. He appears independently and his wife is identified as the ancient goddess Ninḫursag. The action takes place not in Eridu but further south, in the land of Tilmun, the coastal area of Arabia on the northern part of the Persian Gulf. The area is outside southern Mesopotamia, but active relations of a commercial nature at least had been maintained with it from very early on. The myth wants to explain how Tilmun changed from a type of desert into a region that was, if not civilized, at least economically productive and capable of feeding "the land," i.e. Sumer.[5] The transformation was due to Enki, who came to settle there with his wife for that very purpose. His first act was to introduce, instead of the *Bitter Water* of the riverline marshes, *Sweet Water* (*drawn*) *from the soil* by digging wells. Soon the land was covered with cultivated and useful grains.

Then we see, among a number of obscurities that are never absent in Sumerian literary texts, how *Enki sleeps with* his wife who *in nine days for nine months* bears him *Ninsar*, the Lady of Vegetables. Then he sleeps with Ninsar *at the bank of the river* and under the same conditions she bears him *NinKUR*, a polyvalent name which in this context must be considered as Lady-of-the-fibrous-Plants(?). After that *NinKUR* bears him *Uttu*, known as the goddess of spinning. When the text becomes intelligible again there is mention of other plants, first for food, then for medicinal purposes. *Ninḫursag* gives the latter to her husband, each one of the plants to heal a certain part of his diseased body. In the end these plants are hypostatized as minor deities, several of whom are known to us as having power in the vegetable world (like *Ab.ú: Father of the herbs*) and its products (e.g. *Nin.kasi: Lady of the beer*).

Of course we do not know what historical implications are hidden in the myth. What strikes us is the role assigned to Enki. He civilized by introducing sweet water—a characteristic perfectly in accordance with his fa-

4. S. N. Kramer, *Enki and Ninḫursag, A Sumerian "Paradise" Myth;* idem, *The Sumerians*, pp. 147ff., and *History Begins at Sumer*, pp. 143–49.

5. See n. 7 below.

miliarity with the Apsû—i.e. artificial irrigation, thanks to which he has "created" in an empty and sterile land the cultivation and the processing of useful plants. In other words he introduced agricultural techniques.

The same role, now extended over the entire universe, as far as it could be easily imagined by the Mesopotamians in those days, and still from the point of view of technology and profit, is the focus of another Sumerian work, of 467 verses, to which we have given the title *Enki and the World Order.*[6] The text, whose first part, in honor of *Enki,* relates it to the liturgy, describes the activities that gave rise to the god's glory. His office was not the government of the world, but he planned the world, organizing every aspect of it so that it had its own purpose. At least he *fixed the destinies* of the latter always to the benefit of Sumer,[7] the center of the world.

It is with Sumer that he begins: he assigns it as a *destiny* to be the greatest, the richest, the most civilized and civilizing. Then he goes to the south, where he takes the city of Ur* as the connecting link with the foreign countries accessible by sea, and he makes the city the commercial harbor of Lower Mesopotamia. Then, as if going from one extreme of the area to the other, he goes east and assigns to Meluḫḫa (at that time the western part of the Indian peninsula) the destiny to prosper because of its gold and its tin. Then, retracing his steps, he assigns the fates of the immediate neighbors of Sumer: in the southwest Tilmun will be blessed—in accordance with the myth just mentioned—with the provision of dates and grains; in the east, on the Iranian plateau, Elam* and Marḫaši* will be the regular producers of semiprecious stones and of silver; in the northwest, the Martu* (seminomadic Semites of Syria) will be the great providers of cattle. This is how Enki on the "international" level organizes his country and its surroundings so that he derives from the latter the consumer goods that are not, or not sufficiently, available in Sumer. In return Sumer will provide the surroundings with its light and its culture. The god plays in fact the role of the steward who plans the balance between labor and exchange inside the domain that he controls. This domain is the universe, and Lower Mesopotamia was its center.

Finally he fulfills the same office in the interior of his own country. He sets in motion its principal cultural divisions, so to speak—first geographical, then administrative and economical. Each of them he confides to a "specialist" god, placed under his command according to the usual system of scaled responsibilities. To *Enbilulu* he assigns the functioning of the Ti-

6. C. Benito, *Enki and Ninmaḫ* and *Enki and the World Order*, pp. 77–160. S. N. Kramer, *The Sumerians*, pp. 171ff; idem, *History Begins at Sumer*, pp. 94–99.

7. In antiquity it was understood that this term referred to the southern part of Mesopotamia, bordering on the Persian Gulf.

gris and the Euphrates; to *Nanna* the marshy area filled with fish in the south; to *Nanše* the sea; to *Iškur* the flow of rain; to *Enkimdu* the work in the fields; to *Ašnan* the sprouting of plants; to *Kulla* the making of bricks; to *Mušdamma* the construction of buildings; to *Sumuqan* the wild animals; to *Dumuzi* (*Tammuz*) animal husbandry; to *Utu*, the Sun god (*Šamaš*), the proper administrative and juridical direction of the land; to *Uttu* the entire area of textiles; to *Aruru* the production of humans; to *Nininsinna* the sector of prostitution, or as we would say "free love," that was considered to be extremely important at that time; to *Ninmug* the work with wood and with metals; to *Nidaba* all that concerns birth—something that was very delicate and dangerous in those days of high infant mortality; and to (another?) *Nanše* writing and the entire cultural domain that depends on it. We have here, in an order whose justification escapes us, a panoramic view of the entire area of civilization. Only one aspect is missing: war. And it is precisely to that aspect, it seems, that the author wants to get, as if to stress that in that country war, or perhaps the divinity on which war depends, is a latecomer. He ends his work in fact with the accusations by the goddess *Inanna* (*Ištar*)* who claims to have been forgotten and to have been left idle by *Enki*. The latter immediately reminds her that she already controls the field of war, and urges her to quiet down or to end its use entirely.

In a broader manner even than in *Enki and Ninḫursag* the god is placed here at the head of culture and the quality of life in Sumer, and, hence, in the rest of the world.

The ancient Mesopotamians seem to have been very conscious of their civilization and at the same time held a high opinion of it. Hence, when they reflected on it and sought to analyze its contents, which they were unable to separate from their religious vision of the world, they were led to develop the concept of the *me*. That term is obscure to us and difficult to understand, as it does not correspond to any of our semantic categories. It translates a point of view that is far removed from ours and that cannot be directly related to ours. A *me* is an entire cultural area, an acquisition of organized and civilized life reduced to an essential feature which sums it up or evokes it. But at the same time it also presents this acquisition as the result of an "invention" and of a divine decision. The *me* are always related to the gods, who are the only ones that *hold* them. In this sense they are like the specific contents of the *divine plans* (giš.ḫur/*uṣurtu*), of the *destinies* (nam/*šimtu*) assigned by the gods to all beings, animate or inanimate. And precisely because they are only in the hands of the gods, the *me* also indicate the power of each of them over a particular domain.

The theologians of the creed had established a catalogue of these *me* in somewhat more than one hundred entries (see pp. 192f.). Here is a short selection that lists only the clearest ones and classifies them according to our way of thinking. Among them *Divinity* appears, to sum up the entire divine world; *Shepherding, Royalty,* the *Exalted Scepter* that indicate various aspects of the royal power and its functioning; various *Priestly functions* for men and for women; the masculine and feminine representatives of their highly valued prostitution with the related fields of *Sexual trade* and *Embracing.* We also find in it social relations, regulating communal life: *the Assembled family; Compulsory Labor; Dispute; Victory; Slander; Flattery* and what we would call "social virtues" and their opposites: *Courage; Superiority; Dishonor; Justice; Happiness; Falsehood; Respect; Attention* and *Respectful silence*, to direct the interactions between inferiors and superiors. And also: *the Ability to give advice; Reflection; the Feeling for justice; Decision.* For military life: various *Arms; Pillaging of towns* with its results for the conquered people: *Lamentation*—which has produced a well-known literary genre; *Revolt by foreign countries; the Condition of peace and the stability of the throne. Trade* was not forgotten, represented by *Expeditions.* The largest selection was reserved for what we would call "technology": *Husbandry* was represented by *the Sheepfold.* The entire cultivation of the earth was summed up by *Irrigation*, portrayed by the *Flood*—the annual rise of the waters—that set irrigation in motion. There was *the Art of lighting fires; the Art of arranging embers* to keep fire alive and to control it, and *the Art of extinguishing* for when it got out of hand; *Woodwork; Smelting; Bronze work* for the entirety of *Metallurgy; Leatherwork; Masonry; the Scribal art; Exorcism* and *Music* suggested by several instruments. Finally as if to dominate this entire area, and also others which were acquired and realized through them: *Intelligence* and *Knowledge*, entries that are essentially practical—we would do well to remember that.

This enumeration appears—even more than once—in another myth in Sumerian which is unusually long (eight hundred lines). Its literary value is mediocre and it is called *Inanna and Enki.*[8] All the *me* are presented in it as the foremost, the natural, and the universal possession of Enki alone. At a certain moment Inanna, goddess of Uruk, wants to have them—in other words, she wants to give to her own city the civilization that is expressed by them—and she cannot think of any better way than to make their keeper drunk during a banquet which she cunningly makes him give for her in Eridu. She takes advantage of his dazed condition to take the *me* away from him and to bring them to her own city. According to the mythological code, this would not mean that, once the theft was completed, Enki and Eridu were deprived of their *me*, but that henceforth Inanna and Uruk would *also*

8. G. Farber-Flügge, *Der Mythos "Inanna und Enki" unter besonderer Berücksichtigung der Liste der me:* Text of the myth on pp. 16–63; study of the list of *me:* pp. 97–213. Also S. N. Kramer, *The Sumerians*, pp. 160–62; idem, *History Begins at Sumer*, pp. 93–103.

have the possession and the use of them. Whatever the actual and historical circumstances immortalized in the accounts may have been, there is no better way to show that the creator, the sole initiator of all civilized life, was Enki, no one but Enki.

And because all the mechanisms of the complex and refined existence of the land were in a sense concentrated in *Enki,* and he was the source and the regulator of the total, he was considered to be the *intelligent* god par excellence. That means that in a system where intelligence was almost entirely polarized by action, production, and success, he was considered to be some type of super-engineer who was the only one able to deal with any "technical" problem and to find at once the most astute and most efficient solution. A number of mythological tales illustrate this prerogative abundantly.

In ancient Mesopotamia one naturally wondered about the origins and the purpose of mankind. The "thinkers" provided a certain number of answers. We have remains of more than one anthropology, each of them conferring the foremost role upon the divinity who was the focus of the work, such as Enlil for instance. The most elaborate version, however, the one that was doubtless considered to represent the common opinion, is the one that regards Enki as the creator of mankind. If he *created* mankind, it was not by accident or goodness, or as a simple demonstration of his power, but to resolve a precise problem, a "technical" problem.

Because it is in Sumerian and although it is rather late in date (somewhat before the year 1500) and only mentions the creation of mankind in passing, we will first point out the short poem of one hundred and forty lines called *Enki and Ninmaḫ.*[9] It introduces us to an anthropogony that is more explicit (and that probably inspired it, namely that of the *Supersage*—see below and p. 221 above) and places the issue in its real context—that of the absolute superiority of Enki in matters of intelligence and technical competence. We find here a battle of power, or more precisely of the capability to create and to adapt, between Enki and his wife, who here bears the name of the ancient goddess *Ninmaḫ, the Exalted Lady.*

We are told that the gods all derive from the universal primordial Mother, who bears here the name of *Nammu,* and that they installed themselves on earth, each in his own plot of land. Married and taking care of families, they had to provide for their sustenance by starting to dig canals, a rather remarkable fact! Only those of a category that was somehow secondary had to devote themselves to work, while the great ones, exempted, spent their time relaxing: *Enki sleeps.* This inequality, not less than their tiredness, made the worker-gods unhappy, and Nammu warned Enki, rec-

9. C. Benito, *Enki and Ninmaḫ . . .*, pp. 9–81; S. N. Kramer, *The Sumerians,* pp. 149ff; idem, *History Begins at Sumer,* pp. 108–10.

ommending that he attend to their replacement. After having thought deeply, Enki "invented" a new being: he made its "mold"—a normal procedure in the land of clay—and he showed Nammu how to use it. With the help of Ninmaḫ and seven other goddesses, a man was made from it, who was clearly developed to resolve a difficulty that was at the same time economical and technical. Enki in the end behaved like an engineer, who on demand draws up the plans for an instrument that has been calculated to provide a certain output with the least effort.

The rest of the account shows the genius of the god even further. It portrays between him and his spouse, who had become lighthearted from the beer drunk during a banquet held to celebrate his victory, one of these duels of prestige that were so well known in ancient Mesopotamia that they gave rise to a literary genre: the *disputes.** By using the "mold" designed by Enki, Ninmaḫ proposed to produce disabled people, and she challenged the god to "heal" them by finding a suitable use for them, *a good destiny* as they would have said. He accepted the challenge and he won six times over his opponent by assigning the creatures the following uses: to the *being-that-was-weak-and-incapable-of-effort* he assigned the *destiny of a court officer*—an ironic feature!; to *the blind* that of the *bard;* the role he assigned to *the lame* is lost in the break of the tablet; *he who cannot hold his sperm* (i.e. who is unable to procreate) is healed by one of these "exorcistic" charms of which Enki was a master, as we know from other sources; he assigned to *the sterile woman* a place among the *prostitutes;* and for the *asexual human being, neither male nor female* he found a place *in the royal court,* very probably as one of the transvestites and cinedes* whose existence is well attested. Afterwards Enki took his turn in challenging Ninmaḫ by making a last "disabled man" who he himself drew from the "mold." It was seemingly a monstrous creature such as is sometimes born: malformed, feeble, and unsalvageable. Ninmaḫ, as was to be expected, could not find him any *good destiny.* The triumph of Enki was not only to have invented mankind, an enormous technical success, but also in finding a function for all the types, even the imperfect but usable ones, such as this "tool." Thus he is at the same time civilizer, inventor, keeper of all cultural values, but also the most intelligent, the most clear-sighted, the prototypical technician, the only one capable of overcoming all hurdles, and of adapting everything for his purposes, of molding matter for every possible use.

We also find the same image in the myths in Akkadian, some of which represent real and full syntheses in contrast to the Sumerian ones. They are not limited to one point, one conflict, or one problem, but cover an entire vision, a large aspect of history or of theology. Among the many personalities that are involved, Enki, or rather Ea as the Akkadians said, is only rarely the protagonist. But his essential characteristics that we have found up till now, remain the same and are even better developed. Two famous works have to be cited first. Although they are half a millennium apart, the role of Ea is the same in them, and each of them sheds a somewhat different light on him.

We usually refer to the oldest one (from the year 1650 at the latest) by the name of its mortal hero, who was very closely associated with Ea: *Atraḫasis,** or the *Supersage* (see above, pp. 221ff.). The long poem, which in its entirety must have contained almost twelve hundred lines, of which we have less than two-thirds, comprised the entire ancient history of mankind, from its "creation" to its present condition—a quite wonderful synthesis.[10] Without involving itself with the theogony, as in *Enki and Ninmaḫ* (above) and *Enûma eliš** (below), it takes matters from the moment that the gods of second rank, obliged to be the only ones to work for the divine community, grow weary and revolt by going on strike, as we would say. In order to deal with this dangerous situation, which might lead all of them to starvation, the gods come together in plenary assembly, but at first they find no solution. Finally, Ea alone relieves their anguish by bringing to the problem the solution that was described above, in *Enki and Ninmaḫ*. He suggests the creation of a new being whose clay will be made soft and malleable with the blood of a god, slain for that purpose. As a result, not only will it have *both the aspect of the gods and of man,* but the divine victim will be chosen to materialize with precision the model that Ea had conceived in his wise mind: the name and the definition of that god—i.e. his own *being* in the land where each name derived from the essence, where it could replace and reproduce the being—will control the *constitution* itself of mankind. As the god answered to the name *Wê-ilu: Wê-god,* man will be *awîlu*, a term that in Akkadian means *man*. And as he had *ṭêmu,* i.e. a certain aspect of intelligence and of psyche, this *Wê* together with *ṭêmu* will produce in man the *(w)eṭemmu,** the *ghost,* this untouchable and fantastic image of all of us that survives after death and that allows us to participate from afar in the divine privilege, certainly not of immortality, but that of longevity. These features show to what degree the project of Ea was wise, complex, subtle, and precise.[11] As always, we have to stress that he was only the *conceiver.* Nowhere, and especially not here, do we see him taking matters in hand to materialize what he has invented. He confides the production to the goddess who is the universal Mother and Matrix, to whom he "dictates" his instructions. But, despite that, he is no less the only and the real creator of mankind, of whom he will become the fierce defender.

That is the subject of the second part of the work. We see in it how men,

10. W. G. Lambert and A. R. Millard, *The Babylonian Story of the Flood;* R. Labat, *Les Religions* . . . , pp. 113–22; J. Bottéro, *Annuaire 1967–1968* . . . , pp. 113–22 and *Annuaire 1968–1969* . . . , pp. 83f.

11. See also "La création de l'homme et son nature dans le poème d'*Atraḫasîs,*" cited above, chap. 6, n.5.

once they are installed on earth and put to work, are so successful in their original calling that they prosper and multiply enormously. Their "noise," their stirring, their racket, disturbs the serene, idle, existence of the gods. Therefore, the king of the gods and the world, Enlil, wants to reduce the number of these troublesome masses, and for that purpose inflicts an epidemic upon them. But Ea, eager to preserve his work though unable to openly oppose the will of the holder of power, acts in his own way: *with cunning.* He secretly warns his protégé who shares with him the title of "Supersage" among the humans. He makes him take proper measures to avoid the calamity. When Enlil, defeated in his aims, sends Famine to decimate mankind, Ea saves it in the same way.

Then Enlil, furious because he was tricked, decides this time to finish off mankind by sending the Flood. To assure that his sinister project will not be betrayed, he demands from all the gods a solemn oath that they will not reveal his plan to mankind. Here also Ea's ingenuity shows. First by his resistance to Enlil, whose short-sighted plans would only lead the gods back to the disastrous situation from which they were saved by the "invention" of mankind. Second, by the equivocal way, as we can easily say, in which he arranges to break his oath without being accused of doing so: he sends to the "Supersage" a premonitory dream, which is not the same as speaking, and he gives him instructions by addressing the reed wall of the house where Atraḫasîs lives, which is not the same as speaking to man! Thus it happens that on Ea's advice his protégé builds a great boat and saves himself from the Flood, with his family and the animals that inhabit the world. The actions of Ea have not only saved the future of his work, mankind, but especially ensured the gods an indefinite opulent life that is free from worries, against the wish of the king, whose blind fury would have plunged them in destitution and ruin. To preserve the reasonable aspects of the decisions of his ruler, however, Ea agrees to slow down the great proliferation of man, but *in his way.* He makes use, not of brute force, but of thought which adapts the means to the end. He introduces on earth not only a shorter duration of human life but also some categories of women who cannot bear children, either because of sterility, or because of a religious state that prohibits it, or by having their children taken away early by the enemy of babies, the cruel demon who extinguishes (Pâšittu). Ea can act this way, if necessary even against the will of the ruler, on condition that it is in the interest of the latter and his subjects. He does not stand up against him, and not having the power he does not use force and command, but he does use calculation, savoir-faire, and cunning.

Written half a century after *Atraḫasîs*, around the year 1200, the famous *Epic of Creation** (*Enûma eliš: When On-High . . .*), of about eleven hundred verses over seven tablets that are almost entirely preserved, constitutes even more so than the poem of the Supersage a real treatise on theology.[12] The purpose is to legitimize the reorganization of the divine personnel which was the result of a political revolution, as were the earlier reorganizations. In a lasting reorganization of the entire country, around the year 1750, Babylon had become, by force, the capital, and Marduk, the city-god of Babylon, had become the supreme deity of the country. The theologians had to justify this promotion which the worshipers had extended from the terrestrial universe to the supernatural world. They thus explained in the *Enûma eliš* that Marduk was unanimously placed by the gods at their head, because he had saved them from a mortal danger, when the Mother of all, the monstrous and primordial *Tiamat,** wanted to annihilate them. And if he became similarly the absolute master of the world, it was because he had the idea of *creating* it by using for its material the enormous body of his defeated enemy. And it was also he who conceived of a project to find a substitute to free the gods, who were his subjects but also his family, from their obligatory work, under conditions that we already know.

What happened to Ea in this history? Far from being removed from center stage, as were Anu and Enlil, who faded away to the status of *dei otiosi* (as Anu had already more or less been when Enlil ruled) because of the fact of Marduk's promotion, Ea maintained his preeminence and his role. First of all because he was the father of Marduk, who inherited from him his intelligence among other qualities. Marduk in the end stresses the excellence of Ea insofar as he is the superlative replica of him. Second, Ea not only showed his son the way by triumphing himself over Apsû, the husband of Tiamat, during an earlier battle, and by using him cleverly once he was "dead" for the building of his dwelling; but also, when the gods were horror-stricken because of the new and frightening menace imposed upon them by Tiamat and looked in vain for a champion against her, it was Ea who discovered Marduk and pushed him into accepting the difficult task. Finally, when the new ruler decided to replace the gods at work and when he conceived a rather precise idea of their substitute, because he already had given it the name of *man*, it was to his father Ea that he gave the project to make it feasible, and it was under the direction of Ea that it was materialized, as in *Atraḫasîs*. In the "new order of things" Ea had thus maintained his indispensable and irreplaceable role of supertechnician, of ingenious conceiver, of the holder of intelligence par excellence.

A few more touches taken from some other mythological accounts in Akkadian allow us to complete this portrait and to show its permanence in Mesopotamia, whose written culture survived for about three millennia. They always involve difficult problems in which the divine society is en-

12. See also above, p. 220.

gaged, either as a group or through one of its representatives. Only Ea can bring a solution, either by the development of new instruments, or simply by the execution of a crafty and efficient technique.

In the *Descent of Inanna/Ištar to the Netherworld,*[13] of which there is a long Sumerian version (about four hundred lines) and one in Akkadian (one hundred and thirty-eight lines) that is somewhat different, Inanna/Ištar falls imprudently into the hands of the ruler of the Netherworld, Ereškigal. As she is the goddess of love, her absence stops all sexual excitement on earth and compromises at once the survival of animals and of man, to the great injury of the gods. To release her, Ea "invents" and "creates" something to seduce the inflexible Ereškigal. It is a human being, but asexual: the prototype of those transvestite and effeminate passive homosexuals of whom we have already heard, "in the royal court," who were somewhat like buffoons (see above, p. 240 and pp. 190f.). It is in this way that he obtains from the amused infernal queen the freedom of her prisoner and that he starts up again the mechanism of generation.

In the myth of *Anzû,*[14] known since the first half of the second millennium, the text of which is not completely preserved, Ea goes to work differently. The problem is the disruption and the freezing of the functioning of the universe because the talisman-like insignia of supreme power have been stolen from their holder, who is still Enlil, by the giant and evil bird of prey Anzû. It is only Ea who can find a champion to defeat the bird: the young god Ningirsu/Ninurta.* The latter fails in his first attempt because Anzû had the time to pronounce an all-powerful spell that reduced the weapons of Ninurta to their original state: the arrow becomes a reed, the arrow's feathers become bird feathers, and so on. Ea teaches the young hero a successful tactic: to take advantage of the dizziness of Anzû, shocked by the winds used in the assault, by cutting off his wings. This mutilation should leave Anzû stupefied, grounded, and *speechless,* in other words without a "magical" defense against the arrows. This is how order is restored in the world thanks to Ea's genius.

Ea even happens to intervene with an astuteness and competence that is so artful and "in eastern fashion," that the apparent defeat of his stratagems hides his real victory to the superficial eye. In the myth of *Nergal and Ereškigal,*[15] of which two recensions in Akkadian are known, a short

13. Sumerian version: S. N. Kramer: "Inanna's Descent to the Nether World . . . ," *Journal of Cuneiform Studies* 5 (1951): 1–17, and *The Sumerians,* pp. 153–55. Akkadian version: R. Labat, *Les Religions* . . . , pp. 258–65. See also J. Bottéro, *Annuaire 1971–1972* . . . , pp. 79–97. And, for the gods, S. N. Kramer, *The Sacred Marriage Rite,* pp. 107–21 and 154–56.

14. R. Labat, *Les Religions* . . . , pp. 80–92; J. Bottéro, *Annuaire 1970–1971* . . . , pp. 116–28.

15. R. Labat, *Les Religions* . . . , pp. 89–123; J. Bottéro, *Annuaire 1971–1972* . . . , pp. 97–110.

one from around the year 1400 and a much expanded one some centuries later, but less well preserved, an explanation is given of how the infernal kingdom, until then the property of the goddess Ereškigal, came to have a male ruler, Nergal,* who had been previously among the celestial gods. We are told that Nergal deeply insulted the infernal queen in the person of her ambassador in heaven. Nergal is summoned by her to be punished, but he becomes in the end her husband and consort. The transformation had to be created to Ea, who advised Nergal first to disguise himself in order not to be recognized by the myrmidon of Ereškigal, and then to boldly confront the latter in her own subterranean palace. In both versions Nergal ends up by staying there, as the husband of the queen of the Below, and it seems thus to be against the wishes and the efforts of Ea, who seems to have done everything to keep the god with his original family in Heaven. But the real triumph of Ea is suggested in the older version by the mistake upon which the entire work turns: Ereškigal demanded the impertinent man *ana mûti: for death,* but she obtains him *ana muti: as husband.* In a world where names and words have such an objective value this is not an amusing pun but a trick by Ea, who plays on the homophony of the two terms. The later version presupposes a more subtle and more psychological play: when Ea returns Nergal to the Netherworld, he knows that Nergal, on his first trip, established tender bonds with Ereškigal and that she will definitely succumb to his charms when she finds him again. He knows it, but he does not say it. He does it so well that his dealings seem to fail, although they are successful. What he wanted without showing it, was in the end to "colonize" the Netherworld by installing as its ruler a member of the celestial divine family.

The procedure is perhaps even more subtle in the *Legend of Adapa,*[16] also in Akkadian and known in three fragmentary versions starting in date from about the middle of the second millennium. The hero is a legendary personality whom we will encounter later and whose name is Adapa, the *Wise One.* He is a creature of Ea, and has become the majordomo of his temple in Eridu. Attacked in his boat by the South Wind, Adapa breaks its wings. Thus he incites the wrath of the King of the world, who was at that time Anu. The latter summons Adapa to punish him. Ea intervenes again to save him. He teaches him how to win the good favor of the two gods who were charged with bringing him before Anu and who will take his side and intercede on his behalf if he knows how to flatter them. Anu will receive him, then, not as an accused but as a guest, and will offer him food and drink, as is the custom—evidently precious offerings for the simple mortal that Adapa is. Ea advises him to refuse so that Anu will be obliged to pre-

16. R. Labat, *Les Religions . . . ,* pp. 287–94; J. Bottéro, *Annuaire 1969–1970 . . . ,* pp. 108–12.

sent him with the food that is reserved for the gods and that would give him immortality. But Anu, who detected the trap, makes an offering of supernatural dishes to Adapa. By refusing them in obedience to Ea, Adapa looses at once the chance to attain immortal life. In this subtle fight with Anu it seems thus that Ea had lost at the expense of his protégé. But if we agree to take into account the finesses and the light and cunning touches, and if we consider the passage in the beginning of the text where Ea at the creation of Adapa seemingly *refuses him immortality when he gives him wisdom,* we read between the lines that he did not want his faithful servant to pass into the ranks of immortals, when he had made him mortal for a very good reason. In reality, there would have been something wrong with his intelligence, his ingenuity, and his cleverness, if these characteristics, as those of a good Oriental, had not been extremely subtle and capable of "ambiguities."

That is the role of Enki/Ea in the position that he occupies in the system of the gods: at the side and just below the holder of rule. What he does, what he has to do, is never defined in terms of power, of government or of political authority, but only in terms of organization, of control, of the promotion of life and, to that goal, of intelligence and technical and practical success—and all this, always, in the supreme interests of the divine society. In the end he was portrayed as being at the head of an enormous and extremely complicated mechanism, which he guarded and animated. Beginning with his infallible directives and passing through his "foremen," the minor deities each of whom he had charged with a section of this gigantic machine, this mechanism reached all the way down to the "workmen," the people who made it actually function. These people were first of all the "technicians." Ea is the *only god* who, according to the entire tradition, is the patron of all of them and of all the technologies, as if he had established all of them: from agriculture and husbandry to writing and exorcism. This is the first well-established fact about him.

If we look now for the model on which this office and the image of Enki/Ea is developed, in other words to which it corresponds in ancient Mesopotamian society—as the king provided the image for the supernatural holder of power over the entire universe—we can make a start with a little-known myth, that of the *apkallu.** It is designed to answer this question: how has Enki/Ea, the "inventor" of civilization and of all technology, inserted these inventions into history and revealed them to mankind?

The myth is not preserved by itself and in one form. We have to partially reconstruct it. We own first of all the outlines to *Berossos,** this "Babylonian priest of Bêl" who around the year 300 B.C. summed up the "philosophy" and the history of his very ancient country in Greek.

He explains:

> in Babylonia a number of people came to install themselves in Chaldea (the part of Lower Mesopotamia that borders on the Persian Gulf) where they lived an irreligious life, similar to that of animals. In the first year an extraordinary monster appeared . . . on the shore of the Red sea, and its name was Oannes. Its entire body was that of a fish, and underneath his head was a second one, as well as feet similar to those of a man—an image that is still remembered and that is still depicted up to today. This being lived among the people without eating anything and taught them writing, science, and technology of all types, the foundation of cities, the building of temples, jurisprudence and geometry. He also revealed to them (how to cultivate) grains and how to harvest fruits. In short, he gave them all that constitutes civilized life. He did it so well that ever since one has found nothing exceptional [in it]. When the sun set, the monster Oannes plunged back into the sea to pass the night in the water, because he was amphibious. Later similar creatures appeared. . . .

There were a total of seven whom Berossos describes as also coming from the Red Sea and as fishmen. To each of them he connects an antediluvian reign.[17]

Berossos is an author who can be trusted. In the literary tradition in Sumerian and Akkadian we easily find several elements that agree with his narrative and that show a venerable tradition. A short mythological account inserted in an exorcistic text[18] alludes to the *seven brilliant apkallu,* who are compared to *carps,* the model of splendor and brilliance in the poetic imagery of belief, and *who assured the success of the plans that the gods had made for heaven and earth.* The famous *Epic of Erra**[19] also recalls the *seven apkallu of the Apsû, pure carps, who, like Ea their lord, had received* (from him) *extraordinary ingenuity.* Another document, a list from the Seleucid period,[20] lists sixteen individuals, each of them associated with the rule of a king, to whom each of them seems to have played the role of those sages, traditionally placed in the Orient at the side of the king as advisers and called "viziers" by the Arabs. They are divided into three groups: the last group includes eight of them and goes back from the reign of

17. P. Schnabel, *Berossos,* pp. 253f.: III.

18. E. Reiner, "The Etiological Myth of the 'Seven Sages,'" *Orientalia,* n.s., 30 (1961): 1–11.

19. *Mythes et rites de Babylone,* p. 233, verse 162.

20. J. Van Dijk, in Lenzen *XVIII. vorläufiger Bericht über die . . . Ausgrabungen in Uruk-Warka,* 1962, pp. 44–52.

Esarhaddon (680–669) to the Flood, and they are given the title of *ummânu*. The second group is from the time of the Flood, and the first group from the period before the Flood. Together they list eight names, but they are called *apkallu*. It is as if the *apkallu* were nothing but the *ummânu* of the mythological period, both diluvian and antediluvian.

Moreover, the Akkadian word *ummânu* refers to people of a certain calibre and includes the sages, the scholars (some of them that are mentioned in the list are known to us from other sources as the writers and "authors," for instance, of the *Epic of Erra* and of the *Epic of Gilgameš**), but also craftsmen who were especially skilled in their special fields. In a land where the purely speculative use of thought and the mind is almost unknown and where knowledge and intelligence are finalized by realization and success, the combining of these notions under one word is not at all surprising. The *ummânu* in question were thus at the same time wise advisers of the king and some type of super-experts in his service. We have some instructive examples in Mesopotamia itself, such as Mukannišum under King Zimrilim of Mari (around 1780),[21] to mention but one. All the holders of power could not without exception have been initiated in their youth in the entire vast area of wisdom or of the knowledge of technical problems. Their role was, however, considerable in such an "industrialized" society, devoted to the production and the transformation of usable goods according to traditional procedures that were efficient and highly developed. The presence of such experts near them was thus indispensable. The myth has taken from the memory of the historical age this figure of the *ummânu*, the illustrious sage, the deep spirit who knows all, who could decide everything with justice and wisdom, who often could promote or invent new technologies. It has transposed him into mythological times, giving him an even more brilliant glory, which is shown by the designation of *apkallu*, a Sumerian superlative of *ummânu*. Supertechnicians, incomparable sages, and famous geniuses, they were considered as civilizing heroes who taught a mankind that was still unpolished all that constitutes *civilized life*, as stated by Berossos. He specified: *writing, science, and technology*, categories that were much more distinguished by the Greeks and by ourselves than by the Mesopotamians, who saw in them first of all the traditional and efficient procedures, without giving much weight to whether they required mostly the use of the hands or of the mind.

These *apkallu* were attached to Ea, their patron, and the first one among them was called Adapa, the *Wise One*, whose name, known from the Seleucid list summarized above, was precisely U'anna: Oannes. Ea used them to introduce culture in the history of his country: the great technical advances, the successive elements of the high civilization that had made,

21. O. Rouault, *Archives royales de Mari*, XVIII.

first Lower Mesopotamia in general, then Babylon, the cultural center of the world. Also here we are unable to isolate the historical memories fossilized in the myth of the *apkallu*. At least we see clearly, not only that it illustrates the idea they had of Enki/Ea, the inventor of all the commodities of life, of all technologies and of all culture, which he taught mankind little by little over time through his special envoys, the *apkallu*, but also that they imagined close affinities between Ea and the *apkallu*.

Precisely one of the traditional titles that had been conferred upon him in devotion or in theology (and which he moreover passed on to his son, Marduk) was *apkal ilî: apkallu of the gods.*[22] We should not translate this as is usually done, as *the wisest of the gods* but literally, as *he who among the gods plays the role of apkallu*, in other words he who is placed as an intelligent and subtle "vizier," as a wise adviser with inexhaustible resources, near the ruler of the gods, who without him would not always be able to make good use of his power—the story of the Flood provides a good example of that. His office was different from that of government—and that is why the two offices were hypostatized in two distinct personalities. But it was the indispensable complement of governing—and so the myth has juxtaposed them. At the side of authority, of power, of efficient command, of commanding appearance, there was indeed need for clear and profound vision, of intelligence, of wisdom, to give a positive sense to these orders—what we can call "the technical function of power," eminently incarnated by Enki/Ea.

Such a disposition stresses strongly, first of all, how the system of the gods in Mesopotamia was nothing but the translation and the reflection of the social, economic, and political organization of mankind. This is true to the extent that this organization, which is better known, can help us to understand more than one obscure aspect of the theology. The development of the theology in turn, properly analyzed and investigated, illuminates many aspects of the practices or the ideologies that directed communal life and the viewpoints of the ancient inhabitants of Mesopotamia. Nothing, for example, gives us a better perception of the form they gave to kingship than the mythology of divine power.

In the same way the image of Enki/Ea, and the unveiling of what it represents, undoubtedly introduces us better than any other consideration to the vision these ancient people had of their own culture, to the social hierarchy of values, and to their own way of conceiving and evaluating the activity of their minds.

It is not the god of war or the god of justice whom they placed inseparably at the side of their ruler of the universe, but the god of technology. For them war and justice were nothing but ways to live better, among many

22. See *Chicago Assyrian Dictionary*, A/2, pp. 171ff.

others, traditional and efficient procedures to obtain security and prosperity—i.e. techniques, as we have seen in *Inanna and Enki*.

If they have chosen the god who commands these techniques to preside, side by side with his ruler, over the evolution of the universe, it is because—many elements of their mythology and their history show it to us—the entire civilization of the country, their entire life and their way of living was first of all based, since the beginning of time, on communal work, the extensive production and transformation of usable goods. In such a system, in the end, everything is directed by a spiritual activity that researches, invents, promotes, and perfects procedures, not so much to *see* better, but to *do* better. All knowledge, all intelligence, was thus polarized by production and action, and was materialized equally well in the "practical judgment" of the artisans, in what we would call "craft," as in the sagacity of the tactician and his ability to adapt, and as in the "good sense" and the astuteness of what was known in the old days as an "upright man"—both on the collective level and in individual achievement.

Under these conditions it was almost inevitable that the god in whom this type of wisdom was incarnated, whose most perfect form was constituted by the technical-knowledge-that-always-succeeds, was placed in the highest rank, just behind the pillar of sovereign power without which no social life would be possible, and that his function would be portrayed as the completion of that power. This god was not "ancient" or an "old man," like Anu, the patriarch of the divine dynasty, to whom one might think of giving the role of adviser, but a younger god, Ea, as if to stress his capacities not only in knowledge but also in action, in speed and in versatility, which cannot be detached from the "technical functions" or from the "functions of government" that formed the double aspect of power.

14

The Dialogue of Pessimism *and Transcendence*

THE TEXT THAT FORMS THE SUBJECT OF THIS CHAPTER IS PERHAPS not well known among non-Assyriologists, and among Assyriologists it has the reputation of being a literary enigma. There is anything but agreement on the definitive sense of it among those who have studied it in depth. I cannot pretend to propose an irrefutable interpretation of it here, but, more prudently, I hope to awaken or to reawaken interest in a work that is original and very suggestive to a historian of religion, whatever his opinion of it may be.

It is a poetic composition, even though the metrics and prosody are very loose and lyricism is entirely absent, as is too often the case in ancient Mesopotamia, at least for our taste.[1] For a number of reasons taken from the manuscript traditions, the language, the ideology, and even from the contents itself of the "poem," it is improbable that the work had been composed before the end of the second millennium, or more likely the beginning of the first millennium B.C. For instance, one striking piece of evidence is that we find in it a mention of an *iron dagger* (52) when work with that metal did not spread in the Middle East before the twelfth century approximately.

Cuneiform literature was written down on clay tablets that were baked or simply sun-dried, that were exposed for various lengths of time in the past to the abuse of more or less frequent use, and were buried for millennia in a

1. The last—and best—edition of the text is the one by W. G. Lambert in 1960 in his masterly work *Babylonian Wisdom Literature*, pp. 139–49.

This chapter first appeared in *Revue de Théologie et Philosophie* 99 (1966): 7–27.

soil that was usually not very suitable for preserving them without damage. Therefore, the surviving literature is often in fragments, with the text riddled with lacunae due to breaks in the clay and to every kind of accident during the transmission. Our "poem" has not escaped that curse, but all in all it has pulled through without much damage. In fact we have pieces of five different manuscripts, one of which is almost complete. With them we have been able to reconstruct more than five-sixths of the entire text: of the eighty-six lines that it contained only some fifteen remain fragmentary and unintelligible. But their context is almost always clear enough for us to imagine at least the broad sense of what was contained in the lacunae.

The entire work is divided into eleven stanzas of unequal lengths. But all of them—except the last one which clearly has the function of a "conclusion"—are constructed on the same pattern. It involves the dialogue between a *master*, we would say a "gentleman," and his *slave*, something like his "valet" or his "footman." In each stanza the master starts by calling his servant, and the latter is at his disposal at once. The master then informs him that he has the intention of devoting himself to some particular activity. The valet not only agrees but also gives him some excellent reasons to encourage him in his intentions. But then, suddenly, the master tells him that he has abandoned the project. The valet approves immediately, with strong conviction, and presents his master with reasons to abstain that are as good as those he had offered to make him act.

Except for the "conclusion," each of the ten stanzas is devoted to a particular activity. The order in which they are presented is not very clear in itself, and it is obscured even more by the uncertainties of the manuscript tradition. For instance, the only manuscript that contains the continuous text of the fourth stanza mixes together two entirely different activities: the setting up of a home (IV, *29–31* and *37–38*) and litigation (ibid., *35–36* and perhaps *32–34*, damaged). In the textual tradition represented by this copy the scribe must thus have skipped from one stanza to another by mistake. If we accept this hypothesis the damage is not great. But there are worse problems: it seems that there were at least two recensions of the text; one represented by Assyrian manuscripts, the other by only one Babylonian manuscript. Each recension seems to have followed an order that is partly different in the distribution of the stanzas, which does not make matters clearer. I have adopted here the order of the "Assyrian recension" which is best attested: drive to the palace; banquet; hunt; setting up a home; litigation; revolution; love; sacrifice; business; philanthropy. To justify this order it seems to me that the author alternated activities according to certain opposites that he noticed in them: thus the first four make up an exchange between activities done outside the home (drive to the palace and hunt) and those done at home (banquet and setting up a home); philanthropy represents an unselfish activity as opposed to that of business. But as these considerations clearly do not explain everything, we should say at least that we will not succeed in looking at the matters in the same way as the author of our "poem."

Here is, first, a complete translation of the piece based on the Akkadian text, reconstructed especially through the efforts of W. G. Lambert.[2]

I. Drive to the palace

[Slave, listen to me!]—Here, I am, master, here I am!
—[Quickly! Fetch me the char]iot and hitch it up:
I want to drive to the palace!
[Drive, master, drive!] It will be to [your advantage]
[When he will see you, the king] will give you honors!
—[O well, slave] I will not drive [to] the palace!
—[Do not drive, mast]er, do not drive!
[When he will see you, the king] may send you [God knows where],
he may make you take [a route that you] do not know,
he will make you suffer agony [day and n]ight!

II. Banquet

Sl[ave, listen] to me!—Here I am, master, here I am!
—Quickly! [Fetch] me water for my hands: I want to dine!
—D[ine], master, dine! A good meal relaxes the mind!
[ ] the meal of his god. To wash one's hands passes the time!
—O well, [slav]e, I will not dine!
—Do not [di]ne, master, do not dine!
To eat (only) when one is hungry, to drink (only) when one is thirsty is the best for man!

III. Hunt

Slave, listen to me!—Here I am, master, here I am!
—Quickly! Fetch me my chariot, I am going to hunt!
—Drive, master, drive! A hunter gets his belly filled!
The hunting dog will break the bones (of the prey)!

2. See n. 1, above.

The [rav]en that scours the country can feed its nest!
The fleeting onager [finds rich pastures]!
—O well, slave, I will not [go] hunting!
—Do not go, master, do no[t g]o
The hunter's luck changes!
The hunting dog's teeth will get broken!
The raven that scours the country has a [hole] in the wall as home!
The fleeting onager has the desert as his stable!

IV. Marriage

Slave, listen [to me!—Here I am, master, here I am!]
—I want to set up [a home, I want to have a so]n!
—Have them [master], ha[ve them! The man who s]ets up a home [. . .] . . .[3]
—How could I set up a home!
—Do not set up a home:
Otherwise you will break up your father's home!

V. Litigation Only fragments of this stanza remain. They allow us to see that the "master" wants to go to court. For that purpose he decides first to let his opponent act, *without saying a word.* Then, changing his mind as usual, he does not want *to remain silent* anymore:

—Do not remain silent, master, [do not remain silent]!
If you do not open your mouth [your opponent will have a free hand],
Your prosecutors will be savage to y[ou, if you speak]!

VI. Revolution

Slave, listen to me!—Here I am, master, here I am!
—I want to lead a revolution!—So lead, master, lead!
If you do not lead a revolution, where will [your clo]thes come from?
And who will enable you to fill your b[elly]?
—O well, slave, I do not want to lead a revolution!

3. Here the copyist's mistake that I mentioned above appears. I have tried to disentangle the two original stanzas from the remains.

—⟨Do not lead, master, do not lead a revolution!⟩[4]
The man who leads a revolution is either killed, or flayed,
Or has his eyes put out, or is arrested and thrown in jail!

VII. Love

Slave, lis[ten] to [me]!—Here I am, master, here I am!
—I want to make love to a woman!—Make love, master, ma[ke love]!
The man who makes love to a woman forgets sorrow and fear!
—O well, slave, I do not want to make love to a woman!
[Do not make] love, master, do not m[ake love]!
Woman is a real pitfall, a hole, a ditch,
Woman is a sharp iron dagger that cuts a man's throat!

VIII. Sacrifice

Slave, listen to me!—Here I am, master, here I am!
—Quick! Fetch me water for my hands, and give it to me:
I want to sacrifice to my god!—Sacrifice, master, sacrifice!
The man who sacrifices to his god is satisfied at heart:
He accumulates benefit after benefit!
—O well, slave, I do not want to sacrifice to my god!
—Do not sacrifice, master, do not sacrifice!
You will teach your god to run after you like a dog,
Whether he asks of you "Rites" or "Do you not consult your god?" or anything else!

IX. Business

Slave, listen to me!—Here I am, master, here I am!
—I want to invest silver—Invest, master, [invest]!
The man who invests keeps his capital while his interest is enormous!

4. This entire verse was omitted by the copyist.

—O well, slave, I do not want to invest s[ilver]!
—Do not invest, master, do not invest!
Making loans is as [sweet] as making love; but getting (them) back is like having children!
They will ta[ke away] your capital, cursing you without cease,
They will make [you] lose the interest on the capital!

X. Philanthropy

Slave, listen to me!—Here I am, master, here I am!
—I want to perform a public benefit[5] for my country!
—So, do it, master, do it!
The man who performs a public benefit for his country,
His actions are "exposed" to the "circle"(?)[6] of Marduk!
—O well, slave, I do not want to perform a public benefit for my country!
—Do not perform, master, do not perform!
Go up the ancient tells and walk about,[7]
See the (mixed) skulls of plebeians and nobles:
Which is the malefactor, and which is the benefactor?

XI. Conclusion What to do?

Slave, listen to me!—Here I am, master, here I am!
—What then is good?
To have my neck and yours broken,
or to be thrown into the river, is that good?
—Who is so tall as to ascend to heaven?
Who is so broad as to encompass the entire world?

5. Variant of the Babylonian recension: *I want to distribute (free of charge) food rations to my country.* Also here the scribe seems to have mixed the contents of two different stanzas by mistake, because the verses that he copies are the same as those of 64ff., and thus concern not free generosity but business affairs for the purpose of gain.

6. The word *kippatu* used here has the meaning of *loop,* or *circle.* Perhaps it involves a type of ring that, together with the "staff," had the function of a talisman-like symbol of royal power. The expression, otherwise unknown, is obscure for a detailed translation, but the general meaning is clear: Marduk keeps account of good works and he will compensate them.

7. This verse is also found at the beginning (Tablet I, i: 16) and at the end (Tablet XI: 303) of the *Epic of Gilgameš.*

85. —O well, slave! I will kill you and send you first!
—Yes, but my master would certainly not survive
me for three days! . . .

What did the author of this beautiful work want to say? For almost fifty years now Assyriologists have not ceased discussing that. Without going into detail about their controversy or about the peculiarities of their individual opinions, we can group them into two diametrically opposed camps: those who take the text "seriously," as they say, and those who do not.

According to the first and largest group,[8] the author has already reasoned like the legendary donkey of Jean Buridan, so to speak, but on a somewhat more metaphysical level, by attaching to his deductions terribly important consequences, by trying to show us that in all aspects of human activity anything goes, and that there does not exist any compelling reason to choose between action and nonaction. When there are as many reasons to act as not to act, no action whatsoever, either positive or negative, will really impose itself; for a logical spirit there is nothing left in the end but to renounce everything, to hit one's head against the wall, and to opt for a "philosophical suicide." That would be the meaning of the last stanza. We can of course wonder why the author preaches voluntary death seemingly without doing anything about it himself. In order to explain such an incongruity, we are free to appeal to the well known illogical character of literary people in general, or to a particular "state of mind" of our author. If we take seriously the lesson that he wanted to give us, we find here the hymnal of a skeptical philosophy, desperate and very dark: "the negation of all values" (Jacobsen, *Before Philosophy,* p. 231).

Others[9] say that the serious and "philosophical" aspects to this work are clearly not the only ones. Several characteristics betray an intention of ridicule, of satire and of criticism, which place the purpose on an entirely different level. Let us first consider the choice of characters. The master is a rich idler. The list of activities that he wants to undertake is instructive: not a single one relates to *work,* to labor that would be necessary for survival. It is true that, if he had to earn a living by hard work, he would not have found the time to worry his head off by asking himself "what would be suitable to do." That first element is already an indication. He clearly does not know how to kill time: he finds nothing to his liking; he is a victim of this indeci-

8. Especially E. Ebeling in *Mitteilungen der deutschen Orientgesellschaft* 58 (1971): 35f., and in *Quellen zur Kenntnis der babylonischen Religion* 2 (1919): 50; B. Meissner in *Babylonien und Assyrien,* 2 (1925): 432ff.; Th. Jacobsen in H. Frankfort et al., *Before Philosophy* (paperback edition of *The Intellectual Adventure of Ancient Man*), 1946, p. 231f. Also W. G. Lambert, *Babylonian Wisdom Literature,* pp. 139–41.

9. Especially E. A. Speiser, "The Case of the Obliging Servant," *Journal of Cuneiform Studies* 8 (1954): 98ff.

sion and of those constant changes in mood that are often found among the well fed and leisurely. Moreover, he can do *nothing*, not even decide anything, without the advice of his valet. When we think about that, it is indeed also ridiculous. And this servant, isn't he also a "character"? When he is analyzed, he is comical: with his answers always ready to support the smallest caprice of his master; with his ingenuity in finding reasons for and against everything without difficulty; with the composure that he maintains in face of the most contradictory views of his master; half-servile, half-mocking; half-robot by his status and his functions, half-disdainful because of his intelligence and his psychological finesse which burst out in the final statement that he shoots off at his persecutor. It is impossible to take the last verses "seriously" as an apology for a "philosophical suicide." What the valet answers to his master, who has decided *to kill him and to send him off before himself*, is not: *It would take you only three days to be also attracted by the supreme good* (or the least of evils!) *of death!* but: *If I disappear, I am so indispensable to you that you will die without delay, because you cannot do without me!*, and element of humor and finesse that reminds us of that of the astrologer of Louis XI in chapter 29 of *Quentin Durward* by Walter Scott, as A. Ungnad has pointed out.[10]

Interpreted in this way the work is not a type of philosophical parable but a satire. First of all a social satire: the choice of characters is significant. Some poignant elements here and there, like the way in which the valet justifies "Revolution" (VI, *41*f.: one cannot escape misery without revolting against the established powers!)[11] show that the author was very critical in the social area.

The author was also critical in the "spiritual" field, and we will return to that later. But the picture that the author draws of these gods cannot be understood otherwise than as a satirical portrayal of the religious beliefs common in the milieu that he has taken as a target. The gods are too spoiled by constant sacrifices, and end up by not being able to go without them. They always have something to ask from their worshipers, like dogs of their masters.[12]

I also wonder to what degree, by developing the work as he has, the author did not want to poke fun at the idea of basing one's life in some formal and narrow-minded way always on commonplaces. It is in fact striking that many of the reasons given by the valet to act or not to act have the flavor and

10. *Archiv für Orientforschung* 15 (1945): 75.

11. Perhaps this passage has not been sufficiently stressed in the perspective of the chronic social misery and the recurring social disorder that we know were rife in Mesopotamia: see *Journal of the Economic and Social History of the Orient* 4/2 (1961): pp. 113–64: "Désorde économique et annulation des dettes en Mésopotamie. . . ." On workers' revolts in Mesopotamia, see *La Voix de l'opposition en Mésopotamie*, pp. 151ff.

12. To better appreciate this image we should recall the disdain that the ancient Semites, including the Mesopotamians, had for dogs, as the Arabs still have today.

the form of proverbs: Especially verses 16; 19b–22; 25–28; 48; 50f.; 56f; 64; 67; 72f. In ancient Mesopotamian literature from before the second millennium, "proverbs" were very popular, although the genre was broader than what we would take it to be.[13] Excavations have yielded fragments of many collections where these sayings were brought together and classified for the use of literate people.[14] It is very possible—as we see elsewhere[15]—that among these people at least a type of aphoristic "morality," preoccupied with basing actions constantly on solid traditional maxims and on infallible truisms, had been developed. Such rules of behavior are by definition limited and they can be expanded only through contradiction. The popular wisdom of which proverbs are the expression, envisions only very concrete situations and very singular circumstances. This wisdom is thus polyvalent and often expresses the black and the white of the same subject. It would say, as we do, "Like father, like son," but then immediately following, "Stingy father, generous son." How should one behave if one takes as a guide not the objective necessity but traditional commonplaces? I have the impression that the author of the piece had noticed this and that he wanted to expose this way of thinking and action by ridicule.

Therefore, it cannot be disputed that the *Dialogue of Pessimism* contains a purpose of humor, irony, and satire.

But is that all? As far as I know the commentators up till now seem to have behaved very jealously and univocally. Either we have to take the work as serious or as amusing. Either it is an apology for pessimism or it is a mocking and entertaining lampoon. To repeat the conclusion of E. A. Speiser's article,[16] either we have before us "Aethelred the Unready, or a Hamlet, even a Schopenhauer or a Spengler," or we have to think of, not to mention Jonathan Swift, "the Honorable Bertie Wooster and his matchless valet, the imperturbable Jeeves, of P. G. Wodehouse."

I wonder whether monolithic reconstructions in history are not the most fragile ones, since the subject of the discipline is man. There is nothing in this world that is more difficult to understand and more complex, if not hopelessly intricate, than human actions and their motivations. Why

13. Compare *Annuaire 1963–1964*, pp. 81f.

14. For Sumerian and Akkadian "proverbs," see E. I. Gordon, *A New Look at the Wisdom of Sumer and Akkad*, in *Bibliotheca Orientalis* 18 (1960): 125ff.

15. Let us recall here the tendency of many theologians or preachers, especially those of the Middle Ages (following in this matter the example of their Jewish predecessors: cf. E. Schürer, *Geschichte des jüdischen Volkes*, 2: 370ff.) and perhaps still in our days, of not mentioning anything in any field of thought without using endless citations from the Bible or from the Church Fathers. In an entirely different culture we can point to the importance of traditional "phrases," such as in Chinese literature and thought (M. Granet, *La Pensée chinoise*, pp. 58ff., etc.).

16. See n. 9 above.

should we insist rigorously that our author had only *one* purpose, when, if we have read and analyzed his work correctly, it shows at least *two* purposes? The fact that it has all the aspects of a satire does not suppress its "philosophical" content, nor does a certain mentality of skepticism and pessimism abolish its purpose as ridicule and mockery. It is clear that the two characters have been put on stage for a critical and humorous purpose. But it is also clear that the general direction impressed upon the dialogue has been deliberately oriented towards concerns that are very serious and of great importance: those of the value of human activity and of the meaning of life itself.

If we admit this coexistence, a first conclusion appears perhaps immediately. We may consider it to be natural that an author mixes amusing and gloomy objectives, but it is more difficult to imagine that a man who is even a little inclined towards humor would at the same time be a master of absolute despair, forgetting his comical sense entirely, and going on to preach "philosophical suicide." Everything is possible here on earth, but such a combination would be really exceptional, and it is not recommended for historians to appeal to exceptional explanations. Thus, I think that those who stress the "pessimism" of our *Dialogue* are mistaken to take it, I would not say seriously, because it is serious, but literally, at least by interpreting its conclusions as a call for voluntary death as the only refuge from the universal absurdity and absence of all meaning in the world and in life. In the state of mind of our author, as it can be discerned through his ability to see and to underline the ridiculous side of things, it is much more likely that the end of the lampoon is a witticism, as I said above.

As we always have to assume a minimum of coherence in the minds with which we deal, this witticism indicates that even though the author toyed with dark ideas about human life and affairs, with doubts over the meaning and the importance of that life and its universal framework, he does not present himself here *ex professo* as a skeptic and a pessimist, preoccupied above all with impressing upon us a system of thought revolving around the absurdity of the world and of existence, and based on the "negation of all values." His pessimism and irony do not form a system by themselves but are only elements among others of a way of seeing things. Can we discover this personal viewpoint of our author, and through it the real purpose and the right sense of his work? I believe we can.

We have to recognize that the first commentators were correct when they compared the work to the Book of Ecclesiastes of our Bible, a book that is also considered to be disenchanted and somber.[17] Perhaps it has been afterwards forgotten in what way Ecclesiastes reminds us of our *Dia-*

17. For instance E. Ebeling, *Quellen* (see n. 8 above).

logue. Here is at least one passage (3: *1–9*) that seems to be like a summary and a transposition of the essential lessons of our *Dialogue:*

1. For everything there is a season and a time for everything
   under heaven:
   a time to be born, and a time to die;
   a time to plant, and a time to uproot;
   a time to kill, and a time to heal;
   a time to break down, and a time to build up;
   a time to weep, and a time to laugh;
   a time to mourn, and a time to dance;
   a time to cast away stones, and a time to gather them
   together;
   a time to embrace, and a time to refrain from embracing;
   a time to seek, and a time to lose;
   a time to keep, and a time to cast away;
   a time to rend, and a time to sew;
   a time to keep silent, and a time to speak;
   a time to love, and a time to hate;
   a time for war, and a time for peace.
   What gain has the worker from his toil?

The last line gives the key to the rest: Ecclesiastes does not at all want to develop the truism "Each thing in its own time." He wants to show that man's actions regarding the same object follow each other and cancel each other out to such an extent that nothing remains in the end and all actions seem to be futile. That is also the "serious" thesis of our *Dialogue.*

But the comparison with Ecclesiastes goes further, in my opinion. After centuries, and even after more than one hundred years of historical and critical exegesis, the general interpretations of Ecclesiastes have also varied, producing diametrically opposed views.[18] The largest group of interpreters has seen in this book the manifestation of a ruthless pessimism, intended to convince us that "life isn't worth living." The other group has transformed it into a handbook of perfect optimism. When I studied the work, this contradiction urged me to wonder whether one could not find justification for both views. Would it not be wiser to consider that the author, who was after all responsible for both views, wanted to indicate that he put the matter on an entirely different level than the one where his thoughts gave the impression of developing into contradictory propositions. In fact, that is, at least, the idea that I have developed.[19] The

18. *Naissance de Dieu*, pp. 248ff.
19. Ibid.

Preacher used the contradictions of the good and the bad side of things to establish the true thesis of his work: not only are contradictions inherent in the order established and willed by God, their author, but they are incomprehensible. This was also willed by the Creator, who is the only one able to understand the plan of the universe. For instance, the passage cited above is followed by: *If God has given the entire universe to* (be investigated by) *man's mind, yet man cannot find out the plan of God from the beginning to the end* (3: *11*). In conclusion, Ecclesiastes begins from the natural weakness of man's mind to demonstrate the limits of our intelligence at the same time as the absolute transcendence of God: "I do not need a God that I understand."

Let us return now to our own subject matter. In the *Dialogue*, just as in the Book of Ecclesiastes, we have also found two lines of development that are, if not contradictory, at least at first glance disparate: a satire of a certain milieu and a pessimistic and negative criticism of human actions. Thus it is possible that also here (even if it is doubtless in a different way) the issue lies on a different and higher level.

Let us reread the "conclusion" of our *Dialogue*. Among the six verses that end it, the pessimists place a lot of emphasis on the first two—especially when they are taken literally:

> To have my neck and yours broken,
> or to be thrown into the river, is that good? (81f.)

The supporters of the "satire" theory return the argument with the last two lines, which they understand, correctly in my opinion, as a witty ending of nonacceptance. But neither side seems to deal much with the two lines in between, and I wonder whether the real meaning of the book isn't revealed here:

> Who is so tall as to ascend to heaven?
> Who is so broad as to encompass the entire world? (83f.)

In order to understand what the author wanted to say in these lines, let us place these two verses in their context. At this stage of the work, attention has been ultimately drawn to thoughts about death (the last verse of stanza X). At the same time the entire development of the ten stanzas had to convince the master that if it is not really possible to choose between action and nonaction in any field whatsoever, the major question is really: What can we do in the end? What is truly good and useful, as everything is at the same time good and bad, useful and harmful, acceptable and debatable? After all that precedes, this question gets no answer—in fact the valet remains silent. It thus seems to the master that, confronted with such a universal confusion, there remains nothing but to break one's head, and to die willingly. If one absolutely does not know what to choose in life, isn't death all that remains to be chosen? That is at least the question that he asks his servant (*81*f.), to which the latter responds with a double "rhetorical question" (in fact, as we will see, it is an indirect negation) cited above, in verses 83f. What does he want to say exactly?

Starting from what he was asked and what concerns only *what is good to do*, i.e. in the end whether one can find in human activity something really useful with an indisputable value and a definitive meaning, the valet rises up to embrace the entire universe. Almost everywhere, but notably in ancient Mesopotamia, *heaven* above and *earth* below is a common figure of speech to indicate the universe.[20] Man is too small to touch heaven, and his view is too limited to embrace the entire world. In other words, the universe is larger than him, indeed too large for him. That is an indirect way of saying that no one in this world can answer the question of the meaning of human life, because man, as he is, is unable to comprehend the course of the cosmos; such a question is one of numberless ones that we ask in vain about the universe and its functioning.

Having said this, the author moreover returns, in fact, to a real religious tradition, which is duly rooted in ancient Mesopotamia (and which in my opinion betrays a Semitic origin rather than a Sumerian one, if we really have to choose between the two influences that made up Mesopotamian civilization). It is the tradition that only the gods, masters of the universe, know and understand its progress; that only they are aware of the system that rules the universe; that only they are able to answer the innumerable and unsolvable questions that we ask about the universe.

To prove such an assertion we should provide here a large sample of texts, or even better group them in such a way that they reconstruct the history of the cardinal idea of transcendence as well as possible, which like so many other Semitic religious ideas seems to have found its full and absolute development only in the religion of Israel. Let us postpone this task that would require a delicate and difficult analysis and would demand much space and time. Let us be satisfied with citing only one example, but one that is most important for our immediate purpose. It involves in fact a work where one "asks questions" about religion and metaphysics, so to speak. Especially since it deals with the same problems and reaches the same essential conclusions as the *Dialogue*, there is such an affinity between the two works that it is very likely that the author of the *Dialogue*, which was probably the later work, could very well have known and have derived directly or indirectly his inspiration from the other. It is a long monologue of several hundred verses, only two-thirds of which are preserved. It was seemingly composed during the second half of the second millennium, and was well known in Mesopotamia under the title (derived from the *incipit*):

20. Examples cited in *Chicago Assyrian Dictionary*, E: pp. 309f.

Ludlul bêl nêmeqi, "I want to praise the Lord of wisdom."[21] It has been famous among Assyriologists since the beginning of the century, and they refer to it very often as the *Monologue of the Righteous Sufferer.*

The protagonist is in fact a pious man who talks for a long time, and recites with a certain emphasis all the accidents that have befallen him, looking for a reason for those accidents. He cannot find the reason. In the theology of the time, there seems to have been an axiom that the gods, who were just, had to treat mankind with justice. They had to punish the evil and the unfaithful and to reward the virtuous and the faithful. The entire issue involves "material" disaster or happiness here on earth, because at this time the idea of a real survival after death had not been formed yet. That he, devoted and irreproachable, was thus exposed to suffering and disaster, seemed to be an intellectual scandal to the hero of the *Monologue,* an inexplicable reversal of values, an incomprehensible enigma. From this enigma he also passed on to many others that are presented to human reflection by the universe and its functioning. And it is remarkable that among them he chooses to illustrate his thesis by a group of situations that are not far removed from those developed in our *Dialogue.*

Here is the passage in question:[22]

> Indeed, I thought (my piety) to be pleasing to the gods!
> But, perhaps what is proper to oneself is an offence to them?
> And what one thinks to be a blasphemy may be proper to them?
> Who can know the will of the gods in heaven?
> Who understands the plans of the underworld gods?
> How could the mortals understand the plans of the gods?
> He who prospered yesterday is dead today.
> (He who) was dejected for a minute, suddenly is exuberant.
> One moment people are singing in exaltation;
> the other they groan like professional mourners!
> An instant (is thus enough) to change (man's) condition.
> When starving they become like corpses.
> When well-fed, one would say they are gods.
> In prosperity they speak of scaling heaven,
> Under adversity they complain of going down to hell.
> With so many (contradictions) I wonder:
> no, I cannot understand their significance. . . .

21. Again, the best version of the text is in W. G. Lambert, *Babylonian Wisdom Literature,* pp. 21–62. A French translation and commentary can be found in *Le problème du Mal en Mésopotamie ancienne. Prologue à une étude du "Juste souffrant,"* pp. 10ff.

22. Tablet II: verses 33–48.

In the end, the same problem bothers both the author of the *Monologue* and the author of the *Dialogue.* The first deals with a reversal of values that makes him wonder about the apparent injustice of the gods towards him; he also raises the issue of the universal enigma that is posed to man by the plan of the gods in its entirety. And as if to prove that the universe, and especially the universe of mankind, is filled with questions that are equally unanswerable, even beyond his own "scandal," i.e. the divine injustice, he touches on a theme that is very similar to the one that the author of the *Dialogue* made his principal subject: the inconstancy and especially the perpetual contradiction that rules all human activities. What is their ultimate meaning? Why are we thus obliged, in a sense by nature, to pass constantly through the pros and cons both of our feelings and of our activities?

The author of the *Dialogue* poses the same questions even more explicitly. But he goes further by stressing that such inconstancy, such an internal contradiction—which he analyzes much better than the other writer—leads to the same unanswerable question: is there a meaning to life?

He answers the question as did the author of the *Monologue:* no one can understand the meaning, because it is part of the mystery of the universe:

> Who is so tall as to ascend to heaven?
> Who is so broad as to encompass the entire world? (83f.)

The only difference that can be seen is that he expresses only the negative side of the conclusion, "Man cannot understand," while the author of the *Monologue* adds the positive side, "The gods know."

Is this omission significant? In other words, do we have to make our author a "skeptic" in the strict sense, and refuse him what we assign to the author of the *Monologue:* a religious feeling of transcendence as the only way to escape the universal confusion? Could we say that by avoiding mention of the gods, in contrast to the author of the *Monologue,* he shows a dislike for that solution, he deliberately remains an "atheist" or "agnostic," preferring a "not decided" stance? I do not think so.

First of all, "atheism" or even "agnosticism," even in the most moderate way, are concepts and elements of a problem that was entirely unknown in ancient Mesopotamia and, furthermore, generally everywhere in the early first millennium B.C.

Second, because the entirety of the *Dialogue,* when carefully examined, does not suggest that its author would have been irreligious or antireligious. He speaks equivalently about the god Marduk, the supreme deity of the Babylonian pantheon at that time, as rewarding the deeds of someone who devotes himself to philanthropy (stanza X, 72–73). We can say, of course, that the underlying idea and likewise the expression *the circle(?) of Marduk*—even if we do not find it elsewhere—were perhaps traditional, and that they do not reflect the beliefs of the person using them. But then, there is stanza VIII. As I have suggested, it is much more likely that our author did not get involved in blasphemy or in mockery of the gods and their cults, but that he wanted to criticize the traditional religiosity of the milieu represented by his principal character, if not the "pressure groups" hidden behind the representations of the gods. Thus he regards such a religious conception, shamelessly based on the principle of *do ut des,* as an aberration that should be mocked and chastised, a real degradation of the gods. To treat the gods in the way that he denounces them is in reality to take them as *dogs,* starved and greedy, driven by their avidity. If that is indeed the meaning of this criticism, does not the author want to defend, *in petto,* a much higher and purer idea of the divine world?

Finally, I wonder if in the antepenultimate verses of our work the deliberate suppression of every allusion to the gods as holders of the secrets of the universe that are inaccessible to mankind, would not make what follows and what leads to the end of the work inexplicable: *O well, I will kill you and send you first!* (85). Does this verse have a meaning *in its context?* The moment the valet declares that there is no answer here on earth for the questions asked by his master, why would the latter threaten to kill him? Surely not to take revenge on him: there is really no reason for that. Nor is it out of pure caprice and cruelty: the character of the master has nothing bloodthirsty in it; he is only idle and indecisive. It is much more likely that, in his opinion, the valet would be useful to him in dying, as he was useful to him up till then: by enlightening his confusion. How could he be useful to him in death? It is spelled out clearly in the text: by going *before his master.* And why? Evidently to give him, from the Hereafter, an answer that cannot be found on earth—somewhat like Enkidu did for his master and friend Gilgameš in Tablet XII of the famous epic. It is certain in fact that in ancient Mesopotamia the spirits of the dead, the *eṭemmu,** or at least some of them, were assigned a supernatural knowledge, inaccessible to man, possibly because of the fact that they visited those among the gods that lived in the area of the netherworld and who ruled the empire of darkness. Otherwise the questioning of these "ghosts" and the practice of necromancy, both well-attested practices,[23] would be inexplicable. Thus when the valet answered to his master that no one here on earth could inform him about the things that worried him, the master replied, in effect, "Well, I will send you

23. See especially *Chicago Assyrian Dictionary,* E, pp. 397ff. (s.v. *eṭemmu*), and L. Oppenheim, *Dreams,* especially p. 223. More recently, I. L. Finkel, "Necromancy in Ancient Mesopotamia," *Archiv für Orientforschung* 29f. (1983f.): 1ff.

to look for the answer where it can be found: in the Hereafter." Here satire takes the upper hand, preparing us for the last verse that is clearly humorous, as we have said. It was not necessary to explain it: at the time everyone understood that it involved the gods, to whom the dead valet could ask these questions and consequently bring answers back to his master when the latter would consult him through the techniques of necromancy. That was understood. This is why I have said that if our author does not name the gods explicitly here, it is only because of the concise style and brevity. It is because he evidently believes that they are the holders of the universal wisdom refused to mankind.

By doing this and by giving divine transcendence as the only answer to the problem raised by his work—in a very original way, moreover—our author stays in a tradition of essential religious thought in ancient Mesopotamia (present, in my opinion, ever since the Semites became dominant). It stresses the difference in nature, and let us say *order*, between men and the gods; it stresses continuously the limits of human intelligence; it recognizes the lowliness of our condition, even of our level of thought; and it stresses the certainty that *we* never have the last word, including that regarding the pure meaning of the world, of our activities, and of our existence. *Others know it*, higher than us, and that should suffice to keep us tranquil.

As I said before, we should pursue the long history of this idea of transcendence to see that in Mesopotamia it still seems to have been, so to speak, in an embryonic state. It could only bear fruit in monotheism, the prerogative of Israel.[24] But even if it is formulated and conceived in a rudimentary fashion, it is in my opinion a religious attitude that is in the end metaphysical, extremely elevated and noble, whatever one's personal attitude towards it. This should make us admire even more the little work studied here—provided that we don't still find it enigmatic.

24. *Naissance de Dieu*, passim.

15

The Mythology of Death

DEATH, A VERY DEPRESSING EVENT, PRESENTS US WITH A GREAT number of speculative problems. First of all on the level of the community where its victims "decease," "become defunct," i.e. in the etymological sense of the words "cease to fulfill their roles" and "retire from the functions" that they occupied on the economic, social and political levels. That is the enormous sector of the sociology of death, which is still too little explored.

But there is also a purely theoretical level that interests men more, perhaps because in the end it directs everything else. From this point of view one can say that there are invariably three types of relationships between all humans and death. The first is universal and, let us say in passing, very unfortunate; one submits to it, and he who is dead cannot communicate his experience and advice—"Death, that is something that happens to others. . . ."

The second and the third types can at least be communicated. One appeals to sentiment, the other to imagination and intelligence. Before submitting to one's own death, or to the sight of someone else's death, the heart reacts to this event: one resents it as an enemy, or sometimes welcomes it as a friend; one fears it, or one challenges it; one deplores it and one pities

This chapter first appeared in *Death in Mesopotamia*, pp. 25–52, under the title "La mythologie de la mort en Mésopotamie ancienne." Here and there I will cite more thorough studies that I have published on the same subject, in particular "Les inscriptions cunéiformes funéraires," in *La Mort, les morts dans les sociétés anciennes*, pp. 373–406, under the direction of G. Gnoli and J.-P. Vernant (henceforth *Inscriptions*); and especially "Les morts et l'au-delà dans les rituels en akkadien contre l'action des 'revenants'," *Zeitschrift für Assyriologie* 73 (1983): 153–203 (henceforth ZA).

those who have been struck by it. That is the area of the psychology of death.

On the other hand, death necessarily confronts each of us with a number of questions: Why do we have to die? How does one die? What happens afterwards? To give answers, we cannot count on those who have passed away, as they are mute and cannot be reached, they are gone to "the land from which no one has ever returned," and we can only resort to conjectures and constructions of the mind. In societies that can only think in images, not in abstract terms, all those operations derive from the type of "calculated imagination" that we call mythology. This is why I speak here of the *mythology of death* and understand by that phrase the totality of answers given by the ancient Mesopotamians to the paradoxes that came to their minds (and that still come to ours today) before this irrevocable and troubling constraint of death.

In order to give an idea of this mythology it has seemed to me useful to draw up a systematic overview of all that we know about, or believe we know about, the Mesopotamian notion of death and the hereafter. It may provide a useful framework even for Assyriologists, and they will be able to improve it by filling in the gaps and by correcting the mistakes and replacing them with more correct or new elements when they are provided by new discoveries.

Before we draw this outline, of which it should be well understood that it cannot take into account evolution over time because of the lack of significant numbers of "datable" documents, evenly divided over time—especially if we work on such a broad scale as we do here—I have to recall the sources of our knowledge in this matter. The archeological sources are numerous,[1] but they only illustrate a material aspect of the problem: the treatment of the corpse. Among the written documentation of first importance are the texts known by everyone and used for a long time: the accounts of the *Descent into the Netherworld*, of the *Flight from Death and the Quest for Immortality*,[2] not to mention legends such as that of Etana, and especially that of Adapa,* which are not relevant here in my opinion.[3] There

1. See, for instance, *Grab, Grabbeigabe, Grabgefäss* in *Reallexikon der Assyriologie*, 3 (1957ff.): 581ff., 605ff., and 609f.

2. Especially, *Inanna/Ištar in the Netherworld*, above, p. 244 and n. 13; *The Epic of Gilgameš** in its various editions, including tablet XII which is an addition and a simple translation of the account in Sumerian called *Gilgameš, Enkidu and the Netherworld;* for the latest translation, in French, see R. Labat, *Les Religions . . .*, pp. 145–226; *Urnammu in the Netherworld* (published by S. N. Kramer in *Journal of Cuneiform Studies* 21 [1967]: 104ff.); *The Death of Gilgameš* (published by S. N. Kramer in *Bulletin of the American Schools of Oriental Research* 94 [1944]: 2ff.).

3. See *Annuaire 1969–1970 . . .*, pp. 113ff. and 108f.

is also an entire mythological literature[4] and even a "paramythological" literature,[5] so to speak. We can even track down, here and there, precious information in the great mass of texts said to be of practical nature: letters, juridical and administrative documents. But there are especially two important types of documents: first the (all too few) texts of a "funerary" character, that are directly associated with tombs;[6] second, a very small dossier (a part of which has been known, or has become better known, only very recently) of exorcisms to chase away the evils thought to be inflicted by the returned dead, a mine of information insufficiently explored and of great value.[7]

A last word, for the sake of honesty and prudence. As we of course, do not have a "Treatise on Death and the Hereafter" by some ancient scholar of Mesopotamia, but only sparse and fragmentary allusions, occasional shreds of a whole that apparently was itself not constructed in a univocal and coherent way (this will be better understood at the end of the chapter), all that we can do with these *membra disjecta* is to attempt to fit them together in order to reconstruct a picture that is very likely to reflect only very badly, even mistakenly here and there, the original view on the matter. Of course, an increase in independent testimonies and their integration into the picture would reinforce our conclusions, but our reconstruction is very fragile and always subject to caution and revisions—as in every historical work. It would be unwise to forget that, here as elsewhere.

DEATH AND THE DEAD

In Mesopotamia death (*mûtu*) was felt as a destiny that was so universal and inescapable for mankind that when the people wanted to create an idea of the gods, imagined on our model, an endless life was reserved for them, to better indicate their distance and their difference. The feeling of the inevitability of death was so strong that, even though a small number of eminent men were made immortal in the image of the gods,[8] this did not prevent them from submitting at least a few gods to death.[9] But these were excep-

4. For example, the end of the *Poem of the Supersage,** above, pp. 223 and 242.

5. In particular the neo-Assyrian political pamphlet entitled *A Vision of the Netherworld* (*Annuaire 1972–1973* . . . , pp. 93ff.).

6. See *Inscriptions*.

7. See *ZA*.

8. That is, for instance, the case of Uta-napištim, the hero of the Flood in *Gilgameš.**

9. The problem of "dead gods" is complex, and we can only say a few words about it here. On the one hand the gods, immortal by nature, never die a natural death. But they can be "killed" by their equals in order to be "used" in some way or another. That is the case for Apsû,* Tiamat,* and Kingu in the *Epic of Creation,** and for Wê in *The Supersage** (p. 241). On the other hand, it seems that especially in the first millennium, and perhaps already earlier, there was a tendency to explain the loss of effective rule by the "ancient gods" by assim-

tional cases, and the formal or implicit answer to the question "Why do we have to die?" was always: "Because it is the nature and the destiny itself of mankind, as the gods have wanted and made it."

I know of nothing that makes us believe that Mesopotamians asked themselves about the "how" of death. It was a fact, a moment of existence that profoundly changed those struck by it. Death was observed, it was not analyzed. It is not surprising that death was related to a total loss of the blood, which was considered to give life. But a passage in a letter from Mari would seem to be more to the point. There is a reference to slaughtering an ox *by making him blow out his last breath.*[10] This makes us believe that, like the ancient Hebrews,[11] the Mesopotamians of the past considered death as the final return of "breath," which had been given *ad tempus* by the gods, and which during the entire lifetime had left and reentered man continuously, but now left him forever.

It seems that they were more interested in determining the nature of this transformation of man by death: what happened afterwards? How did one exist? Difficult even for minds like ours that are familiar with a certain abstraction, nothingness could not be imagined by people whose knowledge was entirely expressed by the concrete, the material, the imaginable. It could also not sink into their minds that death was the definitive and total disappearance of the dead. Someone who died continued to exist as a person. But what remained of him, since clearly the visible and tangible parts of his being, the body (*zumru, pagru*), became a corpse (*šalamtu*) and disintegrated relatively fast by the disappearance of the flesh (*šîru*)?

What remained was first of all what they considered to be the framework and the support of a live person: the *bones* (*eṣemtu*). From this idea derives the extreme respect for tombs, evidenced especially by the funerary inscriptions. One had to leave in peace (*nâlu, pašâḫu*) what still constituted the dead person, who was as if *asleep* (*ṣalâlu*) when death overtook him.[12] This is why the remains of ancestors were taken along when one left the country.

Something else remained that represented the dead more immediately and undoubtedly more essentially: his *phantom*, his *ghost*, his *soul*, his *spirit* (the last two terms are used in their folkloristic sense rather than in their philosophical sense)—what was usually called his *eṭemmu*.* In or-

ilating them to the kings on earth, whose reigns were usually ended by their deaths: hence the presence in the Netherworld of gods, especially of older date. The "esoteric" theological commentaries even speak of the *eṭemmu** of these gods (*Mythes et rites de Babylone*, p. 275).

10. The letter in question appears in M. Birot, *Archives royales de Mari*, XIV, pp. 26f., no. 5: 17f.

11. For the biblical point of view, see especially Ecclesiastes, 12: 7 (*Naissance de Dieu*, p. 247).

12. *Inscriptions*, pp. 381ff.

der to understand what would represent this *eṭemmu*, and first of all how its existence came to be posited, we are forced to formulate conjectures based on what we are told, as our documents give us no clear information. Moreover several sources allude to appearances by the dead, seen and perceived in a dream or otherwise. The odds are good that they are more or less vague silhouettes, imprecise and phantom-like, but still recognizable and poorly distinguished from the material and actual objects of vision and of real perceptions. They have given the idea of the "survival" of the dead in an airy, impalpable form that resembles the person, represents him, and *substitutes for him* (*ardanân mîti*). It was a *breath* (*zaqîqu, ziqîqu; šâru*), a *shadow* (*ṣillu*)—an *eṭemmu*. The corresponding Sumerian term gedim is attested at least from around the year 2500, but we do not know its fundamental meaning. All that we know is that in cuneiform writing itself, at least from the second millennium on, the sign gedim is barely or not at all graphically distinguished from the sign udug, which indicated a type of *demon* (*utukku*), a supernatural being—certainly also having an imprecise and unseizable silhouette. In fact, not only are the *eṭemmu* sometimes mentioned together with demons, as if they were easily mistaken for each other, at least by their imaginary presentation and their way of acting, but it happened that they were referred to with the word udug/*utukku*. They seem even to have been given, occasionally, the epithet of *ilu* (literally: *god*) with the meaning of supernatural being, sometimes with the "classifying" sign reserved in the script for the gods.[13]

Whatever the value of this hypothesis regarding the possible origin of the idea of *eṭemmu*, related to the idea that they had of the entire imaginary supernatural population, it is certain that in the thoughts of the Mesopotamians only two things remained of man after death: one was plainly material, numb and paralyzed and then subject to gradual erosion—his skeleton; the other formal, airy, a shady and volatile image of what he was during life, but permanent: his *ghost*, his *phantom*, his *spirit*, his *eṭemmu*, active and mobile in its own way, as we will see later on. The relations between the two remains were certain and very close, because it still involved the same person who still bore the same proper name after his death. But these relations have never been defined as far as I know: every mythology necessarily contains various areas that are obscure and vague. Perhaps they were imagined more or less consciously on the model of what each of us experiences all the time: our body, localized and immobile, does not prevent our spirit from roaming around, when we are awake as well as when we are asleep.

The importance of the *eṭemmu* in the mythology of death and in the idea that existed about mankind, does not only appear in the activities that

13. Especially in personal names. See *Chicago Assyrian Dictionary,* I/J. p. 202a: 6.

they were considered to undertake, which we will discuss in more detail later, but also in the fact that in the *Poem of the Supersage* at least, the authors of that remarkable synthesis on the nature and destiny of mankind thought it necessary to include the *eṭemmu* in the creation of mankind (I: 208–30). They stressed that, in the plan of Ea, the "inventor" of our condition and structure, our existence is brought about in two successive stages: one where we are alive and fully active in service of the gods, under the name of *awêlu;* the other after the termination by death of all our functions, under the name of *eṭemmu.*[14]

THE HEREAFTER

The Environment of "Survival"

How was the existence of a dead man, after his decease and in the state of *eṭemmu,* imagined? And first of all, in what milieu was it supposed to take place?

This is one of the cases where a certain coherence seems to have been striven for and a system outlined through the basing of one myth on the others. Traditionally the ancient Mesopotamians had made a conception of the universe that was, so to speak, vertical and bipolar; they saw it as an immense globe composed of two symmetrical hemispheres horizontally separated in the middle, i.e. the *On-High* (an/*šamû*) or, if you want, *Heaven,* and the *Below* (ki/*erṣetu*) or the *Netherworld.* In its center, encircled like an island by the *bitter waters* of *the sea* (*tâmtu*), and lying on a sheet of sweet water of the Apsû,* was what we call the earth: the earth of living humans. The lower hemisphere was given as a space and an environment for the existence of the dead. Such a view certainly has to be related to the traditional way in which corpses were treated in Mesopotamia: they were always shrouded, and put in the earth in a trench, in a tomb, or in a cave. With the exception of a small number of doubtful archeological examples, for which we have no correspondence in the written documentation, burials on or above ground, exposure to the air, or cremation were never used, unless it was done deliberately because one wanted to "mistreat" the dead for reasons of disdain or of vengeance. Placed underground, the deceased was in a way introduced to his new environment, both as body and as *shade.*

The new environment had different names, several of which are not clear to us: what is the exact meaning of *Arallû, Lammu,* and *Ganzer?* They often said ki, or kur/*Erṣetu* ("Earth"), the global name of the lower hemi-

14. See "La création de l'homme et son nature dans le poème d'*Atraḫasîs*" (cited above, chap. 6, n. 5), pp. 31f.

sphere, or also ki.ta(meš)/*Šaplâtu, The regions down below,* sometimes ki.gal/*Kigallu, The Great-Below* or perhaps *the Socle* supporting our own earth; to these words of similar meaning were related *Danninu* (*the "Platform"*) and *Qaqqaru* (*the Earth*). It happened that the Netherworld became more or less confused with the *Apsû*, which can also be located underneath the earth. *Kukkû*, clearly derived from the Sumerian ku_{10}.ku_{10}, *Darkness,* is easy to understand. Similarly with the popular name of kur (or ki).nu.gi_4(.a)/*Erṣet* (or *Ašar*) *lâ târi, the Land* (or *Place*)*-of-no-return*. Another series of designations is drawn from the material and political organization that was assigned to the Kingdom of the Dead, to which we will return later on: unu_x.gal; uru_x.gal; eri/iri_{11}.gal/*Irkallu, the Great City,* to which they seem sometimes to have given the name of the city here on earth whose ruling god was also the one of the Netherworld, *Nergal,** Kutû. We also find as an allusion to the principal Entrance to the infernal area ki.u_4.$šu_4$, for ki.^{d}Utu.šú.a, *the Place where the Sun goes down.*

This hemisphere symmetrical to heaven was not imagined as an immense empty space. It was occupied not only by the Apsû, the domain of the god *Enki/Ea,** but also by residential quarters for the gods who were assigned to it.[15] These gods were called the *Anunnaki** to distinguish them from the *Igigi** who, "in the same number," occupied the "region On-High." It is probable that they had a very confused idea of the internal disposition of the Netherworld, because everything that is related to the Hereafter was in itself uncontrollable. In Mesopotamia, as elsewhere, the Hereafter found itself in the same approximation, the same haziness, the same vagueness, and perhaps even more than in other sectors of mythology, ideas about it were full of inconsistencies and variable or contradictory elements. When, doubtless rather late, some theologians wanted to introduce some order in this confusion, they divided the hemisphere of the Below, as well as heaven, into three vast levels, assigning the lowest one, the one most remote from our earth, to the court of the Anunnaki, the middle one to the Apsû, and the upper one, immediately underneath our earth and in which tombs were dug, to the *residence* (the verb used, *šurbuṣu,* almost evokes the image of *laying down*) of the *spirits of men* (*ziqîqi amêlûti*). But other

15. Without attempting to give more than a short list of the deities presented as being infernal, let us only mention *Nergal* (also called *Erra**) and *Ereškigal,* king and queen of the Land-of-no-return, and the *Anunnaki*—sometimes the collective name of all the gods "Below," sometimes a group of seven gods that fulfill the function of "judges": *Šamaš,** the Sun god, who on his nocturnal trip underneath the world came to play a role among the dead, and *Gilgameš* in person, who seems to have been placed among the dead to exercise some authority. Also found there are *Namtar* ("Destiny"), *Pêtû* (still referred to by most Assyriologists as *Nedu*), the "Doorman" of hell, and an entire string of minor deities. Plus the (couples of) "ancient" and "dead" gods (cf. n. 9, above): *Duri-Dari, Laḫmu-Laḫamu, Alala-Belili,* etc. See ZA, pp. 197ff.

documents that do not deal with the location of the Apsû, seem to connect the *eṭemmu* and the infernal gods, especially in matters of space.

The same uncertainties and same disagreements exist about *the entrance to the Netherworld (nêreb Erṣetim)*. In the absence of explicit evidence (I, at least, do not know of any), "logic" would have it that each tomb acted as the point of passage for the deceased who was deposited in it, the lobby and the doorstep to the Netherworld: hence the impossibility, proclaimed here and there, for the unburied dead to reach their proper residence.

But they also seem to have imagined that cracks, crevices and holes (ab.làl/*takkapu; nigiṣṣu; ḫurru*) could give access to the Netherworld; it is through them that in Uruk* the insignia of power, *pukku* and *mekkû*, fell, and that the *spirit* of Enkidu came up.

Another fantastic idea is reflected elsewhere: it was imagined that the entry or the return of the *eṭemmu* to the Netherworld was done in the extreme west of the world where the Sun went down into the earth each day, in order to travel underneath it at night and to reappear the next morning at the other side. In fact, Šamaš, the Sun god, was often closely associated with the dead, with whom he had to occupy himself as much as with the living. Even though, at least according to tablet XI of the *Ninivite version of Gilgameš** (col. iv: 46ff.), the subterranean road of Šamaš is a sort of unending tunnel that seems to have been dug separately and has nothing to do with the Netherworld, it is easily understood that the entrances to the two would be more or less confused.

The same perception agreed with the geography as it was then known. An enormous and dismal desert—the desert that bordered Mesopotamia in the west—was thought to extend to the place where the Sun disappeared and to end at an enormous body of water, which was perhaps called *Saḫan/Irḫan*, but more often *Ḫubur*. The latter, as stated by Tiamat* in *Enûma eliš** (I: 133), designates almost certainly the Sea that encircles the Earth and separates it from the gloomy border of the Hereafter, so distant and so poorly visible that one did not know whether the cosmic sea was *beyond* or *beneath* it.

The "Voyage"

The space assigned to the dead was the Netherworld. To express it otherwise, the last breath took the dead away from the rule of the gods On-High and made them pass into the control of the gods Down Below. Therefore, the *eṭemmu*, the human phantom, had to have a way of going to his new land as soon as he replaced the *awêlu* in death. How? Here the variants and disagreements already noticed with regard to the entrance of the Netherworld reappear. Insofar as the individual tomb—or the family tomb (*kimaḫ kimti*)—formed the first step of the stairway leaving the Earth, a burial should suffice to allow the dead to go to his final homeland. This "transfer" is nowhere explicitly documented, as far as I know. But, as I have said before, the fact itself that corpses left on the surface of the earth were thought to be unable to go to their new destination, and were condemned to wander miserably and spitefully above, instead of disappearing below the earth, shows quite well that their transfer was a *descent* (*arâdu*)[16] assured by their ritual inhumation.

We are not informed of other "ways" of gaining access to the Netherworld such as those that must have been used by the divinities who were said to have left it, such as the *chargé d'affaires* (*sukkallu*) of the Queen of the Netherworld in *Nergal and Ereškigal*, or to have descended into it, like Nergal in the same myth, or like Inanna/Ištar and later *Dumuzi** in the famous *Descent*. We do not know whether all the crevices and holes in the earth could lead to the Kingdom of the Dead. On the other hand, the documents that place *The Great Gate* (ka.gal ^{d}Utu.šú.a/*Abul erêb* ^{d}*Šamši*) of the Netherworld in the extreme west, are more explicit. They foresee a long and painful journey leading to the entrance, for which outfits (clothes, sandals, waterbags, and sacks) and *provisions for a journey* (*ṣudû, ṣuddû*) were needed.[17] One *set out to* the west; one had to cross a gloomy, endless desert, an area of desolation, of hunger and thirst, filled with wild animals and demons, where one was exposed to all sorts of attacks and constantly tempted to turn back. At the end one reached the sinister banks of the *Ḫubur*, which one still had to cross, doubtless in the boat of the *Boatman of the Netherworld* named *Ḫumuṭ-tabal* (*Bring fast!*), in order to finally cross the border of the Land-of-no-return.

The Stay in the Netherworld

Having arrived in whatever way, what did one find? Here also the mythopoetic fantasy could put together this unknown and unknowable universe by transposing to it the images familiar in a positive or negative way from the earth.

First of all, the subterranean environment as well as the images of the dead forced them to replace our light by darkness, our noise and our movement by immobility and silence, the brightness of all that surrounds us by dust and filth. This is the often-cited picture that is given in the beginning of *Ištar's Descent to the Netherworld* and in *Gilgameš, Ninevite version*, tablet VII, whose characteristics can be found here and there in other texts.

16. The movement in the opposite direction is indicated with the verb *elû, to* (*re*)*ascend*, whose "causative" form is *šûlû, to make* (*re*)*ascend*. The conjurers of the spirits of the dead are called *mušēlu eṭemmi*/*ṣilli, those who make re-ascend the phantom*/*shades*.

17. See ZA, pp. 191f.

To the Land-of-no-return, the area of Ereškigal,
Ištar the daughter of Sîn* was determined to go:
The daughter of Sîn was determined to go,
To the dark house, the dwelling of Irkalla;
To the house which those who enter cannot leave;
On the road where traveling is one-way only;
To the house where those who arrive are deprived of light,
Where mould is their food, dust their bread,
They dwell in darkness, they never see light.
They are dressed like birds, with feathers,
While over the door and the doorbolts dust has
settled. . . .[18]

This gives the idea clearly: whatever was thought about the existence that follows death and its environment, one could only judge it to be extremely sad, gloomy, torpid, and as the extreme opposite of our *joie de vivre*, which is clear and loud even in its worst disasters.

Even the gods who lived in this enormous, dirty, and dark cavern had something oppressive, severe, and morose about them, as we see from the sad Ereškigal in *Nergal and Ereškigal*, or from the dreadful gods in the infernal court in the *Vision of the Netherworld*. They were not "dead," however, and they laid claim as much as their celestial counterparts to respect and to the opulent life free of worries—even if they were sometimes presented as also being afflicted by the negative signs. Be this as it may, they had to be provided like the other gods with all their needs, and an abundance and luxury is suggested by the *Infernal Palace of lapis lazuli* that was assigned to them. Whether or not this palace was placed in the depths of the Below, it was usually seen as being in the middle of an enormous subterranean citadel, enclosed by an awesome wall. No one could enter it except through a Gate, closely guarded by the merciless Pêtû, the chief gaoler, who was assisted by an entire team of minor deities in order to assure security and surveillance. To improve upon this image, driven by the incurable tendency in works of imagination towards exaggeration, they had even multiplied this rampart by seven, and the seven concentric walls that protected the central palace of the infernal rulers were each provided with a gate, guarded by its own Cerberus. This organization, transposed from the capital cities here on earth, apparently explains the name of *Great-City, Metropolis*, given to the Netherworld—a city in which even *streets* (*sulû*) were imagined to exist. The [*plan*] of the City of the Dead, which an exorcistic ritual urged to *draw* ([*uṣurta*] *eṣêru*), apparently to direct better the haunting ghost that one wanted to send back, was doubtless like that.

18. *Ištar's Descent to the Netherworld: 1–11//Gilgameš*, Ninevite version, VII/iv: 33–39.

It is probable that what is told in *Inanna/Ištar's Descent to the Netherworld* about the gradual undressing of the newly arrived goddess, who at each gate had to leave something of herself behind until she was entirely naked in the final circle, where she was to be detained, expresses a development of the same basic idea that death takes everything away from us, adapted to "topography." Once the deceased passes the Gate or the Gates of the Land-of-no-return, he is informed of the "laws" that will henceforth govern him. He is behind closed doors and under strict surveillance, in other words unable ever to leave—at least in principle.

Here the inevitable question arises, whether at this entry into the Netherworld each dead person was subjected to a real judgment, as scholars have often suggested, using doubtful or false arguments. It is true that the infernal Anunnaki, and perhaps the highest placed of them sometimes grouped in a council with seven members, were often presented as "judges" (di.kud/*daiiânu*), *rendering verdicts for the people below and delivering judgments to the entirety of humanity,* whenever humans arrived in their kingdom. But in Mesopotamia these expressions covered a semantic field that is broader than the simple exercise of judicial power. The latter in our opinion consists of applying the laws to each person brought before a court, and of determining the person's fate based on his behavior. In Mesopotamia, to judge is especially to decide: to assign, to impose a *destiny* without necessarily taking into account the merits and the demerits of those on whom the destinies are imposed. It is not an act of logic or of morality, but of power. When in *Inanna in the Netherworld* the *Anunnaki pronounce their judgment*, it is their decision to detain the goddess, treating her *according to the laws of the Netherworld*, in other words like the other dead there. They were considered to play the same role vis-à-vis each dead person by notifying him at his arrival in their domain of his final destiny, a destiny which settled him forever in his dead state and assigned him an eternal stay in the Land-of-no-return. We are far from the "individual judgment" of the Christian tradition, or even from the psychostasy of the ancient Egyptians.

"Condemned" in a sense, i.e. being confined once and for all in the world of the dead, the *eṭemmu* were thought to have an existence in their new kingdom that was nothing but dull and negative: asleep, powerless, immobile, and cadaverous, they were similar to the nocturnal birds that live in "hole" and caverns. They had nothing but mud to sink their teeth into, and as drink only the foul water of low-lying grounds—conditions entirely opposite to those of living people on earth.

Because the universal destiny of men is death, this existence should logically be exactly the same for everyone; this is suggested by the total undressing mentioned above that was imposed on the dead at their entering the Netherworld. But in a society as hierarchically structured as the Mesopotamian one, where differences in life-style were commonplace and considered to be normal, it was difficult not to transpose these differences into the Hereafter. Hence differences were introduced in this new way of living—or better of existing—that was dusty, obscure, torpid, and negative. These differences were of the kind that exist here on earth, separating rulers from subjects, powerful from weak, and rich from poor.

Such a fantasy is ancient: It must have been what, in the end, led the Mesopotamians to pile up the treasures and commodities of life, even to kill domestic personnel around the remains of the rulers of the First Dynasty of Ur* and of the rulers of Kiš, around the year 2500. Thus kings remained kings after death; and why not others? Even if soon afterwards they refrained from pushing this maxim to its most bloody consequences by sacrificing for the king's attendance his entire court or only part of it, and even if what was given to the dead king in his tomb was reduced in quantity and splendor, if the kings and the great of this world were richly endowed in their tombs, and the little people modestly,[19] was this not because both groups counted on maintaining their different conditions of life into the Hereafter? This is what we find, for instance, in the *Death of Gilgameš* and in *Urnammu in the Netherworld* (above, n. 2). Both these men at least were able to arrange a more comfortable existence for themselves by sumptuous offerings to the infernal divinities. *Gilgameš, Enkidu, and the Netherworld* drew the conclusion of such an axiom, by introducing among the dead an entire hierarchy of situations and fates, based not on their own merits but in the end on chance; in short, on the *destiny* that is a reproduction of what prevailed on earth. This is a perfect contradiction, but it will be better understood at the end of this discussion, and it is not the only one in the mythology of death, in Mesopotamia as elsewhere.

The Dependence of the Dead

The inequalities in the fate of the dead during their eternal existence can also be partly explained by the difference in treatment that they received from those they had left behind on earth. The *eṭemmu* was in fact extremely dependent on his survivors, and the latter had obligations towards the dead.

These obligations were based of course on family solidarity, which is always powerful in a patriarchal society. Among the ritual exorcisms against the *eṭemmu* we find an evocation of the ancestors and family members: grandfather and grandmother, father and mother, brothers and sisters, and then the other members summed up under the collective term of *kimtu*, *nišûtu*, and *salâtu*: *family, relations*, and *kindred*. If these catalogues do not

19. See the articles in the *Reallexikon der Assyriologie*, 3, mentioned above (n. 1).

go further than the third generation it is not because the earlier ancestors were neglected, even if they were only indirectly and increasingly less known because of the distance in time. But one of the texts in question adds: *everyone as many as there are asleep and on earth,* and a few other texts invoke also the *bânu qab*[*ri*] which referred to the *founders* of the family and *of the family tomb.* Moreover, we know that at least when it involved the ruling dynasty, one could go back much farther by listing a long line of ancestors whose names were doubtless better retained in the collective memory or in the official "papers." Moreover, the burial inscriptions do not place any limit in time on the age of the bones for whose peace they demand respect. The entire deceased part of the ancestry, without limitation or exception, had the collective name of *eṭem kimti, family eṭemmu,* or if you like, *Manes.* The survivors, regardless of generation or sex, and especially the *children* (*mâru, mârtu*), even the adopted ones, and certainly especially the *oldest one* (*aplu*) were thus charged with taking care of the Manes. The latter, who passed from the state of *awîlu* to the state of *eṭemmu* were henceforth unable to provide for their own paltry existence, and inasmuch as the *offspring* (literally, *the hearth*) were not *extinct* (*kinûnu balû*), the Manes expected everything from their heirs.

First of all the descendants had to mourn their dead. They had *to weep* (*bakû*) and *to bury* (*qebêru*) them according to the established rituals—to put them in the ground so that they, as we understand it, could reach their *supreme place* (ki.maḫ/*kimaḫḫu*), their *place of sleep,* their *residence of peace, of rest,* their *eternal dwelling* (*bît salâli*/*qûlti*/*tapšuḫti; šubat darâti*). Under the worst of threats nobody could disturb the arrangement of the *supreme place,* or remove the dead from it, except out of hatred and hostility.[20] To be left unburied was an extremely heavy punishment. It was used, for instance, to punish a woman who had committed abortion and who had been first impaled.

Necropolises of various sizes had been created near the settlements, and especially in the cities, apparently for reasons of convenience, but it seems that they were always at the borders of the social space. And it is even possible that they would have sometimes prepared burials within the cities not far from the temples and the palace, or erected mausoleums for the great of this world. But the custom of burying the dead underneath the family houses themselves (or on the family property) also survived, from the rulers to their subjects, down to the lowest one. A passage of an exorcistic ritual may suggest that these burials were more likely situated in one area of the house; in the *wing* of the building that was called for that purpose *wing of the dead of the family* (*šiddi eṭem kimti*), and also served as the domestic chapel.

20. See *Inscriptions*, pp. 381ff.

We have already said that each body was usually provided with a certain number of objects in the tomb. The latter were usually individual ones, but that did not exclude successive reuse, at which we have some examples. These objects included vessels, ornaments, tools for work, war, or play, clearly put at the disposal of the deceased not only because they remained his property (sometimes his name was written on them), to which he was thought to have been attached and to be still attached, but also because it was thought that they could be useful to him in his new existence. Let us say in passing that such an existence was not free from supernatural dangers, since more than one of these presents had only the value of a charm: for example, the seals, when they had not been the property of the dead, and very likely the cuneiform tablets placed near them at the time of burial, the contents of which had by all indications nothing to do with the person buried. For several good reasons I remain convinced that the famous "funerary tablets" found in a tomb in Susa* had a connection with the "voyage" of the dead to the Hereafter.[21] In my opinion, moreover, it is especially for this voyage—and the rituals of exorcism show it very clearly—that the food (and doubtless also the drink) were provided, traces of which archeologists have sometimes found in the vessels deposited near the dead.

After the dead were buried, the survivors were not discharged from their duties, perhaps especially those among them that by their rank in the family or by their connections to the dead were *in charge* (*pâqidu, sâḫiru*), without excluding the others of course. One had to protect the survival of the dead in some way, first of all by *pronouncing his name here on earth so that he would not sink into oblivion*. In other words, in the land where a name was the same as a substance, one called up his person, and conferred reality, presence, and existence upon him. It is in the same spirit that one always had to *treat him with respect, with honor, with regard* (*kunnû, šurruḫu, kubbutu*).

But most of all the dead had to be provided *down-below* with the indispensable goods for consumption—as, with due respect to proportions, one had to do for the gods. We have to imagine that from time to time, according to a schedule that we do not know, the living were busy with *feeding* and especially with *giving drink* to the dead by *pouring fresh water* for them. There is even mention of a type of pipe, called *arûtu*, inserted into the tomb, through which one could pour liquids for the dead—an arrangement for which, perhaps, some archeological remains exist. It is possible that certain terms, such as *kisikkû* (ki.sì.ga), designated these occasional offerings of food and drink reserved for the dead. The exorcistic rituals prescribe them more than once.

For this reason an institution existed, especially founded for the benefit

21. See *Inscriptions*, pp. 393ff.

of the dead it seems, celebrated usually in a part of the family house that was devoted to it: *the wing of the Manes* (*šiddi eṭem kimti*, see above), or the *place of the kispu* (*bît kispi*) where the surviving members of the family came together periodically. The preferred moment for this gathering was the end of the month, when the disappearance of the moon turned the attention naturally towards death and the dead. But it seems also to have been celebrated in other circumstances, in particular when there was a need felt to conciliate the dead in such ceremonies. This is what was called the *kispu*, in Sumerian ki.sì.ga (Akkadianized as *kisikkû*, but perhaps with a slightly different meaning—see below).[22]

This ceremony could be accompanied by the offering of a certain number of objects: various accessories, jewelry, etc. But, as its name indicates (*kasâpu, to break, to divide* food), it was essentially a meal. It is possible that originally it had been, and had always fundamentally remained, in spite of its secondary application, one of these meals of solidarity that were taken on some occasions by the reunited members of a family, and which in the ways of the ancient Semites had the purpose of reinforcing their vital bonds to the extent that they drew life from the *same food broken* and *divided* among them. That is in short the type of *monthly* banquet, that all the members of the divine family had in *Nergal and Ereškigal*, with the absent gods sending their agents to pick up their shares. Among the gods everyone was present or duly represented. Among the humans the dead were called to come and join in a meal with the living and to share it. We see it very well in Mari* where the *kispu* is regularly *celebrated for the kings* by the royal family, and often (if not always) also *for the maliku* of the Netherworld, an unclear term, but the choice of which in this context could be indicative.

This is how their survivors regularly provided the *eṭemmu* with the goods that were considered to be indispensable for maintaining them in their feeble existence. Those who were neglected by their descendants were pitied, even if they had been properly buried, and also those who had no one to prevent them from *sinking into oblivion* and who would therefore lead a very miserable "life" in the Netherworld. They were pitied, and they were feared, as were all the dissatisfied in the Hereafter.

The Reactions of the Dead

If the survivors had the advantage over the dead, the latter could act against the living—another "illogicality." How could the dead, sent for eternity to the Land-of-no-return, kept behind the enormous walls of the infernal citadel, still involve themselves with the affairs *here-above?*

22. See, on this subject, the article in *L'Histoire* 85 (1986): p. 64ff., "Le plus vieux festin du monde."

The universal folklore is full of "visits" of the dead to the living. The latter see the dead in a dream or otherwise; they feel that they are close, they hear them talk, cry, or complain; they feel persecuted, haunted, terrorized, and sometimes appeased or consoled by them. This airy and phantom-like appearance in which the dead were encountered did not only give an idea of their new state as shadows and *spirits*, it also gave rise to, or reinforced, the belief in their interventions and their "returns" to earth. In spite of their belief that death indicated the definitive transfer to another universe, the ancient Mesopotamians, impressed by such experiences, could not resist the fantastic imaginings that these experiences aroused. Thus they were convinced that, as such, the *eṭemmu* could really act among the *awîlu*, in a double way.

The first way was to the advantage of the living. The helping attitude doubtless had its basis both in the family relations between the dead and the living and in a type of gratitude that the dead were supposed to have towards those who, by paying their respects to them, helped to make their life as shades bearable. But also—and the graphic similarity of the signs udug and gedim, with the consequences indicated above (p. 73) points us in this direction—one had to assimilate the *eṭemmu* more or less *de facto* to the various demoniacal supernatural beings that, without having the prestige or the powers of the gods, were endowed with the supernatural capacities to accomplish the missions that the gods assigned to them, both to do good and to do evil. *Eṭemmu* and demons of all kinds often appear together in a more or less stereotypical list of exorcisms. This is why one invoked and prayed to the dead for favors to the living, whether or not the dead *belonged to the family.* The dead were thought to be *standing up in the Netherworld before the Council of the Anunnaki* and interceding for their descendants. They could free patients from the evil they suffered. Moreover, from very early on the Mesopotamians seem to have assigned the dead, among other superhuman powers, a much more extensive and penetrating knowledge than ours, perhaps because of their familiarity with the infernal gods. They were thought to have in particular a knowledge of the future, about which they were consulted just as diviners were consulted. For this purpose one could even *make them return,* literally *reascend* (šulû; see above, n. 16) from their Netherworld, as we see with the *spirit* (*utukku!*) of Enkidu in *Gilgameš, Enkidu, and the Netherworld.* To practice this skill there were *recallers of the eṭemmu* (*mušêlu eṭemmi;* literally *who make* (*re*)*ascend the ghosts*), necromancers for whom, we might note, there is no indication at all of a sinister reputation.

But the dead could also turn against the living and harm them. They could appear in the night and scare them; they could get hold of them and haunt them, plunge them into fear, inflict all sorts of tortures upon them both "psychological" and physical, to such a degree that the diagnosticians knew what we would call *the syndrome of the eṭemmu* (*qât/ṣibit/manzaz eṭemmi*). Perhaps because so many formulas for fighting such evils are preserved, we are well informed about these misdeeds. Some scholars have wondered whether the evil deeds of the returning spirits did not largely outweigh their good deeds. For every *good eṭemmu* (*eṭemmu damqu*) the number of *evil ones* (*eṭemmu lemnu*) is enormous, to the extent that the simple appearance (in a dream or hallucination) of one of these ghosts was considered to be in itself a bad omen.

These attacks and nuisances were blamed on *foreign eṭemmu* (*aḫû*), i.e. without family ties to the patient and who doubtless had never been buried for various reasons—either because they had died in an uninhabited region, or because they had died of hunger or thirst in an area rarely visited, or because they had been drowned, burned, or executed and were therefore *wandering* and *vagrant* (*murtappidu, muttaggišu*). They were vindicative, quarrelsome, and capable of jumping upon the first victim walking by to take revenge for their own misery. It could also be a ghost properly buried but neglected by his descendants and leading a miserable existence in the Hereafter. He also took revenge, in a sense, either on a stranger or on a member of his forgetful family.

In order to haunt, to "possess" and to persecute their victims, it was necessary for the *spirits* to get near them, and hence they had to leave the *Land,* even if it was *of-no-return,* after they had *descended* into it. It is never explained to us what unusual circumstances allowed this, what way or what mysterious means were used. It seems to have been assumed that it happened with the permission, or even the orders of the gods, to whom the *eṭemmu,* no less than the numerous demons, served as agents for punishing those who had incited the rage of the gods. Like the demons the *eṭemmu* could under these conditions come and go outside the borders of the awful prison that had been constructed by the mythology of death. The exact purpose of the exorcistic rituals was to send them back through all sorts of procedures, and a study of these rituals sheds light on many aspects of that mythology.[23]

For instance, one threw the persecuting *eṭemmu,* in the shape of a substitute figurine, into the river, so that it could be carried far away and become lost—a method that was also used for other evildoers. Alternatively, they were buried in some part of the desert in the west, or they were provided with clothes and travel provisions so that this burial or reburial resulted in the returning spirit's *redescent* to the Netherworld, either directly or by getting the departure signal for a new voyage to the Great-Gate of the Netherworld in the west. One could also treat the spirit—through its substitute figurine—as a prisoner to be returned to his cell. When it in-

23. See especially ZA, pp. 174ff.

volved an *eṭemmu* who was thought not to have been buried, to have been abandoned and wandering, he was offered the family tomb as a type of adoption *post mortem,* so to speak, in order to make his condition normal. He was given, belatedly, a ritual burial that would finally allow him to enter the Netherworld, and he was promised the normal gifts that he had the right to expect from his own descendants. Finally, to mention only the most interesting procedure, one could take advantage of the celebration of the "death" and the disappearance into the Netherworld of the god Tammuz, in the last days of the month named after him (June–July). The haunting spirit could be given to the god somewhat like a sheep is given to a shepherd, which Tammuz still was, so that he would take the spirit back with him; once back in the Hereafter, Tammuz could lock up the Spirit there forever. It should be said in passing that this "forever" was not certain at all. Among the same exorcistic rituals we find some that foresee the failure of the first and even of the second procedure! In any case, when we go through our dossier, we see that the mysterious ways of this Hereafter, even though it was called the *Land-of-no-return,* were filled with a perpetual coming and going of the dead, who returned sometimes to help but more often to persecute the living, and who were sent back to their subterranean homes.

The Two Ideas of the Netherworld and the Contradictions of the Mythology

It if is true that this evil aspect of the activities of the dead was much stronger than their helpful good nature, the Netherworld could only seem to the ancient Mesopotamians as a region with forces hostile to mankind. With their limited freedom, the dead were capable of *ascending to earth to eat the living,* as is shown in *Ištar's Descent.* That is undoubtedly one of the reasons why the apparitions of the dead were so terrifying. Even the infernal gods, from the greatest down to their demon-agents, took on fearful shapes and incited terror. To get an idea of this, it suffices to glance at the description in the Neo-Assyrian *Vision of the Netherworld* (above, n. 5).

However, if we consult other texts, such as *Urnammu in the Netherworld* (above, n. 2), a different image is given. There, the place is much more serene, but sad, gloomy, and dull, where existence tends to be a caricature of the one we lead on earth. Its life is nothing but a melancholic shadow, with ceaseless regret over the loss of real life forever. But the place, the inhabitants, and the gods have nothing cruel and terrible about them.

These two presentations of the Hereafter, one simply negative and pitiful, the other fully hostile and terrible, were they contemporaneous or do we have to imagine an evolution of thought from one to the other? After all, there are perhaps a good one thousand years between *Urnammu in the Netherworld* and the *Vision!* It is possible that the infernal gods, especially the most important ones, became more and more dangerous and frightening to mankind, due to the fact that they were busy, ex officio, populating their empire by provoking the great hecatombs of epidemics, catastrophes and wars here on earth, that are described in the *Erra epic.** The role of these demons, a large number of whom had close connections with the Netherworld, could have been focused more and more on the evil and frightening aspects in the communal conscience, from the moment that they were imagined to play essentially the role of henchmen of the gods who were irritated with mankind. The *eṭemmu* "took advantage" of this, so to speak, since they were closely related to the demons, as we have seen. Therefore one can postulate a change in the ideas of the Netherworld: first it was the home of the ex-living, later, little by little, of the anti-living.

I wonder whether the suggestion is not too simplistic and much too logical. Not only are we missing the stages of this transformation, which greatly weakens this hypothesis, but in the text itself of *Ištar's Descent in the Netherworld,* for instance, we find dead who are at the same time threatening and terrible on the one hand, and immobile and prostrated in the dust of their dark and silent cavern on the other hand—two visions that are entirely oppossed.

Thus it would be better to wait for more documentation that was spread out over time, and in the meantime to consider this double image of the Netherworld as one more contradiction to be added to those that we have already found in the mythology of death among the ancient Mesopotamians. Those contradictions include the entrance to the kingdom of the dead, both through numerous individual tombs and through the unique entrance at the end of a long voyage to the west; the dead being either numb and as if paralyzed, or aggressive and active; the *Land-of-no-return* that lets its inhabitants continuously "return"; the equality of everyone in this essentially negative condition, yet the continued hierarchy of great and small, of rich and poor, etc.

The typical aspect of all mythological thought, in contrast to logical thought, is that it provides different answers to the same question, even opposing answers, because the answers are imaginary, exact, and calculated, *toties quoties,* without concern for coherence; they envision, not truth, but the probable. In the field of death and the Hereafter, the only basic belief that has "preceded" and influenced all mythological elaboration is that death had to put an end to all that is positive, bright, noisy, joyous, active, comforting, and happy in our existence. On that point the ancient Mesopotamians never wavered. And we still think like them!

GLOSSARY-INDEX

accidents of daily life (divination through the)

A branch of *deductive divination* which extracted its oracles from the phenomena of the geographical, mineral, botanical, animal, and human world in the setting of daily life. See p. 33.

acrophony

A procedure that consists of giving as a phonetic value to a pictogram the phoneme (syllable or element of a syllable) by which the name of the object that it represents begins. Thus, in the "Phoenician" alphabetic writing, the sign of "the house," which was read "bêt," indicated the consonant *b*. See pp. 80 n. 10 and p. 90.

Adad

The Semitic name of a god who had control over the rain, hurricanes, storms, and other weather conditions. By *syncretism* he absorbed the personality of his Sumerian counterpart, Iškur. See pp. 215 and 233.

Adapa

An epithet of unknown origin that meant "the Wise one." This epithet was used for the first of the *apkallu*, whose name was U'anna. See pp. 247 and 248. A legend existed about him (pp. 245 and 269) which often has been erroneously considered to be a myth.

Akkad/Akkadian

Agade is the name of an ancient city (the location of which is not yet determined; perhaps not far from Sippar?): p. 167f. It became the capital of the First Semitic Empire, the Empire, or Dynasty of Akkad (p. vii). The name of its inhabitants, Akkadians, is conventionally extended to the oldest *Semites* settled in Mesopotamia. The upper half of Lower Mesopotamia, the region where they were originally in the majority, has been called Akkad. Hence the name Akkadian for the local Semitic language (pp. 48, 60 and 204) which, in its oldest stage before the second millennium, defines the so-called Old Akkadian period of the history of the country (p. vii). This language was later divided into two principal dialects: Babylonian in the south and Assyrian in the north (p. 60 n. 2). Those who made common use of the language are known as the speakers of Akkadian.

Amurrû/Amorites

The Akkadian name for the members of the seminomadic Semitic tribes who entered Mesopotamia, individually or in groups, in order to settle there, starting from the end of the third millennium (p. vii). They were called Martu in Sumerian (p. 236). Martu/*Amurru* is the designation for "the west" (p. 145). The language that they used, Amorite, which was related to *Canaanite*, was replaced by Akkadian.

An/Anu

An is a Sumerian word; it means "(the) above," "the heaven," and *Anu* is its Akkadianized form. It was the name of the god of Heaven, the oldest member and the founder of the ruling divine dynasty. He resided in *Uruk* in his "Temple of Heaven" (É.anna), which he shared with his courtesan, *Inanna*. See pp. 213, 225f and 234.

Anarchy (Time or *Period of)*

The traditional designation for the last century of decline of the Empire of Akkad (p. vii).

Anunnaku/Anunnaki

Derived from the Sumerian A.nunna(k), "Offspring of the divine Prince" (by whom we perhaps have to understand *Enki/Ea?*). It is the collective name of a group of higher divinities, ranking above the *Igigu/Igigi* (p. 222). Beginning with the second half of the second millennium the term was more readily used for the gods of the *Netherworld* (p. 278). Sometimes the word refers to the totality of the gods.

apkallu

A designation of Sumerian origin for the seven "Sages" (the exact meaning of the word is unknown), the civilizing heroes sent by *Enki/Ea* to teach culture to the archaic inhabitants of Mesopotamia (pp. 247f). The first of these sages was U'anna/*Adapa*.

apodosis

A definition, especially in the language of the *Treatises*, of the principal proposition introduced by a conditional clause which is itself called *protasis:* "If a man dreams that he is a leather tanner (*protasis*): he will be successively rich and poor (*apodosis*)." Presented in this way, the two together form the basic element of these *Treatises*, both stylistically and logically.

apography

Reproduction of the traces of the cuneiform signs as they appear on the original tablet. This term is preferable to "autography," which is more generally used.

Apsû

Word of unknown origin, as is its synonym Engur. In Mesopotamian cosmology it applied to the immense body of sweet water underneath the earth (p. 215). It was the realm and the habitat of *Enki/Ea* (p. 233). In the *Epic of Creation* it represented the male half of the primordial couple, while *Tiamat*, "Sea," was the female half (p. 220).

Arameans

A group of Semitic people coming from the northwest, who were originally seminomadic and started to settle in southern Mesopotamia from the second half of the second millennium on (p. viii). There they became progressively sedentary and then mixed with the autochthonous population. Their language, Aramaic, was written in an alphabetic script derived from the "Phoenician" alphabet. Starting in the middle of the first millennium, Aramaic came to replace Akkadian in daily use, step by step. It reduced Akkadian, which was still written in cuneiform, to the state of a literary and scholarly language.

Asalluḫi

Written Asari.lú.ḫi. A Sumerian compound of unknown meaning of which the first element, *Asari*, is not clear either (p. 88 n. 2). Asalluḫi was an archaic deity of the city Ku'ar, whose personality and name were later absorbed by *Marduk*, especially in his function as patron deity of the rites of *exorcism*. This function he exercised together with his father *Enki/Ea* (p. 234).

Asari

See the preceding entry.

Assur (Aššur)

Name (of Semitic origin but of unknown meaning) of the patron deity of Assyria (pp. 1 and 214), the northern part of Mesopotamia. The same name also indicated the first capital city of Assyria (*Aššur:* pp. 49 and 206). Assyria became an independent kingdom, especially starting from the second half of the second millennium, and remained so until its disappearance in the year 609 (p. viii). The Assyrian language was a dialect of Akkadian, and its development subdivides the history of the kingdom: Old Assyrian was used during the first half of the second millennium, Middle Assyrian during the second half, and Neo-Assyrian later (pp. viif.). Even while it was politically triumphant, Assyria always remained culturally dependent on Babylonia.

Assurbanipal

One of the greatest kings of Assyria, who reigned between the years 669 and 629. In his palace in *Nineveh (Kuyundjik)* he collected the entire current literary production of his time in a famous library. This library was found in some 30,000 tablets and fragments, and is now in the British Museum in London.

astrology

A branch of *deductive divination* that drew its oracles from the aspects and the movements of the stars and the meteorites (pp. 34 and 141).

Atraḫasîs (The Supersage)

This epithet, belonging to *Enki/Ea,* was also used to indicate his devotee, who was saved from the Flood by *Enki/Ea* in order to preserve the human race. Atraḫasîs is the subject of a long mythological poem, of 1,200 lines on three tablets, about three-quarters of which is preserved, composed apparently around the year 1700. The poem is of considerable importance, especially for the study of the creation of mankind (pp. 221ff. and 241ff.).

Babylon/Babylonians

A city almost entirely unknown in its early history but one that left obscurity under its First Dynasty (between the years 1894 and 1595; see p. vii). Babylon then became the capital of the kingdom which *Ḫammurabi* had established around the city. When the kingdom of Assyria emerged, Babylonia became the name of the southern part of the country (p. 1). As with the Assyrian dialect, Babylonian follows the great periods of the history of Babylonia: Old Babylonian used before the year 1500, Middle Babylonian used during the second half of the second millennium, and Neo-Babylonian used in the first millennium (pp. viif.). Late Babylonian refers to the literary language in use during the first millennium.

Bêl

An Akkadian word that refers to *Marduk*, and that means "The Lord."

Bêlet-ekallim

"Lady of the palace" in Akkadian: epithet of *Ištar* (p. 111).

Berossos

Babylonian scholar who, shortly after the year 300, recorded in Greek the history and the traditions of his country. Although the fragments that are preserved of his *Babyloniaka* are only scraps, they are precious, considering the importance of their author (pp. 139 n. 6, and 246f.).

Canaanite

Derived from Canaan, the ancient name of Palestine. It refers to a linguistic branch of north Semitic (like the later Aramaic) to which Hebrew, Ugaritic, and the even older Amorite are related (p. 66).

canonicity

Relates to a type of choice in the corpus of the written works of liturgical, literary, and scientific nature, that took place in Mesopotamia starting in the second half of the second millennium. These works were from that moment on diligently copied in the same general form that was established once and for all at that time. Thus the *Epic of Creation* was canonically divided into seven tablets, and the *Epic of Gilgameš* was divided into eleven tablets, to which later a twelfth was added.

catamite
A term derived from an ancient Latin name of Ganymedes, which came to refer to passive homosexuals.

Chaldea
The Chaldeans (Kaldu) were the tribes that were seemingly Semitic, possibly the forerunners of the *Arameans*, to whom they must have been more or less related. The Chaldeans came to settle in the southern part of Babylonia, which later came to be called Chaldea. The name Chaldea was later extended to include the entirety of Babylonia. Sometimes the last independent dynasty of the land, which ruled after the year 609, is referred to as "Chaldean."

cinedes
A word derived from Greek and more or less synonymous with *catamite*.

city-state (urban-state)
A political regime in which the country was divided into independent units comprising a rural countryside with scattered villages around a capital city, where the central power was located. See pp. 48, 69, and 205f.

classifying (signs)
Another designation of *determinative* signs.

"Code" (of Ḫammurabi)
See *Ḫammurabi*.

copyists
Among the indigenous users of the cuneiform script one has to distinguish between the crowd of copyists (scribes, notaries, redactors, secretaries, who worked by the job and were satisfied with copying and storing various documents) and the scholars, learned men who created ideas and new works. The latter were able to make "active" use of the script, and thus surpassed by far in ability the copyists, who relied on routines. See p. 89.

Creation (Epic or *Poem of)*
See *Epic of Creation*.

cuneiform
The word refers to the local script of Mesopotamia, where the marks impressed on soft clay by a stylus cut in the shape of a bevel give the impression of "wedges" or "nails." See p. 56.

Dagan
God of the highest order in the pantheon of the *Canaanites* and the *Amorites*, who is attested in that capacity in *Mari* (p. 111).

deductive/inspired divination
The difference between these two types of mantic in ancient Mesopotamia is explained on pp. 106f. and 125f.

Descent of Innana/Ištar to the Netherworld
This is the name given to a myth that relates how *Inanna/Ištar*, who wanted to go to the Kingdom of Hell, was taken prisoner there and could be saved only by a trick of *Enki/Ea*, at the expense of the "life" of her lover, *Dumuzi/Tammuz*. A complete Sumerian version of more than 400 lines, and another version in Akkadian that is much shorter, are extant. See pp. 194f., 244, and 277.

determinative (signs)
Also called *classifying signs*. In cuneiform these are signs placed rather regularly before or after a word to indicate the class of objects to which the word belongs. See pp. ix, 59, and 89.

diacritic (signs)
Graphic signs (accents or index numbers) intended to differentiate homophonous characters. Their presence has no relationship at all to the pronunciation: sa, sá, sa_6 are all equally pronounced SA. See pp. ix and 95 n. 4.

disputes
A particular genre of the ancient Mesopotamian literature: a type of duel in dialogue form. See pp. 30f.

divination
See *deductive/inspired divination*.

Dumuzi
See *Tammuz*.

Ea
See *Enki*.

Ebla/Eblaite
Modern Tell Mardikh, located some 60 kilometers southwest of Aleppo. The capital of a Syrian state flourishing around the middle of the third millennium. Around 12,000 cuneiform tablets were found

there, written partly in Sumerian and partly in Eblaite, the local Semitic idiom (pp. 10 and 22).

Elam/Elamites
A state located in the southwestern part of Iran, bordered by different political entities—such as *Marḫaši*—and known primarily from the city of *Susa*, which has been the most extensively excavated Elamite site. Elam seems to have been at the same time one of the most stubborn adversaries of Mesopotamia, which ultimately subjugated Elam, and one of its oldest cultural subordinates. It borrowed first of all the idea of the pictographic writing system from Mesopotamia, which still remains undeciphered, and later adopted the real cuneiform script. The local language, Elamite, is still badly understood, and is linguistically as isolated as is Sumerian. See pp. 10, 22, 58f, 236.

Enki/Ea
The first of these two terms is Sumerian, but its exact meaning is not certain. The second term is of Sumerian outlook but was used only by the speakers of Akkadian, and seems to have been a popular etymology that tried to render something like *Ayya, Aya, Ya*. For this major god, one of the best characterized of the Mesopotamian pantheon, "inventor" and protector of mankind and of all technical achievements, master of all the works of the exorcists, father of *Marduk*, and the one who resided in the temple of the *Apsû* in the city of *Eridu*, see especially pp. 213 and 232ff.

Enlil
In Sumerian "Lord atmosphere" (p. 233 n. 3), sovereign deity of the universe according to the ancient system of the pantheon (pp. 213f., also p. 209). His residential city was *Nippur*, where the main temple was named "Temple [of the] Mountain" (É.kur), referring to one of Enlil's epithets.

Enûma eliš
See *Epic of Creation*

Epic of Creation
This poem was referred to in antiquity by its *incipit: Enûma eliš*, "When on high. . . ." It is a long work of some one thousand verses, on seven tablets, composed probably around the year 1200 in Babylon. It described, starting from the beginning of the universe, the accession of *Marduk* as ruler of the gods and of the world. See pp. 88, 214, and 242f.

Epic of Gilgameš
Gilgameš was the Sumerian name (of unknown meaning) of a king of Uruk, dating to the second quarter of the third millennium, who very

soon became the hero of a certain number of legends in Sumerian, and who later became deified (p. 274 n. 15). The content of the majority of these legends was taken up again in Akkadian and put together in one continuous story which has great strength and a real poetic character: it is what we call the *Epic of Gilgameš*. In it were depicted the prowess of Gilgameš and of his friend Enkidu, a wild man who was introduced to civilization; how, after the premature death of Enkidu, Gilgameš went to search for a means to have eternal life; and how he returned home empty-handed. This work is best known from the version that was found in the library of Assurbanipal, known as the Ninevite version. This version is written on eleven tablets, about three-quarters of which are preserved (p. 193). Older fragments (especially the "Pennsylvania" and "Meissner" fragments, etc.) lead us to believe that there could have existed one (or more) Old Babylonian version(s) or edition(s) of the work (pp. 111f.). Later a twelfth tablet was added to the work, an Akkadian translation of a Sumerian legend: *Gilgameš, Enkidu, and the Netherworld* (p. 219).

Ereškigal
"Lady of the Great-Earth" (one of the names of the *Netherworld*) in Sumerian. She was the queen of the Kingdom of the Dead. She first ruled by herself, but later was joined by her husband, *Nergal* (pp. 216, 244f., 274 n. 15).

Eridu
Ancient city in the south of Mesopotamia, whose tutelary deity was *Enki/Ea*.

Erra (or *Irra*)
Another name for *Nergal*. He was the hero of a long composition of around 700 lines, on five tablets, the *Poem* or *Epic of Erra*, of which about a third is lost. It was written around the year 850 and explains the misfortunes of *Babylon* by the destructive will of Erra, and its resurrection when he was appeased at the end. See pp. 247f.

Esagil
The major temple of *Marduk* in *Babylon*.

eṭemmu
Akkadian for the Sumerian gedim, indicating the "spirits" of the dead, who lived in the *Netherworld* after passing away (pp. 271ff.).

exorcism
Often inappropriately called "magic." It was the totality of the procedures executed to avoid the evils of life, using a mixture of mutually reinforcing manual and oral rites (pp. 177, n. 12, and p. 230).

extispicy
Synonym for *haruspicy.*

Fara
Modern name of the ancient city of Šuruppak, seat of the dynasty under whose rule the Flood was thought to have taken place. Tablets and fragments from around 2700/2600 have been found there, as well as in the neighboring site of *Abu Salābīkh*. Among these tablets were several hundred that represent the oldest stage of Sumerian literature. See pp. 70f. and 83.

full words
See *hollow/full words.*

Gilgameš
See *Epic of Gilgameš*

Gudea
A Sumerian name, meaning something like "Prophet." It is the name of a ruler of Lagaš (ca. 2144–2124), for whom we have found a number of documents and especially inscriptions on cylinders of clay (now in the Louvre museum) containing two long poems which he composed to celebrate the local temple of his god *Ningirsu* (p. 85).

Ḫammurabi
King of *Babylon* (1792–1750) and founder of the kingdom whose capital was Babylon (pp. vii, 48f., and 206). Author of a famous collection, mistakenly taken for a "Code" of laws. See on this pp. 156ff.

haruspicy
A branch of *deductive divination* that derived its oracles from the appearance of the entrails of sacrificed animals. See pp. 34 and 141.

Ḫatti
See *Hittites.*

hepatoscopy
A branch of *extispicy* that derived its oracles from the shape of the liver of sacrificed animals (p. 34).

Hittites
An Indo-European population that settled from the seventeenth century on in Anatolia, where it created a powerful empire for half a millennium. The Hittites borrowed from Mesopotamia its cuneiform script, among other institutions and technologies. However, the Hittites invented simultaneously an original system of hieroglyphic character. We have the remains of a considerable written documentation from these people. See pp. 10, 22f., 63f.

hollow/full words

In any given language the full words indicate the actual realities (the beings and their movements), the hollow words indicate their mutual relations, by themselves or from our own point of view (pp. 68f., 78).

homophony

A phonetic coincidence of two different signs or words, which seem to have been particularly frequent in Sumerian and which thus appears often in the *cuneiform* script (pp. 79f.).

Ḫurrians

From the end of the third millennium on, the Ḫurrians descended from the mountains to the north and the northwest of Mesopotamia. They were scattered for more than 1,000 years, not only throughout Mesopotamia, but also throughout Syria, where they founded short-lived kingdoms. They also wrote their language in *cuneiform*. This language is isolated (related only to its descendant, Urartean) and we are only starting to master it. See pp. 10 and 65.

Iamenites

In Amorite, "people of the south." Seminomadic tribe(s) that settled in the region of the Upper and Middle Euphrates, at least during the first half of the second millennium (p. 110).

ideography

A system of writing where the signs, at first simple pictograms, became differentiated from the primitive sketch by a certain stylization on the one hand, and on the other saw their original restricted meaning extended to a real semantic constellation (pp. 38 and 73 n. 7).

Igigu/Igigi

A term of unknown origin and meaning that ended up by indicating in some instances the entirety of the gods, and sometimes more commonly those that occupied heaven. See p. 222. See *Anunnaku*.

Inanna/Ištar

Inanna is Sumerian for "Lady of the sky"; *Ištar* is the Semitic divine name used by the speakers of Akkadian. She is a composite divinity in whom *syncretism* joined a Sumerian goddess of "free love" (pp. 188ff.) and a Semitic deity of discord and war (p. 237), as well as a goddess (Dilbat or Delebat) of the planet Venus. One of her high residences was in Uruk (p. 238) but she had worshipers and sanctuaries almost everywhere (compare with *Bêlet-ekallim*), and her importance was so great that she eventually absorbed the majority of other goddesses. See also *Descent of Inanna/Ištar to the Netherworld*.

incubation
We have a few attestations of this practice, which tried to provoke divinatory dreams: see pp. 34 and 112.

Ištar
See *Inanna/Ištar.*

Kalḫu
Modern Nimrud, some forty kilometers south of Mosul. It was the second capital of Assyria starting around the year 850.

Kassites
Invaders of whom little is known, who came from the mountains of the east and the northeast and who, under a Kassite dynasty, occupied Babylonia between the years 1600 and 1200 (pp. vii and 49).

Kingdom of the dead
See *Netherworld.*

Kuyundjik
Modern name of the mounds of *Nineveh* where *Assurbanipal* had his palace and his library.

Land-of-no-return
See *Netherworld.*

lists
The first known presentation of "scientific" works in Mesopotamia. The lists contained catalogues of signs and words, duly classified according to various criteria. In the beginning they were only in Sumerian, but later they were expanded with a parallel column to indicate the Akkadian equivalents. See pp. 29f.

Ludlul (bêl nêmeqi)
In Akkadian: "I want to praise [the Lord of wisdom]." Incipit of a type of monologue on four tablets and almost 400 verses in length, in which a devotee searches in vain for the reasons of the misfortunes which suddenly overcame him. In the end *Marduk* removes his misfortunes. The text was composed during the second half of the second millennium, and most of it is preserved. See p. 264.

magic
See *exorcism.*

mantic techniques
Another name for divination.

Marduk
Name (with a disputed origin and etymology) of the god of the city of *Babylon,* who was originally obscure but became later the official pa-

tron deity of the kingdom of *Ḫammurabi*. Finally he came to be recognized, in the cult and in theology, as the highest deity of the gods and the people. See *Epic of Creation*. He was the son of Ea and shared with him more particularly the patronage of *exorcism*, preferring in that role the name of *Asalluḫi*. He resided in *Babylon* in his famous temple "On the raised platform" (*Esagil*) with his wife, Ṣarpanîtu or Zarpanîtu. See pp. 209, 214, and 234.

Marḫaši
See *Elam*.

Mari
An ancient city on the Middle Euphrates, which was for a long time an independent (Amorite) kingdom, and which was destroyed and incorporated by *Ḫammurabi* around the year 1760. Numerous administrative archives were found there as well as an enormous international diplomatic correspondence, dating to around 1780. See pp. 22, 110f., 142, and 282.

Martu
See *Amurrû*.

Middle Assyrian "Laws"
Fragmentary tablets found in *Assur* and dated around 1100, where statements analogous to those of the "Code" of *Ḫammurabi* were collected. These statements were, however, much more detailed and rigorous than those of Ḫammurabi.

mythology
An intellectual procedure which consists of responding to the great questions about the origins and the meaning of the universe and our existence, as well as the role and the activity of the gods, who are considered to have directed everything. This procedure worked not by rational and conceptual analysis, in order to find the truth, but by imaginative activity that gave answers that were no more than probable but that were considered to be sufficient. See pp. 194, 218. After a long oral tradition which is entirely unknown to us, but later undoubtedly accompanying this oral tradition, a great number of myths came to be present in Mesopotamian literature. These myths are the products of the mental activity of authors who remain unknown to us and whom we sometimes qualify as mythographers (p. 11).

Nabû
Name (Akkadian, but of unknown etymology) of a god who appeared rather late in the Mesopotamian pantheon. He was made the "son" of *Marduk* and had as a feudal estate the city of Borsippa. In certain mi-

lieus in the first millennium there was a tendency to make him the successor of his father at the head of the gods (p. 214).

namburbû

Akkadianized form of the Sumerian nam.búr.bi "appropriate dissolution (of evil)". It was used for exorcistic procedures, a great quantity of which have been preserved. The procedures were intended and executed to avert the evils foreseen by divination. See pp. 124 n. 12, pp. 142f. n. 14.

Nanna(r)

Sumerian name of the Moon god, called Sîn by the Akkadian speakers.

Nergal

Derived from the Sumerian name nè.eri$_{11}$.gal, "Authority of the Great-City" i.e. the *Netherworld*. Nergal, who also used the name *Erra*, was the husband of the queen of the Netherworld, *Ereškigal*. See pp. 216, 244f., 274 n. 15.

Netherworld (Kingdom of the dead, Land-of-no-return)

Subterranean space, in symmetry with heaven, where the "phantom"-*eṭemmu* went after death, and resided for eternity. See pp. 273f.

Nimrud

Modern name of *Kalḫu*.

Nineveh

The last capital of Assyria, starting from the reign of Sennacherib (704–681) (pp. viii, 1).

Ningirsu/Ninurta

The first of these Sumerian terms is an epithet ("Lord of the city of Girsu") for the second name ("Lord of the earth"), which applied to an ancient god who was originally considered to be the patron of agriculture. He experienced his period of greatest celebrity and devotion in the third millennium. He was considered, somewhat like *Marduk* later on, to have been the champion of the gods and the savior of the land from the barbarian peoples of the mountains in the north and the northeast.

Nippur

An ancient city, without any direct political influence, whose role seems never to have been more than religious. It was the seat of *Enlil*, the supernatural lord of the world and of Mesopotamia.

oneiromancy

For this branch of divination, which derived its oracles from dreams, see especially pp. 105ff.

phonetism

Said of script where the signs (qualified in such a system as phonograms; therefore the term "phonography" is also used) express the sounds, i.e. phonemes. See especially pp. 79ff.

physiognomy

Sector of *deductive divination* where the oracles were derived from the appearance of the body of the interested party (physiognomy in the strict sense) or from its behavior (physiognomy in the broad sense).

pictography

Refers to the oldest stage of writing where the characters consist of sketches of the objects that they signify, directly or indirectly. See especially pp. 79ff. and 99.

polyphony

In the cuneiform writing system it is the ability of the characters to indicate several different realities, due to the picto-/ideographic origins, and as many different syllabic phonemes, following the discovery of their phonetic values, each of them derived from one of the names of these realities. See especially pp. 82 and 91f.

protasis

See *apodosis*.

Ras Shamra

Modern name of *Ugarit*.

Rosetta Stone

This is the name of a trilingual document, the last column of which contained a text in Greek, thereby allowing J.-F. Champollion to break the code of the hieroglyphs in the first column (p. 4).

Šamaš

The Semitic name of the Sun god, known as *Utu* in Sumerian (pp. 209f., 274 n. 15).

Sargonids

The name is used to refer to the successors of Sargon II (721–705) in Assyria, under whose rule the country reached its apogee, before its disappearance in the year 609 (p. viii).

Sargon the Great, or *the Elder,* or *Sargon I*

Founder of the Akkadian empire (p. vii).

scholars

See *copyists*.

Semites

An ethnic group characterized by an original common language and culture, which spread since prehistory (at the latest the fourth millennium) in the area around Arabia in successive linguistic and cultural waves: in Mesopotamia (the original inhabitants, then the "Akkadians," then the Amorites, then the Arameans), in Syria and Palestine (Eblaites, then Amorites, then Canaanites, then Arameans), and finally starting in the first millennium in Arabia itself, the South Arabians and the Arabs. See pp. viif., 47, and 204.

Sîn
Semitic name of the Moon god. See *Nanna(r).*

Sumer/Sumerians
The name *Sumer* is the original designation of the southern part of Lower Mesopotamia. The name *Sumerian* was applied to those people who had arrived probably from the south or the southeast, and who inhabited Sumer as a majority in the beginning of history (around the year 3000) (pp. vii, 1, 47f., 69, 204). The term *Sumerian* is also used for the linguistically isolated language that they spoke and wrote (thus the qualification *speakers of Sumerian* that is sometimes used for them) (pp. 47, 63). They disappeared quickly in the course of the third millennium, and were absorbed by the Semites in Mesopotamia, to whom they left, besides a number of inventions, the use of their language for literature, liturgy, and science.

sumerograms
The name Assyriologists give to the ideograms in the cuneiform script to the extent that each of them indicates a Sumerian word by its proper origins (p. 86 n. 15).

Supersage
See *Atraḫasîs.*

Šuruppak
See *Fara.*

Susa
Capital of *Elam* (pp. 114, 159, 281).

syllabary
The totality of the signs in a syllabic script. Each sign refers to a sound that is basically pronounceable (syllabograms) and together they form a syllabary. The cuneiform script is only partly syllabic (p. 61).

syncretism
A synthesis of cultural elements which took place by the contact of cultural systems. This happened very often in Mesopotamia as a result of the original Sumero-Semitic symbiosis. We have numerous examples

of syncretism, especially in the religious sphere. See p. 216 and above, *Inanna/Ištar*.

Tammuz

Akkadianized form of the Sumerian *Dumuzi* ("legitimate" or "faithful son"). The name referred to an ancient and partly legendary ruler who was made the first lover of *Inanna/Ištar* by the mythology. A month of the year was named after him (the fourth month: June-July). See p. 285.

teratomancy

A branch of *deductive divination* that draws its oracles from the abnormal appearance of animals and humans at birth, both in premature births and full-term births (p. 34).

Tiamat

In Akkadian, "sea." In the *Poem of Creation* it is the female half of the primordial couple, whose male counterpart was *Apsû* (p. 220).

tocomancy

A branch of *deductive divination*, partly covered by *teratomancy*, whose oracles were derived from the appearance of newborn animals or humans (p. 34).

treatises

The usual presentation in ancient Mesopotamia of "scientific" material. Treatises took the form of long lists of analytic and varied descriptions of the studied objects. Sometimes they are also called "manuals." See pp. 31f., 127f., 169f.

Ugarit

Modern *Ras Shamra* on the Syrian coast. It was a city and a state in Syria that flourished after the middle of the second millennium. An especially great number of documents was found in this city. These are not only in a particular Semitic language of the Canaanite type, known as Ugaritic, but also in a cuneiform alphabetic script (p. 65).

Ur

A famous city in the south of Lower Mesopotamia, which was the seat of several dynasties (p. vii). It was the feudal holding of the Sumerian Moon god *Nanna(r)*, p. 236.

Urartu/Urartean

The ancient name of Armenia. The language used there in the first millennium, Urartean, is known to us only from a small number of intelligible documents. It was written in *cuneiform* and was derived from Ḫurrian (pp. 65f.).

urban-state

See *city-state.*

Uruk

One of the most important archaic cities of Lower Mesopotamia; especially celebrated for its "Temple of Heaven" (É.anna) where *An* resided (pp. 225f.) with his hierodule *Inanna.*

Utu

The Sumerian name of the Sun god, called *Šamaš* by the Semites.

Vision of the Netherworld

A sort of lampoon in Akkadian dating to around the year 650, of which only half is preserved. In it a political message is thought to have been given to the crown prince (probably *Assurbanipal*) during a dream(?). In the dream he saw himself summoned by the court of horrifying gods that preside over the Netherworld. See p. 270 n. 5, and p. 285.

REFERENCES

Acta antiqua Academiae Scientiarum Hungaricae. Budapest.

Akkadica. Brussels.

Annales du Centre d'Étude des Religions. Brussels.

Annali della Scuola Normale superiore di Pisa. Lettre e Filosofia. Pisa.

Annuaire 19..–19.. de la IVe section de l'École practique des Hautes Études. Paris.

Annuaire de l'Institut de Philologie et d'Historie orientales et slaves de l'Université Libre de Belgique. Brussels.

Archives royales de Mari, 10: G. Dossin-A. Finet, *Correspondance féminine.* Paris, 1978.

______14: M. Birot, *Lettres de Yaqqim-Addu.* Paris, 1974.

______18: O. Rouault, *Mukannišum.* Paris, 1977.

Archiv für Orientforschung. Graz/Horn.

Bulletin of the American Schools of Oriental Research. Baltimore, Md.

C. A. Benito. *"Enki and Ninmah" and "Enki and the World Order"* (Microfilm). Ann Arbor, 1969.

Robert T. Biggs. *Inscriptions from Tell Abu Ṣalābīkh.* Chicago, 1974.

______ŠÀ.ZI.GA. Ancient Mesopotamian Potency Incantations. New York, 1967.

Bibliotheca Orientalis. Leiden.

R. Borger. *Assyrisch-babylonische Zeichenliste.* Neukirchen-Vluyn, 1978.

J. Bottéro. *L'Epopée de la Création.* L'Arbresle, 1979.

______*Mythes et rites de Babylone.* Paris, 1985.

______*Le Problème du Mal en Mésopotamie ancienne. Prologue à une étude du "Juste souffrant."* L'Arbresle, 1977.

______*La Religion babylonienne.* Paris, 1952.

E. Burrows. *Ur Excavations, Texts.* 2: *Archaic Texts.* London, 1935.

G. Cardascia. *Les Lois assyriennes.* Paris, 1969.

Catalogue de l'exposition Naissance de l'Écriture. Paris, 1982.

Chicago Assyrian Dictionary. New York.

A. T. Clay. *Epics, Hymns, Omens, and Other Texts.* New Haven, 1923.

Cuneiform Texts from Babylonian Tablets . . . in the British Museum. London.

Death in Mesopotamia, ed. B. Alster. Copenhagen, 1980.

A. Deimel. *die Inschriften von Fara.* Leipzig, 1922–24.

Dictionnaire archéologique des techniques. Paris, 1963–66.

(La) Divination en Mésopotamie ancienne et dans les régions voisines. Paris, 1966.

Divination et rationalité, ed. by J.-P. Vernant. Paris, 1974, pp. 70–197 ("Symptômes, signes écritures en Mésopotamie ancienne").

G. R. Driver-J. C. Miles. *The Babylonian Laws.* Oxford, 1955–56.

E. Ebeling. *Quellen zur Kenntnis der babylonischen Religion.* Leipzig, 1918.

______*Die akkadische Gebetsserie "Handerhebung".* Berlin, 1953.

______*Keilschrifttexte aus Assur religiösen Inhalts.* Leipzig, 1915–23. (*KAR.*)

E. Ebeling-F. Köcher. *Literarische Keilschrifttexte aus Assur.* Berlin, 1953.

R. S. Ellis. *A Bibliography of Mesopotamian Archaeological Sites.* Wiesbaden, 1972.

A. Falkenstein. *Archaische Texte aus Uruk.* Berlin-Leipzig, 1936.

______*Sumerische Götterlieder,* I. Heidelberg, 1959.

G. Farber-Flügge. *Der Mythos "Inanna und Enki," unter besonderer Berücksichtigung der Liste der* me. Rome, 1973.

J.-G. Février. *Histoire de l'écriture.* Paris, 1948.

A. Finet. *Le Code de Hammurapi.* Paris, 1973.

H. Frankfort et al. *Before Philosophy.* Harmondsworth, 1949/1951.

H. D. Galter. *Der Gott Ea/Enki in der akkadischen Überlieferung.* Graz, 1983.

M. Gauchet. *Le Désenchantement du monde.* Paris, 1985.

Genava. Geneva.

T. Ghirshman. *Archéologue malgré moi.* Neuchâtel, 1970.

A. Goetze. *Old Babylonian Omen Texts.* New Haven, 1947.

J. Goody. *The Logic of Writing.* Cambridge-New York, 1986.

______*The Domestication of the Savage Mind.* Cambridge-New York, 1977.

M. Granet. *La Pensée chinoise.* Paris, 1950.

A. K. Grayson. *Assyrian and Babylonian Chronicles.* New York, 1975.

A. Haase. *Die keilschriftlichen Rechtssammlungen in deutscher Übersetzung.* Wiesbaden, 1963.

R. F. Harper. *Assyrian and Babylonian Letters belonging to the Kouyundjik Collection of the British Museum.* London-Chicago, 1892–1914.

(L')Histoire. Paris.

Hommes et bêtes. Entretiens sur le recisme, ed. by L. Poliakov. Paris, 1975.

G. Ifrah. *Histoire universelle des chiffres.* Paris, 1981.

Iraq. London.

Journal of Cuneiform Studies. Cambridge, Mass./Philadelphia.

Journal of Economic and Social History of the Orient. Leiden.

Journal of Near Eastern Studies. Chicago.

J. Koenig. *L'Herméneutique analogique du Judaïsme antique d'après les témoins textuels d'Isaïe.* Leiden, 1982.

S. N. Kramer. *Enki and Ninḫursag: A Sumerian "Paradise" Myth*. New Haven, 1945.

______*History Begins at Sumer*. New York, 1956.

______*The Sacred Marriage Rite*. Bloomington-London, 1969.

______*The Sumerians*. Chicago, 1963.

F. R. Kraus. *Königliche Verfügungen in altbabylonischer Zeit*. Leiden, 1984.

R. Labat. *Traité akkadien de diagnostics et pronostics médicaux*. Paris, 1951.

______*Manuel d'épigraphie akkadienne*. Paris, 1948/1976.

W. G. Lambert. *Babylonian Wisdom Literature*. Oxford, 1960.

W. G. Lambert-A. R. Millard. *Atra-ḫasîs. The Babylonian Story of the Flood*. Oxford, 1969.

B. Landsberger et al. *Materialien zum sumerischen Lexikon/Materials for the Sumerian Lexicon*. Rome, 1937–.

S. Langdon. *Die neubabylonischen Königsinschriften*. Leipzig, 1912.

______*Pictographic Inscriptions from Jemdet Nasr*. . . . Oxford, 1928.

E. Laroche. *Catalogue des textes hittites*. Paris, 1971.

E. Leichty. *The Omen Series* šumma izbu. New York, 1970.

H. Lenzen. *XVIII. vorläufiger Bericht über die . . . Ausgrabungen in Uruk-Warka*. Berlin, 1962.

M. Mauss. *Sociologie et anthropologie*. Paris, 1950.

G. Meier. *Die assyrische Beschwörungssammlung Maqlû*. Berlin, 1937.

Mitteilungen der deutschen Orient-Gesellschaft. Berlin.

(La) Mort, les morts dans les sociétés anciennes, ed. by G. Gnoli and J.-P. Vernant. Cambridge. 1982.

S. Moscati, ed.. *Le antiche divinità semitiche*. Rome, 1958.

F. Nötscher. *Haus und Stadtomina*. Rome, 1928.

______*Die Omen-Serie* šumma âlu ina mêlê šakin. Rome, 1930.

L. Oppenheim. *Ancient Mesopotamia*. Chicago, 1977.

______*The Interpretation of Dreams in the Ancient Near East*. Philadelphia, 1956.

Orientalia. Rome.

S. Parpola. *Letters from Assyrian Scholars to the Kings Esarhaddon and Assurbanipal*, I and II. Neukirchen-Vluyn, 1970 and 1983.

Reallexikon der Assyriologie. Berlin.

Recherches et documents du Centre Thomas More. L'Arbresle.

E. Reiner. Šurpu, *a Collection of Sumerian and Akkadian Incantations*. Graz, 1958.

Revue d'Assyriologie. Paris.

Les Religions du Proche-Orient asiatique. Paris, 1970.

J. J. M. Roberts. *The Earliest Semitic Pantheon*. Baltimore, 1972.

V. Scheil, *Textes élamites sémitiques, 2. Mémoires de la Delegation en Perse*, 4: Paris, 1902.

———*Textes élamites-sémitiques*, 5. *Mémoires de la Mission archéologique en Susiane*, 14: Paris, 1913.

P. Schnabel. *Berossos und die babylonisch-hellenistische Literatur*. Leipzig, 1923.

E. Schürer. *Geschichte des jüdischen Volkes im Zeitalter Jesu Christi*. 1901/1964.

J. Seux. *Hymnes et prières aux dieux de Babylonie et d'Assyrie*. Paris, 1976.

A. Shaffer. *Sumerian Sources of Tablet XII of the Epic of Gilgameš* (microfilm). Ann Arbor, 1963.

Societies and Languages of the Ancient Near East. Studies in Honour of I. M. Diakonoff. Warminster, 1982.

E. Sollberger-J. R. Kupper. *Inscriptions royales sumériennes et akkadiennes*. Paris, 1971.

M. Stol. *Altbabylonische Briefe*, 9. *Letters from Yale*. Leiden, 1981.

Symbolae ad jura Orientis antiqui pertinentes Paulo Koschaker dedicatae. Leiden, 1939.

K. Tallqvist. *Akkadische Götterepitheta*. Helsinki, 1938.

Textes cunéiformes du musée du Louvre, 6: Fr. Thureau-Dangin. *Tablettes d'Uruk à l'usage des prêtres du temple d'Anu au temps des Séleucides*. Paris, 1922.

R. C. Thompson. *The Reports of the Magicians and Astrologers of Nineveh and Babylon*. London, 1900.

F. Thureau-Dangin. *Les inscriptions de Sumer at d'Akkad*. Paris, 1905.

———*Rituels accadiens*. Paris, 1921.

(L')Univers. Histoire et description de tous les peuples. Chaldée, Assyrie, Médie, Babylonie, Mésopotamie, Phénicie, Palmyrène. Paris, 1852.

Ch. Virolleaud. *L'Astrologie chaldéenne*. Paris, 1905–12.

(La) Voix de l'opposition en Mésopotamie, colloque de Bruxelles, 1973.

W. von Soden-W. Röllig. *Das akkadische Syllabar*². Rome, 1967.

S. D. Walters. *Water for Larsa*. New Haven, 1970.

Wörterbuch der Mythologie, ed. H. W. Haussig, I. *Die alten Kulturvölker*, Stuttgart.

Zeitschrift für Assyriologie und vorderasiatische Archäologie. Berlin.

J. Zimmern. *Beiträge zur Kenntnis der babylonische Religion*, 2. Leipzig, 1901.

ABBREVIATIONS

AO	*Antiquités orientales*, Louvre Museum
K	*Kuyundjik* collection, British Museum
KAR	E. Ebeling-F. Köcher, *Keilschrifttexte aus Assur religiösen Inhalts*
Sm	*G. Smith* collection, British Museum
VAT	*Vorderasiatische Abteilung*, *Tontafeln* collection, Museum of Berlin.

BIBLIOGRAPHICAL ORIENTATION

For readers who are eager to broaden, a little or a lot, their knowledge of ancient Mesopotamia I offer here a few titles of works that are able to give a more detailed, yet still accessible, idea of the country's geography, people, economy, its long political, economic, and cultural history, its mentality and its entire culture. There are few works available for such a purpose and many of them are of either secondary or even tertiary nature, are outdated, or they are indigestible and overpowering with their heavy load of scientific exposition. Those that I will list seem to me to be largely free of these problems.

First of all there are two books that have a broad horizon and that should be able to introduce the entire issue of ancient Mesopotamia. The best up till now, the most up-to-date methodical, and complete, the easiest to read, and in my opinion the most indispensable, is that by Dr. G. Roux, *La Mésopotamia. Essai d'histoire politique, économique et culturelle* (Paris: Éditions du Seuil, 1985).

Ancient Mesopotamia. Portrait of a Dead Civilization, by L. Oppenheim (Chicago: University of Chicago Press, 1977), is a masterful and original synthesis and in any case as suggestive as instructive, even if its author, an Assyriologist of renown in his day, was not always able to control his imagination and his weakness for paradoxes (for an example see above, chap. 12, n. 1).

In *Les Civilisations de l'Orient ancien* (Paris: Arthaud, 1969; generously illustrated) J. Deshayes, an excellent archeologist, but in that capacity cut off from any personal familiarity with the enormous mass of written documentation, has painted a praiseworthy image of Mesopotamian history, starting from the depths of prehistory, and placed in its native surroundings.

The two volumes by A. Parrot in the collection "The Arts of Mankind" (New York: Golden Press): *Sumer: the Dawn of Art* (1961) and *The Arts of Assyria* (1961) are especially valuable for their abundant and beautiful illustrations.

In the field of archeology the most magnificent and useful collection remains that by E. Strommenger, *5,000 Years of the Art of Mesopotamia* (New York: H. N. Abrams, 1964): the photographs and the reproductions are numerous, varied, and first-rate, and they are discussed briefly but accurately.

The *Dictionnaire archéologique des techniques* (Paris: Éditions de l'Accueil, 1963–64) contains in its two volumes a mass of information, often with illustrations, about all aspects of material life and the many technologies used in Mesopotamia.

To understand particular areas of the written documentation, half of the

Catalogue de l'exposition Naissance de l'Écriture (Paris: Éditions de la Réunion des Musées nationaux, 1982) is devoted to cuneiform writing and is a treasure of pictures and explanations on the subject.

On pp. 109–55 of the collective work *Écrits de l'Orient ancient et sources bibliques* (Paris: Desclée, 1986) J.-M. Durand has given an overview of both Sumerian and Akkadian literature under the title "Les écrits mésopotamiens."

The recent *Dictionnaire des mythologies* (Paris: Flammarion, 1981) presents some succinct studies of problems that deal with the mentality and the world vision of the ancient Mesopotamians, and here and there they open up into the field of religion: "Le champs de l'étude" of the religious area (vol. 2: 99f.); "La Religion comme expression de la condition humaine" (2: 100f.; by E. Cassin); "La Souverainité divine et la division des pouvoirs" 2: 455–65; same author); "La Cosmogonie" (1: 228–35; same author); and "Le Problème de Mal: mythologie et 'théologie'" (2: 56–64; my "L'Intelligence et la fonction technique du pouvoir" from the same volume has been reprinted above as chapter 14). The dictionary has been translated into English as *Mythologies*, 2 vols. (Chicago: University of Chicago Press, 1991).

Almost all the articles by Mme. E. Cassin collected in her book *Le semblable et le différent* (Paris: La Découverte, 1987) have as subject matter an original, penetrating, and extremely fruitful "entry" into Mesopotamian anthropology.

A few blunders and archaisms, excusable thirty years ago, do not seem to have outdated the short synthesis of the religious thought, the religious ideology, and the religious behavior that I attempted to give in *La Religion babylonienne* (Paris: Presses Universitaires de France, 1952).

To become better acquainted with such an ancient world one should perhaps become familiar with authentic texts and documents, properly rendered in a modern language and made accessible. There are a certain number of these translations. Here are a few that are not pedantic, heavy or annoying, as is usually the case.

The best anthology of texts written in the Sumerian language —although it offers only extracts—remains that by the great Sumerologist S. N. Kramer, *History Begins at Sumer* (with illustrations) (New York: The Falcon Wing Press, 1956), revised by the same author in 1975 and 1981. The author selects from the enormous corpus of "belles-lettres" pieces that he renders in a pleasing way and that he discusses, thus introducing with intelligence the life and the ideas of their authors.

By the same author is *The Sacred Marriage Rite* (Bloomington: Indiana University Press, 1969) also illustrated, and with longer translations of poems (including on pp. 108–33 almost the entire text of the Sumerian version of *Inanna's Descent into the Netherworld*) that are sometimes still moving and that illustrate the emotional life and the religious life of our ancient ancestors.

The collection "Littératures anciennes du Proche-Orient" (Paris, *Éditions du Cerf*) contains to date only four volumes that fall in our area. First, *Les Inscriptions royales sumériennes et akkadiennes*, by E. Sollberger and J. R. Kupper (1971). Second, in the field of literature in the Akkadian language, *Le Code de Ḫammurapi*, by A. Finet (1973, 2d edition 1983). The scholarly apparatus of the *Lois assyriennes*, by G. Cardascia (1969), and of *Hymnes et prières aux dieux de Babylonie et d'Assyrie*, by J.-M. Seux (1976) runs the risk scaring away laymen.

The most extensive, the most up-to-date, and the best-translated collection of Akkadian works of interest for religion remains that of R. Labat on pp. 13–349 of the collective work entitled *Les Religions du Proche-Orient asiatique* (Paris: Fayard/Denoël, 1970). In particular, one can find there the majority of the texts (or what has survived of them) of the principal documents often cited above: *Atrahasîs* or *The Supersage* (pp. 26ff.); *The Descent of Ištar in the Netherworld* (pp. 258ff.); *The Epic* or *Poem of Creation,* alias *Enûma eliš* (pp. 36ff.); *The Epic* or *Poem of Erra* (pp. 116ff.); *The Epic of Gilgameš* (pp. 145ff.); *The Legend of Adapa* (pp. 287ff.); *The Myth of Anzû* (pp. 80ff.); *Nergal and Ereškigal* (pp. 98ff.); and *A Vision of the Netherworld* (pp. 94ff.).

Allow me to mention the promise made above of the publication in translation, with S. N. Kramer, of the most complete collection possible of myths in Sumerian and in Akkadian (there are about fifty of them) as they have come down to us, and without too much of the forbidding erudition that has been so responsible for making this world inaccessible, a world, that is, in the end, so close to ours. (Now published, under the title *Lorsque les dieux faisaient l'homme* [Paris: Gallimard, 1989].)